Revolutionary Movements in Africa

'An incredible book ... Activists whose voices have long been silenced, many of them Africans with first-hand knowledge of political struggle, here recall their demands and their actions to confront oppression, and how they organised workers, students, and other collectivities of the repressed. Thought-provoking and powerful.'

—Janet Bujra, *Review of African Political Economy*

'A remarkable volume on the vicissitudes of the revolutionary left in post-independence Africa. The volume bravely attempts to tell an untold story which continues to unfold in the more repressive milieu of neo-liberalism in the midst of the beating of new "cold war" drums. A pioneer work which hopefully will inspire a couple more to complete what is essentially a "work in progress".'

—Issa Shivji, Professor Emeritus at the University of Dar es Salaam, Tanzania

'This collection covers over a dozen French- and English-speaking countries from all parts of Africa [enabling] readers to grasp the true revolutionary moment of the African anti-colonial and anti-neocolonial political and social movements. A majority of the authors are African academics with activist credentials [who] present genuine new information gained from original historical research. Twenty-first-century radicals should find new inspiration for action in this untold history.'

—Jean Copans, anthropologist and sociologist

'Without rejecting Marxism-Leninism as a useful theory of popular emancipation and political transformation, the essays in this book show that it is not the only theory of successful political change ... From the Tubu nomads of northern Chad to peasants, workers and students throughout the African continent, we see how the leaders of these social strata can use old and new ideas to mobilise emancipatory struggles for change. The editors of this volume are to be congratulated for making it possible. We hope to read more studies of great revolutionary movements leaders like Amilcar Cabral, Chris Hani, Ibrahima Abatcha, Thomas Sankara, Ruben Um Nyobe, and Pierre Mulele.'

—Georges Nzongola-Ntalaja, Professor of African and Global Studies, University of North Carolina at Chapel Hill

Black Critique

Series editors: Anthony Bogues and Bedour Alagraa

Throughout the twentieth century and until today, anti-racist, radical decolonisation struggles have attempted to create new forms of thought. Figures from Ida B. Wells to W.E.B. Du Bois and Steve Biko, from Claudia Jones to Walter Rodney and Amílcar Cabral produced work which drew from the historical experiences of Africa and the African diaspora. They drew inspiration from the Haitian revolution, radical Black abolitionist thought and practice, and other currents that marked the contours of a Black radical intellectual and political tradition.

The Black Critique series operates squarely within this tradition of ideas and political struggles. It includes books which foreground this rich and complex history. At a time when there is a deep desire for change, Black radicalism is one of the most underexplored traditions that can drive emancipatory change today. This series highlights these critical ideas from anywhere in the Black world, creating a new history of radical thought for our times.

Also available:

Against Racial Capitalism:
Selected Writings
Neville Alexander
Edited by Salim Vally and Enver Motala

Ere Roosevelt Came:
The Adventures of the Man in the Cloak –
A Pan-African Novel of the Global 1930s
Dusé Mohamed Ali
Edited by Marina Bilbija and Alex Lubin

Moving Against the System:
The 1968 Congress of Black Writers and
the Making of Global Consciousness
Edited and with an Introduction by
David Austin

Anarchism and the Black Revolution:
The Definitive Edition
Lorenzo Kom'boa Ervin

After the Postcolonial Caribbean:
Memory, Imagination, Hope
Brian Meeks

A Certain Amount of Madness:
The Life, Politics and Legacies of Thomas
Sankara
Edited by Amber Murrey

Of Black Study
Joshua Myers

On Racial Capitalism, Black Internation-
alism, and Cultures of Resistance
Cedric J. Robinson
Edited by H.L.T. Quan

Black Minded:
The Political Philosophy of Malcolm X
Michael Sawyer

Red International and Black Caribbean
Communists in New York City,
Mexico and the West Indies, 1919–1939
Margaret Stevens

The Point is to Change the World:
Selected Writings of Andaiye
Edited by Alissa Trotz

Revolutionary Movements in Africa

An Untold Story

Edited by
Pascal Bianchini, Ndongo Samba Sylla
and Leo Zeilig

in association with CODESRIA, Dakar

First published 2024 by Pluto Press
New Wing, Somerset House, Strand, London WC2R 1LA
and Pluto Press, Inc.
1930 Village Center Circle, 3-834, Las Vegas, NV 89134

in association with CODESRIA, Avenue Cheikh Anta Diop, Angle Canal IV,
BP 3304 Dakar 18524, Senegal. www.codesria.org

www.plutobooks.com

We are thankful to CODESRIA for its important support.

British Library Cataloguing in Publication Data
A catalogue record for this book is available from the British Library

ISBN   978 0 7453 4786 8   Paperback
ISBN   978 0 7453 4789 9   PDF
ISBN   978 0 7453 4788 2   EPUB

This book is printed on paper suitable for recycling and made from fully
managed and sustained forest sources. Logging, pulping and manufacturing processes are expected to conform to the environmental standards of the country of
origin.

Typeset by Stanford DTP Services, Northampton, England

Simultaneously printed in the United Kingdom and United States of America

Contents

About CODESRIA

The Council for the Development of Social Science Research in Africa (CODESRIA) is an independent pan-African organisation that was established in 1973 to facilitate research in the social sciences and humanities, promote research-based publishing, and create multiple forums geared towards the exchange of views and information among African researchers. All these efforts are aimed at reducing the fragmentation of research on the continent through the creation of thematic research networks that cut across linguistic and regional boundaries.

CODESRIA publishes several noteworthy journals, including *Africa Development*, the longest-standing Africa based social science journal; the *African Sociological Review*; *Africa Review of Books* and the *Journal of Higher Education in Africa*. The results of its research and other activities are also disseminated through various channels, including its Working Paper Series, Book Series, Policy Briefs and the CODESRIA Bulletin.

All CODESRIA publications are accessible online at www.codesria.org

Introduction: Remembering a Forgotten History

Pascal Bianchini, Ndongo Samba Sylla and Leo Zeilig

THE LONG MARCH OF THIS BOOK – 2018–23

The process that made this book possible started in December 2018 when a call for contributions for a conference planned for October 2019 in Dakar, Senegal was written and made public by Ndongo Samba Sylla, Leo Zeilig and Pascal Bianchini. Ndongo Sylla is senior researcher at the Rosa Luxemburg Foundation, well known for his radical economic writings, especially on monetary issues,[1] social movements and democratic mobilisations in Africa.[2] Leo Zeilig is an editor of the *Review of African Political Economy* and its website who has published on student movements and class struggles in Africa, and is also the author of several biographical works on Fanon,[3] Lumumba,[4] Sankara,[5] and recently, Walter Rodney.[6] Pascal Bianchini is an independent researcher who has written books and articles on the sociology of education and social movements, especially student movements in Africa,[7] and for a decade has conducted research on the revolutionary left in Senegal.[8]

About 40 proposals were received, and among them 21 were selected by a committee and the organisers. Then, for three days (30 and 31 October and 1 November) about 30 contributors, activists and discussants gathered in Dakar. During the first day, after the opening session, former members of Senegal's revolutionary left (including one from Mauritania) presented intimate testimonies and debated and discussed their former activism. During the following two days, the selected papers were presented and debated. It was an exquisite mix of academic discussion and militant memories. This particular and unique atmosphere motivated us to publish this volume.

We must thank all the participants who contributed to the success of the event. Among them, we dedicate the collection to Eugénie Rokhaya Aw and Moctar Fofana Niang, who took part in the discussion on the first day and unfortunately have since passed away. In the same vein, Lila Chouli, a friend and comrade to all of us, well known for her invaluable contributions on the social struggles in Burkina Faso, died in 2016 and would have taken part in the symposium if she had lived. We also have to acknowledge the efforts of the committee for the conference and the reviewers who helped us to enhance the quality of this volume (Jimi Adesina, Hakim Adi, Kate Alexander, Janet Bujra, Jean Copans, Thierno Diop, Ibrahim Abdullah, Abdoulaye Dragoss Ouedraogo, Françoise Raison-Jourde, Mor Ndao and Alexis Roy – each were indispensable to the final volume). Several chapters originally written in French were translated by Carole Ann Small Diop and Cheikh Hamala Diop. We also appreciate the skills of Florian Bobin, who made the website for the conference where the programme with the abstracts of the contributions was published.

This book would not have been completed without the contribution of the *Review of African Political Economy* and its website, https://roape.net, which published the call for contributions as well as a conference report written by Adam Mayer, nor without the Rosa Luxemburg Foundation, which financially supported the conference and the translation of several chapters of this book. The project also received the enthusiastic support of David Shulman and Pluto Press, who have been companions and comrades to us as the book was being written.

THE INCONSPICUOUS HISTORY OF THE REVOLUTIONARY LEFT IN AFRICA

The history of revolutionary left movements in Africa is largely ignored and disregarded even among political scientists, historians and across the academic literature on Africa. Most of the existing literature consists of memoirs from former activists. However, most of the rank-and-file activists and even some of the leaders of these movements went to their graves without having an opportunity to tell their own stories. Moreover, the views expressed in these books are inevitably partial. Another limitation is the scarcity of original documents. Here lies a paradox, because an important part of all militant activity is the dissemination of pamphlets or leaflets. Though miraculous discoveries are always possible and documents are found, the reality is that most of the time, pamphlets and leaflets no longer exist for various reasons: because of the fear of repression (during the revolutionary years those found in possession of these materials could be detained in police custody and sent to jail), together with the harshness of the climate and also the 'gnawing critique of mice' ... and termites.

The invisibility of the African revolutionary left in the existing literature contrasts with the situation prevailing on other continents, where we find a rich collection of books on this subject. In place of serious research on this issue, we find research and writing on related issues such as African revolutions and uprisings,[9] invariably guerrilla warfare launched by liberation movements against colonial or neocolonial armies.[10] Other publications have focused on revolutionary regimes.[11] Still more research can be found on prominent figures, not to say tragic revolutionary heroes, such as Amílcar Cabral[12] or Thomas Sankara[13] who lost their lives in the struggle (and those like Patrice Lumumba who lost their lives at the start of independence). Finally, some contributions have shed light on the relations developed between African activists and revolutionaries and the former state socialist countries and the attraction exerted by this model[14] of socialism, and more recently on the relations between African liberation movements and Western communist parties.[15]

AN ATTEMPT TO DEFINE THE AFRICAN REVOLUTIONARY LEFT

Generally speaking, orientation to the left implies a position in favour of equality, not only in terms of rights or opportunities for the individual, but also as an organising principle of society, especially at the socio-economic level. It also refers to progressive values opposed to conservative, traditionalist, jingoist conceptions which tend to maintain the domination of men over women, elders over youth, etc. and to reject and stigmatise minorities in the broad sense of this word. These ideological commitments were to be found among the African revolutionary left. However, colonial rule and imperialist domination had an impact on this 'universal', commonly accepted, definition. Class relations were not the same as in Western societies. The classic cleavages between proletariat and bourgeoisie were obscured by colonial rule and post-colonial state-building. The anti-colonialist and anti-imperialist struggles were essential factors in the emerging political arenas from the 1930s. Moreover, the initial social basis for leftist organisations (trade unions and political parties) was to be found among urban workers, and even more specifically in the student movements which increasingly initiated and occasionally led the struggle against colonialism and neocolonialism and which were in a specific position to nurture internationalist relationships.

Regarding the term 'revolutionary', a revolution means a radical change in the social order. In practice, revolutionary politics in the Western world came to be seen as 'non-conventional politics', challenging 'formal' and 'bourgeois (or capitalist) democracy'. Participation in elections was mainly considered as an opportunity to popularise ideas and to achieve momentum in favour of the revolutionary processes. Yet in the case of colonial or post-colonial conditions, representative, multi-party democracy and fair elections did not last particularly long if they had ever really existed. In these circumstances, the idea of taking up arms logically appeared as a response to the one-party state and dictatorship (see, for instance, the case of the Front de libération nationale du Tchad [FROLINAT, National Liberation Front of Chad] in Chapter 7 on Chad). However, launching guerrilla war was easier to say than to do, as shown in most cases (see, for instance, the case of the Sawaba evoked in Chapter 4 on Niger). In other cases, radical democratic movements emerged which, in specific contexts marked by a strong centralisation of state power under military or single-party rule, appeared as revolutionary in the broad sense of the expression (see, for instance, the case of the Movement for Justice in Africa [MOJA] developed in Chapter 6 on Liberia). These considerations explain why the contours of our subject have had to be extended to avoid limiting our scope to a narrow definition of the revolutionary lefts in Africa.

Although the 1960s and 1970s were golden years for revolutionary movements in Africa, one must take into account earlier developments associated with the radicalisation of anti-colonial struggles at the end of the 1950s (see, for instance, the birth of the Parti africain de l'indépendance [African Party of Independence] evoked in Chapter 1 on Senegal). On the other hand, the 1980s were also for some countries a period of revolutionary organising in its various forms (as well as the case of Niger, we must mention the case of the Parti communiste revolutionnaire voltaïque [Voltaic Revolutionary Communist Party] discussed in Chapter 3 on Burkina Faso).

THE OBSTACLES TO UNDERSTANDING THE HISTORY OF AFRICA'S REVOLUTIONARY MOVEMENTS

In contrast to the rest of the world, where essays, monographs and histories have been written on radical left movements during their heyday,[16] this is not the case for their African counterparts. At first glance, the history of African revolutionary movements seems less epic. Compared to the Cuban revolution in Latin America or to the Vietnamese popular war that inspired

revolutionary movements during the 1960s and 1970s,[17] the African continent might appear unfavourable terrain for revolutionary struggles.

Che Guevara, the most iconic figure of the 1960s, himself expressed
reservations about the prospects of revolutionary victories in Africa. After
his unsuccessful attempt in Congo, he wrote: 'Africa had a long way to go
before it achieved real revolutionary maturity.'[18]

However, many revolutionary movements around the world during the
1960s and the 1970s, even if they have been able to challenge the state, were
finally defeated – for example, the Naxalites in India[19] and the Tupamaros
in Uruguay,[20] not to mention the Black Panthers in the USA. Yet their experience influenced revolutionaries from other countries. The idea of a 'lack
of maturity of the African people' imbued with localist traditional values is
still an underlying prejudice about the revolutionary perspectives in Africa
among many commentators, though it is a terrible misconception, especially
when it is expressed in general for a whole continent.

Moreover, the extraordinary anti-colonial struggles and the creation of
new independent states occurred during the Cold War. Anti-colonial movements and radical organisations within these movements were considered
by mainstream observers as Soviet proxies rather than independent actors.
In this way, a well-known American commentator could write:

> The Soviet Union has supported nationalist development in Africa as part
> of its global strategy to create situations of instability and weakness within
> the Western world, to train and indoctrinate Communist leadership
> cadres with the expectation that by manipulating mass discontent and
> nationalist symbols they could seize power in African Soviet Republics,
> and, in general, to carry out Lenin's dictum to attack the West through its
> dependent territories.[21]

For several decades, the reference to Marxism in these liberation movements was still considered as fundamental, and according to this view,
radical movements and politics could not survive the collapse of the Eastern
Bloc.[22] However, such conceptions ignore the ability of African activists and
intellectuals to embrace, create and adapt revolutionary doctrines for their
own sake. The idea that activists and revolutionaries simply imported ready-
made doctrines from a Marxist-Leninist blueprint is at best a narrow point
of view, at worst a deeply patronising and colonial idea.

Of course, this position of principle must not lead us to ignore the
numerous hurdles faced by left movements in Africa, whether from external

or internal causes. During the twentieth century, the penetration of communist ideas in the contemporary sense of the word was linked to the establishment of colonial institutions and the labour force necessary for the colonial economy. Then, the major issue raised for the development of left-wing organisations (mainly communist) was the relationship with the emerging nationalist movements, though even when the colonial period came to an end, many areas remained out of reach for communist-inspired organisations:

> Communist influence was found in the north and south and to a lesser extent in the west, but there was virtually no communist influence in East Africa. Generally, the continent's predominantly rural and peasant population made the diffusion of communist ideas difficult or even impossible.[23]

If we go back to Marx himself, we know that he was among the few European theorists of his generation who did not try to conceal his 'debt' to Africa, but celebrated such knowledge as foundational. Recent work by the Nigerian scholar Biko Agozino shows how people of African descent were central to the theory, practice and writings of Marx, including in *Capital*.[24] In addition to his major writings were the letters he wrote from Algeria at the end of his life, or more significantly, the articles on African-Americans during the Civil War in the United States.[25] Although it has been considered Eurocentric, his work was inspirational for many African-American and African thinkers, so that Marxist ideas have deeply influenced the 'making of a Black radical tradition'.[26] Even more unexpected, if we take a closer look at such an iconic figure as Cheikh Anta Diop, often associated with 'Afrocentricity', we note that his writings did not ignore Marxist analysis[27] and that his own involvement in Senegalese politics with the Rassemblement national démocratique (National Democratic Rally) during the late 1970s occurred in relation with Marxist activists from the Parti africain de l'indépendance (PAI, African Independence Party) and from Maoist groups which joined the party he had created.[28]

In Africa, the 'boom' of Marxist revolutionary ideas occurred especially during the decades examined in this book. Later on, these ideas retreated from the continent, which can give the utterly false impression that it was mainly a Western fad. However, this ideological decline of Marxism is not unique to Africa, rather it was a more general and global phenomenon that goes beyond the scope of this introduction and volume.

A CHRONOLOGICAL FRAMEWORK FOR THE HISTORY
OF THE REVOLUTIONARY LEFT IN AFRICA

In order to give an outline of the historical development of revolutionary movements in Africa, we propose a division into three periods.

First, we identify pioneers who challenged triumphant colonialism in calling for Pan-Africanist solidarity (from London in 1900 to Manchester in 1944) and also for some of them, in developing connections with Communist organisations during the interwar period, especially since the creation of the Soviet Union and the Third International. This early period of the revolutionary left embodied by activists often based in Europe, in the colonial metropolis, such as Lamine Senghor or Tiemoko Garang Kouyate for the French colonies or Wallace Johnson for the British colonies, is not within the scope of this book. However, these figures have been rediscovered and celebrated by the generations that followed, especially in the 1970s. The main debate for this generation was 'Panafricanism or Communism?', as suggested by a famous book written in the late 1950s as a reassessment of this period.[29] However, if tension has existed between the two orientations, they were not always in contradiction.[30]

We then identify a second period which is shorter and more difficult to delineate, during the late colonial era and the aftermath of the struggle for independent states. During this time, anti-colonial movements became more radicalised, especially when confronted with delaying tactics from colonial powers. In parallel, during this period, the influence of communist and progressive forces grew to the point that the centre of gravity shifted from the diaspora to African territories, even when they were not yet mass parties. At the same time, the Union of Soviet Socialist Republics (USSR) and the People's Republic of China began to appear as attractive counter-models to Western capitalism.

Finally, we see in the 1960s and the 1970s a third wave of activism sweeping across Africa, as it did throughout the whole world, and the Global South. These 'anti-systemic' movements were not only directed against Western imperialist domination, but also against 'bureaucratised' states claiming to stand for socialism.[31] In Africa, this New Left developed during and after 1968 and jostled with the Old Left, still aligned with the USSR. Clandestine movements were burgeoning in every part of the continent, and a spirit of rebellion was challenging the political order.[32] This historical development has remained largely ignored for decades. However, recent publications have emphasised the role played during these years by certain 'capitals of the revolution' where emblematic revolutionary figures such as Che Guevara, Stokely Carmichael, Eldridge Cleaver and others travelled or settled, for example in Algiers,[33] Brazzaville,[34] Conakry[35] or Dar es Salaam.[36] These countries became new bases or refuge sanctuaries for freedom fighters against the apartheid system, the counter-insurgency campaigns and assassinations launched against the Black Power movement in the United States, Portuguese colonialism, and exiled nationalist activists and revolutionaries from struggles in Southern Africa. This solidarity frequently exposed these states to attacks from the South African or Portuguese armies or secret services which were waging a dirty war against their opponents, as was shown with the assassination of Eduardo Mondlane in Tanzania in 1969[37] and of Amílcar Cabral in Conakry in 1973.[38] However, beside these 'spectacular' headline developments, less noticeable radical experiences are to be found in every African country. This book will shed light on these forgotten realities, with most of our chapters centred on this third revolutionary age.

SEVERAL PROBLEMATIC ISSUES

If this framework is suitable to situate the history of the African revolutionary left movements, some problematic issues must also be broached for deeper understanding.

The first key question to be raised is the social basis of these movements. Historically, in Western countries, the left had its roots in the labour movement. But in African territories, radical organisations originated initially from the diaspora, students,[39] urban workers, and more generally the African 'petty bourgeoisie' who suffered colonial discrimination. In addition, the industrial proletariat which was supposed to be fundamental to the class struggle was numerically weak compared to the rural masses or even the urban lumpenproletariat (though this is not to say that working-class struggles, strikes and politics were not significant, and often vital to early nationalist movements). Moreover, the colonial state used indigenous chiefs and traditional authorities (including the religious customary power) as intermediaries to help run colonial society. It was theorised in the British colonies as 'indirect rule'. But French authorities, allegedly preferring 'direct rule', did not act in any fundamentally different manner. Later, post-colonial states often maintained this 'tradition'. Consequently, conquering the 'heart of the masses' was a significant challenge for revolutionary activists who sought to establish cells or bases among the popular classes. During the 1970s, these efforts were important, but not always successful.

Another major thematic focus was the conquest of state power and the exercise of revolutionary power. For both internal and external reasons, the strategy of armed struggle became emblematic of the 1960s and the 1970s. The closure of political systems and the use of violence by neocolonial states were compelling reasons for activists to turn to armed struggle. Also, emblematic movements from Africa (armed struggles against Portuguese colonialism and the apartheid system) or from Latin America, or even direct support from the Cubans or the Chinese, had the effect of influencing this 'turn' to armed struggle. However, as mentioned earlier, implementing guerrilla warfare was not so easy. A favourable context was found in a very limited number of cases.

There also appeared during these years a one-stop solution to the lifelong presidencies and one-party systems, with 'progressive' military coups overthrowing neocolonial governments and setting up so-called 'revolutionary' power. The alliance of revolutionary organisations with military groups has been an issue of considerable debate. For some commentators, such a shortcut to revolution was in fact a dead end because the military, whether 'progressive' or 'revolutionary', had their own political rationales and their own agendas for taking power.[40] For others, several cases, from the DERG (Coordinating Committee of the Armed Forces, Police and Territorial Army, a coalition of apparently progressive military organisations) in Ethiopia to the Sankarist regime in Burkina Faso, demonstrate that military power was able to implement radical (if not revolutionary) transformations in their countries.[41] In fact, the issue of alliance with some military factions and the militarisation of the revolutions should lead us to a more general reflection on the exercise of power in a revolutionary situation and an alleged revolutionary regime.

The Ethiopian revolution that upheld Haile Selassie's monarchy was a case in point. The student movement gained momentum during the 1960s and 1970s, and became more radical during the 1960s. During the years before the revolution in 1974, several revolutionary parties appeared. The two main organisations at that time were the Pan-Ethiopian Socialist Movement (Mei'son) and the Ethiopian People's Revolutionary Party (EPRP). The former chose to back the revolutionary DERG, whereas the latter chose to fight against the regime that they did not consider revolutionary. In 1977, the Red Terror started, with EPRP members first targeted in a bloody campaign, but later on, Mei'son was also suppressed.

Several decades later, the debate is still raging among Ethiopian historians about the balance of the revolutionary process, its heavy death toll and the responsibilities of the revolutionary activists in these events. For one historian who was also active in the revolutionary student movement, the students were fighting for their ideals and played a major role in putting forward the slogans inspired the revolution (for instance, 'the land to the tiller') and were not directly responsible for the bloody crackdown during the Mengistu regime.[42] By contrast, for other scholars, revolutionary intellectuals never played a fundamental role in the revolutionary process.[43] Another view has argued that activists had a narrow and Eurocentric view of their own society inspired by a European-based Marxist ideology.[44]

Another significant illustration of the debate on how to gain influence and to seize power in an African context was the case of the Sudanese Communist Party (SCP). Formally created in 1952, the party grew during the late 1950s and the 1960s, and played an important part in the revolution in 1964. Later on, the SCP chose to back the military progressive regime headed by Nimeiry, who was inspired by the Egyptian President Nasser's Arab socialism. In 1971, a left-wing coup took place in the army led by allegedly pro-communist officers. After the failure of the coup, the SCP was heavily suppressed and the party went into decline.[45] Apart from suffering from a military crackdown, the SCP was also marginalised for its supposed atheism by its Islamic critics, when in reality most of the SCP members practised their religion without thinking it was in any way a contradiction of their political ideology.[46]

LIMITATIONS OF THIS VOLUME

Apart from the two important examples discussed above – Ethiopia and Sudan – which are not included in this volume, there are other major revolutionary experiences, such as the Congo (formerly Zaïre) during the 1960s with the 'second independence movement' led by Mulele, Soumialot and Kabila,[47] the revolution in Zanzibar in 1964[48] and the revolutionary process in Dahomey, which became Benin in 1975, which also do not appear in this book.[49] In addition, the Lusophone countries which remained later under the domination of Portuguese colonialism could have inspired one or two chapters, whereas the absence of North African case studies is always questionable.[50] These vital gaps in our coverage warrant a second volume on the Revolutionary left in Africa which remains to be written. Even though we are exhausted by the task of publishing this volume, plans for a second volume are being hatched.

We also need to note that the issue of gender does not occupy the place it deserves as we had initially hoped. A panel was planned in 2019 on the central question of gender, but it was cancelled due to the absence of two contributors who had sent their proposals but could not attend the conference, and eventually were unable to submit their planned papers. However, instead of scholarly contributions, we heard the testimonies and statements of women who were active in the Senegalese Maoist movement in Senegal during the 1970s. What they said, in a nutshell, was that they had to fight against patriarchy as a *pervasive* social and institutional phenomenon – including within revolutionary circles and organisations where women were often relegated to subservient positions.

However, women did play an important part in the struggles for emancipation in Africa and in revolutionary movements, and vibrant figureheads have emerged, such as Eugenie Aw from Senegal, to whom we pay tribute in this volume's final chapter. Their role was prominent during exceptional moments, for example at the end of the 1970s with the student struggles against Moussa Traoré's dictatorship in Mali[51] or during the events of May 1972 in Madagascar (see Chapter 9 by Irène Rabenoro), and in other countries African feminism developed within the radical left (see Chapter 5 on Nigeria by Baba Aye and Adam Mayer).

Given these important gaps, this volume should be considered as an effort to unearth the rich story of the revolutionary movements in Africa. More volumes will be needed in order to complete the intellectual (re)construction it has started.

OVERVIEW OF THE BOOK

The chapters in this volume cover different countries and themes. Authors come from various political and academic backgrounds – philosophy, history, anthropology, etc. Some of them are activists or scholar-activists, others academics. Such a diversity represents for the editors a fertile space to open up various and diverse radical avenues and prevent the potential erasure of the historical memory of the African revolutionary left movements.

In Chapter 1, Ibrahima Wane depicts the cultural dimension of the struggles led by the radical left in Senegal, a country ruled by a powerful head of state who was also a poet and an ideologue of Negritude whose cultural prestige was immense. This cultural fight started with the first radical left-wing party – in 1957 the PAI was born, and challenged Senghor's power from the start. It relied on the celebration of African languages as a political tool of emancipation. This struggle developed further during 1968 in Senegal with the birth of cultural clubs that became cradles for the politicisation of the youth. Later, in 1977, when the Maoists became more or less hegemonic among organisations of the revolutionary left (though harshly suppressed in 1975), the Senegalese Cultural Front was also an important initiative. These activists tried to bring to light a popular anti-colonial culture with poems, songs and dramas in African languages. Moreover, they praised anti-colonial figureheads who were forgotten, marginalised and ignored by Senghor's regime that was labelled by activists a neocolonial state.

Chapter 2 is written by Issa N'Diaye, a philosopher who was a direct participant and activist in Mali's left politics. It gives a well-informed, though critical, insider view of Malian revolutionary movements in the 1960s and the 1970s. As in most African countries, the Malian radical left emerged during the anti-colonial struggle. Then, just after independence, when the Union soudanaise-rassemblement démocratique africain (Sudanese Union-African Democratic Rally) with Modibo Keita came to power with an anti-colonial programme that contrasted with the policies followed by many other governments that remained within a neocolonial framework represented by Senegal or Niger, the radical left in Mali represented by the PAI was pressed into joining the single party. However, some of them refused and created a new organisation, the Parti malien du travail (Malian Workers Party). In 1968, a military coup put an end to the socialist hopes led by Keita, and a harsh dictatorship cracked down on left activists and militancy. In 1991, when the dictator Moussa Traoré was overthrown by a popular uprising, a new cleavage appeared between the former activists supporting the party that won the elections, the Alliance démocratique du Mali – Parti africain pour la solidarité et la justice (Alliance for Democracy in Mali-African Party for Solidarity and Justice), and radicals from the student movements of the 1980s and the 1990s.

This issue of the left's confrontation with the exercise of power, and more generally the issues of violence and hegemony (with, on one hand, the military coups, and on the other hand, the influence of religion), return several times in Mali's history. Although his reflections and conclusions may appear pessimistic, Issa N'Diaye gives us a far-sighted contribution whose scope goes beyond the case of Mali.

In several African countries, the hotbed of revolutionary activists was the student movement. This was especially true in Burkina Faso, where different generations of activists have cut their teeth in the historical organisation of the student movement: the Union générale des étudiants voltaïques

(General Union of Voltaic Students). In Chapter 3, Moussa Diallo reminds us of the struggle between different 'political positions' during the 1960s and the 1970s. Through the ideological disputes that took place in the succeeding congresses, the most radical line embodied by the Parti communiste révolutionnaire voltaïque (PCRV, Voltaic Revolutionary Communist Party), born in 1978, became an important pole of attraction for the radical left at the time. However, the internal cleavages inside the student movement had important political consequences: the split of the student movement gave birth to the Union de luttes communiste (ULC, Union of Communist Struggles), whose leaders became the ideologues of the Sankarist revolutionary regime, while the PCRV remained underground in the opposition, where it was active in the Front syndical (Trade Union Front) in 1985 which gathered together trade unionists opposed to Sankara's government. Paradoxically, whereas the ULC eventually disappeared after Sankara's assassination, the PCRV has remained influential in the trade unions for decades, especially with the creation of the Confédération générale du travail du Burkina (General Confederation of Labour of Burkina) in 1988.

In Niger, a first moment of radicalisation occurred during the early 1960s with the experience of guerrilla warfare launched (without success) by the Sawaba in the context of French neocolonialism that maintained a tight grip on African governments across its former colonial territories. Later, a second wave of radicalisation occurred in the 1970s and the early 1980s, whose hotbed was the student movement. Then underground organisations germinated from student activism. The two main groups were the Groupe des révolutionnaires nigériens (GRN, Group of Nigerien Revolutionaries) and the G-80, which appeared around 1980. Tatiana Smirnova's Chapter 4 is a well-grounded contribution that captures the revolutionary atmosphere through interviews with former members of GRN and G-80. This unknown history is all the more important since these groups gave birth to the Parti Nigérien pour la démocratie et le socialism (PNDS, Nigerien Party for Democracy and Socialism), one of the main political parties in the multi-party system that took shape during the 1990s and which has been in power since 2011. It also shows the interaction between revolutionary movements in neighbouring countries such as Burkina Faso and the dividing political lines between the two national communities.

Chapter 5 on Nigeria by Adam Mayer and Baba Aye traces the origins of the Nigerian radical left in the nationalist movement, but also in the history of the trade unions. In 1963, the first Nigerian organisation that claimed to be Marxist-Leninist appeared. However, the development of the revolutionary left has been affected by the vicissitudes and constraints of Nigeria's tumultuous post-colonial political economy: the internal/regional cleavages which gave rise to the Biafra civil war, the military coups and the suppression of political opposition and civil society organisations.

In the 1970s, the development of the higher education system became a breeding ground for an emerging intelligentsia who expressed a radical critique in Marxist terms against the capitalist accumulation in Nigeria and the imperialist domination that continued unabated after independence. However, the revolutionary left, once influential among the students and some sections of the urban working class, has remained divided between various groups and has failed to become a force on the political scene, which has been dominated by army and civilian politicians. Yet today, the radical left remains active in Nigeria and has been at the forefront of anti-neoliberal movements that developed in Nigeria for several decades.

The study of the Movement for Justice in Africa in Liberia by George Klay Kieh, Jr in Chapter 6 explores the border between the 'hardcore' revolutionary left and the 'progressive' and 'democratic' movements that may play a revolutionary role in particular contexts. Liberia had never been colonised by Europeans, but instead a colonial administration established an authoritarian state ruled by an elite of freed African-American slaves who settled in independent Liberia in 1822. The MOJA was initially focused on solidarity with African liberation struggles, but its actions shifted later to domestic politics. It played a significant role as a popular educational movement. It was only during its later years in the 1980s that the MOJA started to launch a political organisation in order to compete for state power. However, George Kieh points out the limitations of this strategy: targeting the local elite in power, the leaders of the movement did not offer a global analysis of imperialism and capitalism. In terms of practice, it shied away from mass mobilisations and it made a fateful choice in backing Samuel Doe's coup in 1980, which contributed to its eventual decline.

In Chad, the FROLINAT was launched in 1966, as described in Chapter 7 by Tilman Musch, Moussa Bicharra Ahmed and Djiddi Allahi Mahamat. Seemingly, it perfectly fits with the Maoist concept of 'popular war'. Guerrilla warfare launched in the northern region by the FROLINAT was grafted onto a history of rebellions by peasants and nomads against the authoritarian colonial administration. Moreover, the desert and the mountains of Tibesti provided the guerrilla struggle with some tactical advantages. On this basis, the chapter demonstrates that the ability of the FROLINAT to control a large part of the country took place without external support (except from

Libya), because it was backed by a population who had long experience of 'relying on its own forces'. However, even though it was an important anti-imperialist rebellion fighting a neocolonial regime backed by the French army, the politicisation of the FROLINAT was essentially limited to the leadership of the movement.

Chapter 8 by Héloïse Kiriakou and Matt Swagler demonstrates that the international and local aspects in revolutionary politics are often closely intertwined. The revolution in Brazzaville in 1963 had an important impact on the regional situation and even further afield. Brazzaville became a revolutionary crossroads for various movements: the Movimento Popular de Libertação de Angola (People's Movement for the Liberation of Angola) and Lumumbists from the former Belgian Congo. The country also developed diplomatic relations with Cuba and China. In fact, this international dimension was closely intertwined with the internal situation, especially the balance of power between the left wing of the revolutionary regime, especially with the youth organisation: Jeunesse du mouvement national de la révolution (Youth of the National Movement of the Revolution) and the right wing in favour of a gentleman's agreement with the neighbouring states aligned with the United States and other Western countries. The youth organisation played a decisive part in preventing the regime from surrendering its radical political agenda. However, the failed attempted coup by Ange Diawara and his followers and their short-lived guerrilla warfare in 1972 ended a period when Brazzaville had become another 'capital of the revolution' in Africa.

In Chapter 9, Irène Rabenoro, a student and activist in the events in 1972 in Madagascar and today a professor at the University of Antananarivo, gives us an intimate account of the Malagasy Revolution of May 1972. The student movement was at the forefront of the struggle to overthrow Tsiranana, the 'father of independence', but it was the convergence of various social forces which compelled the head of state to resign. The regime denounced the manipulation of the movement by communist activists who had allegedly infiltrated the movement. However, though the movement had political claims, especially the democratisation and the Malagasisation of the educational system, in a broader context of rejection of the neocolonial links with France, it was essentially spontaneous. The collapse of the regime can be explained by its own political mistakes, especially when the demonstrations were harshly suppressed, resulting in a heavy death toll.

In Chapter 10 on South Sudan, Nicki Kindersley raises the issues of the influence of leftist ideas and the presence of leftist activists in a geographic space and a historical moment where they were not expected to emerge. The Sudanese Communist Party, whose history is relatively well known, did not develop in South Sudan. The Anya-Nya rebellion which was active in the 1960s was backed by Israel and was opposed to 'progressive' Arab states such as Nimeiry's Sudan or Nasser's Egypt. However, through various archives, Kindersley has traced the influence of the left and even of Marxist ideas on certain intellectuals and more widely the educated youth in South Sudan during the 1960s and the 1970s. Her study reveals the inconspicuous presence of the revolutionary left even in unpropitious contexts during this period.

In Chapter 11 on Uganda, Adrian Browne traces the origins of the radical left in a country that used to be a stronghold for conservative powers such as the monarchy of Buganda and the Christian churches. Unsurprisingly, the first Ugandan communists appeared within the diaspora in Great Britain at the end of the 1950s, especially among students who were in contact with the Communist Party of Great Britain. Then the radical left took root in Uganda itself, especially among trade unions and youth organisations. Later, the left could be found in the Uganda's People Congress which came to power after independence. The left wing of the party gained momentum in 1963–64, but failed to lead the party. This example is revealing of the paradoxical existence of the revolutionary African left: they were fast-growing forces for several years, but they failed to become hegemonic within the institutionalised political arena.

This volume includes two complementary chapters focused on the University of Dar es Salaam during the late 1960s and the 1970s. In Chapter 12, Patrick Norberg pinpoints the role of the University Students African Revolutionary Front (USARF), a radical group of students that organised conferences with internationally renowned intellectuals such as Walter Rodney and John Saul and also published a magazine, *Cheche*. Founded in 1967, the group was tolerated by the head of state, Julius Nyerere, as a Marxist-Leninist left wing within the frame of *Ujamaa* socialism (a version of African socialism, meaning 'familyhood'). The main cleavages between Nyerere and his dissenters were about the nature of socialism (scientific versus African), the analysis of post-colonial society (class-based versus community-based) and internationalism (USARF opposed Tanzanian nationalism). In 1970, as the critiques of Nyerere's regime became harsher, and the regime's repression more severe, USARF was banned – a unique experience that has left its mark not only in Tanzania, but also in the neighbouring countries in East Africa.

In Chapter 13, Zeyad el Nabolsy attempts to summarise the 'Dar es Salaam debates' that took place during the 1970s among Marxist intellectuals at the University of Dar es Salaam who opposed the communalist vision of African Socialism advocated by Nyerere, and rather rooted their analyses in terms of class positions and control over the means of production, and stressed the need to take into account external domination by imperialist forces. However, from these premises, they had divergent views, for example about the issue of the national ruling class and its level of autonomy from/ dependency on the international capitalist system. These debates were not merely theoretical, as they implied different revolutionary strategies, especially on the issue of class alliances with the petty bourgeoisie.

In Chapter 14, Heike Becker covers particular periods in the history of anti-apartheid struggles. She focuses on two distinct sets of events: the Durban strikes in 1973 and the workers' strikes in Namibia backed by the student movement. Both have to be considered landmarks in this history: the former saw the reawakening of social movements that led to the uprising in Soweto in 1976 and the mass mobilisations of the 1980s, and the latter, in Namibia, saw the awakening of social movements that boosted the rejection of apartheid in Namibia and support for the claim of independence. Both examples demonstrate the pioneering role of the radical left in events that paved the way to the development of large socio-political movements strong enough to overthrow the existing political order.

In Chapter 15, through the extraordinary case of Dimitri Tsafendas who stabbed to death South Africa's apartheid Prime Minister, Hendrik Verwoerd, in 1966, Harris Dousemetzis raises the issue of individual revolutionary action. Dousemetzis's biographic point of view shows us that such an individual deed must be understood within the global history of anti-apartheid struggles. During his whole life, the man who executed the 'architect' of apartheid had always been an anti-colonial communist activist fighting against the Portuguese in Mozambique, then against apartheid in South Africa. However, Tsafendas was presented as a solitary terrorist, and even as insane, because the aim of the authorities was to deny him any political agency or motivation. This occurred at a moment when anti-apartheid forces had been defeated after the non-violent demonstrations of the late 1950s and the (relatively) unsuccessful armed struggle launched by the African National Congress in the early 1960s. Tsafendas's act was intended to tell the apartheid leaders that they could not live in peace as long as the racial discrimination system continued to exist.

As a work in progress, to be completed by future research and volumes, we are conscious of the limitations and omissions of this book. Let us also emphasise that this collective intellectual effort is not an activist's book nor a 'politically neutral' academic publication. This volume has been written by committed intellectuals, in the broad sense of the expression: although the contributions are written from a historical perspective, we have refused to turn our backs on involvement in militancy or to give up on the ideals of emancipation for African peoples against colonialist, post-colonial or imperialist domination and the search for radical alternatives to global capitalism. We believe that understanding, exploring and debating Africa's radical left history and politics are central to this commitment. This volume is an invitation to (re)think African radical leftist projects and utopias that we hope will reach a large audience of readers.

NOTES

1. Fanny Pigeaud and Ndongo Samba Sylla, *Africa's Last Colonial Currency: The CFA Franc Story*, London: Pluto Press, 2021; Maha Ben Gadha, Fadhel Kaboub, Kai Koddenbrock, Ines Mahmoud and Ndongo Samba Sylla (eds), *Economic and Monetary Sovereignty in 21st Century Africa*, London: Pluto Press, 2021.
2. Ndongo Samba Sylla (ed.), *Les mouvements sociaux en Afrique de l'Ouest: entre les ravages du libéralisme économique et la promesse du libéralisme politique*, Paris: L'Harmattan, 2014.
3. Leo Zeilig, *Frantz Fanon: The Militant Philosopher of Third World Revolution*, London: I.B. Tauris, 2015.
4. Leo Zeilig, *Lumumba: Africa's Lost Leader*, London: Haus Publishing, 2008.
5. Jean-Claude Congo and Leo Zeilig, *Thomas Sankara: Voices of Liberation*, Johannesburg: National Institute for the Humanities and Social Sciences, 2017.
6. Leo Zeilig, *A Revolutionary for Our Time: The Walter Rodney Story*, London: Haymarket Books, 2022.
7. Pascal Bianchini, *École et politique en Afrique noire*, Paris: Karthala, 2004.
8. Pascal Bianchini, 'The 1968 Years: Revolutionary Politics in Senegal', *Review of African Political Economy*, 46(160), 2019, 184–203; Pascal Bianchini, '1968 au Sénégal: un héritage politique en perspective', *Canadian Journal of African Studies*, 55(2), 2021, 307–329.
9. Françoise Blum, *Révolutions africaines: Congo-Brazzaville, Sénégal, Madagascar, années 1960–1970*, Rennes: Presses universitaires de Rennes, 2014; Willow J. Berridge, *Civil Uprisings in Modern Sudan: The 'Khartoum Springs' of 1964 and 1985*, London: Bloomsbury Press, 2015.
10. Gérard Chaliand, *Armed Struggle in Africa: With the Guerrillas in 'Portuguese' Guinea*, New York: Monthly Review Press, 1969; Basil Davidson, *No Fist Is Big Enough to Hide the Sky: The Liberation of Guinea-Bissau and Cape Verde, 1963–74*, London: Zed Books, 1974.

11. David Ottaway and Marina Ottaway, *Afrocommunism*, New York: Africana Publishing House, 1981.

12. Patrick Chabal, *Amilcar Cabral: Revolutionary Leadership and People's War*, Trenton, NJ: Africa World Press, 2003. For a broader scope than Chabal's views, see Antonio Tomas, *Amílcar Cabral: The Life of a Reluctant Nationalist*, London: Hurst, 2021.

13. Bruno Jaffré, *Biographie de Thomas Sankara: la patrie ou la mort ...*, Paris: L'Harmattan, 2007; Ernest Harsch, *Thomas Sankara: An African Revolutionary*, Athens, OH: Ohio University Press, 2014.

14. Maxim Matusevich, 'Revisiting the Soviet Moment in Sub-Saharan Africa', *History Compass*, 7(5), 2009, 1,259–1,268. Eric Burton and Constantin Katsakioris, 'Africans and the Socialist World: Aspirations, Experiences, and Trajectories: An Introduction', *International Journal of African Historical Studies*, 54(3), 2021, 269–278.

15. Françoise Blum, Marco Di Maggio, Gabriele Siracusano and Serge Wolikow (eds), *Les partis communistes occidentaux et l'Afrique: une histoire mineure?*, Paris: Hémisphères, 2021.

16. For the United States, see Max Elbaum, *Revolution in the Air: Sixties Radicals turn to Lenin, Mao and Che*, London: Verso, 2002, and for a synthetic view on the revolutionary left in Latin America, see Verónica Oikión, Solano Eduardo Rey and Tristán Martín López Ávalos (eds), *El Estudio de las Luchas Revolucionarias en América Latina (1959–1996), Estado de la Cuestión*, Zamora: El Colegio de Michoacan, 2013.

17. Two books in particular were bedtime reading for the generation of the 1960s: Che Guevara, *Che Guevara on Guerrilla Warfare*, New York: Praeger, 1961, and Vo Nguyen Giap, *People's War People's Army: The Viet Cong Insurrection Manual for Underdeveloped Countries*, New York: Praeger, 1962.

18. Che Guevara, *The Congo Diary: Episodes of the Revolutionary War in Congo*, Melbourne: Ocean Press, 2011.

19. Prakash Singh, *The Naxalite Movement in India*, New Delhi: Rupa, 2006.

20. Lindsey Churchill, *Becoming the Tupamaros: Solidarity and Transnational Revolutionaries in Uruguay and the United States*, Nashville, TN: Vanderbilt University Press, 2014.

21. James S. Coleman, 'Contemporary Africa Trends and Issues', *Annals of the American Academy of Political and Social Science*, 298, 1955, 96.

22. Arnold Hughes, 'The Appeal of Marxism to Africans', *Journal of Communist Studies*, 8(2), 1992, 4–20.

23. Allison Drew, 'Comparing African Experiences of Communism', in Norman Naimark, Silvio Pons and Sophie Quinn-Judge, *The Cambridge History of Communism, Vol. II: The Socialist Camp and World Power, 1941–1960s*, Cambridge: Cambridge University Press, 2017, 519.

24. Biko Agozino, 'The Africana Paradigm in *Capital*: The Debts of Karl Marx to People of African Descent', *Review of African Political Economy*, 41(140), 2014, 172–184.

25. Kevin B. Anderson, *Marx at the Margins: On Nationalism, Ethnicity, and Non-Western Societies*, Chicago, IL: Chicago University Press, 1992.

26. Cedric J. Robinson, *Black Marxism: The Making of the Black Radical Tradition*, London: Zed Books, 1983.
27. Thierno Diop, 'Cheikh Anta Diop et le matérialisme historique', in *Marxisme et critique de la modernité en Afrique*, Paris, L'Harmattan, 2007, 145–175.
28. Pascal Bianchini, 'Cheikh Anta Diop et les marxistes au Sénégal: des relations ambivalentes entre démarcations et rapprochements, entre intégrations et scissions', *Revue d'histoire contemporaine de l'Afrique*, 4, forthcoming, 2023.
29. George Padmore, *Panafricanisme ou communisme? La prochaine lutte pour l'Afrique*, Paris: Présence africaine, 1962.
30. On this period and the relation between Pan-Africanism, Pan-Negrism and communism in the African diasporas, see: Philippe Dewitte, *Les mouvements nègres en France, 1919–1939*, Paris: L'Harmattan, 1985; Jonathan Derrick, *Africa's 'Agitators': Militant Anti-Colonialism*, London: Hurst, 2008; Hakim Adi, *Panafricanism and Communism: The Communist International and the African Diaspora*, Trenton, NJ: Africa World Press, 2013.
31. Immanuel Wallerstein, 'New Revolts against the System', *New Left Review*, 18, 2002, 33–34.
32. Heike Becker and David Seddon, 'Africa's 1968: Protests and Uprisings across the Continent', https://roape.net/2018/05/31/africas-1968-protests-and-uprisings-across-the-continent.
33. Elaine Mokhtefi, *Algiers, Third World Capital: Black Panthers, Freedom Fighters, Revolutionaries*, London: Verso, 2018.
34. See Chapter 8.
35. Amandla Thomas-Johnson, *Becoming Kwame Ture*, Cape Town: Chimurenganyana Series, 2020.
36. George Roberts, *Revolutionary State-Making in Dar es Salaam: African Liberation and the Global Cold War, 1961–1974*, Cambridge: Cambridge University Press, 2022. See also Chapters 12 and 13.
37. George Roberts, 'The Assassination of Eduardo Mondlane: Mozambican Revolutionaries in Dar es Salaam', in *Revolutionary State-Making in Dar es Salaam*, 135–172.
38. Peter Karibe Mendy, 'The "Cancer of Betrayal": The Assassination of Amílcar Cabral, 20 January 1973', in *Amílcar Cabral: A Nationalist and Pan-Africanist Revolutionary*, Athens, OH: Ohio University Press, 2019, 166–182.
39. From the 1950s to the 1980s, the student movements were the recruitment pool for revolutionary clandestine organisations. See Chapter 3 on Burkina Faso and Chapter 4 on Niger. For a more general view of the socio-political role of student movements, see Pascal Bianchini, 'Student Movements in Sub-Saharan Africa: Key Socio-Political Stake-Holders. From Corporatist Mobilisations to Avant-Garde Positions', *Journal of Civil Society*, 18(3), 2022, 263–285.
40. Bjorn Beckman, 'The Military as Revolutionary Vanguard: A Critique', *Review of African Political Economy*, 13(37), 1986, 50–62.
41. Paulo Gilberto Fagundes Visentini, 'African Marxist Military Regimes, Rise and Fall: Internal Conditioners and International Dimensions', *Brazilian Journal of African Studies*, 5(2), 2020, 33–52.

42. Bahru Zewde, *The Quest for Socialist Utopia: The Student Movement, 1960–1974*, Rochester: James Currey, 2014.

43. Messay Kebede, 'The Civilian Left and the Radicalisation of the Dergue', *Journal of Developing Societies*, 24(2), 2008, 159–182.

44. Tibebu Tishale, 'Modernity, Eurocentrism, and Radical Politics in Ethiopia, 1961–1991', *African Identities*, 6(4), 2008, 345–371.

45. Alain Gresh, 'The Free Officers and the Comrades: The Sudanese Communist Party and Nimeiri Face-to-Face, 1969–1971', *International Journal of Middle East Studies*, 21(3), 1989, 393–409.

46. Abdelwahab Himmat, *A History of the Sudanese Communist Party*, PhD thesis, University of South Wales, 2019, https://pure.southwales.ac.uk/ws/portalfiles/portal/5206971/Himmat_last_Version_7march.%20%20pdf.

47. George Nzongola-Ntalaja, *The Congo from Leopold to Kabila: A People's History*, London: Zed Books, 2002, 121–140.

48. Amrit Wilson, *The Threat of Liberation: Revolution and Imperialism in Zanzibar*, London: Pluto Press, 2013.

49. In 2022, for the 50th anniversary of the events of 26 October 1972, a conference was organised at the University of Abomey Calavi, https://calenda.org/989838.

50. For this part of Africa, we can refer to published volumes on the Arab communist parties or the Arab lefts, for example: Tareq Ismael, *The Communist Movement in the Arab World*, London: Routledge, 2005; Laure Guirguis, *The Arab Lefts: Histories and Legacies, 1950s–1970s*, Edinburgh: Edinburgh University Press, 2020.

51. Ophélie Rillon, 'Quand les filles s'en mêlent: le mouvement étudiant à l'épreuve des rapports de genre au Mali (1977–1980)', in Françoise Blum, Pierre Guidi and Ophélie Rillon, *Etudiants africains en mouvements: contribution à une histoire des années 1968*, Paris: Publications de la Sorbonne, 2016, 213–231.

1

Political Struggle in Senegal in the 1960s and 1970s: The Artistic and Literary Front

Ibrahima Wane

The alliance between politics and art is not a new phenomenon. Extensively theorised by Karl Marx and Friedrich Engels,[1] it has, in many parts of the world, guided the practice of revolutionary parties seeking to harness cultural production for social change. In Senegal, various left-wing movements have made creativity a key instrument of political awareness-raising and mobilisation, convinced that 'it is above all at the level of the superstructure, and particularly in the fields of art and literature, that the influence of the bourgeoisie is the most profound and lasting'.[2] This strategy was especially used by the underground movement, where the language of art served both as a refuge and as a vehicle for dissenting discourse. Political parties have thus practised the use of art as a weapon, from the era of the struggle for independence to that of the fight against post-colonial power, with variations dictated by both sensibilities and circumstances.

Senegal, which was represented by a deputy in the French National Assembly beginning in 1848, already had a fairly lively political life during the colonial period. The epicentre of this competitive political scene was Dakar, which became the capital of French West Africa in 1895. The election of Blaise Diagne, the first black deputy, in 1914 marked the end of the hegemony of whites and biracials on the Senegalese political scene. At the end of the Second World War, another turning point was reached with the adoption of the Lamine Guèye Act, which established French citizenship for all nationals of the 'overseas territories' in 1946. This legal provision added a new dimension to the electoral contest. The two major parties contending fiercely for the seats of Senegalese representatives in the French parliament were the Fédération sénégalaise de la Section française de l'internationale ouvrière (Senegalese Federation of the French Section of the

Workers' International) and the Bloc démocratique sénégalais (Senegalese Democratic Bloc), until the framework law established territorial governments in 1956.

Upon independence in 1960, the multiparty system was still in force, but within a few years the political landscape was entirely dominated by the ruling Union progressiste sénégalaise (UPS, Senegalese Progressive Union), as some opposition parties had merged with the UPS and others had been banned. The 1970s dampened the euphoria of international sovereignty and the government's optimistic plans for the future. Drought, oil crises and a groundnut crisis led to the implementation of an Economic and Financial Recovery Programme followed by Structural Adjustment Programmes. This period also saw the opening of a new page in national political life with the introduction of a tripartite system and later a quadripartite system. This codification of the democratic space, which excluded several left-wing parties from the official sphere and forced them to organise and operate underground, was reconsidered when President Léopold Sédar Senghor resigned in 1980. Senegal then returned to a fully pluralist system with the official recognition of the political organisations in existence.

THE SEEDS OF DISSENT

In the aftermath of the Second World War, which had rocked the foundations of the colonial edifice, the intensification of the struggle for emancipation was not confined to the trade union and political fronts alone. The yearning for social justice and international sovereignty was also a key driving force in the West African art scene.

The work of the Guinean Keïta Fodéba, who was a schoolteacher in Tambacounda, then Saint-Louis, after training at the William Ponty Teachers' College, and who was primarily known for his talents as a musician and playwright, is particularly revealing of the correlation between political action and artistic creation. The messages contained in his Théâtre africain, which echoed his convictions as a member of the Rassemblement démocratique africain (RDA, African Democratic Rally), did not fail to arouse the suspicions of the colonial administration, which promptly prohibited the performance of his play Aube africaine ('African Dawn') throughout the French West African territory, to take just one example.[3]

The plays of his Senegalese colleague Thierno Bâ, another graduate of William Ponty, suffered the same fate.[4] The young intellectual, a former member of the Groupes d'études communistes (Communist Study Groups),[5] remained faithful to his political commitment, which led him to join the Union démocratique sénégalaise (Senegalese Democratic Union, the Senegalese section of the RDA), the Bloc populaire sénégalais (Senegalese Popular Bloc) and later the Parti du regroupement africain-Sénégal (PRA-Sénégal, African Regroupment Party-Senegal), which advocated immediate independence in 1958. His party comrade Assane Sylla shared similar views. As a student in Grenoble, he already combined philosophical reflection with poetic production in Wolof. His poem 'Moom sa réew', a call to fight for independence written during this period, was adopted by the Parti africain de l'indépendance (PAI, African Independence Party) and used as the lyrics of its anthem. The PAI was created in 1957 as a Marxist political party and a federal party covering both Senegal and Sudan (present-day Mali). However, the party soon lost its Sudanese territorial section, which joined the Union soudanaise-rassemblement démocratique africain (US-RDA, Sudanese Union-African Democratic Rally) in 1959.

The slogan 'Moom sa réew' ('national independence') resonated in the country during the 1958 referendum period, when the PAI conducted a strong 'no' campaign. The echoes of this call can be seen in the number of *navétanes clubs*[6] that were founded in various Senegalese towns under the name Moom sa réew. However, the PAI did not have time to develop the cultural aspect of its political strategy and programme any further as it was forced to go underground by a dissolution order after barely three years of existence. The party was banned in Senegal after the municipal elections of 31 July 1960, which were marred by clashes between PAI and UPS activists in Saint-Louis. PAI leaders, including its Secretary General, Majhemout Diop, were imprisoned. Others went into exile. According to their interests and opportunities, party members, individually or in small groups, carried out initiatives aimed at promoting national languages, literature and artistic creation. The translation of the *Manifesto of the Communist Party*[7] into Wolof by Majhemout Diop and Madiké Wade during their imprisonment in Saint-Louis was one of the first strong signals. The *Ijjib volof (syllabaire volof)*,[8] written by a group of Senegalese students in Grenoble, was immediately adopted by PAI members as a literacy tool for workers. A similar dynamic was set in motion by a group of Fulani activists who met in Paris, under the leadership of Amadou Malick Gaye, to draw up an inventory of the Pulaar alphabet and a transcription method.[9] The pamphlet, which bore the French title *Inventaire de l'alphabet poular et méthode de transcription* ('Inventory of the Pulaar Alphabet and Method of Transcription'), was used to set up literacy classes in Saint-Louis and Dakar in 1960. The process continued with the development of a Pulaar alphabet at the outcome of the Mbagne Congress in Mauritania, which brought together Senegalese and Mauritanian students and researchers with an interest in the harmonisation of Pulaar writing in 1962.

Ousmane Sembène[10] took up the struggle through the medium of cinema, which became a substitute for his literary work that the language barrier made inaccessible to the majority of his people. Xala,[11] for example, portrays the impotence affecting the Senegalese political and economic ruling classes, who, despite appearances, were disconnected from national realities and remained intricately linked to French imperialism following independence. In the film, the Wolof language, which coexists in conflict with the official language, French, overtly symbolises nationalistic demands. The writer and filmmaker went on to publish the Wolof-language newspaper Kàddu[12] ('speech' or 'word') with other comrades in struggle, including the linguist Pathé Diagne. Alongside his participation in the newspaper, Pathé Diagne also produced a significant body of scientific material.

In the field of literature, one of the most distinguished figures is Cheik Aliou Ndao.[13] A member of the group that developed the Wolof syllabary, he focused on nationalist and Pan-Africanist poetry in the early 1960s.[14] Later, in parallel with his work in French, Ndao committed himself to demonstrating the capacity of national languages to generate quality works of literature in all the other genres as well (novels, short stories, theatre and essays).

David Diop, another Marxist poet, is noted for the courage and lucidity with which he tackled the question of the linguistic medium used by African writers.[15] The avenues he explored in terms of using the French language as a tool for transition did not go unnoticed.

The work of this author, who only had time to leave a single volume of poetry[16] to posterity, is among those that have had the greatest impact on schoolchildren and university students alike. Hamidou Dia, who viewed him as the greatest poet of his generation,[17] revealed in his doctoral thesis his intellectual debt to this bard and warrior of the new Africa. Landing Savané, leader of the Maoist movement And-Jëf ('unite to act' in Wolof), dedicated his first collection, written during his incarceration, to this 'pioneer of activist poetry',[18] adding that 'his youthful ardour', 'his boundless commitment to the African cause' and 'his revolt against the restraint of the "fathers"'[19] chimed well with the fiery spirit of the generation of secondary school and university students who took up the torch of the revolutionary struggle at the end of the 1960s.

THE CIRCLES AND THE STAGE

The 1960s were marked by the invasion of youth into the public sphere. The events of May 1968 in the French-speaking world were a reflection of their desire to challenge the establishment and a sign of the social and political changes already underway. Black power in the USA and the wave of liberation movements in Africa and Asia confirmed the trend.

In Senegal, however, the political horizon appeared dim. In the 1968 elections, the UPS, as the only party,[20] won all the seats in the National Assembly, and its Secretary General, Léopold Sédar Senghor, the only candidate for the presidency of the Republic, was re-elected with 100 per cent of the vote. The PAI, the main opposition force, was driven underground, with some of its leaders in exile, and was plagued by differences that led to a series of splits. This state of unease was conducive to the emergence of hotbeds of protest among the country's youth.

The Foyer artistique, littéraire et culturel du fleuve (FALCF, Artistic, Literary and Cultural Home of the River), founded in 1967 in Saint-Louis as a framework for reflection bringing together students with a love of literature from the city's four secondary schools, gradually became an instrument of struggle. Its performances, combining poetry recitals, theatre and musical evenings, were politically oriented. Patriotic and anti-colonialist monologues took precedence over romantic, symbolist or negritude-influenced poems. In his novel *Les sanglots de l'espoir*, former FALCF leader Hamidou Dia shared the story of the ideological evolution of the 'Damnés de la terre' ('the wretched of the Earth'), which was the core leadership group of the FALCF:

> Marxism, Fanonism and the Black Panthers were the new idols of the group. This did not detract from their love of literature but intensified their love for revolutionary combat poetry. The group was not at all bothered by the contradictory nature of their multiple ideological references. Not only did they easily accommodate them, but they found it normal to draw on all sources, without questioning any of them, since they all revolved around independence and revolution.[21]

Thus, many of these students came to their revolutionary engagement through the cultural movement. The FALCF combined cultural activities and trade union activism. Its role in the school strikes resulted in its leaders' expulsion from boarding school in 1968. Former FALCF members, arriving in university in Dakar or in France after completing their second-ary education, did not fail to make use of their experience in the emerging underground left-wing organisations and cultural clubs.

This turning point coincided with the start of the Great Proletarian Cultural Revolution. The impact of the Chinese cultural revolution[22] in Africa and the world, Mao's *Little Red Book*[23] and the broadcasts of Radio Peking were not easily ignored. Study circles were formed by young people fascinated by the experiment, who dreamt of a 'New Left'. Thus, in 1969, the Mouvement des jeunes marxistes-léninistes (MJML, Movement of Marxist-Leninist Youth) was born of the meeting of a core group of secondary school students inspired by Maoism with university students who had formed a Marxist study group in Paris and decided to return to Senegal to 'join the struggle'.

Alongside the underground ideological study circles formed in Dakar, Thiès and Saint-Louis, the members of the MJML set up cultural clubs, which were more open organisations allowing them to spread messages through literacy sessions, 'awareness theatre' or 'theatre of truth', and poetry readings designed to 'educate the people' and encourage them to 'break the chains of oppression'. The activities of the cultural clubs featured 'red dances', set to the rhythm of black American revolutionary music, interrupted from time to time by harangues and poetry recitations extolling the popular masses and announcing 'the Big Night'. In so doing, they applied the princi-ples stressed by Mao Zedong during the Yenan forum on literature and art:

> to ensure that literature and art fit well into the whole revolutionary machine as a component part, that they operate as powerful weapons for uniting and educating the people and for attacking and destroying the enemy, and that they help the people fight the enemy with one heart and one mind.[24]

Within the clubs, where various persuasions could be found, the unifying theme was nationalism, anti-imperialism, and anti-neocolonialism. Among the most active organisations in Dakar were the Lat Dior Club, the Fanon Club and the Africa Club.

The role of these cultural clubs as opposition forces was not lost on the regime in power. Moustapha Niasse, Chairman of the National Youth Com-mittee of the UPS and Chief of Staff of the President of the Republic, in his report to the eighth congress of the party, called on his comrades to remain vigilant and to closely monitor the deployment of such groups:

'youth centres were gradually becoming "centres of leftist agitation". Under the guise of apparently educational meetings, political training courses were taught which ultimately served to create a breeding ground for future so-called progressive activists.'[25]

These clubs were disbanded during 1972–74 due to the break-up of the MJML. Some of their members joined the Rassemblement national démocratique (RND, Democratic National Rally) led by Cheikh Anta Diop. Another group formed a movement that led to the creation of And-Jëf. This 'national-democratic, anti-imperialist and anti-feudal organisation' was built around the newspaper *Xarebi* ('the struggle'). After the publication of about ten issues, this clandestine organ[26] was seized and several of the movement's leaders and members were detained following a series of arrests between December 1974 and July 1975.

THE FRONT OF THE PEN AND THE BRUSH

This crisis gave rise to a phase of introspection within And-Jëf known as the Critical Assessment and Rectification Movement. The main conclusion of these conclaves was that there was a need for a real presence among the popular masses and the diversification of the party's bases. Accordingly, the party moved into the youth and student movements, sports and cultural associations, women's organisations, the trade union movement etc., while also moving closer to political organisations such as the Union pour la démocratie populaire (Union for Popular Democracy), which emerged from the MJML, and the Organisation pour la démocratie prolétarienne (Organisation for Proletarian Democracy), which was founded by former leaders of PRA-Sénégal with a view to 'unifying the Senegalese Maoist Left on a new foundation'.

This redeployment was achieved with the 'new culture' movement ('caada gu bees' Wolof) popularised under the name Caada gi, as its main tool for agitation, propaganda and mobilisation.[27] The Caada gi movement was driven by the Front culturel sénégalais (Làngug Caada Senegaal in Wolof, Senegalese Cultural Front in English),[28] which was founded in 1976 on the initiative of a group of young poets, activists and sympathisers of And-Jëf who had decided to continue the struggle in other forms in the face of police repression. The Senegalese Cultural Front claimed its identity as a front of the pen and the brush, symbols of literary and artistic creation.[29]

Informed by the lessons drawn from the actions of left-wing political organisations and the activities of previous cultural clubs, and inspired by the work of the Kàddu group, the leaders of the Senegalese Cultural Front sought, in their organisational process, to take things further by clarifying their approach by means of a collective work of theory. Thus, the line, objectives and strategy of the Senegalese Cultural Front were defined in a manifesto published in 1977.[30] Their first brochure, *Teerebtannu-taalifu xare Senegaal*[31] ('Anthology of Senegalese Combat Poetry'), was an illustration of the struggle 'against imperialist cultural domination and the vestiges of feudal culture'. The authors,[32] equally obsessed by beauty and expression, drew from the recesses of popular culture to describe the suffering of the masses and urge them to rise up and change their destinies.

Consciousness-raising also relied heavily on the power of music. Music was viewed as one of the best ways to sow the seeds of lucidity and combativeness in the minds of youth in the light of the threat posed by the influx of Western cultural products. One transitional idea of the nascent creative workshops was to set messages promoting the revolutionary ideal to popular traditional tunes or songs by contemporary singers. This experiment, which led to the production of two cassette tapes,[33] was continued and expanded through the cultural and sports associations that the Senegalese Cultural Front became involved in from the outset to ensure 'liaison with the masses' and allow it to gain a national dimension.

The launch of the Caada gi movement was accompanied by the creation of a so-called 'new type'[34] of cultural and sports associations – associations that truly fulfilled their cultural vocation. That is how the Pencum Tilléen[35] cultural and sports association was created in the Médina neighbourhood of Dakar. In existing associations, such as the Niayes of Pikine in the Dakar suburbs, cultural sections[36] were set up. These cultural and sports associations benefited from the contributions of students and pupils who returned to their respective towns, villages and neighbourhoods to run activities during school holidays.

The university campus was also immersed in this atmosphere in the late 1970s. During that period, when the forces of the left were vying for influence, And-Jëf managed to gain control of the Union nationale et patriotique des étudiants sénégalais (UNAPES, National and Patriotic Union of Senegalese Students) created in 1979.[37] This influence was reflected above all in the circulation of publications in national languages and the sudden explosion of Wolof and Pulaar poetry on campus. Cultural evenings provided a setting where the names of unsung heroes who did not appear on the official list of heroes of the anti-colonial struggle or in school textbooks could be heard.[38]

The activities of the Senegalese Cultural Front also extended to France, in the university circles where its members were active. Its influence could be seen in the cultural activities of the Association des étudiants sénégalais en France (AESF, Association of Senegalese Students in France), where the Maoists were one of the dominant currents between 1975 and 1980.[39] The contents of the pamphlets published by the Maison d'Afrique[40] section and the repertoire of the Troupe du 26 mai[41] attested to the affinities between the people in charge of the cultural activities of the AESF and the leadership of the Senegalese Cultural Front.

THE NEW STANDARDS OF HEROISM

In its endeavour to reclaim African history, the 'patriotic cultural movement' took a particular interest in figures who had stood in violent opposition to the colonial system that had monopolised the pen in the writing and teaching of the continent's history. From this desire to re-examine the history of Senegal arose a project aimed at rearranging the pantheon by placing, alongside the heroes already sanctified for their resistance to colonisation and/ or their contribution to building the national identity, other 'valiant sons of the people' whose actions had also influenced the country's destiny. The memory of several 'patriotic and revolutionary figures' who took part in the 'liberation struggle', especially at the beginning of the twentieth century, was revived and rehabilitated. We will mention only two, who are among those who have provided the most inspiration for poets and singers alike: Aline Sitoé Diatta and Lamine Senghor.

Aline Sitoé Diatta, an Icon of Civil Disobedience

Aline Sitoé Diatta[42] joined the circle of national heroes through the will of segments of the population in search of a symbol of radical opposition to the colonial order. As a priestess, she came to the fore in an environment of resistance in Casamance, where France, in the midst of the Second World War, was seeking to extract maximum human and cereal resources from its colonies. Her conflicts with the colonial power contributed to making her an 'icon of civil disobedience'. The administrative authorities, whose recruitment operations, food requisition campaign, tax collection and vaccination campaigns in 1942 did not sit well with the people of Lower Casamance, quickly recognised her as an enemy whose influence needed to be quelled by removing her from the territory.

The conditions of the deportation that followed her arrest had the opposite effect,[43] as the mystery of Aline Sitoé Diatta's fate served instead to build a myth around her figure. In the mid-1970s, her name began to be heard, especially in left-wing circles engaged in the fight against 'neo-colonialism'. Voices rose both in tribute and to demand the truth about the circumstances of this atypical woman's disappearance. In a study on intertextuality, Bassirou Dieng gave an account of the fixation surrounding her figure:

> The many questions in the newspapers some years ago about the fate of the Joola heroine, Aline Sitoé Jata, deported by the colonial authorities, reflected the networks of manifestations of the horizon of expectations. Historical memory called for facts and for her glorification.[44]

Young intellectuals denounced the 'conspiracy of silence' surrounding her person and set about reversing the trend by overstating the subversive aspect of her actions. In Landing Savané's poem 'Sénégal', Aline Sitoé is placed on the same lofty plane as monarchs and key protagonists of the resistance against colonial penetration in the nineteenth century.[45] The Senegalese Cultural Front produced a 20-page pamphlet on her in 1980.[46] This biography was followed by plays and novels by well-known authors.[47] These publications established her as a key figure in the political history of Casamance and Senegal, but her legacy took shape with the songs to her glory produced by the Senegalese Cultural Front and the cultural and sports associations. In these odes, Aline Sitoé was raised to the rank of queen due to the desire for sublimation on the part of young revolutionaries magnifying her opposition to the rule of the 'Whites' over the land of her ancestors and her individual sacrifice for the freedom and peace of the community. The chorus of praise emanating from many centres of artistic creation cast a spotlight on a figure who was not just a priestess reciting mystical litanies, but also and above all a rebel with a 'highly anti-colonial' message.[48]

Lamine Senghor, a Pioneer in the Struggle for Independence

Lamine Senghor was rescued from the dark recesses of history by his self-proclaimed heirs who undertook to inform their compatriots of the significance of his political and trade union career, which was conducted entirely abroad.[49] Since the metropolis had no interest in honouring him and the post-colonial regime did not claim responsibility for his actions, activists in the Front culturel sénégalais (FCS, Senegalese Cultural Front), the Association of Senegalese Students in France and cultural and sports associations strove to remove him from the list of unsung heroes by dint of monologues and poems about his life and 'the sacrifices he made for the cause of peoples around the world'.[50]

The verses they dedicated to him reflected their determination to 'wrest Lamine Senghor from the shadows into which he had been thrust'.[51] These lyrical writings were part of an effort to posthumously establish the career of a hero destined for immortality. They symbolically repatriated the 'Lion of the Sine'[52] and returned him to his roots, recalling the origins of his struggle. References to the 'kingdom of childhood' also introduced an implicit comparison with another Senghor – Leopold – who originated from the same region, but was seen as an ally of France, in contrast to Lamine Senghor, a worthy son of the nation and a thorn in the side of the colonial system.

Indeed, Lamine Senghor tenaciously fought 'the collaborationist position of Blaise Diagne',[53] Secretary of State for the colonies, whom he criticised for his role in the recruitment of the Tirailleurs (colonial troops) in 1918. Indeed, the first African deputy elected to the French Constituent Assembly, whom official history portrayed as a defender of indigenous rights, was, in the words of the 'first African communist cadre',[54] a 'zealous servant of the interests of French imperialism'.[55] In his pamphlet *La violation d'un pays*,[56] published in 1927, Lamine Senghor highlighted the cultural aspects of the colonial problem and lambasted the metropolis and its African accomplices.[57] In this he was, as Guy Ossito Midiohouan points out, 'the first French-speaking African writer to raise the problem of the acculturation of the colonised through schooling and the compulsory use of the language of the white master'.[58]

The voice of the Senegalese Cultural Front extolled the courage of the activist who fought for the people's right to self-determination. Lamine Senghor's entry into the pantheon was rationalised by associating him with a well-known and recognised hero, El Hadj Oumar Tall. Although they could not remove him from the provincial cemetery in France where he rested in obscurity and grant him a 'place of honour in a Senegalese cemetery', as Guy Ossito Midiohouan[59] recommended, artists and poets strove to write his name into the annals of history as one of the few Africans who openly raised the question of independence between the two world wars.

These figures were established in the collective unconscious through musical, poetic, and theatrical productions that challenged the official version of history. Through these works, a generation of creators and intellectuals shattered the state's monopoly on the creation of national heroes.

THE LABOURS OF THE NEWLY LEGAL PARTY

And-Jëf became legal in 1981,[60] under the name And-Jëf/Mouvement révolutionnaire pour la démocratie nouvelle (AJ/MRDN, And-Jëf/Revolutionary Movement for New Democracy). It was supported in its efforts to occupy the political landscape by the newspaper *Jaay doole bi/Le prolétaire*.[61] This new status led to readjustments and choices that would cause some friction. Positions diverged on the policy of unity of action with other parties, participation in elections, strategies for building a proletarian party, and more. Differences of opinion were also voiced as to how to meld cultural activities with the political struggle. The emphasis on intervention in businesses and the building of a workers' movement was perceived by several FCS leaders as a relegation of cultural work to the sidelines. The will of the party leadership to incorporate democratic cultural organisations into basic party committees meant the disintegration of the FCS.

Some of the former members of the FCS who were active in the party then set up a theatre company, known as Troupe Aliin Sitooy, which participated in the activities of And-Jëf (rallies, conferences and cultural events). It also produced a cassette tape in 1982 titled *Dama yàgg fekke*, containing songs in Wolof and Pulaar.[62]

Although the vocations inspired or confirmed by the 'new culture' movement were not adequately encouraged or supported, several artists continued to perform works created by the 'patriotic cultural movement' after becoming professional and popular musicians. Thus, these works were able to make their way onto records and even the national radio station. Many of the songs performed by Baaba Maal or the group Pape & Cheikh, for example, bear the hallmark of 'red' events. Echoes of this vibrant era can be heard even in the lyrics and compositions of the Y en a marre ('fed up') movement, which came to the forefront of the Senegalese political scene in the 2010s.

The connection between these two generations lies in their focus on words and images that speak to the lives and dreams of the disenfranchised, not unlike the spokespersons for the Kenyan working masses whose role the writer Ngugi wa Thiong'o illustrated in *Decolonising the Mind*.[63]

The production and dissemination of works that can simultaneously elicit aesthetic enjoyment and foster political awareness is a valuable tool. Cultural activities have served the forces of the Senegalese left as a framework for expression and a means of raising awareness among broad swathes of the population, and not least as a means for recruiting new members.

The actions of the heroes and heroines of resistance to colonisation and the resources of the national languages have been widely used to awaken national pride, stir the patriotic fibre and fan the flames of revolution.

SELECT BIBLIOGRAPHY

AESF (1979), *Francophonie et néocolonialisme: le combat linguistique dans la libération du peuple sénégalais*, Paris: AESF.

AESF (1979), *Recueil de chants et poèmes patriotiques*, Paris: AESF.

Dia, Hamidou (1987), *Les sanglots de l'espoir*, Paris: L'Harmattan.

Diop, Boubacar Boris (1990), *Les tambours de la mémoire*, Paris: L'Harmattan.

Diop, David (1973), *Coups de pilon*, Paris: Présence africaine.

Front culturel sénégalais (1977), *Manifeste du Front culturel sénégalais*, Dakar: Front culturel sénégalais.

Front culturel sénégalais (1979), *Lamine Senghor: vie et œuvre*, Dakar: Front culturel sénégalais.

Front culturel sénégalais (1980), *Aliin Sitooye Jaata: vie et œuvre*, Dakar: Front culturel sénégalais.

Front culturel sénégalais (1980), *Les braises rouges qui chantent (anthologie de poèmes révolutionnaires)*, Dakar: Front culturel sénégalais.

Sagna, Olivier (1986), *Des pionniers méconnus de l'indépendance: africains, antillais et luttes anti-colonialistes dans la France de l'entre-deux-guerres (1919–1939)*, doctoral thesis, Paris: Université Paris VII.

Savané, Landing (undated), *Luttes et lueurs*, Dakar: Editions Xamle.

Senghor, Lamine (1927), *La violation d'un pays*, Paris: Bureau d'éditions, de diffusion et de publicité.

NOTES

1. Karl Marx and Friedrich Engels, *The German Ideology* (English translation), Amherst, MA: Prometheus Books, 1998 (1845).
2. Landing Savané, *Luttes et lueurs*, Dakar: Editions Xamle, undated, 4.
3. Ndoumbé Ndiaye, *Le contrôle politique et administratif de la production et de la circulation des œuvres intellectuelles en AOF de 1906 à 1958*, master's thesis in History, Dakar: Université Cheikh Anta Diop de Dakar, 2002, 47. 'Aube africaine' recounts the Thiaroye massacre of 1944.
4. Ibrahima Thioub and Ndiouga A. Benga, 'Les groupes de musique "moderne" des jeunes Africains de Dakar et de Saint-Louis, 1946–1960', in Odile Goerg (ed.), *Fêtes urbaines en Afrique: espaces, identité et pouvoir*, Paris: Karthala, 1999, 222.
5. See Jean Suret-Canale, *Les groupes d'études communistes (G.E.C.) en Afrique Noire*, Paris: L'Harmattan, 1994.
6. The *navétanes clubs* were originally football teams formed for 'inter-neighbourhood tournaments' at the end of the 1940s. As the competitions

grew, the clubs developed into sports and cultural associations in the 1970s, eventually competing in a 'people's national championship'.

7. Karl Marx and Friedrich Engels, *Manifesto of the Communist Party* (English translation), 1850 (1848).

8. Association des étudiants sénégalais en France, *Ijjib volof (syllabaire volof)*, Grenoble: Imprimerie des deux ponts, 1959.

9. Groupe d'étude du poular, *Inventaire de l'alphabet poular et méthode de transcription*, Paris, 1960.

10. A member of the General Confederation of Labour and the French Communist Party since his early years in France, Ousmane Sembène participated in the creation of the PAI section in Marseilles in 1957. He continued his political activism outside the framework of political parties from 1960 onwards on his return to Senegal.

11. A work of fiction produced in 1974, adapted from the novel by Sembène Ousmane, *Xala*, Paris: Présence africaine, 1973.

12 The newspaper *Kàddu* was published quarterly, then monthly, from 1971 to 1978.

13. A member of the PAI section in Grenoble, Cheik Aliou Ndao was also in charge of the Fédération des étudiants d'Afrique noire en France (Black African Students Federation in France) theatre group at the time.

14. These poems were published in Assane Sylla's anthology *Poèmes et pensées philosophiques wolof, tome IV: de l'oralité à l'écriture*, Dakar: IFAN, 1996, 25–30, and in two collections by Cheik Aliou Ndao, *Lolli-Taataan*, Dakar: IFAN/Enda-Editions, 1999, and *Bàkku xaalis* (undated).

15. 'He knows that by writing in a language that is not the language of his brothers, he cannot truly render the heartfelt song of his country. But by asserting the presence of Africa with all its contradictions and its faith in the future, by fighting through his writing for the end of the colonial regime, the French-speaking black creator contributes to the rebirth of our national cultures'; David Diop (1956), 'Contribution au débat sur la poésie nationale', *Présence africaine*, 6, 1956, 115.

16. David Diop, *Coups de pilon*, Paris: Présence Africaine, 1973.

17. Hamidou Dia, 'Littératures nationales et écriture poétique', doctoral thesis, Quebec: Université Laval, 1995, 169.

18. Savané, *Luttes et lueurs*, 8.

19. Amadou Ly, *La poésie sénégalaise d'expression française de 1945 à 1985: écriture et thématique*, Dakar: IFAN Ch. A. Diop, 2012, 147.

20. After the dissolution of the PAI in 1960, the merger of the ruling UPS with part of the Bloc des masses sénégalaises (Bloc of the Senegalese Masses) in 1963, the banning of the Front national sénégalais (Senegalese National Front) in 1964 and the integration of the PRA-Sénégal into the UPS in 1966, Senegal was effectively under a one-party regime.

21. Hamidou Dia, *Les sanglots de l'espoir*, Paris: L'Harmattan, 1987, 58–59.

22. They drew on both the 'New Culture Movement' led by Chinese youth in 1917–1919 and the 'Great Proletarian Cultural Revolution' launched by Chairman Mao in 1966.

23. A collection of quotes summarising the thoughts of Mao Zedong.

24. Mao Zedong, *Talks at the Yenan Forum on Literature and Art (May 1942)*, *Selected Works, Vol. III*, 84.

25. Moustapha Niasse, 'Nouvelles structures et nouvelle politique du mouvement des jeunes du parti ou "Jeunesse et vie politique"', Dakar: VIIIème congrès de l'Union progressiste sénégalaise, reprod., 16–18 December, 1972, 13.

26. Senegal returned to a multiparty system in 1974 with the recognition of the Parti démocratique sénégalais (Senegalese Democratic Party) led by Abdoulaye Wade and the return to legality of a divided and weakened PAI in 1976. This democratic liberalisation was enshrined in the 1976 law on the creation of political parties, which established three ideological and doctrinal orientations: 'the social-democratic current, the liberal-democratic current and the Marxist-Leninist or Communist current'.

27. *Caada gi* is a neologism derived from the contraction of the expression *ci aada ji* ('in culture, about culture'). This lexical creation expresses both a desire to break with tradition and a constant harking back to tradition, hence a call for cultural renewal.

28. *Làngug caada Senegaal* in Wolof.

29. The logo of the Senegalese Cultural Front is a raised fist clutching a pencil and brush, and its motto is 'Fer̃ent mën na taalug daay', a translation of the Chinese proverb, 'A single spark can start a prairie fire', used by Mao Zedong in a famous letter to his comrades in 1930.

30. *Manifeste du Front culturel sénégalais*, 1977.

31. *Làngug caada Senegaal/Front culturel sénégalais, Teerebtannu-taalifu xare Senegaal*, 1977.

32. The poems, which were distributed clandestinely, are anonymous or signed with pseudonyms.

33. The cassettes were tape-recorded and distributed through the network of cultural and sports associations and political circles.

34. Despite their name, cultural and sports associations had continued to focus on football, which had become the country's most popular sport.

35. Pencum Tilléen was the first cultural and sports association created by members of the Senegalese Cultural Front. From the time of its inception in 1977, it distinguished itself by its particular focus on its cultural vocation: setting up a theatre company and a band, organising poetry recitals, publishing brochures and a newspaper (*Baatu penc mi*), etc.

36. In addition to its artistic activities, the cultural section of the Niayes organised holiday courses for pupils and literacy sessions in national languages.

37. 'Echos du congrès de l'UNAPES', *Jaay Doole Bi-Le prolétaire*, 3, 1980, 3; Pascal Bianchini, 'Le Mouvement étudiant sénégalais: un essai d'interprétation', in Momar-Coumba Diop (ed.), *La société sénégalaise entre le local et le global*, Paris, Karthala, 2002, 374.

38. See next section, 'The New Standards of Heroism'.

39. Abdoulaye Guèye, 'Les étudiants sénégalais en France', in Momar-Coumba Diop (ed.), *Le Sénégal contemporain*, Paris: Karthala, 2002, 220–221.

40. The members of the AESF who were most sensitive to cultural issues met at the Maison d'Afrique, a university residence in the 14th arrondissement of Paris

(later renamed Résidence Lucien Paye). The section published the following two pamphlets in 1979: *Francophonie et néocolonialisme: le combat linguistique dans la libération du peuple sénégalais* ('Francophonie and neo-colonialism: the linguistic combat in the liberation of the Senegalese people) and *Recueil de chants et poèmes patriotiques* ('Collection of patriotic songs and poems') in Wolof, Pulaar and French.

41. The name of this theatre company refers to 26 May 1972, the date of the death of Al Ousseynou Cissé, who was part of the group of students expelled from the University of Dakar and forcibly enrolled in the army following the strikes of 1971. The Troupe du 26 mai produced two cassettes: *Chants & poèmes patriotiques du Sénégal, tome 1: Doom noppil* and *Chants & poèmes patriotiques du Sénégal, tome 2: Joxante loxo.*

42. Aline Sitoé Diatta was born around 1920 in Kabrousse, in the department of Oussouye in south-western Casamance. As a young girl, she worked as a docker in the port of Ziguinchor, then as a domestic worker in Dakar. It was in Dakar that she received her revelation in 1941, and returned to Casamance to become a rain priestess. Pilgrims flocked to her neighbourhood, Mosoor, in western Kabrousse. This excitement coincided with the first acts of open defiance by the people against the colonial power. Accused of fomenting the uprising, Aline Sitoé was arrested in January 1943, sentenced to ten years' imprisonment, and deported to Kayes and subsequently to Timbuktu in French Sudan, now Mali.

43. Aline Sitoé, of whom the population has had no news since her deportation, has become a kind of ghost. A commission of enquiry set up by the Senegalese government in 1983 returned from Timbuktu with a document stating that the famous prisoner had died in 1944, but that information did not dispel the doubts.

44. Bassirou Dieng, 'Les genres narratifs et les phénomènes intertextuels dans l'espace soudanais (mythes, épopées et romans)', *Annales FLSH*, 21, 1991, 92.

45. Savané, *Luttes et lueurs*, 19.

46. Front culturel sénégalais, *Aliin Sitooye Jaata: vie et œuvre*, 1980.

47. Inspired by the approach of the Senegalese Cultural Front, Boubacar Boris Diop, in his novel *Les Tambours de la mémoire*, Paris: L'Harmattan, 1990, portrayed the fascination exerted by Aline Sitoé on a fringe of the Senegalese left. Marouba Fall produced a play celebrating the actions of the heroine: *Aliin Sitooye Jaata ou la Dame de Kabrus*, Dakar: NEAS, 1996).

48. Front culturel sénégalais, *Aliin Sitooye Jaata*, 11.

49. Lamine Senghor was born in 1889 in Joal, where he spent his childhood working in the fields before moving to Dakar in his late twenties to look for work. He was enlisted in the French army in 1916 and took part in the First World War. At the end of the war, he returned to Senegal and was discharged in 1919 for health reasons. After obtaining French citizenship, he returned to France in 1921, where he found a job as a letter carrier for the French Post. Lamine Senghor joined the Intercolonial Union and the French Communist Party. In 1926, he created the Comité de défense de la race nègre (Committee for the Defence of the Negro Race). The following year, he was elected to the executive committee of the French League against Colonial Oppression and

Imperialism and became the head of the Paris League for the Defence of the Negro Race. On the political activities of Lamine Senghor, see David Murphy, 'Tirailleur, facteur, anticolonialiste: la courte vie militante de Lamine Senghor (1924–1927)', *Cahiers d'histoire: revue d'histoire critique*, 126, 2015, 55–72.

50. Front culturel sénégalais, *Lamine Senghor: vie et œuvre*, 1979, 6.

51. Ibid., 8.

52. This periphrastic expression was coined by the Senegalese Cultural Front; see ibid., 28.

53. Amady Dieng, *Blaise Diagne, premier député africain*, Paris: Editions Chaka, 1990, 106.

54. Olivier Sagna, *Des pionniers méconnus de l'indépendance: africains, antillais et luttes anti-colonialistes dans la France de l'entre-deux-guerres (1919–1939)*, doctoral thesis, Paris: Université Paris VII, 1986, 320.

55. Front culturel sénégalais, *Lamine Senghor*, 25.

56. *La violation d'un pays*, Paris: Bureau d'éditions, de diffusion et de publicité, 1927, tells the story of the colonisation of black peoples in narrative form. In it, the author condemned the role of Blaise Diagne, depicted as a traitor who made a pact with the invader at the expense of his own brothers.

57. In this caricature of Deputy Blaise Diagne, portrayed by the main character Dégou, who spoke to his brothers in French, Lamine Senghor asked his readers to imagine 'the effect that a speech delivered in the language of the "pale man" would have had on the minds of ebony-coloured men, even when spoken by a brother'.

58. Guy Ossito Midiohouan, 'Lamine Senghor (1889–1927), précurseur de la prose nationaliste négro-africaine', in Papa Samba Diop (ed.), *Sénégal-Forum: Literature and History*, Frankfurt: IKO, 1995, 166.

59. Ibid., 167.

60. The legalisation of the party came with the advent of the full multiparty system introduced by Abdou Diouf, who succeeded Léopold Sédar Senghor in power in January 1981. Other left-wing organisations were also officially recognised, including the Rassemblement national démocratique, the Parti de l'indépendance et du travail (Party of Independence and Labour), the Ligue démocratique/ mouvement pour le parti du travail (Democratic League/Movement for the Party of Labour), the Mouvement pour la démocratie populaire (Movement for Popular Democracy), the Union pour la démocratie populaire (Union for Popular Democracy), the Organisation socialiste des travailleurs (Socialist Organisation of Workers), the Ligue communiste des travailleurs (Communist League of Workers), and the Union pour le socialisme et la démocratie (Union for Socialism and Democracy).

61. A legal newspaper founded in February 1980 by members of the And-Jëf leadership.

62. The party's events were accompanied by Troupe Aliin Sitooy until the early 1990s.

63. Ngugi wa Thiong'o, *Decolonising the Mind: The Politics of Language in African Literature*, Harare: Zimbabwe Publishing House, 1986.

2

The Revolutionary Left in Sub-Saharan Africa: The Case of Mali

Issa N'Diaye

The history of the Malian left often remains unknown. Little has been written, except for what one can find in a few clandestine newspapers of the period. The archives held by left-wing leaders or activists are private property. They are very poorly kept in boxes or distributed in bags that are easy to hide or remove in case of police searches. Many have been lost with the death of their holders. Others have become the property of their families who do not see their historical significance. Poorly preserved, they remain, for the most part, little used, sometimes unusable. However, they remain full of suffering or hope, sometimes both at the same time. They remain the few precious testimonies of this part of the country's recent history.

Unfortunately, few activists who witnessed and acted during these periods write or agree to talk about them. Few also are those who agree to give the documents they have to younger activists or to researchers. These jealously guarded archives often end up disappearing with their holders. Rare also are the families who realise the inestimable value of these documents thrown in a jumble and sometimes devoured by time.

Many also are the comrades who have redeployed in the field of the management of the political apparatus of the moment. They ended up being 'oxidised' there, digested by the ruling elites in power or in opposition. Few are those who have remained faithful to their former convictions. Many have ended up converting to neoliberalism. While they do not deny their revolutionary past, many have shifted to the new political 'realism'. Few are willing to be self-critical. Some sing the praises of this heroic period in the history of the Malian left and equate any criticism or even self-criticism with denigration. Others simply prefer to turn the page, uncomfortable with their own reversal, thus discrediting in the eyes of their fellow citizens the speeches that no longer reflect the values and struggles of the left.

Desperate left-wing Malian activists have ended up sinking into alcohol. Misunderstood by their immediate entourage, abandoned by the organisations that structured their lives as activists, they became marginalised. Others, over time, became 'mosque rats'. It is surprising to see the Marxist-Leninists of yesterday disserting on the virtues of the Koran and vigorously discussing this or that passage of the hadiths. This seems to be the 'tragic fate of communists', according to their liberal critics.

On the other hand, the failure of the left-wing regimes that our geographical space has known, the deviations and disillusionment with the promises of yesteryear, the abandonment of previous militant commitments and the brutal conversion to neo-liberalism have made a good number of former left-wing militants revert to 'political realism'. One is almost ashamed to assume one's past or to say that one is a leftist. In some cases, one does not even dare to evoke the slightest terminology referring to it. The words communism, Marxism, socialism and class struggle are banished from the vocabulary of the day, as if referring to them would be a sign of political archaism. One goes so far as to celebrate the 'death of ideologies' in the face of triumphant neoliberal globalisation.

Nowadays, the left and its discourse have become barely audible. It is sometimes at union level that we still discover some survivals, notably among some teachers' or students' unions. And even there, the theoretical level of the discourse of the moment is largely, qualitatively speaking, behind those of yesteryear. Neoliberal globalisation has shrivelled many things, starting with the collective memory and the sharing and solidarity impulses that already permeated our cultures and civilisations. It is true that the citizen, trade union, political and other organisations that existed before have been swept away by the structural adjustment programmes and privatisation policies imposed by international institutions and donors. Today, we are still struggling to recover. The current proliferation of political parties (currently close to 300 in Mali) and trade unions (close to 100), the flourishing of associations with multiple vocations (more than 10,000, mostly religious), do not reflect the vitality of the 'democratic' renewal. The quality of intelligence and political commitment seems to have given way to the quantity of circumstantial groupings and the lure of easy and immediate gain. Rare also are the organisations for citizen remobilisation and re-grounding. They are dealing, most of the time, with cultural fields which seem to regret the past values of our societies, ignored or trampled by the young people, victims of the Western mimicry and the drifts of absolute permissiveness. The failure of the educational system, the disintegration of the social fabric, the trampling of societal and civilisational values and the loss of reference points have aggravated the disintegration of the backbone of our societies and the references of our collective memory.

THE LEFT AND THE ANTI-COLONIAL STRUGGLE: FROM THE AFRICAN PARTY FOR INDEPENDENCE TO THE MALIAN LABOUR PARTY

Let's first go back in time to better decipher the present. The history of the Malian left is partly in line with the history of national liberation struggles in the French colonies of Africa. It experienced a period of incubation under the colonial administration thanks to the multiple links of solidarity that French left-wing progressives present in the colonial administration were able to weave: teachers, doctors, civil servants and others. They helped to structure the first local union movements and to create the first Marxist study circles. Jean Suret-Canale, a communist activist and historian of Africa, was one of the main leaders of the 'Marxist study groups'. One can find testimonies on the communist study groups in Black Africa in his book *Les groupes d'études communistes (G.E.C.)* published in 1994.[1] However, according to the Senegalese economist and writer Amady Aly Dieng,[2] the discovery and then the specifically African appropriation of Marx and Marxism were made by Africans residing in France, intellectuals and students, before acquiring a more autonomous life on African soil. On the whole, this was mainly the work of militants of left-wing political and trade union organisations from the metropolis, especially those close to the French Communist Party. The Marxist study circles had a strong impact on student youth and the few local executives who worked in the colonial administration. For many young students of the time, it was like a compulsory rite of passage. It was mainly within the schools and the trade unions that the first leftist militants and leaders were trained. Those who supervised them, both nationals and expatriates, were subject to a lot of bullying by the colonial power.

But it was the struggles for national independence that served as a crucible for the training and emergence of the first left-wing militants. The end of the Second World War gave a boost to the political awareness in favour of the emancipation of colonised peoples. The militants and forces of the left will make their mark in spite of the impediments of the colonial administration and the multifarious support to the proponents of the status quo.

In the case of Mali, formerly called French Sudan, it is the Parti africain de l'indépendance (PAI, African Party for Independence) that will serve as a matrix for the fertilisation of the militants and forces of the left. Born in the heat of the struggles, notably those of the railway workers of the Dakar–Niger railroad line in 1947–48, the PAI was established on 15 September 15 1957 in Thiès, Senegal through a manifesto signed by 23 African patriots from Guinea, Mali, Niger and Senegal. They were mainly teachers, medical doctors, pharmacists, dentists, civil servants, workers, engineers, students and artists. Organised into territorial sections, the PAI split after the break-up of the Federation of Mali in 1960. A good part of them joined the Union soudanaise – Rassemblement démocratique africain (US-RDA, Sudanese Union – African Democratic Rally) of Modibo Keita and formed what was called the 'left wing of the RDA'. Its leader was Amadou Seydou Traoré, known as Amadou Djicoroni, one of the first militants of the Sudanese section of the PAI. A teacher by training, he was disbarred from the civil service for his stance. He was the founding director of the Librairie populaire du Mali during the First Republic, and his political current participated in the 22 September 1960 Congress, which proclaimed Mali's independence and decided on the socialist option for development. This left was strongly involved in trade unions and youth organisations.[3]

If the original PAI fiercely advocated immediate independence of the former French colonies, the RDA was a political movement that wanted to federate the political parties operating in the former French colonies at the local, regional and African levels. It thus created national sections. Initially affiliated with the French Communist Party, the RDA existed in Guinea, Côte d'Ivoire, Benin, Burkina Faso, Senegal (Senegalese Democratic Union), Mali, Niger (Niger Progressive Party) and as far as Central Africa, Chad (Chad Progressive Party), in the Middle Congo (Congolese Progressive Party then Democratic Union for the Defence of African Interests), in Gabon (Gabonese Mixed Committee then Gabonese Democratic Block) and in Cameroon (Union of the Populations of Cameroon) in the former French territories of equatorial Africa. In Mali, it took the name Union Soudanaise-rassemblement démocratique africain.

The RDA was crossed, since its creation, by two lines of divergence which ended up fracturing it definitively. These two lines had opposite ideological contours. The first was the idea of federation. The progressive current supported the idea of going together towards independence as federated states in a geographical space grouping the former French colonies of West Africa and Equatorial Africa. Modibo Keita and Sékou Touré were the main leaders. They were initially supported by Senegalese political leaders. The anti-federalist current within the RDA was led mainly by the Ivorian Houphouët-Boigny who was close to French interests. He strove to torpedo all efforts undertaken by Modibo Keita and his supporters. He succeeded in getting Upper Volta (later Burkina Faso) and Dahomey (later Benin) to give up the initial project of the Federation of Mali.

The former, like Modibo Keita, advocated a more marked break from the colonial system, while the latter were more in favour of the status quo. From then on, the logic leading to the failure of federalist projects both within the Federation of Mali and on a regional and African scale was put in place, projects torpedoed by France, which worked to overthrow progressive regimes in Africa in complicity with the French government networks of Françafrique. The long list of coups d'état in Africa (more than 50) globally matches that of French military interventions in Africa. This chapter is far from being closed today. The ongoing chaos in the Sahel and Mali is a perfect illustration.

The break-up of the Federation of Mali caused a split within the original PAI. There were serious differences of opinion within the PAI as to the direction taken on the issue of African independence. The PAI was in favour of immediate independence, while the US-RDA was in favour of independence for federated states. This required more time. The 'No' vote of Sékou Touré's Guinea was in line with the PAI's position, which initially explained the massive support of PAI cadres for the young Guinean state.

However, the ideological proximity between the progressive current within the RDA and the PAI allowed a good number of left-wing leaders and activists who were later persecuted in Senegal, Guinea and elsewhere to find refuge in Modibo Kéita's Mali. Thus Majhemout Diop, the main leader of the PAI, persecuted in Senegal, was able to find refuge for a while in Bamako. Other Senegalese left-wing militants such as Baïdy Ly, former director of the Lycée de jeunes filles de Bamako under Modibo Kéita, and Mamadou Talla, the first director of Radio Soudan, which became Radio Mali, held high positions within the Malian administration until the military coup of 1968. The same is true of left-wing political opponents from Niger such as Bakary Djibo and Abdou Moumouni, an internationally renowned physicist who was the first director of the Solar Energy Laboratory in Mali and author of the famous book *Education in Africa*.[4]

The split in the PAI led some of its members to join the US-RDA, whose ideological orientation they influenced during and after the 22 September 1960 Congress which proclaimed Mali's independence. This left wing of the

RDA, reinforced by militants from the PAI, was at the origin of the US-RDA's main ideological, political and economic choices. It was very active inside trade union organisations and youth movements. It was the driving force behind the choice of the socialist option for the development of the young Malian state, the nationalisation of major essential sectors of the national economy and the establishment of state-owned companies and enterprises. It was also this left that favoured the abandonment of the franc Communauté financière d'Afrique (Financial Community of Africa franc) and the creation of the Malian franc. The left also inspired the decision to close and withdraw French military bases from the national territory on 20 January 1961. It was also the inspiration for the policy of reforming the Malian education system in 1962. These measures helped to anchor the young Mali in the progressive camp on the African and international level.

The other tendency within PAI which refused to integrate the US-RDA took the name Parti malien de travail (PMT, Malian Labour Party). Following Sékou Touré's 'No' during the 28 September 1958 Referendum which led to Guinea's independence, many of its leaders went to lend a hand to Guinea, which was facing hostility from France. They spontaneously put themselves in the service of the new state, the colonial administration having decided, in retaliation, to withdraw its own cadres. The newly born Guinean state was threatened with collapse due to the brutal withdrawal of the colonial administration's executives and technicians, and the economic and financial reprisals undertaken against the new Guinean regime. Sékou Touré's regime was subject to a real economic and financial blockade. Its future evolution ended up weakening its links with the PAI.

THE MALIAN LABOUR PARTY AND THE REVOLUTIONARY LEFT IN MALI

The PMT, of Marxist-Leninist persuasion, was for a long time the main political force of the left in Mali after the fall of the regime of Modibo Kéita, following the military coup of 19 November 1968. Although its main militants were known to the leaders of the RDA during Modibo Keita's tenure (1960–68), the organisation remained underground, and the RDA leadership avoided repressing them.

The PMT has remained an underground party throughout its history. Although opposed to the RDA, which it described as a petty bourgeois movement, the PMT was the first political organisation to voice its opposition to the 1968 coup d'état in a leaflet distributed by its clandestine newspaper *L'abeille* ('The Bee'), which later became the organ of the Alliance démocratique du Mali – Parti africain pour la solidarité et la justice (ADE-MA-PASJ, Alliance for Democracy in Mali – African Party for Solidarity and Justice), one of the main components in the forces that contributed to the fall of Moussa Traoré's military dictatorship in March 1991. Following the distribution of this leaflet in 1968, its main local leaders were arrested, convicted and deported to prisons throughout the country. The best-known were Abdramane Baba Touré, a doctor in physics and former director of the Advanced Teacher Training School, Marie Bernard Cissoko, a doctor in philosophy and professor at the Advanced Teacher Training School, Mamadou Doucouré, a professor in physics at the National School of Engineers, Santigui Mangara, a student in philosophy at the Advanced Teacher Training School, Kadari Bamba, an engineer, National Director of Industry, Oumar Yattara, a controller at the Post and Telecommunication Office, and Monobem Ogoniangaly, an engineer at Sonarem (the national company for research and operation of mining resources of Mali).

Other left-wing leaders such as Ibrahima Ly, a doctor in mathematics, former leader of the Federation of Black African Students in France, author of the famous book *Toiles d'araignées*[5] ('Spider Webs') and *Les noctuelles vivent de larmes*[6] ('Noctuaries Live on Tears'), were arrested, deported and savagely tortured, as was Kari Dembélé, a doctor in sociology and professor at the Advanced Teacher Training School and at the National School of Administration. The list of victims of the dictatorship of Moussa Traoré's regime was long and bloody. Arrests, arbitrary detentions, transfers and disbarment, all equally arbitrary, were often the lot of many left-wing activists, including the author of this chapter. The list of victims of the dictatorship of Moussa Traoré is long and painful. The Comité de défense des libertés démocratiques au Mali (CDLDM, Committee for the Defence of Democratic Freedoms in Mali) published a non-exhaustive list of the victims of the regime's repression after the fall of the regime. It was a period of 23 years of tears and blood.

The Malian Labour Party, although not legally existing, was a real laboratory for the training and structuring of militants of the Malian left. Many of them had their baptism of fire as left-wing militants there. They discovered there Marxist theory and served their organisational apprenticeship and that of clandestine militant. Thus the chain was extended and the new cadres contributed greatly to the dissemination of left-wing thinking and principles throughout the country, where new schools were created and new companies and state enterprises were established. In these circles were recruited most of the militants and executives who were to serve as the driving force during the long resistance against Moussa Traoré's bloody dictatorship.

Outside the capital, it was mainly in working-class and peasant circles that the PMT managed to spread left-wing ideas, particularly in the textile factories of Segou, at the Malian textile company COMATEX, and in peasant circles in the Office du Niger, the country's agricultural granary. Further west, it was in the SOCIMA cement production plant at Diamou, not to mention the Railway Company, which was a great school for anti-colonial resistance and the emergence of the Malian left.

Malian trade unions, first and foremost the National Union of Workers of Mali, were also a privileged place for the training and maturation of the Malian left. It was in the trade unions, especially among teachers and schoolchildren, health workers, cultural workers, press workers and justice workers, that the left-wing battalions were trained that eventually overcame Moussa Traoré's ferocious military dictatorship.

The PMT experienced several splits within its ranks. Ideological differences within the international communist movement exacerbated the contradictions within the party. The debates were virulent, particularly within the diaspora, between Stalinists, Trotskyists, pro-Soviet, pro-Chinese, pro-Albanian and others. The PMT did not recover from this. Exclusions were also pronounced, such as that of Dr Aly Nouhoun Diallo by the French Section of the PMT led by Professor of Mathematics Yoro Diakité, for 'sectarianism and fractional work'. He was later reinstated by the internal leadership of the party. Other members of the PMT were co-opted and integrated by the military regime under the guise of the 'theory of entryism', which claimed to change the system from within. Thus, among the best-known are Ngolo Traoré, who served for a long time as Minister of Foreign Affairs under the dictator Moussa Traoré, Fagnanama Koné, who was appointed to the Ministry of Agriculture, and Oumar Issiaka Ba at the Ministry of Education, who exercised ferocious repression against teachers without any qualms.

Within the Malian diaspora, left-wing activists were the main leaders of various initiatives such as the CDLDM and the Liaison Committee for Student Workers which were the origin of literacy campaigns in the homes of immigrant workers, such as Bassirou Diarra, an activist who was close to the French Communist Party's newspaper *L'Humanité*.

Other debates took place on other topics, about the stages in the struggle to be defined, as the 'National Democratic and Popular Revolution' or 'Democratic and Popular Revolution', where some advocated going directly to socialism – theoretical jumps of formidable complexity! Some positions, sometimes bizarre, also led to the condemnation of certain national liberation movements, describing them as 'petty bourgeois'.

THE SANFIN GROUP

From the PMT, a dissident group was created and affiliated with the international Stalinist group based in Canada, whose journal was called *On the Way to Bolshevism*. It eventually gave birth to the Sanfin ('The Cloud' in the Bamanankan language) group, named after its newspaper, *Sanfin*. This group was especially active in student circles in France. During the period of the dictatorship, this newspaper was distributed in the networks of left-wing circles. *Sanfin* had a radical discourse that appealed to the student youth of the time. Its criticism was virulent, both against the regime and against other left-wing opponents. *Sanfin* crossed swords with the other tendencies of the Malian left. It denounced in no uncertain terms the 'theory of entryism' advocated by certain currents in the domestic leadership of the PMT, according to which it was necessary to enter the power structure of the military junta in order to change it from within. This tactic was also prevalent in the trade unions. It created cracks and irreconcilable oppositions within the left. Those who joined Moussa Traoré's government tried to drag the others into it, and if they refused, became their denouncers. This tactic divided the leadership and created serious divergences within the PMT. In spite of this, some entryists remained in the government of Moussa Traoré until his bloody fall in March 1991. The party fell apart, and worse, some of the entryists ended up turning against their former comrades, whom they denounced to the regime's police. Their collaboration with the dictatorship contributed to discrediting the PMT on the left-wing scene in Mali. *Sanfin* strongly contributed to the denunciation of the party leadership, which it already described as revisionist. Sanfin's rhetoric, its excessive methods, its virulence, its chainsaw analysis, however, contributed to further fragmentation within the left. Some of its leaders ended up joining the pro-Albanian current in the international communist movement. While its denunciations of the dictatorship rang true for many left-wing activists, its treatment of the contradictions within the Malian left eventually isolated it. Within the movement, dissent emerged. This internal struggle within Sanfin was merciless. The ferocity of the internal struggle went so far as to publicly denounce certain leaders of the movement and to disclose their code names in hiding, in a context of generalised police surveillance. This triggered a violent controversy. The PMT took advantage of this to denounce ultra-leftism within the resistance movement against the dictatorship.

Within the student movement, Sanfin also advocated 'revolutionary syndicalism' and described the students' demands for greater wellbeing as 'corporatist'. This occasionally led to vigorous theoretical fights. These fierce debates left some young students stunned, and contributed to alienating them from the movement. Stalinists, Trotskyists, pro-Albanian, pro-Chinese and pro-Soviet clashed virulently at student meetings and conventions. Sometimes national issues were relegated to the background. This also contributed to the loss of influence within the student movement and the left as a whole. Thus, Sanfin's influence was eroded over time and became marginal within the democratic movement. When Moussa Traoré fell, the Sanfin group chose to remain in opposition. While some of its criticisms of the democratic movement remained well-founded, its 'ideological and political purism' distanced it from the spaces where the political struggle took place. It never managed to regain the influence it had previously had within the Malian left. Despite all the criticisms that could be levelled at it, Sanfin endures in the political history of the Malian left in the early 1970s as a political movement that had the longest life. It has remained constant in its political line even if its theoretical rigidity has often led it into serious tactical errors. The main leaders were Mohamed Tabouré, an activist and leader of the Association des étudiants et stagiaires maliens en France (Association of Malian Students and Trainees in France), who later returned to the country, as did Salia Konaté, a computer scientist, and Amadou Tiéoulé Diarra, a legal expert trained in Dakar who ultimately left the group.

When Amadou Toumani Touré fell in March 2012, Sanfin joined forces with Solidarité africaine pour la démocratie et l'indépendance (SADI, African Solidarity for Democracy and Independence), led by Cheick Omar Sissoko, then by Oumar Mariko, and with other movements and associations within the Mouvement populaire du 22 mars (MP22, Popular Movement of 22 March) and later Coordination des organisations patriotiques du Mali (COPAM, Coordination of the Patriotic Organisations of Mali). The resolute and indiscriminate support that Sanfin and SADI gave to the military junta of Captain Sanogo that overthrew Touré has raised many questions. The tactic of keeping a defector from the Union démocratique du peuple malien (UDPM, Democratic Union of the Malian People), a party created by Moussa Traoré, in the leadership of COPAM was also misunderstood by many comrades in the left.

But it was over the analysis of the national situation that the differences clashed most violently. Sanfin denounced the petty bourgeoisie in its rhetoric. Its analyses consistently emphasised the working class, while for others it was necessary to be more nuanced in terms of class analyses and alliances. Sanfin's ideological purism and theoretical rigidity eventually made it a marginal movement within the Malian revolutionary left.

THE TIÉMOKO GARAN KOUYATÉ GROUP

Within the PMT, other splits occurred. Some of their militants ended up organising within the Groupe Tiémoko Garan Kouyaté (TGK, Tiémoko Garan Kouyaté Group), named after a Malian communist militant who was shot in 1942 by the Nazis during the occupation of French territory during the Second World War. Some members of this group, originally Sur la voie du bolchevisme militants, played an important role in the fall of the dictatorship of Moussa Traoré. It worked mainly in the underground. Its activists were involved in the trade union struggles of teachers, pupils and students, the judiciary, the health service and other unions. On many occasions, they were the driving force behind the general mobilisation during the popular uprising that eventually brought down the military dictatorship.

The TGK was mainly composed of militants who had broken with the PMT, whose ideological reversals and collaboration with Moussa Traoré's regime they denounced as part of the 'theory of entryism' mentioned above. The leading figures were Professor Yoro Diakité, the filmmaker Cheick Omar Sissoko, the anthropologist Bréhima Béridogo, the historian Dean Drissa Diakité and the magistrate Hamidou Diabaté, joined by others from within the country such as the medical student Oumar Mariko, one of the main leaders of the student movement Association des élèves et étudiants du Mali (Association of Pupils and Students of Mali) in the 1990s, and Tiébilé Dramé, a professor of literature who fled to France to escape the dictatorship of Moussa Traoré.

TGK also denounced the theory about the need for the creation of a national bourgeoisie as an indispensable step in the process of the national democratic and popular revolution. Thus, some leaders and cadres of the PMT advocated facilitating the enrichment of an elite for the 'emergence of a national bourgeoisie'. Some put their money where their mouths were and became businessmen. They took advantage of their position within the apparatus of Moussa Traoré's regime to set up a vast network that served as a 'real money pump', often within state-owned enterprises. They ended up setting up what some people called the 'CMDT clan', named after the Compagnie malienne de développement du textile (Malian Company for the Development of Textiles), which had a major role in the country's economy. After the fall of Moussa Traoré, the CMDT clan gained importance within the state apparatus. It took advantage of this to position its executives within the political and economic apparatus of the new ADEMA regime and to seize the most lucrative sectors of the national economy during the implementation of privatisation policies imposed by the World Bank and the International Monetary Fund. They became the main and new shareholders in the privatised sectors – hotels, Pari mutuel urbain (commonly known as 'tiercé'), telecoms, mines and others. The deviations and abandonments of the left-wing line by the ADEMA government stem from this. So did the buying of ballots and the widespread corruption.

After the fall of the dictatorship in March 1991, the main leaders of the TGK ended up creating the Congrès national d'initiative démocratique (CNID, National Democratic Initiative Congress), an association that gave birth to a party of the same name. Later, in 1995, the left-wing elements split from the liberals within the party to create the Parti de la renaissance africaine (PARENA, Party of the African Renaissance), led by Professor Yoro Diakité and later Tiébilé Dramé. This party experienced several splits which led to the creation in 1996 of the Bloc des alternatives pour le renouveau africain (Bloc of Alternatives for African Renewal), led by Yoro Diakité, and SADI, under the leadership of Cheick Omar Sissoko, then Oumar Mariko.

THE MALIAN PARTY FOR REVOLUTION AND DEMOCRACY

Another left-wing party, the Parti malien pour la révolution et la démocratie (PMRD, Malian Party for Revolution and Democracy), composed mainly of former Malian students from the former Soviet Union and Eastern European countries, merged with the PMT to create ADEMA-PASJ.

The PMRD had a generally pro-Soviet political line, although some of its members were somewhat critical of the Soviet Union. It recruited its activists mainly from student and trade union circles and from cadres trained in the former East European countries and Russia. Its leaders were very popular, especially in academic circles, such as Professor of Philosophy Mamadou Lamine Traoré.

The PMRD played an important role in the resistance struggle against the dictatorship of Moussa Traoré. Abdoulaye Barry, a linguist by training, was one of the main domestic leaders. Among its leading figures were Cheick

Pléah, a sociolinguist and son of Dr Koniba Pléah of the US-RDA, Samba Sidibé, a public works engineer, Kléna Sanogo, long-time Director of the Institute of Human Sciences, Bakary Bouaré, an economist by training, as well as Kassa Traoré, former Director of the Rural Polytechnic Institute in Katiboubou, and Mohamedoun Dicko, former Secretary General of ADEMA. From 1974 to 1978, some of its militants and leaders were arrested, tortured and deported to the northern prisons in the middle of the desert for having distributed a leaflet hostile to the constitutional referendum which made the UDPM a constitutional party. Many PMRD leaders and officials also suffered under the dictatorship.

The PMRD experienced its first crisis at the birth of ADEMA. Some of its cadres and leaders were in favour of building a party front rather than dissolving all left-wing underground parties and movements within ADEMA. In their view, this would have opened up the party to opportunist currents with no real left-wing identity and would have allowed them to eventually seize the political leadership of the democratic movement at the time. This minority current, represented by Abdoulaye Barry, was dismissed from the leadership, but events later proved him right. In 1994, following a crisis within ADEMA, the party in power, the former PMRD members broke from the presidential majority and created a new party, the Mouvement pour l'indépendance, la renaissance et l'intégration africaine (MIRIA, Movement for Independence, Renaissance and African Integration), under the leadership of Professor Mamadou Lamine Traoré. This party also experienced crises with the departure of some founding executives and militants. Some of the main figures of this dissidence returned to ADEMA. Others disengaged from political action. Over time, MIRIA lost its leadership within the student and political movement and became an appendage of the presidential party. Some PMRD activists were behind the 1975 leaflet denouncing the regime's 1975 constitutional referendum project. They suffered four years of detention and deportation, as can be seen in the book *Toiles d'araignées* ('Spider Webs') by Ibrahima Ly, later made into a film. Among them, in addition to Ibrahima Ly and Mohamedoun Dicko already mentioned, we can note Oumar Ly, Director-founder of SOMIEX, Jean Etienne Diendéré, an economist by training, Bakary Konimba Traoré, known as Bakary Pionnier, an economist, Adama Samassékou, a linguist, Samba Sidibé, a public works engineer, Cheick Sadibou Cissé, an architect, Seydou Thiéro, Director of the Sports Club, Bourama Traoré, an urban planner, Cyr Mathieu Samaké, Director General of Liptako-Gourma, Mamadou Lamine Kouyaté, Director of the Omnisports Stadium, and Mani Diénépo, Inspector General of Youth and Sports.

In the end, the CDLDM drew up a list of more than 300 victims of the repression of Moussa Traoré's regime.

SHORT-LIVED EXPERIENCES OF THE LEFT

On the domestic front, from 1968 to 1991, other left-wing organisations had, for the most part, a short-lived existence, such as the group created around the 'Manifesto for the Motherland' launched in 1994, which was already denouncing the betrayal of the 26 March 1991 ideals by the ADEMA government. Among its main leaders were Professors Issa N'Diaye and Cheick Pléah. The same was true for the Parti des travailleurs du Mali (PTM, Mali Workers' Party), which claimed to be part of the PMT's legacy but denounced its excesses. PTM was created in 1975 by militants from the Malian Communist Party, itself the result of a merger between former PMT dissidents (Professors Many Camara, Djibonding Dembélé, Issa N'Diaye and Fadel Diop, a chemical engineer and former employee of COMATEX in Segou. The latter went into exile for a while in the Congo during the period of Marien Ngouabi's revolution. To this nucleus were added various small parties such as the Party of Popular Unity led by a former PMT militant, Diatrou Diakité, established especially in the working-class environment at the Diamou cement factory near Kayes, in the western region of Mali, and at the marble factory in Bamako. Its organ, the newspaper *Avant-garde*, ran to only one issue. The PTM had a rather short existence. Some of its executives and leaders ended up in ADEMA, SADI and on other fronts of struggle, notably trade union, cultural and others. It should be noted that the current Malian Communist Party is different from its predecessor of the 1970s. It is composed essentially of former Malian students from the 1980s and 1990s. Its influence is quite marginal.

THE *BULLETIN DU PEUPLE*

Another grouping was formed around a press organ, *Le Bulletin du Peuple*, published in Dakar. Its publications disturbed the peace of the military dictatorship, and the hunt for the paper led to arbitrary arrests, including those of Professors Yoro Diakité, Many Camara and Issa N'Diaye of the Higher Education Union. *Le Bulletin* played a significant role in raising awareness and mobilising left-wing forces, especially against the military dictatorship.

It had a vast network of clandestine whistleblowers right up to the heart of the state apparatus. It was distributed to the mailboxes of members of the ruling junta. Each of its publications provoked the fury of the regime and its disarray. Its editor, Mohamed Lamine Gakou, a Malian political refugee who settled in Dakar during the dictatorship of Moussa Traoré, was for a long time a collaborator of the Franco-Egyptian economist and left-wing activist Samir Amin. After the fall of the dictatorship, he returned to Mali and became an advisor to the President of the Republic.

If the clandestine political organisations, unions and associations contributed greatly to the fall of the military dictatorship and the advent of democracy, their mutation and gradual transformation into a multitude of political parties led to a paradoxical ultraliberal turn. Today, the disaster is obvious. The responsibilities now deserve to be allocated.

The Left Facing the 2012 Coup D'état

The differences that arose during the struggles had important consequences for the maturation and progress of the democratic process in Mali.

The fall of Amadou Toumani Touré and the coup d'état by the junta led by Captain Sanogo in March 2012 was a missed opportunity for the reconfiguration of the Malian left. The coup was greeted by strong popular mobilisation for change. The militants and forces of the left were still the main animators. They regrouped under the banner of MP22. If the leading figures of this movement were left-wing, it remained a heterogeneous movement where all those discontented with the system cohabited, up to the religious. The duo of Sanfin and SADI, not without difficulty, ended up taking control of the political leadership of the movement. Differences emerged within MP22. The duo supported the military junta in no uncertain terms, although no political agreement had been reached between MP22 and the junta. SADI was in fact the liaison between the movement and the junta. The planned meeting between a delegation from MP22 and the head of the junta to clarify the foundations of a partnership based on a shared political programme never took place. The erring ways of the new power created strong concerns, which were swept aside each time by Sanfin and SADI. Gradually, many activists and leaders of the left and of the associations and parties that were members of MP22 ended up distancing themselves from it. Nevertheless, the mobilisation carried out during this period by the various components of the movement made it possible to defeat France's manoeuvres which had used the leaders of the Economic Community of West African

States as a tool. The street demonstrations created strong concerns. They explain the real reason for the French military intervention in Mali, in order to stop the popular revolution that was looming on the horizon. The popular movement was in danger of taking over power in Bamako. This is what precipitated the French military intervention, Serval, in order to block this popular process, which risked inspiring democratic and popular forces in French-speaking West Africa and elsewhere. The cloak of the anti-terrorist struggle came to camouflage the real intentions of French imperialism.

SKETCHING A LEFT FRONT IN MALI

Despite this failure, attempts to regroup in order to constitute a left front took place in Ségou. Three consecutive years, 2013–15, were devoted to this. Its secretariat was entrusted to SADI. The exchanges were chaotic and used as a tool, sometimes by SADI, sometimes by both Sanfin and SADI. One of the major stumbling blocks was the critical assessment of MP22. SADI and Sanfin used every possible means to justify their strategic alliance with the military junta led by Captain Sanogo. Their arguments were overwhelmingly defeated. However, they continued to use various subterfuges to block the summary documents. It was a real ordeal to obtain these documents and to see that they had been falsified. Confidence was no longer required. It was also realised that SADI had withheld a lot of information about the African Left Networking Forum for which SADI acted as the secretariat.

Today, the Malian left is in tatters, mainly because of the theoretical and tactical errors of its leaders, coup-supporting temptations and ego issues. The only structure that still has some consistency is the one grouped within the Popular Front created in June 2016 around the Convention nationale pour la solidarité en Afrique (National Convention for Solidarity in Africa), led by Zoumana Sacko, former prime minister of the 1991 transitional government. The Popular Front, born of the desire for a healthy reconfiguration of leftist forces, unfortunately has not led to the expected results. Its weakness, beyond a certain theoretical rigidity, lies in its small popular base. It is above all a movement of executives and intellectuals. It has not escaped the quarrels of leadership because, once again, of over-inflated egos.

CONCLUSION: THE CHALLENGES OF THE MALIAN LEFT

One of the major challenges for the Malian left remains its ability to go beyond the urban intelligentsia. In its heyday, SADI succeeded in building a rural base among the farmers of the Office du Niger and the CMDT. But it failed to manage this precious capital. It was also one of the few political parties to take an interest in social movements. Radio Kayira was able to capture the attention of the working classes. Many people of modest means came to talk about their concerns. It was the 'people's radio', and its pro-grammes were relayed throughout the country by a network of community radio stations and were well followed. The management of this precious tool for the convergence of popular struggles is today threatened by being chal-lenged in court by its board of directors. SADI's mistakes are not unrelated to this.

In the course of its history, the Malian left, in its various segments, has often been tempted by leftist adventurism. Its spectacular stances, failure to respect mass opinion, the temptation of the cult of personality, the lack of democracy in the internal operation of its bodies, the dubious circumstan-tial alliances and ego conflicts have largely contributed to reducing the trust and credibility accumulated over several decades. Basically, all these issues indicate a deficit in the ideological training of its executives and leaders. The question of training has become crucial today for the Malian left. In reality, this observation is valid at the political, trade union, associative and civil society levels. It is a prerequisite for the rebirth of a true left-wing political pole in Mali. Unfortunately, it seems to have been abandoned. It is essentially from the lack of ideological and political training that the current strategic and tactical errors stem, and many other things besides.

Moreover, the Malian left cannot prosper without its integration within the population. Today, the trade union movements are mired in blind cor-poratism and their leaders lack a real political and ideological culture. At the level of the peasantry, the situation is the same. It is in the urban peripher-ies and in the mining areas that social movements are the most significant. One needs to analyse and understand them. There is a need to get them to go beyond the stage of spontaneity, and this requires time and strategy. However, the Malian left seems more concerned with the immediate seizure of power. To this end, it often enters into opportunist and unnatural alli-ances. Thus, most of the time it plays into the hands of the liberals, whom it helps to bring to power. Once in power, yesterday's allies become their exe-cutioners. This is still the case today within the 5 June Movement-Patriotic Forces Rally, which contributed to the coup that overthrew the power of Ibrahim Boubacar Kéita.

The left would benefit from developing its own agenda and getting down to work with perseverance and thoroughness. But this requires a clear strategic vision and appropriate tactics. This is currently far from being the case. Activism alone will not suffice. The tactic of alliance with religious circles is also, in the long run, counterproductive. In March 1991, religious leaders had virtually no influence on the ongoing struggles. It was the failure of the leadership of the political parties and the populism adopted as a strategy for gaining power by Amadou Toumani Touré in 2002 that propelled the religious leaders to the forefront of the scene, with the dramatic consequences that we know today.

For the rebirth of the left, the task is immense. It must plough its own furrows in the long term and without intermediaries within the popular strata.

The question of its relationship with the military must also be examined in depth because of the recurrent coup-supporting temptation within the left. The case of Mali is a perfect illustration. And each time, the backlash is terrible. The bloody repression of left-wing forces and the physical liquidation of all left-wing elements within the Malian military, starting with Captain Diby Silas Diarra and his comrades-in-arms after the 1968 coup d'état, have created a de facto mistrust that persists in spite of everything.

The question of civil society also remains to be rethought in our societies. In the current context of loss of credit for political parties, it is appropriate to reflect on this. To what extent could it be a factor of popular mobilisation for the forces of change? The question remains open, especially since Malian civil society is also affected by a wave of general discredit. It has become a refuge for notorious opportunists seeking funding from Western donors.

The international context also bears its share of responsibility. The failure of left-wing experiments in various countries has contributed to the decline of left-wing forces in many countries. Similarly, the validation of the liberal model of winning power through the ballot box has contributed greatly to diluting the revolutionary potential of the masses. The question deserves to be analysed in the light of the failure of experiments since the case of Allende's Chile, the failure of Lula in Brazil, that of Syriza in Greece, of Podemos in Spain, the serious threats to Venezuela of Chavez and Maduro, and Evo Morales's Bolivia. Despite many difficulties, only the Cuban way seems to be prospering. We should learn from this. Why can't left-wing parties, bringing about real change, manage to prosper through the ballot box? This question remains essential, in spite of the positive changes currently underway almost everywhere in the world, particularly in Latin America, where the latest elections have brought left-wing forces to power in Mexico, Colombia and elsewhere, opening up new prospects favourable to popular forces.

The other critical issue lies in the analysis of the failure of left-wing experiments that could not be brought to a conclusion. It is important to make an exhaustive and thorough analysis.

How to lead revolutionary change in a context of globalisation of liberal capitalism?

Is a rupture possible?

In any case, exit from the current world capitalist system seems indispensable. This path needs to be explored in order to give ourselves the chances of an effective transformation of the world in order to remove our societies from the domination of capital. So many theoretical and practical questions remain to be put on the agenda.

By questioning the current realities of the world, it appears more and more that the spark of changes to come will arise in the countries of the South. But there is little doubt that it cannot prosper without the solidarity of the struggles of the forces of the left at the sub-regional and regional levels and in the countries at the centre of world capitalism.

Today, tectonic fractures are crossing the world, especially in Asia, Latin America and Africa. They are shaking the very foundations of Western domination over the world. The awakening of popular consciousness puts on the agenda the tipping of the world towards new horizons, rejecting the neoliberal capitalist model. A new world order is in the making. The de-dollarisation of the world economy and the rise of BRICS (Brazil, Russia, India, China and South Africa) are a sign of the upheavals underway. Federating the forces of the left in our neighbouring countries and on the African scale is an urgent challenge. Making the connection at the global level is an absolute necessity.

But all this requires theoretical creativity. But it is not in the manuals of Marxism-Leninism that we will find the answers to the challenges of the moment, even if revisiting the fundamentals today is indispensable.

A popular adage in the Bamanan environment in Mali says that 'Thinking is what turns millet into beer!'

SELECT BIBLIOGRAPHY

Koné, Souleymane T. (1998), 'Les partis politiques et la démocratie au Mali', *Africa Development/Afrique et développement*, 23(2), 185–208.

Touré, Abderhamane Baba, and Bamba, Kadari (2002), *La contribution du Parti malien du travail (PMT): à l'instauration de la démocratie pluraliste au Mali*, Bamako: Editions Jamana.

Traoré, Amadou Seydou (2005), *Devoir de mémoire, devoir de vérité*, Bamako: La ruche à livres.

Traoré, Amadou Seydou (2008), *Le salaire des libérateurs du Mali*, Bamako: La ruche à livres.

NOTES

1. Jean Suret-Canale, *Les groupes d'études communistes (G.E.C.)*, Paris: L'Harmattan, 1994.
2. Amady Aly Dieng, *Mémoires d'un étudiant africain, tome 1: de l'école régionale de Diourbel à l'université de Paris 1945–1960)*, Dakar: Codesria, 2011; Amady Aly Dieng, *Mémoires d'un étudiant africain, tome 2: de l'université de Paris à mon retour au Sénégal (1960–1967)*, Dakar: Codesria, 2011.
3. Amadou Seydou Traoré, *Le salaire des libérateurs*, Bamako: La ruche à livres, 2008, 237.
4. Abdou Moumouni, *L'éducation en Afrique*, Paris: Présence africaine, 1964.
5. Ibrahima Ly, *Toiles d'araignées*, Paris: L'Harmattan, 1985.
6. Ibrahima Ly, *Les noctuelles vivent de larmes*, Paris: L'Harmattan, 1988.

3

The History of the Upper Volta Revolutionary Left: From Ideological Struggles within the Student Movement to the Creation of the PCRV and the ULC

Moussa Diallo

INTRODUCTION

This chapter is not written by a professional historian, but a researcher in political philosophy, and aims essentially to explore the ideological, political and policy line struggles that ran through the student movement, the communist circles and the workers' unions in Burkina Faso in the 1960s and 1970s. Thus, in order to understand the history of the Upper Volta revolutionary left, one must go back to the history of the student movement in Upper Volta in the 1960s. It was there and then that the leaders of the communist circles that supported the coup d'état of the Conseil national de la révolution (CNR, National Council of the Revolution) forged their ideological and political weapons. It is also where the leaders of the clandestine communist party, the Parti communiste révolutionnaire de Volta (PCRV, Revolutionary Communist Party of Upper Volta) gathered their ideological and political experience. Let us put it in a nutshell: it was within the student movement of the 1960s that all types of struggles were waged: ideological struggles between revolutionaries and reformists, political struggles between the militants of the Mouvement de libération nationale (MLN, National Liberation Movement) and the Parti africain de l'indépendance (PAI, African Independence Party), and policy line struggles between supporters of reformist class collaborationist trade unionism and those of revolutionary class struggle trade unionism. This chapter intends to present a brief historical analysis of the Upper Volta revolutionary left. It will limit itself, on the one hand, to recalling the ideological, political and policy line struggles within the powerful Union générale des étudiants de Volta (UGEV, General Union of Upper Volta Students), the Organisation communiste voltaïque (OCV, Upper Volta Communist Organisation) and the workers' unions, and on the other hand, to highlight the evolution of the various communist groups that emerged from the 1979 divide.

IDEOLOGICAL, POLITICAL AND POLICY LINE STRUGGLES WITHIN THE UPPER VOLTA STUDENT MOVEMENT

After its creation, the General Union of Upper Volta Students experienced ideological struggles within its ranks before being stabilised as a revolutionary anti-imperialist association. After recalling the context of its birth, we will analyse the ideological struggles and lines that have crossed it.

The Context of the Creation of the UGEV

The UGEV, born on July 27 1960 in the heat of the struggle of the African peoples for 'national independence and true social progress', is the result of the regrouping of the Étudiants de Volta en France (AEVF, Association of Upper Volta Students in France), created in 1950, and the Association des scolaires voltaïques (ASV, Association of Upper Volta Students) in Dakar, created in 1956. Through the AEVF, the UGEV is a member of the Fédération des étudiants d'Afrique noire en France (FEANF, Federation of Black African Students in France), which was created in 1950 in the metropolis. Today, the UGEV practises revolutionary class struggle unionism. Here is the testimony that Roger Moussa Tall gives about the context of the UGEV's creation in his *Memoirs*:

On August 5, 1960, there was the independence of Upper Volta. A few days before, the Upper Volta students, who at that time only came from France and Dakar, held the constitutive congress of UGEV.... The authorities of the time did not allow for the holding of the congress; therefore this one took place at the residence of I. Thiombiano, the brother of the late A. Thiombiano, a very committed student of Dakar; from Dakar, I remember that there was also C. Tamini.[1]

He then specifies:

> For the establishment of the Union's first board, the analysis of the situation had led the congressmen to choose the first UGEV leaders among the militants of AEVF, for the good reason that the freedoms of assembly and expression were much greater in France than in Dakar. Also, upon a proposal of AEVF's Chairman, our comrade A. Ouedraogo, were elected: R. Meda as President, S. Diallo as Secretary General, R. Tall as Treasurer General. This Board had not been able to function because its members lived in different localities.[2]

Ideological, Political and Policy Line Struggles within the UGEV

Before arriving at its anti-imperialist and revolutionary orientation of class struggle in 1971, the UGEV was riven by ideological struggles (between revolutionaries and reformists), political struggles between militants of the MLN and the PAI and policy line struggles between partisans of reformist class collaborationist unionism and those of revolutionary class struggle unionism. We can assign three time periods to these policy line struggles:

- from 1966 to 1971 – a period characterised by the struggle against the Ancien courant réformiste (ACR, Old Reformist Current);
- from 1972 to 1976 – the struggle against the Nouveau courant réformiste (NCR, New Reformist Current);
- from 1976 to 1979 – the struggle against the Nouveau courant opportuniste et liquidateur (NCOL/M21, New Opportunist and Liquidating Current).

The period 1966–71 was characterised by the manifestation within the UGEV, especially at the level of its leadership, of a reformist trend driven by the militants of the MLN in the student milieu. The MLN is the political movement created by Joseph Ki-Zerbo which contributed to the struggle for independence of the colonised countries in French-speaking Black Africa. When the UGEV had to assess the national political situation resulting from the 3 January 1966 events, including all the political parties and groups (according to their constitutions, programmes, actions, declarations, leaders etc.), the Executive Committee, which was composed of elements influenced by the MLN, made various manoeuvres to prevent any analysis of the national situation. As the UGEV's newsletter and training bulletin *Jeune Volta* stated:

Under the influence of this reformist line, UGEV meetings consisted in the study of general, very ambitious and fundamentally reformist themes. These studies did not allow the students to understand the neo-colonial nature of the Upper Volta society, the real source of their ills.[3]

The following themes were studied at the second (1966), third (1967) and fourth (1968) UGEV congresses: 'The African student in the face of underdevelopment', 'Upper Volta youth, their education and responsibilities' and 'The Upper Volta peasant, his place and role in political and economic life'.[4] But the most significant fact that exposed the predominance of the reformist line within the UGEV, and more particularly at the level of its leadership, is the assessment of the 3 January 1966 events. For the reformist Executive Committee of the time, this popular movement co-opted by the army constituted the 'New Year's Revolution', and the reactionary neo-colonial army was given the title of 'people's army'. Against this reformist line defended by the UGEV leadership at the time, the AEVF opposed a policy line struggle. Indeed, the first manifestations of the policy line struggle within the UGEV appeared at the 1966 Christmas congress of the AEVF, which had carried out an analysis of the national situation and an objective assessment of the various political parties, particularly the MLN. This assessment provoked an outcry from the pro-MLN elements. This was the first manifestation of a nefarious political current that the UGEV would later call the Old Reformist Current. This line or ideological struggle covered the second, third and fourth UGEV congresses held respectively in 1966, 1967 and 1968. It was willingly fuelled by the reformist UGEV leadership and exacerbated by the AEVF motion adopted during its 1967 Christmas congress. This motion stated:

We, the congress:

- note that in its practice this party (MLN) seems not to have adopted a consistent anti-imperialist stand,
- express our serious reservations about the progressive character of the MLN,
- launch a call on AEVF militants and the working masses of Upper Volta to be more vigilant in the face of this movement.[5]

Moreover, the fourth UGEV congress was to be the culmination of ideological contradictions within the UGEV, with undermining work by its reformist leadership (blocking debates, attempting to isolate AEVF from other sections and refusing to publish the proceedings of its 1967 Christmas congress in the union's struggle newsletter). This undermining work basically aimed at paralysing the UGEV. This resulted in the freezing of activities, and consequently, the 1969 and 1970 congresses did not take place. It was not until the historic fifth congress in August 1971 that the ACR was finally defeated and the UGEV was put on a solid anti-imperialist, patriotic and revolutionary footing. If the fifth congress was allowed to defeat the ACR, it made a political error in overestimating the student movement by making it the 'vanguard' of the struggle for the national and social liberation of the people of Upper Volta. It also made the political mistake of launching the slogan 'integration with the working and peasant masses'. This is what the PCRV maintained in its message to the ninth congress of the General Union of Upper Volta Students:

> What the above-mentioned slogans (integration with the masses and the call to intellectuals and workers to put themselves under the political and ideological leadership of UGEV) reveal is the overestimation of the role of the student movement, and UGEV even had to believe and affirm that: '... under the current specific conditions of the struggle of our people, it merely plays the role of a vanguard.' The ideological root of such a point of view is the desire of the petty-bourgeoisie to push aside the proletariat and usurp the leadership of the revolution.[6]

In brief, this overestimation of the UGEV's role consisted of making it a political organisation, even a political party, whereas it is only a mass organisation.

The second period of the line struggle within the UGEV was characterised by the struggle against the reformist positions defended by the PAI and its youth organisation, Ligue patriotique pour le développement (LIPAD, Patriotic League for Development). The current defended by PAI and LIPAD has been called the New Reformist Current.

According to Harouna Toguyeni, the UGEV's eighth congress clarified the relationship between the UGEV and LIPAD, which claimed to be part of the revolutionary camp:

> On the national level, the aim was to determine the link that could exist between the student revolutionary movement and organizations such as LIPAD, which also claimed to be part of the revolutionary movement.

After analysing their manifesto, UGEV found that on many political points they differed from LIPAD.[7]

The main political points of divergence included the nature of the revolution to be carried out in Upper Volta, the nature of feudal forces and their role in a modern state, and the issue of international relations. These differences of opinion on these issues led the UGEV to call LIPAD the New Reformist Current.

The third period of line struggle within the UGEV was characterised by the struggle against the New Opportunist and Liquidator Current. In addition to the NCR, the UGEV Board of Directors' meeting held in August 1978 revealed the birth of a new protest movement within the Upper Volta student movement: the June 21 Movement (M21). The leaders of this new movement questioned the political line hitherto defended by the UGEV and at the same time denounced practices that they considered contrary to the revolutionary spirit. The ideological debate was controversial and heated. The defenders of this new current were accused by the UGEV of leading the NCOL. Here is the testimony given by Adama Saba in his memoirs:

> But a devious current was preparing to attack the Federation of Black African Students in France (FEANF) with the obvious but still unavowed goal of liquidating it. The main proponents of this current were a group of African students, especially Upper Volta students. This current was to shake FEANF and its territorial sections and allow Valéry Giscard D'Estaing's government to declare FEANF's dissolution. Within AEVF, this current was called the 'June 21 Movement' (AEVF/M21). Its calling card was 'One divides into two', a famous sentence that featured prominently in its manifesto and announced the objective of its proponents vis-à-vis AEVF and FEANF: to break these associations.[8]

This is why, Adama Saba explains, the AEVF had called this movement the New Opportunistic and Liquidator Current. According to him:

> It all began in Paris, and quite naturally within the central management of the FEANF, to then spread throughout France. For the needs of their cause, they had also baptized AEVF that is to say us, 'the National Populist and Liquidator Movement' (MONAPOL). African and French historians as well as independent historians should look into FEANF's life and death to enlighten Africa on this part of its history.[9]

It was the ninth congress in August 1979 that would definitively decide between the supporters of the NCOL and the UGEV leaders of the time. After this congress, a split took place within the UGEV. The leaders of the NCOL created the AEVF/M21 in France and the UGEV/M21 in Ouagadougou. They would also accuse the then leadership of the UGEV of coaching the National Populist and Liquidator Movement. Thus, at the end of its ninth congress, the UGEV adopted its induction as a revolutionary anti-imperialist organisation. Since its anti-imperialist and revolutionary orientation of class struggle operated during its ninth Congress of August 1979, the General Union of Upper Volta Students is recognised today as the most representative and the most combative of schoolchildren's and students' associations in Burkina Faso.[10] Moreover, it is even considered by Lila Chouli as the main political counter-power among the student associations of Burkina Faso.[11]

FROM THE MARXIST-LENINIST GROUP OF UPPER VOLTA TO THE UPPER VOLTA COMMUNIST ORGANISATION

To examine the birth in Upper Volta of the revolutionary current that animated and influenced the Upper Volta student movement during 1973–76, it is necessary to take a look back to allow us to note that the leaders of the Upper Volta student movement set up the Marxist-Leninist Group of Upper Volta, which between 1973 and 1976 organised study groups bringing together the most politically advanced elements among the students and pupils. This group was mainly coached by the future militants of the African Party for Independence Amidou Thiombiano, Adama Touré, Philippe Ouédraogo, among other emblematic figures, of the Union des luttes communistes (ULC, Union of Communist Struggles) Valère Somé, Basile Guissou, Firmin Diallo etc., and of the PCRV, a party that has remained clandestine until today. The group has organised cells in France, Dakar, Ouagadougou, Lomé, Canada and the Russian Federation in order to prepare the creation of the future communist party.

In this context, the Upper Volta Communist Organisation was created in August 1977 in Ouagadougou. The OCV adopted a programme and theses for the future party. At the same time, the eighth UGEV congress was held, where communist militants and sympathisers (supporters of the PCRV) had the wind in their sails. Under their leadership, the student organisation began to perceive the erroneous nature of some of its positions and recognised that most of its slogans could only be assumed by a political party, in this case a Marxist-Leninist communist party. The UGEV contended:

If a communist party is born in Upper Volta that mobilizes and leads the masses in the struggle against imperialism, mainly French and their Upper Volta henchmen, for the realization of the National Democratic and Popular Revolution (RNDP), we will support such a party and in a conscious way.[12]

But during the same year, 1977, the International Communist Movement faced new contradictions within it, leading to the breaking of relations between Albania and China. Obviously, the situation, which had repercussions on the Upper Volta communists, led to an open crisis within the OCV from January 1978 onward. Two ideological trends clashed. And in September 1978, the split was consummated with the creation of the Union of Communist Struggle on the one hand and the Upper Volta Revolutionary Communist Party on the other.

The latter aligned itself behind Enver Hoxha and considered Albania 'the only bastion of the Revolution'. From now on, 'Mao Tse-Tung is a peasant deceptively draped in the Marxist-Leninist cloak and China, a revisionist, social imperialist country.'[13]

THE CREATION OF THE PCRV AND THE ULC

The project to create a communist workers' party in Upper Volta was compromised as a result of ideological and political differences within the OCV. For some, it was necessary to aim for the creation of the Revolutionary Communist Workers' Party of Upper Volta and for the others, the conditions were not met for the creation of the party in question. Thus, a split in the OCV took place.

From the OCV to the Birth of the PCRV

The PCRV originated from the Marxist-Leninist Group of Upper Volta, which was influenced by Mao Zedong's thought. This group and the Marxist-Leninist group Le Prolétaire worked to create the OCV, which in turn worked to lay the ideological and political foundations for the creation of the PCRV. However, ideological and political differences within the OCV led to its implosion in 1978. Thus, the OCV which still carried the ideological shortcomings of the Marxist-Leninist Group of Upper Volta (mainly coached by the future militants of the PAI) and the Marxist-Leninist group The Proletarian (mainly coached by the future militants of the ULC) set about purging itself of its Maoist elements. After patient work of ideological and political clarification, the OCV created the conditions for the creation of PCRV on 1 October 1978. The PCRV is a Marxist-Leninist party of Stalinism and Hoxhism. In its struggle to defend the purity of Marxism-Leninism and against Khruschevian and Titian revisionism, the PCRV espoused the positions developed by the leader of the Party of Albanian Workers, Enver Hoxha, who published a book in 1980 with the provocative title *Eurocommunism Is Anti-Communism*. Since its inception, it has remained underground to this day. The justification for this posture is as follows: 'The PCRV did not deliberately choose to fight underground: it was the enemies of freedom who forced them into it.' Moreover, the PCRV states: 'The struggle for the legalisation of PCRV is inseparable from the consequent struggle for political freedom and a true rule of law.'[14] After its creation on 1 October 1978, the PCRV led a policy line struggle within itself for its ideological, political and organisational construction. On the ideological level, it had to wage a merciless struggle against all right-wing and revisionist deviations in order to remain a 'genuine and pure Marxist-Leninist party'. On the political level, it had to elaborate and adopt 'a revolutionary Marxist-Leninist strategy and tactics'. On the organisational level, it was a question of elaborating and implementing the ways and means to adopt the PCRV's line. This line struggle within the PCRV led it to sincere self-criticism and recognition of its ideological errors when it had adopted from the Marxist-Leninist Group of Upper Volta the thoughts of Mao Zedong – which, by the way, had an undeniable influence on revolutionary youth across the world. This is why, in June 1980, it published a special issue of its newspaper *Bug-Parga* on 'Mao Tse-tung Thought', which it presented as the 'source of Chinese revisionism'. After the adoption of its fundamental line, the PCRV specified that its 'theoretical basis is Marxism-Leninism: it is the teachings of Marx, Engels, Lenin and Stalin that guide the theory and practice of our party'.[15] Presenting itself as a detachment of the international communist movement, the vanguard of the proletariat's struggle, its general staff in the struggle for the realisation of the National Democratic and Popular Revolution, the PCRV advocated the seizure of power through general armed insurrection.

The PCRV, a Clandestine Party to Be Destroyed

Since its creation in 1978, the PCRV has been ostracised by the various neo-colonial governments that have followed one another at the head of the Burkinabe state. Although clandestine, the party remains an important and recognised political force in popular mobilisation. On 1 October 22, the PCRV turned 44. Its armed wing, the Union de la jeunesse communiste de Haute Volta (UJCHV, Union of Communist Youth of Upper Volta), turned 42. Since its birth in 1978, the PCRV, like the UJCHV created two years later, on 1 October 1980, has evolved, far from the prying eyes of the political police.

While its detractors and most provocateurs see in this tactic a lack of political courage on the part of the leaders of this ideological current, Ludo Martens argues otherwise: 'Africa is the land of twists and coups d'état. If they want to hold on to their heads, it is in the interest of the communists to be discreet.'[16]

This has been confirmed by the main party concerned, the PCRV, in a brochure titled *Pour une république démocratique moderne* published in June 2000, stating that as early as 1979, the PCRV was outlawed by the Prime Minister of the Third Republic, Dr Issouf Conombo, and ostracised.

From then on, all the workers, pupils and students of Burkina Faso suspected of belonging to this party were subjected to harassment and numerous repressions. In this regard, Augustin Loada emphasises that the PCRV, which has remained orthodox and uncompromising since its creation, has been one of the favourite targets of the various regimes that have come to power, in particular the Sankarist regime, which was denied any revolutionary legitimacy, believing that a coup d'état could not be equated with a revolution.

About the Creation of the ULC

The Union of Communist Struggle was born from the Upper Volta Marxist-Leninist Group The Proletarian. It was created in October 1979 during its first congress, one year after the PCRV's creation. Since its establishment, it has had a draft political programme. The ULC justified the need for a communist political programme for Upper Volta in these terms:

This necessity arose from the very needs of the communist movement in Upper Volta. The publication of a petty bourgeois program by the PCRV imposes on us the task of presenting to the Upper Volta and world proletariat a truly Marxist-Leninist program of the Upper Volta communists. Taking this sentence from the Communist Manifesto and adapting it to the situation of our country, we say that it is high time that the Upper Volta communists expose to the face of the Upper Volta people and the whole world, their goals and tendencies; that they oppose to the narrative of the communist spectrum a program of the communists.[17]

In reality, the ULC was not a political party, but a political organisation that would evolve into the Communist Workers' Party of Upper Volta. Here is what ULC itself says in its draft programme:

> This program that the Union of Communist Struggle presents to the workers and people of Upper Volta, to the workers and people of the world, is the outcome of six months of discussions within the former Marxist-Leninist group 'The Proletarian' and with authentic communists in Upper Volta. This program sets out the fundamental conceptions of ULC on the character, objectives and tasks of our communist movement in Upper Volta. These concepts should serve as the flag of our organiza-tion, consolidating its unity and cohesion despite the differences that may exist among its members on matters of detail. They will have to serve to realise in fact and not in words the union in the fight of all the authen-tic communists of our country with the view to create the Party of the Proletarian Revolution in Upper Volta, the Communist Workers' Party of Upper Volta.[18]

The ULC also specifies that its programme is based in both form and content on the fundamental teachings of the great educators of the world proletariat, Marx, Engels, Lenin and Stalin.

In 1981, after publishing a declaration against the power of the Comité militaire de redressement pour le progrès national (CMRPN, Military Com-mittee of Recovery for National Progress), ULC leaders were arrested, imprisoned and tortured. After their release, they dissolved the ULC. It was not until the advent of the National Council of the Revolution on 4 August 1983 that the ULC was reborn from its ashes under the name Union de lutte communiste reconstruite (ULCR, Union of Communist Struggle Union Reconstituted). The ULCR is thus part of the numerous commu-nist circles that coached the CNR. The ULCR, whose main leaders include Valère Somé, Basile Guissou, Simon Compaoré and Roch Marc Christian Kaboré, supported the coup d'état of the captains as soon as it took place on 4 August 1983, contributed to labelling it a democratic and popular rev-olution, and set up the CNR and the Committees for the Defence of the Revolution. Thus, the ULCR, the Regroupement des officiers communis-tes (ROC, Regrouping of Communist Officers) and the PAI were the main communist groups that coached the CNR. After a few months of handling the CNR's power, the ULCR and ROC joined forces to exclude the PAI from the exercise of power.

At the advent of the Popular Front, which resulted from Blaise Compaoré's coup d'état against Thomas Sankara, the ULCR leaders, Valère D. Somé and Basile Guissou in particular, were arrested, detained at the gendarmerie and tortured. Valère D. Somé gave a fairly exhaustive account of this detention in his book *Les nuits froides de décembre: L'exil ou ... la mort* ('The Cold Nights of December: Exile or ... Death'), which it would not be useful to revisit here. What is important to remember from this pathetic account is that the ULCR dissolved itself at the end of this repression and some of its leaders (Basile Guissou, Roch Marc Christian Kaboré and Simon Compaoré, to name only the most emblematic) joined the Popular Front, then the Organisation for Popular Democracy/Labour Movement, and even the Congress for Democracy and Progress of Blaise Compaoré. Only Valère D. Somé was forced into political exile in France. Since then, the ULC and ULCR have completely disappeared from the political landscape of Burkina Faso.

THE INFLUENCE OF LEFT-WING POLITICAL PARTIES ON TRADE UNION STRUGGLES IN UPPER VOLTA, BURKINA FASO

The Upper Volta trade union movement is considered one of the most combative in the West African sub-region. Before formal independence, African trade union organisations, notably the Union générale des travailleurs d'Afrique noire (General Union of Black African Workers), including its Upper Volta section, the Union syndicale des travailleurs voltaïque (USTV, Trade Union of Voltaic Workers) contributed to the struggle for independence alongside political parties such as the Rassemblement démocratique africain (RDA, African Democratic Rally), the PAI and the MLN. These struggles had a resounding impact after Upper Volta gained its independence on 5 August 1960. We will briefly review some of the major dates in these trade union struggles.

Trade Union Struggles under the First, Second and Third Republics

Since formal independence in 1960, workers in Burkina Faso have fought many battles against attempts by successive governments to enlist, control and even liquidate the unions. These struggles were influenced by leftist political parties (revolutionary and reformist): the PAI and MLN in particular during the First, Second and Third Republics, and the PCRV from 1978 until today.

In fact, as early as April 1964, Upper Volta trade unions rejected the Act of 27 April 1964 requiring workers' trade union organisations to merge into a single trade union central body that was to be under the control of a single party, the ruling Union démocratique voltaïque/Rassemblement démocratique africain (UDV/RDA, Voltaic Democratic Union/African Democratic Rally). Similarly, at the USTV congress on 28 December 1965, an umbrella union was created and the unions, acting in concert, formed a bloc against the iniquitous Finance Act of 1965, and with the support of political parties (the PAI and MLN in particular) carried out the popular uprising of 3 January 1966 which put an end to the First Republic.[19]

In December 1975, in the face of General Sangoulé Lamizana's National Movement for Renewal plan for a single party, the trade unions achieved extraordinary unity of action, which led to a general strike and 'dead city' days on 17 and 18 December 1975, and General Lamizana was forced to abandon his single-party project.

From 1978 to 1980, under the regime of the Third Republic, many grass-roots unions and trade union central bodies engaged in struggle against attacks on trade union freedoms and anti-strike bills etc. Despite the repression, the struggles led to the release of arrested union leaders and the withdrawal of the anti-strike bill from the National Assembly, among other concessions.

Trade Union Struggles under the Successive Emergency Regimes from 1980 to 1999

From 1980 to 1982, under the CMRPN, despite the ferocious repression of the unions, the struggle against repression and for the unrestricted exercise of freedoms continued. This struggle strengthened the unity of action between workers, pupils and students after the publication of Country Strategy Papers 1 and 2 (82–83) under the CNR from 1983 onwards.

From 1983 to 1987, under the CNR regime, the Front syndical (Trade Union Front) revealed on 28 January 1985, through a now historic declaration bearing its name, that it would defend the free exercise of democratic and trade union freedoms, respect for individual and collective freedoms, and improve workers' purchasing power that had been largely damaged by the various measures of the CNR. This trade union front was the forerunner of the General Confederation of Labour of Burkina Faso, which was created on 29 October 1988.[20]

After the assassination of journalist Norbert Zongo and his three companions in Sapouy on 13 December 1998, the Collectif des organisations démocratiques de masse et de partis politiques (Collective of Democratic Mass Organisations and Political Parties) was created. The heroic struggles of this collective have greatly contributed to creating the conditions for the Burkinabe people's struggle against impunity and corruption and for more freedom, including the popular uprising of 30 and 31 October 2014 and the popular and victorious resistance to the 16 September 2015 coup d'état.

CONCLUSION

The history of the Upper Volta revolutionary left, or should we say, of the Burkinabe revolutionary left, is rich in lessons. But writing it remains a tedious task given the complexity of the subject. We have experienced enormous difficulties in obtaining the information necessary for the writing of this chapter, difficulties linked to the reluctance of the actors who do not want to be exposed (this is notably the case with the PCRV). As for the PAI and ULC, they were initially suspicious before agreeing to collaborate with us. But we had a lot of trouble obtaining publications from the PAI and ULC. This explains the lack of references to the publications of these two organisations, which would have shed more light on certain important moments in the history of the Upper Volta revolutionary left. All in all, we have succeeded in gathering information that will be indispensable for writing the history of the Upper Volta revolutionary left. That said, we must admit that the history from the 1960s to the 1970s sketched here needs to be continued and deepened. And it is up to professional historians to make this a new field of research.

BIBLIOGRAPHY

Chouli, Lila (2018), *Le contre-pouvoir étudiant au Burkina Faso: l'ANEB face à l'usage de la violence d'état et à la discrimination du campus de Ouagadougou (1990–2011)*, Paris: Fondation Gabriel Péri.

Hoxha, Enver (1980), *L'eurocommunisme c'est de l'anticommunisme*, Tirana: Éditions Nentori.

Fédération des syndicats nationaux des travailleurs de l'éducation et de la recherche (F-SYNTER, Federation of National Unions of Education and Research Workers) (2017), *Le travailleur de l'éducation et de la recherche*, 1, spécial 1er congrès fédéral.

Kaboré, Roger Bila (2002), *Histoire politique du Burkina Faso*, Paris: L'Harmattan.

Loada, Augustin (1999), 'Réflexion sur la société civile en Afrique: le Burkina de l'après-Zongo', *Politique africaine*, 76, 136–151.
Martens, Ludo and Meesters, Hilde (1989), *Sankara, Compaoré et la révolution burkinabè*, Berchem: Éditions EPO.
Muase, Charles Kabeya (1989), *Syndicalisme et démocratie en Afrique noire: l'expérience du Burkina Faso*, Paris: Éditions Karthala/Inades éditions.
PCRV (1980), *Bug-Parga*, numéro spécial, June.
PCRV (1981), *Bug-Parga*, 13, October.
PCRV (1991), *Bug-Parga*, 44, August.
PCRV (2017), *Bug-Parga*, 119, June.
PCRV (1985), *Déclaration du 10 février 1985*.
PCRV (1979), *Message au IXème congrès de l'Union générale des étudiants voltaïques*.
Saba, Adama (2015), *Mémoires: histoire d'une vie socio-professionnelle au Burkina Faso*, Ouagadougou: Éditions Céprodif.
Somé, Valère D. (1990), *Thomas Sankara: l'espoir assassiné*, Paris: L'Harmattan.
Somé, Valère D. (2015), *Les nuits froides de décembre: l'exil ou … la mort*, Ouagadougou: Les éditions du millénium.
Syndicats nationaux des travailleurs de l'éducation et de la recherche (SYNTER, National Unions of Education and Research Workers) (1983), *Le travailleur de l'éducation et de la recherche*, 1, spécial 1er congrès, 27, 28 and 29 July 1983.
Tall, Moussa Roger, *Mémoires, tome I: une merveilleuse aventure. La vie de Moussa Roger*, Ouagadougou: Éditions découverte du Burkina Faso.
Toguyeni, Harouna (2018), *En quête de progrès social: combat d'un militant*, Ouagadougou: Éditions Céprodif.
Union générale des étudiants burkinabè (1983), *L'étudiant burkinabè*, spécial XIe congrès.
UGEV (1972), 'La situation politique en Haute-Volta et l'orientation de la jeunesse', *Jeune Volta*, new series, 1, July.
UGEV (1981), *Jeune Volta*, spécial Xe congrès.
UGEV (1982–83), *L'étudiant voltaïque* (Ouagadougou), 1.
ULC (1981), lettre ouverte, *Le prolétaire*.

NOTES

1. Moussa Roger Tall, *Mémoires, tome I, une merveilleuse aventure: la vie de Moussa Roger*, Ouagadougou: Éditions découverte du Burkina Faso, 2018, 143.
2. Ibid., 144.
3. UGEV, 'La situation politique en Haute-Volta et l'orientation de la jeunesse', *Jeune Volta*, new series, 1, 1972, 26.
4. Ibid., 27.
5. Ibid.
6. UGEV, *Jeune Volta*, spécial IXe congrès, 10–15 August 1979, 26.
7. Harouna Toguyeni, *En quête de progrès social: combat d'un militant*, Ouagadougou: Éditions Céprodif, 2018, 82.

8. Adama Saba, *Mémoires: histoire d'une vie socio-professionnelle au Burkina Faso*, Ouagadougou: Éditions Céprodif, 2015, 133.

9. Ibid., 134.

10. Lila Chouli, *Le contre-pouvoir étudiant au Burkina Faso: l'ANEB face à l'usage de la violence d'état et à la discrimination du campus de Ouagadougou (1990–2011)*, Paris: Fondation Gabriel Péri, 2018, 16.

11. Chouli, *Le contre-pouvoir étudiant au Burkina Faso*.

12. UGEV, *Jeune Volta*, 1979, 25.

13. PCRV, 'La "Pensée Mao Tsé Toung", source du révisionnisme chinois', *Bug-Parga*, special issue, June 1980, 22.

14. PCRV, *Bug-Parga*, 44, 1991, 4.

15. PCRV, *Ligne fondamentale: le parti*, June 1979, 3.

16. Ludo Martens and Hilde Meesters, *Sankara, Compaoré et la révolution burkinabè*, Berchem: Éditions EPO, 1989, 85.

17. ULC, *Le prolétaire*, 1, 1979, 1.

18. Ibid., 3.

19. Charles Kabeya Muase, *Syndicalisme et démocratie en Afrique noire: l'expérience du Burkina Faso*, Paris: Éditions Karthala/Inades éditions, 1989, 91.

20. Confédération générale du travail du Burkina (CGT-B), *Archives de la CGT-B, tome 1*, Ouagadougou: Éditions Céprodif, 2016, 127.

4

Student and 'Post'-Student Activism in Niger, 1970s–80s

Tatiana Smirnova

INTRODUCTION

It is formed in Niger by revolutionary militants entirely devoted to the defence of the interests of the working class and the entire people, a political organization named Organisation des Révolutionnaires Nigériens (ORN) [Organisation of Nigerien Revolutionaries].[1]

This chapter focuses on a brief and almost forgotten period of Niger's history connected with the emergence of clandestine political groups that contributed to forging the dominant socialist political party the Parti nigérien pour la démocratie et le socialisme (PNDS-Tarayya, Nigerien Party for Democracy and Socialism – Gathering). While the origins of these groups date back to the period of student activism in the 1970s, they took form only in the late 1980s. Today, the factual existence of such groups in Niger is under question and presented as an artificially constructed discourse seeking to multiply social and symbolic resources in order to reinforce the political legitimacy of PNDS-Tarayya. Indeed, there is a very limited amount of written evidence. However, it is important to take into account that it is mainly because of the clandestine character of such groups that much of the activist literature was systematically destroyed, lost and forgotten. Without engaging explicitly in the debate on the existence of the groups, this chapter illustrates activist life in Niger during the 1960s–80s, while locating it in the larger historical perspective of the counter-hegemonic post-colonial narrative. It also shows the conditions of student activism of that period and demonstrates how, over time, students contributed to reinforcing the clandestine dimension of the movement by destroying evidence of discussions and meetings. The secrecy has also contributed to nourishing strong bonds within the core structure of the movement. Finally, this chapter is about ideas of social radical transformation through educational, economic and socio-political independence that managed to find a specific political expression with the emergence of multipartism in December 1990.

BEGINNING OF STUDENT MOBILISATIONS: END OF THE 1950s–60s

> He [the director] hits us, he is forcing us to harvest for him strawberries, he eats the strawberries and tomatoes – and we are not allowed to have a single strawberry or a single tomato that we are working on and produce! He gives us nothing! Then, when he wants to punish us, he says that we don't have a scholarship and he cuts it! At the end of the month, we are supposed to receive some pocket money and at the end of the year – money to go on the leave to see parents – all this, he cuts, he cuts![2]

This testimonial brilliantly conveys the deep feelings of injustice and frustration that have progressively taken a more conceptual and organised form as part of activist anti-imperialist discourse. Although the first school strikes in Niger were connected in some way to the Sawaba movement,[3] in almost every case mobilisations were driven by the conflicting relationships between teachers and students. Students perceived the attitudes of teachers – who were often former colonial officials – as hostile and violent.

For example, in 1957, students of the Union fraternelle des élèves de Tahoua (Fraternal Union of Tahoua Students) launched a strike asking the director of the school to leave:

> It was the director who was too hard. But very competent. But tough. He was a real military man. Yes! Those were military methods. But I affirm that the Cours normal de Tahoua [Tahoua Normal Course] had the best results of the AOF [Afrique occidentale française, French West Africa]. So he was tough. But we couldn't stand his extreme rigour. We made him leave. Yes-yes [laughter]. We said that the school would not function if he doesn't leave. The French government was forced to make him leave. It was under the colonization period.[4]

It is noteworthy that the strike of 1957 at the Tahoua school began during the visit of a delegation of deputies from Niamey with the participation of Djibo Bakary. At that moment, the Sawaba movement, led by Bakary, was gaining social support, aiming for immediate independence. Djibo Bakary was the first elected mayor of Niamey in October 1956, and in 1957 he was holding the position of vice-president of the council of government. It was most probably thanks to his support that the students' demands to replace the director of the Tahoua school were met.

Similarly, on 17 January 1959, students demanded the departure of the principal of the Collège moderne de Niamey (Niamey Modern College). They considered his behaviour 'racist', even though Niger was no longer formally a French colony and the demand for his departure was clearly expressed by the participants in the strike.[5] As the authorities feared further mobilisations, 14 of the most active participants were sent directly to Abidjan to complete their secondary studies.[6]

In 1962, a conflict between students and a teacher at the Cours normal de Zinder was specifically violent, as commented by *Gaskiya*, Sawaba's magazine:

On March 10 1962, Colonel Mauget, a teacher at the Cours normal de Zinder [Zinder Normal Course], gave a grade that the student considered unfair; Mauget then slapped him ... started beating him with his fists and feet, to the point that the boy managed to grab a letter-opener and scratched his attacker. Immediately, all the repressive forces, French armies, gendarmerie, police, were mobilised. The school was closed until 9 April 1962 and the pupils were sent back home; 12 exclusions were pronounced: 8 definitive and 4 temporary; the boy at the origin of the conflict was sent to a correctional centre for seven years. As for his aggressor, he is obviously ready for an asylum, unless one accepts that he has the right of life and death over Nigerien citizens.[7]

The first school protests in Niger transcended the injustice and violence perceived by students as part of the school routine, but these strikes also had a political dimension. At different levels, they were related to other social movements claiming independence and more autonomy from France. The connections with Sawaba, with the Union générale des étudiants d'Afrique Occidentale (UGEAO, General Union of West African Students) and the Fédération des étudiants d'Afrique noire en France (FEANF, Federation of Black African Students in France) played an important role in further formalisation and structuring of the student movement in Niger.

The Union des scolaires nigériens (USN, Union of Nigerien Students) was born in this context. According to Djouldé Laya, one of its founding members, the USN project dates back to July 1958 – before independence.[8]

However, the statute of the organisation was adopted on 16 July 1960, which is recorded in the history of the movement as its date of birth, and this date is systematically quoted in various activist documents.

Very quickly, the USN took a radical position, openly criticising Diori Hamani's government. In 1961, *Gaskiya* published an 'Open Letter to the Republic of Niger Government'. It was signed by the USN and demonstrated its anti-government position:

> Since its installation by Colombani and by General de Gaulle, the PPN-RDA [Parti progressiste nigérien, Nigerien Progressive Party] of the Nigerien Government expressed its docility by acts masterminded in Paris. The Sawaba party was dissolved, its leaders – doctors, engineers – are now in prison; its fearless leader, Djibo Bakary, is in exile.[9]

The Sawaba activists were indeed systematically eliminated: by the end of the 1960s, there were thousands of Sawaba detainees in Niger, and some were put in prison and executed, sometimes even without due trial.[10]

The early years of Diori Hamani's rule were marked by a climate of terror, reinforced by the reputation of the Nigerien secret service and its methods of torture. This general context explains the important role of secrecy as one of the driving elements in the organisation of the student movement in Niger. It possibly also explains why so little written evidence of the activities of the student movement of the period of the violent repression against Sawaba has been preserved.

However, while Sawaba militants were systematically persecuted, the leading figures of the USN and the founding members of FEANF were not violently repressed. The example of sociologist Djoulé Laya, a founding member of the UGEAO and USN, is perhaps the most striking: on his return to Niger after pursuing his studies, he managed to build a brilliant career while being particularly close to Boubou Hama, the General Secretary of the PPN. Abdou Moumouni Dioffo, a FEANF cofounder and Sawaba sympathiser, on his return in 1969 from the USSR, where he studied possibly with the *Sawaba* scholarship, was appointed as a director of the Office national de l'énergie solaire (National Office of Solar Energy).[11] Therefore, there was no systematic violent repression of the very first generation of student leaders in Niger.

Niger, like most of the countries that had just achieved independence, was in need of qualified professionals. Repressing students could be also seen as counterproductive, and the authorities hoped to manage the protests through political co-optation. For example, from 1964 to 1971, the USN was recognised by the authorities as a legitimate body, while it continued to openly criticise the regime, regarded as 'neo-colonial'. In 1964, members of the USN obtained a non-permanent vote at the National Fellowships Commission,[12] and in 1971, two permanent votes.[13] The USN's involvement in scholarship commissions corresponded to a populist strategy that was particularly noticeable from the examples of co-optation of other unions that were rapidly placed under control after independence. For example, the workers' organisation that shared some of Sawaba' views, the Union nationale des syndicats du Niger (National Union of Trade Unions of Niger) was dissolved. It was replaced by the Union nationale des travailleurs du Niger (USTN, National Union of Nigerien Workers). The new organisation was presided over by a bureau member of the PPN.[14]

In the 1960s, the Nigerien authorities wrongly perceived the USN as part of the hegemonic order and hoped to co-opt the movement – as it had co-opted other unions and popular organisations – through recruitment of former activists. A certain degree of freedom for the students was deliberately allowed by the authorities, and it contributed to reinforcing the organisation rather than dominating it. However, the subsequent increases in student protests led to greater repression while promoting the context of secrecy.

INCREASES IN STUDENT PROTESTS, 1970–80

The development of the education system in Niger occurred in parallel with increasing protests. In the early 1970s, Niger had only a few university students: 103 in 1971–72, and 282 in 1973–74.[15] The Centre d'enseignement supérieur (Higher Education Centre) in Niamey was not founded until 1971, and became a university two years later.[16] Simultaneously, by the beginning of the 1980s, there were eight high schools dispersed throughout the territory of Niger in the most important regional centres: Niamey, Zinder, Tahoua, Dosso, Diffa and Maradi.[17] Being more numerous, high school students played an important role in triggering mobilisations throughout the country, but specifically in the capital, with its three high schools and the emerging university.

While activists were pursuing their studies benefiting from the development of the secondary and higher education in Niger, they persisted with contesting the curriculum as well as teaching methods. Throughout the 1970s, the student journal *L'Étincelle* included a special section titled

'Regarding the Reform of the Education System',[18] where the criticism of the education system was presented from different angles:

> The neocolonial school, on the other hand, is merely an extension of the colonial school in both its aims and its nature. It was concerned with training a carefully selected bureaucratic 'elite' to manage the neo-colonial apparatus, executive agents for the needs of the administration. It gave little importance to technical training (health, agriculture, animal husbandry) and favored the development of Western cultures. In most African countries, education is characterized by the maintenance of the language of the colonizer as an official language. ... The control of neo-colonialism over the educational system in our countries is legalized by the maintenance of cooperation agreements that allow some countries like France to control the specializations of the training system, and to impose selection.[19]

An issue of the USN magazine was presenting similar ideas in 1975:

> Today we are unanimous on this point: the school in Niger is unsuited to the realities of the country, more precisely to the interests of the Nigerien people. Indeed, the Nigerien school, a copy of the colonial school, retains these objectives; destruction of our cultural values, alienation of a social category formed to serve imperialism.[20]

According to the students, in order to reform the educational system, it was necessary to destroy all neo-colonial structures, to break up with the cultural adjustment. By accusing the regimes of Diori Hamani and Seyni Kountché of being caught up in a 'puppet game', students questioned their ability to carry out a real reform of education because it could 'endanger their own existence and the interests of their French masters'. Therefore, this position openly questioned the legitimacy of the regime.

In addition to criticising the education system, activist literature dealt with other matters of national interest – for example, it likened the 1967 uranium treaties with France to the 'selling of a nation'.[21] It also discussed more pragmatic issues of daily life, such as increases in the price of rice, and denounced the 'waffling' discourse of the state-controlled newspapers *Le Sahel-Hebdo* and *Le Sahel-Dimanche*. One of the USN leaders of that time recalled:

We understood very quickly that the regime didn't like leaflets ... so those who were in charge of the regime did not like to hear things that were contrary to what was being said on the national media. Because these were the real analyses with precise data, precise figures. All this information seriously undermined the very demagogic and false discourse of the regime. So there was a need for information other than that of the state.[22]

The typewriters that produced militant literature were a secret arm of the students and were systematically hidden in order not to be found by the government intelligence services.

Through the 1970s and 1980s, despite their relatively small numbers, students managed to position themselves as a real power, questioning the legitimacy of Nigerien authorities and political authorities in general. The relative success of student mobilisations contributed to reinforcing the legitimacy of the movement, structuring the identity of the organisation as a counter-hegemonic actor resisting the dominant political order. For example, the 1972 mobilisation on the occasion of the French President Georges Pompidou's official visit to Niger has become symbolic of the student power of that moment: one of the activists threw a tomato that landed on Pompidou's jacket. This gesture was most probably inspired by the example of the Diop brothers, young Senegalese protesters who tried to attack the presidential motorcade during Pompidou's visit to Dakar in February 1971. Unlike Senegal, where the perpetrators were severely repressed, nothing like that happened in Niger. Paradoxically, no major repression was organised by the government despite the important strikes that broke out in schools in 1972 and continued during 1973–74. The drought that affected the Sahel and the progressive loss of legitimacy of the regime contributed to its weakening and to the coup d'état organised in April 1974 by Seyni Kountché.[23]

The new leader of Niger, the militarist Seyni Kountché, was relatively unknown and was looking for legitimacy and recognition. Like his predecessor, at the beginning of his rule Kountché adopted a number of measures designed to co-opt the USN. For example, he liberated students and teachers imprisoned after the 1973–74 strikes and tried to involve USN activists in the committees for food distribution in 1974. The regime even allowed the USN to organise its third congress that took place on 5–12 August 1975.[24] It was an unprecedented event, as a USN congress had never happened before on the territory of Niger. Apart from visible populist measures, Kountché also offered important positions in the government to student leaders like Mamane Brah, who was the USN President for 1972–73 and a political prisoner during 1973–74.[25] In February 1976, while the country was going through a significant drought, Mamane Brah accepted the strategic job of State Secretary for Rural Development.[26]

However, despite superficial resemblances between Diori's and Kountché's methods in managing students, there were clear differences between them. Diori's attitude was paternalistic, treating students as 'poor children' deprived of any political agency, while Kountché regarded them as political peers. This transformation was reflected first of all in the repressive methods. Indeed, when Seyni Kountché finally realised that all attempts to control the movement had failed, on the first occasion of student mobilisation in 1976 the USN was violently repressed, and subsequently, 1976–77 was proclaimed a 'blank year' in secondary schools. The USN was also banned.

Following a brief period when militants had to reinforce the clandestine dimensions of their activities, a new wave of mobilisations started at the beginning of the 1980s. The triggers of protest were always similar and deeply related to the process of teaching and the curriculum itself: students contested evaluations, professors' behaviour or administrative decisions. The connection of these triggers to the education system was obvious, as it was perceived as an extension of the established (post-)colonial order. Events preceding the official visit of the French head of state François Mitterrand, scheduled for 19–22 May 1982, allowed the movement to gain unprecedented political force.

According to one senior state official of that time, it was very important for the Kountché government not to have incidents similar to those that happened ten years ago with George Pompidou when a student had thrown a tomato at him.[27] Student leaders were quite aware of these preoccupations, and decided to use them to negotiate a better position.

Strikes began after the public seminar on educational reforms known as 'the Zinder Debates' that took place on 22 February–31 March 1982. The USN launched its first strike on 26 April. It was supported by principal schools as well as by university students. The following day, the USN organised a march in order to 'denounce the anti-social policies of the CMS [Conseil militaire suprême, Supreme Military Council]'.[28] Meanwhile, demonstrations continued for several days and took place throughout the regions of Niger: Dosso, Zinder, Tahoua, Diffa, Dogon Doutché, Say and Kollo. In Niamey, activists distributed leaflets disapproving of the luxury lifestyle of political leaders. According to one of them, issued on 7 May 1982, there were several thousand students and pupils, facing police, the republican guard, riot police and firefighters, who did not hesitate to 'use tear gas even in classrooms'.[29] On 8 May 1982, the USN distributed a paper titled 'Explosion of anger in Nigerien schools'. It denounced the exorbitant public spending on youth festivals, sports infrastructure, socio-cultural complexes and the organisation of championships. According to the leaflet, the regime was preoccupied by 'strengthening its international image'.[30]

The mobilisations lasted from 26 April until 10 May, when the authorities finally decided to negotiate with the students as it was now only nine days before Mitterrand's official visit. The four ministers representing the authorities were all important and trusted figures in the Kountché government.[31] Mamane Brah, President of the USN, and another student leader, Abdou Ibo, represented the activists. The negotiations lasted for five days (10–14 May), ending just five days before the official visit of the French head of state. This precedent was a clear indication of a break with the dominant political order: now, it was students who made political authorities negotiate with them, not the other way around. Abdou Ibo himself recalled this historic moment:

> At first we did not agree on the location. It took a lot of debate for them to agree to let us come to Issa Korombé High School. And there we brought the pupils from the area for them to stay in the courtyard since if they [security forces] would hit us, they could have hurt the children too. We wanted to feel safe and we didn't believe in the regime, which is used to robbing people, to make people disappear without knowing where they are. And throughout the debates, almost at every concluding point, before we say yes, they had to call the president to inform on the negotiations. So we could discuss like that until 9 p.m., because every time they would pretend to go to drink water or go to the toilet, but it was to call Koutnché to seek his approval of a certain negotiated point. Sometimes he approved, sometimes he did not, but we persisted. So the last and the most important point that remained was the recognition of the USN. We were uncompromising.[32]

The USN's strategy of putting the military regime under pressure had been a success. In exchange for stopping the mobilisations, several of Seyni Kountché's ministers signed a memorandum of understanding with the USN leaders promising to officially recognise the organisation.[33] These accomplishments of the USN delegation exceeded all expectations, demonstrating the government's willingness to use any means to stop the student mobilisations in order to protect Mitterrand's visit and hence the image of Seyni Kountché on the international arena.

However, the act of recognition of the USN was not effective, and strikes continued. On 3 May 1983, police intervened on the campus and violent clashes began. Confrontations resulted in the death of a student, Amadou Boubacar, under inexplicable circumstances. While the Minister of Higher Education and Research released a statement announcing the arrest of 14 students,[34] it is possible that this figure was an underestimate: according to other sources, 300 students were arrested and detained in severe conditions for many days,[35] and others were imprisoned for years.[36]

However, several USN leaders managed to hide and escaped to Burkina Faso because of its 'revolutionary context', as they explained their choice of destination. Disguised as peasants, with their identity cards hidden in their clothing, the group left Niamey and travelled on foot through the desert, risking their lives as the trip was extremely dangerous.[37] On their arrival in Ouagadougou, they received financial support from the local USN section as well as from another one based in Dakar. Nigerien activists were also assisted by the Union générale des étudiants burkinabè (General Union of Burkinabé Students),[38] and managed to obtain student identity cards at the University of Ouagadougou. With the support of some former USN leaders (one of whom was working for an international organisation), they obtained a political refugee status. This was particularly important, as the Kountché government tried to negotiate with Thomas Sankara, President of Burkina-Faso (1983–87) for their return to Niger.[39] But this was in vain.

The university reopened on 16 May 1983, but repression continued: arrests, dismissals and threats to families, among other measures, were a common feature. This situation prevailed until Kountché's death in 1987, but contributed to a far more organised and politically sophisticated ideo-logical struggle. Its premises and foundations were tested in struggles within the movement through the 1970s and early 1980s.

SOCIAL CONTROL AND STRUGGLES FOR A RULING IDEOLOGY WITHIN THE MOVEMENT

Ideological tensions within the Nigerien student movement through the end of the 1970s resembled those in student movements elsewhere, and were nourished by the Sino–Soviet split. However, unlike in other universities of West Africa, in Niger student leaders maintained unity and managed to use ideological beliefs as a tool of social control over ordinary activists. To a certain extent, these internal struggles, together with the growing clandestine nature of activism, contributed to the formation of political groups.

Amongst three principal trends within the global left discourse – pro-Soviet, pro-Maoist and pro-Albanian – the last one was prevailing on the Niamey campus because it was promoted by the Burkinabe students who represented the dominant nationality.[40] They aligned themselves with the model of Albanian communism advanced by Enver Hoxha,[41] a movement that contributed to the founding of the Parti communiste révolutionnaire voltaïque (PCRV, Voltaic Revolutionary Communist Party) in 1978. Meanwhile, the Nigerien students, especially the ruling circle, were close to the 'pro-Soviet' trend, remaining under the influence of the Parti africain de l'indépendance (PAI, African Independence Party).[42]

Tensions between Nigerien and Burkinabé students were important, threatening the unity of the movement and its strength. According to Nigerien leaders, the long theoretical discussions during the general assembly prevented students from taking important decisions.[43] L'Étincelle noted that the general assembly held at the beginning of the 1977–78 academic year was dedicated 'in vain to discussions on the declaration of the general position regarding the USSR and China'.[44] Another general assembly held in 1978 lasted more than six hours, and 'only a few minutes were devoted to practical problems of students, while the whole discussion was marked by a sterile debate'.[45]

In order to preserve the USN's unity, student leaders decided to forbid any open ideological debate so that no opposition tendency could develop.[46] Indeed, the USN was supposed to function in accordance with the Leninist principle of democratic centralism, allowing only a limited degree of freedom for members to debate. The official position of the leaders was reinforced by the publication in L'Étincelle of these words: 'Saying that USSR, China or Albania present the only "bastion" of struggles is bizarre and, on the contrary, leads to turning away from the internationalist duty'.[47] That strategy did not work immediately: the 'pro-RNDP' Burkinabé students were not used to adhering to the decisions of the student union, whose leadership was dominated by 'pro-Soviets'. Therefore, one of the problems faced by the USN leaders was the systematic refusal of the Burkinabé students to go on strike together with the Nigerien students. To address the issue, the USN used a specific procedure, forcing students to participate in activist activities. As one of the leaders of that time recalled:

There were other nationalities who are not required to go on strike. There were the Burkinabés, there was a very important quantity. So we had to use the strong methods. So, when you look at the campus buildings, you have at least three floors. On each floor, we organised the Nigeriens, what we call 'corridor structures', with a person in charge of the corridor, who we call the 'corridor leader'. This corridor, along with all the other corridors, meets and elects a 'building manager'. When there are instructions to be given to the 'building managers', they decide at the level of the building. On all issues, as minimal as they may be: from building maintenance, toilets, toilet paper to national issues introduced at the government level. It is with these structures that we organise the picket lines in order to force Burkinabé students.[48]

The way the USN organised strikes had also contributed to reinforcing mechanisms of social control over ordinary activists within the movement. It was also supported by other practices that were deeply embedded within ideological beliefs of activists. The ideological training played a critical role in this process:

It was necessary that on all questions we could have a committee of analysis. It took us some time, by '78. The work of Marxist political formation was systematised with methods not far from those practised in Latin America .... We had the alcoholics among us, but we didn't go to bars, we had young people who had girlfriends all over the place, but we forbade that at the level of the activist structures. In other terms, all that lacked was weapons.[49]

Ideological education of ordinary activists was provided through special committees systematising the Marxist political worldview, essentially pro-USSR.[50] The ideological training and guerrilla-inspired forms of activist organisation were at the core of the USN's modus operandi and played an important role in organising strikes, specifically those at the very beginning of the 1980s:

So the strikes followed and we developed a system: when you organise a strike, you must never leave free time to the students so that they would start thinking and would be discouraged. During the strikes, we established a schedule: all the activist structures had to perform a programme from 8 a.m. to 9 a.m. For example, to organise a lecture on a political topic, then from 10 a.m. to 12 noon there could be a karate demonstration etc. And we were so well organised that each building on the campus had what we call a 'building manager'. And the whole week would be occupied by different activities during the daytime. And for the night, in order not to give people time and to give them a real feeling of participation in the struggle, we introduced a system of patrolling the campus: students who were in the building would make these patrols on a rolling basis (from 1 a.m. to 2 a.m., from 2 a.m. to 3 a.m. and so on) – and it's not because they could protect the campus against something, but in order to give them a real feeling of participation and to maintain the dynamics of the struggle.[51]

Ideological convictions were deeply ingrained in bodily practices, as can be illustrated by numerous examples. Drinking alcohol or dancing was not encouraged because all free time was supposed to be filled by activism.[52] As one of the student leaders recalled:

We led a very hard, clandestine life in the clandestine cells, because in Zinder we stopped drinking, taking alcohol, dancing and so on. We only concentrated on militant activities, as we had to rebuild the USN after '76. Yes, and we continued with similar practices in the politics. When you take a party like PNDS-Tarayya, it was born out of the clandestine structures of this generation of activists.[53]

Activists were required to be 'physically fit' and available whenever the 'nation will need you'.[54] Therefore, the internal organisation of the movement was marked by the imposition of a code of conduct and discipline: corruption or stealing were strictly reprimanded and punished. For example, one of the student leaders explained that when it was discovered that a leader had stolen most of the local USN budget, they forced him to reimburse all of it, subsequently rehabilitating him.[55]

Therefore, activist discipline was a key feature of social control that contributed to reinforcing student organisation and constituted a means of resistance and subversion of the dominant order incarnated by Seyni Kountché's rule.

By the end of the 1970s, academic relations between Niger and Burkina Faso had considerably deteriorated: because of their radicalism, the Burkinabé students were considered dangerous revolutionary activists and were systematically expelled.[56] That contributed to the progressive disappearance of Burkinabé students from the activist landscape[57] and to preserving the coherence of the student movement in Niger.

CLANDESTINE POLITICAL GROUPS IN NIGER IN THE 1980s

Shared experiences of activism contributed to the emergence of forms of political expression that went beyond the student organisation. According to interviews, starting in the 1980s, at least two clandestine activist groups were formed. The first was referred to as G-80 and was less structured than the second one, the Groupe des révolutionnaires nigériens (GRN, Group of Nigerien Revolutionaries) that became the Organisation des révolutionnaires nigériens. In 1990, the two groups (G-80 and the ORN) participated in the creation of the Syndicat national des enseignants-chercheurs et chercheurs du supérieur (SNECS, National Union of Teacher-Researchers and Higher Education Researchers) and a major political party, PNDS-Tarayya.

G-80, was created during the school holidays in the early 1980s, and was composed of the 12 'most committed, reliable and trusted comrades'.[58] In the beginning, most of its members were scattered abroad, in France and Belgium, as well as in the countries of the West African sub-region. From the mid-1980s, the majority of activists were in Niger, and some occupied high-level positions.[59] The group managed to function in conditions of extreme secrecy:

> If at our level, we meet, but with the greatest discretion, because you could not even know that we are organised. For example, I am very connected to X. So we can be seen with X, but not with the others. But when we have meetings, we know how to do it – that is, we say the meeting place is at such and such a place. So everyone manages to be there, because our meetings are held in the bush, on the road to Say, on the road to Tillabéry, on the road to Filingué, or in certain concessions.[60]

Because of these extreme precautions, no written trace concerning the activities of the group was kept,[61] which makes it difficult to provide in-depth analysis of its ideas and functioning.

This was not the case with the other clandestine group, the GRN. According to interviews, the GRN originated from the ideas of three student leaders. During 1981–82, they started to hold informal but regular meetings reflecting on their political future.[62] In 1982, they created a clandestine structure 'above the steering committee of the USN, but without a statutory link to it,[63] but after the May 1983 strike, they left Niger for Burkina Faso, and in July 1983 founded the GRN, with support from USN sections outside Niger (specifically in Dakar and Lomé). At the end of the meeting held in 1988 in Tahoua, the GRN was transformed into the ORN.

Unlike G-80, the GRN/ORN had a written activist output. However, documents covering the period 1983–87 were lost.[64] Today, their absence is interpreted as a proof of non-existence of the structured group. It appears, however, that the GRN/ORN was rooted in Niger. As one of its founding members explained in a book chapter, 'there were clandestine political circles throughout the territory of Niger'.[65] A G-80 activist confirmed that their comrades in the GRN were nurses, teachers and civil servants, and that 'they were everywhere in the country'.[66] Another element testifying to the existence of GRN/ORN structures on the territory of Niger was the 'infiltration' tactics, widely used by its activists.[67] One of its members was arguing for the necessity 'to infiltrate the teachers' union'.[68] As a teacher, he influenced the union's delegates by contesting the principle of federation of the Syndicat national des enseignants du Niger (SNEN, National Union of Teachers of Niger). For him, the splitting of the union into two structures (primary and secondary education) would weaken its protest force.[69] In 1987, several ORN activists and sympathisers joined the SNEN executive committee.[70] In 1989, the order was given 'to infiltrate the steering committee of the USTN'.[71] The strategy of infiltration was productive as it allowed the members of the ORN to recruit a solid social base, notably within the USTN and the SNEN.

At least four documents from the period 1988–89 were preserved.[72] The language and factual references in them overlap with the discourse of GRN members. Article 1 of its statute explained: 'It is formed in Niger by revolutionary militants entirely devoted to the defence of the interests of the working class and the entire people, a political organization called: Organisation des révolutionnaires nigériens'.[73] The document set out that the ORN was calling to overthrow the authorities through a national democratic revolution 'led under the banner of the proletariat', undertaking 'permanent agitation among people, legal and illegal action'.[74] The revolutionary process was to be carried out through alliance with the 'middle bourgeoisie, which occupies an intermediary position between the exploitative social classes allied with imperialism and the people, but also with a part of the army'.[75] The final objective was 'to found a powerful democratic pole in Niger with a view to overthrowing the neo-colonial power subservient to imperialism, and the establishment of a new society, a socialist society'.[76]

The ORN copied the structure of the USN. It was organised into cells, sub-sections and sections located on the territory of Niger.[77] Management was provided by the Sécretariat executif révolutionnaire (Revolutionary Executive Secretariat), headed by the first secretary, a political leader of the ORN. It was composed of four departments dedicated to security, propaganda, finance and external relations. The ORN statute also provided for specific security precautions that reflected the climate of terror of that time: 'The ORN militant must know how to endure all humiliations, all threats and torture, and even the need to sacrifice his life to preserve the secrecy of the organization and the lives of his comrades in struggle.'[78]

On 23 December 1990, members of the ORN and G-80 founded PNDS-Tarayya.[79] The idea of the party was born out of a meeting between activists from the two groups in Ouagadougou in 1989. According to militants, it turned out that although they had known each other for a long time, they did not know that each of them were members of the other clandestine group. In fact, it was a G-80 activist who had helped the founding members of the GRN to obtain political refugee status in Burkina Faso. One of the participants of the 1989 meeting recalled: "So it was during one of my missions to Ouaga [Ouagadougou] and during my discussions with [X], that I told him that we were working discreetly and that we had a group .... He too had told me about the existence of a group at their level.'[80] A year later, the activists created PNDS-Tarayya, which would become one of the major parties in Niger's political life.

CONCLUSION

This chapter has focused on a poorly studied period of socio-political history of Niger through the lens of the student protests and their critical role in structuring the contemporary political arena. It has described the context preceding the formation in the 1980s of Niger's clandestine political groups whose existence is still debated today. Without engaging with these debates, the chapter presented the documents of the GRN/ORN as well as interviews with members of the groups that it was possible to collect. The general climate of secrecy has largely contributed to the fact that most documents were lost or destroyed by the militants, who were very few in numbers but occupied important positions in different socio-political structures (including trade and teachers' unions) or were located abroad and were able to return to Niger in the 1990s to take up key positions in the activist, political or academic life of the country.

The most important lesson that can be taken from Niger's socio-political history is the significance of activist experiences in framing the plurality and flexibility of approaches to power, coercion and violence. The current debate on the existence of secret political groups beyond the student movement should be seen as a logical consequence of what such groups really were and the conditions of their existence as well as their effects on structuring the contemporary political arena.

NOTES

1. ORN, *Statuts de l'Organisation des révolutionnaires nigériens*, 1988, private activist archives, Niamey.
2. Interview with a former student of the Cours normal de Tahoua who participated in the 1957 strike, conducted on 28 June 2008.
3. Sawaba was founded in the mid-1950s by Djibo Bakary, who was aiming for immediate independence from France. The movement developed a campaign to vote 'no' in order to remain in the French community at the 1958 French referendum. The party was formally banned in 1959, and its activists were preparing for a guerrilla war to overthrow Diori Hamani, Niger's president after independence in 1960, and his ruling Parti progressiste nigérien. As part of this preparation, some activists were sent abroad for military or other types of training with scholarships negotiated by Djibo Bakary. In the autumn of 1964, armed Sawaba commandos attempted an insurrection. It was severely repressed, and some commandos were arrested and sentenced to death. In April 1965, another attempt at a coup was made by a young Sawabist who tried to assassinate Diori Hamani with a grenade. It was the definitive failure of the Sawaba movement, which since then has stopped playing a role as an important political force. For more on the Sawaba movement, see K. Van Walraven, *The Yearning for Relief: A History of the Sawaba Movement in Niger*, Boston, MA: Brill, 2013.
4. Interview with a former student of the Lycée National de Niamey in the 1960s, one of the ministers of Seyni Kountché's government in the 1980s, conducted on 24 June 2008 in Niamey.
5. Interview with one of the leaders of the 1959 strike at the Collège classique et moderne de Niamey, who was also one of the leaders of the Fédération des étudiants d'Afrique noire en France during the 1960s–70s, and subsequently in the 1970s, a civil servant and teacher, conducted on 23 June 2008 in Niamey. Interview with a former student of the Lycée de Niamey in the 1960s, a professor at the University of Niamey since the 1970s, conducted on 1 June 2008 at Niamey.
6. Interview with one of the leaders of the 1959 strike at the Collège classique et moderne de Niamey who was also one of the leaders of the FEANF during the 1960s–70s, and a civil servant and teacher in the 1970s, conducted on 23 June 2008 at Niamey.

7. 'Le gouvernement du Niger contre la jeunesse', *Gaskiya*, 25 March 1962, 4, translated from French by the author.

8. See the interview with Djouldé Laya, one of the founding members of the USN, in Jean-Dominique Penel and A. Mailele, *Littérature du Niger, tome 3: rencontre*, Paris: L'Harmattan, 2010, 44.

9. 'Lettre ouverte au gouvernement de la République du Niger', *Gaskiya*, 1 June 1961, translated from French by the author.

10. Klaas Walraven, *The Yearning for Relief: A History of the Sawaba Movement in Niger*, Boston, MA: Brill, 2013, 771.

11. Several years later, under Seyni Kountché's rule in 1979, he became Chancellor of the University of Niamey, a job he held until 1983.

12. Decree 64-173/PRN, *Journal officiel de la République du Niger (JORN)*, 1 September 1964, 2.

13. Decree 71-165, *JORN*, 11 November 1971, 772.

14. The Union nationale des syndicats du Niger was also affiliated to the Confédération générale des travailleurs, diffusing radical communist ideas. See Mamoudou Gazibo, *Les paradoxes de la démocratisation en Afrique: analyse institutionnelle et stratégique*, Montreal: Presse de l'Université de Montréal, 2005.

15. Pierre Foulani, *Amélioration de l'efficacité de l'Université de Niamey, Niger: remplacement de l'enseignement bloqué par un système d'unités de valeur*, Paris: Institut international de planification de l'éducation, 1994, 5.

16. Law 71-31, *JORN*, 15 September 1971, 620; Law 73-23, *JORN*, 1 October 1973, 437.

17. Here is a list of public high schools in their order of creation: 1960 – Lycée national de Niamey; 1969 – Lycée Kassay in Niamey; 1973 – Lycée Amadou Kouran Daga in Zinder; 1977 – Lycée Aggata in Tahoua; 1980 – Lycée Mangou in Dosso; 1980 – Lycée Alaoma in Diffa; 1982 – Lycée Dan Baskoré in Maradi; 1984 – Lycée Franco-arabe in Niamey; 1986 – Lycée Tagama in Agadès; 1989 – Lycée Tillabéry. See M. Tidjani Alou, *Les politiques de formation en Afrique francophone: école, état et sociétés au Niger*, PhD thesis in Political Science, University of Bordeaux I, 1992, 235.

18. *L'Étincelle*, 1975, 1976, 1977 and 1978.

19. USN magazine, 1975–76, 2, 16, USN/UENUN archives, Niamey.

20. USN magazine, 1975, 14, USN/UENUN archives, Niamey.

21. 'Le sac de mil à 2500F: qui en profite?', *L'Étincelle*, February 1976, National Archives of the Republic of Niger, Niamey.

22. Interview with Abdo Ibo, one of the USN student leaders from 1970 to 1980, who participated in the 1982 negotiations, conducted on 6 June 2008 at Niamey.

23. Tatiana Smirnova, 'Les mobilisations des scolaires et étudiants nigériens dans les années 1957–1974: les imaginaires, l'enseignement supérieur et "l'extérieur"', in Françoise Blum, Ophélie Rillon and Pierre Guidi (eds), *Étudiants africains en mouvement: contribution à l'histoire des années 68*, Paris: Publications de la Sorbonne, 2016.

24. 'Une date une histoire: le 22 octobre 1973: journée de lutte du scolaire nigérien', USN leaflet, 22 October 1982.

25. Ibid.

26. Brah Mamane occupied positions in different governments from February 1976 to November 1983. Decree 76-24, *JORN*, 1 March 1976, 125; Decree 83-157/ PCMS, *JORN*, 15 November 1983, 847.

27. Interview with a minister in Seyni Kountché's government in the 1980s, conducted on 24 June 2008.

28. Ibid.

29. 'Au Niger il est devenu chose courante, pour le pouvoir de développer la calomnie et le mensonge à travers la radio, la télévision et les journaux afin de mystifier l'opinion démocratique nigérienne', USN leaflet, 7 May 1982, student archives, Niamey.

30. 'L'explosion de la colère des scolaires nigériens', USN leaflet, 8 May 1982, student archives, Niamey; 'Le système capitaliste mondiale traverse une crise structurelle sans precedent', USN leaflet, 2 January 1983, student archives, Niamey.

31. Annou Mahamane was the Minister of Mines and Industry and also head of the delegation on behalf of the government; Illa Maikassousa was formerly the headmaster at Issa Korombé High School, and in June 1982, just after Mitterrand's visit, he became the Minister of Higher Education; Oumar Diallo was the Minister of Public Works; Maman Oumarou was the Minister of Youth, Sports and Culture.

32. Interview with Abdo Ibo, one of the USN student leaders from 1970 to 1980, who participated in the 1982 negotiations, conducted on 6 June 2008 at Niamey.

33. CD/USN, 'Procès-verbal des négociations du 10 mai 1982 au 14 mai 1982 entre le gouvernement et le Comité directeur de l'USN', 17 May 1982, USN/UENUN archives, Niamey.

34. 'Déclaration du Ministre de l'enseignement supérieur et de la recherche', *Le Sahel-Hebdo*, 16 May 1983.

35. Claude Raynaut, 'Trente ans d'indépendance: repères et tendances', *Politique africaine*, 38, 1990, 330, at 27; Christiane Montandon, *Le Niger*, Paris: L'Harmattan, 2002, 235.

36. Interview with one of the student leaders of USN at the beginning of the 1980s, conducted in October 2016.

37. Interview with one of the leaders of Issa Korombé High School during the late 1970s, conducted on 24 June 2008 at Niamey.

38. Interview with one of the student leaders from the end of the 1970s to the beginning of the 1980s, conducted on 15 June 2008 at Niamey.

39. Interview with one of the student leaders in the 1970s, conducted on 18 June 2008 at Niamey.

40. The demographic composition of the university students reflected the socio-historic configuration of higher education in Niger, and the Burkinabé students largely predominated.

41. Enver Hoxha was the communist leader of Albania from 1944 until his death in 1985, serving as the first secretary of the Party of Labour of Albania.

42. The PAI, a left-wing socialist political party born in Senegal in 1957, defined itself as Marxist-Leninist in its early days. It aimed for immediate independence, and was banned in 1961, but continued to exist under clandestine conditions;

Pascal Bianchini, 'Les paradoxes du Parti africain de l'indépendance (PAI) au Sénégal autour de la décennie 1960', 2016, https://www.academia.edu/24370358/ Les_par adoxes_du_Parti_africain_de_lind%C3%A9pe ndance_PAI_au_S%C3 %A9n%C3%A9gal_aut our_de_la_d%C3%A9cennie_1960.

43. Interview with one of the student leaders at the end of the 1970s and a union and political leader throughout the 1990s–2000s, conducted on 29 June 2008 at Niamey.

44. 'De la crise organisationnelle à l'Université de Niamey', L'Étincelle, 1980.

45. Ibid.

46. Interview with one of the student leaders at the end of the 1970s, who was a union and political leader throughout the 1990s–2000s, conducted on 29 June 2008.

47. 'De la crise organisationnelle à l'Université de Niamey'.

48. Interview with Abdo Ibo, one of the USN's student leaders from 1970 to 1980 who participated in the 1982 negotiations, conducted on 6 June 2008 at Niamey.

49. Ibid.

50. Ibid.

51. Interview with a student leader in the beginning of the 1980s, who was also a civil society activist, conducted on 26 June 2008 at Niamey.

52. Interview with one of the student leaders at the beginning of the 1980s, conducted on 26 June 2008 at Niamey.

53. Interview with a student leader in the beginning of the 1980s who was also a social activist, conducted on 26 June 2008 at Niamey.

54. Interview with one of the leaders of Issa Korombé High School during the late 1970s, conducted on 24 June 2008 at Niamey.

55. Interview with one of the student leaders at the end of 1970s who was a union and political leader throughout the 1990s–2000s, conducted on 29 June 2008 at Niamey.

56. Pascal Bianchini and Gabin Korbéogo, 'Le syndicalisme étudiant, des origins à nos jours: un acteur permanent dans l'évolution socio-politique du Burkina Faso', Journal of Higher Education in Africa/La Revue de l'enseignement supérieur en Afrique, 6(2 and 3), 2008, 3360, at 39.

57. Out of 782 students enrolled in the university in 1977–78, only 422 (54%) were Nigeriens. In 1982–83, out of 2,142 students, 1,907 (89%) were Nigeriens; Direction de la programmation et de l'evaluation des projets, Programme intérimaire de consolidation 1984–1985, tome 2, Niamey: National Archives of Niger, 1984, 242.

58. Interview with one of the student leaders from the Lycée national de Niamey in the 1970s, a founding member of G-80 and a member of PNDS-Tarayya, conducted on 18 June 2008 at Niamey.

59. Ibid.

60. Ibid.

61. Ibid.

62. Interview with a student leader from 1970 to 1980, a founding member of the GRN, conducted on 1 June 2008 at Niamey.

63. Ibid.

64. Ibid.
65. Nigerien historian Malam Issa also notes: 'Once in Burkina, these students, together with others from France, Dakar and Lomé, created the Groupe révolutionnaire Nigérien (GRN), whose presence on national soil was marked by clandestine political circles. These structures served as a basis from which the Parti nigérien pour la démocratie et le socialisme (PNDS-Tarayya) was later formed'; Malam Issa, 'Le régime militaire de Seyni Kountché (1974–1987)', in I. Kimba (ed.), *Armée et politique au Niger*, Dakar: Codesria, 2008, 144161, at 159.
66. Interview with one of the student leaders from the Lycée national de Niamey in the 1970s, a founding member of G-80, member of PNDS-Tarayya and also a politician, conducted on 18 June 2008 at Niamey.
67. Interview with one of the student leaders in the late 1970s, who was also leader of the USN section abroad in the 1980s and a founding member of the GRN and PNDS-Tarayya, conducted on 29 June 2008 at Niamey.
68. Ibid.
69. Ibid.
70. Ibid.
71. ORN, *Brève analyse du cours politique national produite par le SER de l'ORN au plenum du CR*, 1989, private activist archives, Niamey.
72. ORN, *Document d'orientation*, 1988, private activist archives, Niamey; ORN, *Statuts de l'Organisation des révolutionnaires nigériens*, 1988, private activist archives, Niamey; ORN, *Le plenum du CE de l'ORN s'est tenu au cours de l'année 1989*, 1989, private activist archives, Niamey; ORN, *Brève analyse du cours politique national produite par le SER de l'ORN au plenum du CR*.
73. ORN, *Statuts de l'Organisation des révolutionnaires nigériens*.
74. ORN, *Document d'orientation*.
75. Ibid.
76. Ibid.
77. ORN, *Statuts de l'Organisation des Révolutionnaires Nigériens*.
78. ORN, *Document d'orientation*.
79. Interviews with various members of the GRN and ORN, conducted in 2008.
80. Interview with a former student at the Lycée National de Niamey in the early 1970s, an activist, professor at the University of Niamey, member of G-80 and also a founding member of PNDS-Tarayya and SNECS, conducted on 19 June 2008 at Niamey.

5

The Labour Movement, Marxism, Northern Leftists, Feminist Socialism and Student Rebels in Nigeria, 1963–78

Baba Aye and Adam Mayer

This chapter presents the development of the labour movement and the left in 1960s–70s Nigeria and puts it in perspective. Taking 1963 as a point of departure marks the first formation of a relatively sizeable socialist labour party, the Socialist Workers and Farmers Party (SWAFP). The first and second All-Nigeria Socialists Conferences were held at Zaria and Lagos in 1977 and 1978 respectively. These were attempts at founding a united working people's party which failed in the context of anti-union legislation and an anti-Marxist purge within trade unions through the Adebiyi Tribunal in 1976.

The first section sets the wider context, presenting the dynamics of developments leading to the period under review. Then socialist feminism and the Northern Leftist movements are introduced. The subsequent section looks at the 1960s in a chronological manner, while the last section of the main body of the text draws together the threads of developments in organised labour, the academic left and efforts at rallying these together with the needle of how the left shaped these and was shaped by them.

EMERGENCE OF TRADE UNIONISM AND THE LEFT

Wage labour was introduced with the nascent steps of capitalism's post-slave trade integration of the region that would come to be known as Nigeria. This appears to have been in the 1830s, and the earliest employers were imperialist adventurers who conscripted a few natives to help them know the region.

The traders who followed in their wake, better informed to pillage, continued the trend of wage employment.[1]

Formal colonisation, which began with the annexation of Lagos in 1861,
saw the beginning of wage employment in the thousands, and by 1871, there
were 2,500 waged workers.[2] The expansion of colonial administration as the
British government took full charge of running the Southern and Northern
Protectorates of Nigeria from the Royal Niger Company in 1890 and construction of the railway line to open up the resource-rich hinterlands which
began in 1889 contributed significantly to the expansion of wage employment in the 1890s (particularly in Lagos and Calabar). The records of what
could be considered as 'the first organisation known to have had an interest
in trade union activities' in the country began in that period.[3] It also witnessed the first spark of trade unionism.[4]

The 8 August 1883 edition of *The Lagos Times* notes that the Mechan-
ics Mutual Aid Provident and Mutual Improvement Association which was
formed in July of that year might well be considered the first trade union
organisation in the country. It is quite significant, not least because its members were most likely *not* waged workers. But the gradual generalisation of
wage employment must have inspired their combination as working people.

The 9–11 August 1897 strike of artisan workmen in the Public Works
Department in Lagos is the first recorded industrial action by salaried
workers. The department's workers stood firm against the autocratic dis-
position of the governor, Mr McCallum, even with the threat of dismissal,
resisting arbitrary changes in working time. They won; the government was
forced to negotiate.

The Southern Nigerian Civil Service Union, formed in August 1912, is
generally considered the first trade union in the country. It appears that 'in
its formative stage, the union seemed to see itself as an elite organisation'.[5]
Two years later, the Southern and Northern Protectorates were amalgamated,
and the union became the Nigerian Civil Service Union (NCSU). That same
year, the First World War between the imperialist powers started. It had the
consequence of increasing the cost of living in colonies like Nigeria, radicalising the NCSU, which took up agitation for civil servants' salaries.

But it was in the wake of the Great Depression that trade unionism became
generalised as 'the economic crisis generated awareness among workers'.[6]
The Nigeria Union of Teachers became the second union to be formed after
the NCSU. This was in 1931, beginning a flood of unions. Within two years
after the formation of the Southern Nigerian Civil Service Union, unions

emerged in the maritime sector and railways. And by 1940, there were 14 unions representing 4,629 workers.[7]

As a means of channelling trade unionism into the safer waters of economism (unionism that shies away from non-economic, i.e. political, problems) and away from the politics of the incipient anti-colonial nationalist movement, the British colonial government passed the Trade Union Ordinance in 1938, making unions legal entities. Economism was not achieved within the ranks!

While the 1930s saw unions' emergence, the 1940s was the decade when they flourished: 'Between 1940 and 1950 some 144 trade unions with a membership of over 144,000 were formed.'[8] The first federations were also formed in this decade, and the left emerged within these, straddling the divide of trade unionism and the nationalist movement. The nationalist movement in the 1940s and unionism were like two strands of a rope, each strengthening the other.

By the early 1940s, socialist left influence can be detected in the labour movement. For example, one of the resolutions passed at the July 1943 conference of the first trade union federation was a call for the nationalisation of the mining industry. This central labour organisation was established as the Federated Trade Unions of Nigeria in November 1942. It changed its name to the Trades Union Congress of Nigeria in July the following year, when that resolution was adopted. Its paper *The Nigerian Worker*, which reached a print run of 10,000 copies by 1944, wielded such influence that it came under the colonial government's censorship.

The African Workers Union of Nigeria formed by Frank Montague Macaulay[9] after his participation in the International Congress of Negro Workers in Hamburg in 1930 might have served in sowing the early seeds of Marxism within the labour movement were it not for his untimely passing. Frank was a son of Herbert Heelas Macaulay, generally considered a founding leader of the liberal nationalist movement behind independence. Another son of Herbert's, Oliver Ogendengbe (Oged) Macaulay, was active in the Zikist (radical pro-independence, nationalist) Movement in the late 1940s.

The year 1945 is generally considered a watershed in the nationalist movement, opening the phase of struggle that led to independence 15 years later. External and internal developments were interwoven in creating this. The end of the Second World War with the victory of the supposedly all-out democratic forces of the West inspired fervent claims to self-determination, in the spirit of the Atlantic Charter.[10] But the internal contradictions were the driving force on the ground. Central to this was the rise of workers' power.

Left trade unionists' involvement in nationalist resistance was cemented with their role in the formation of the National Council of Nigeria and the Cameroons[11] in 1944. The 2 June–4 August 1945 general strike for the Cost of Living Allowance defined the working-class movement's power as a formidable force, courted by factions of the nascent bourgeois class that were the leadership of the nationalist movement.

By 1948, the trade union movement witnessed its first split in what became a history of splits for three decades. Short-lived reunification in 1950 produced the first Nigeria Labour Congress (NLC). Within two years, the movement was split again. This time, the camps were pro-communist/socialist ideas versus anti-communist, 'moderate' reformists. This would largely remain the case until 1975.

The Zikist National Vanguard (an organisationally loose but politically radical cluster of young journalists, teachers, clerks and union persons) formed in 1946 represents the 'highest articulation' of 'militant nationalist politics' up to that time in Nigeria's history,[12] including even the core north. While a number of revolutionary socialists played leading roles in its movement, it was essentially a radical African nationalist platform. In 1948, it issued 'A Call for Revolution', and the following year it played an energetic role in efforts to forge a united front of labour and nationalist forces after 21 coal miners were shot dead in the eastern capital city of Enugu (Igboland). By 1950, it was repressed by the colonial government after an alleged attempt to assassinate Sir Hugh Foot, Chief Secretary of the colonial government, and activists received jail sentences.

In the 1950s, the mainstream nationalist leaders ditched the radical labour movement as it became clear that the colony's British overlords would sooner than later be leaving them with the reins of self-government. They thus no longer needed the cannon fodder of the trade union movement as foot soldiers.

The earliest attempts at forming what could be considered Marxist parties were in 1945. These were the Talakawa Party by Amanke Okafor and the Nigerian National Socialist Party of Fola Arogundade. The 1950s was the apogee of such efforts. These included the Freedom Movement, the Nigeria Convention People's Party and the Communist Party of Nigeria and the Cameroons in 1951, the People's Committee for Independence in 1952, and the United Working Peoples Party in 1955.

Like the earlier two 'parties' in 1945, these groups, even though some of them included a few trade unionists, were largely transient localised groupuscules which had little or no effect on the movement. However, the fact that such efforts were made reflected the distancing of relations between the trade union movement, particularly the left within it, and the nationalist movement, and a tacit belief that the left had come to be established within the political firmament of colonial Nigeria.

This feeling of ripening influence of the socialist left in the country was shared by the state. The colonial government (and private employers in commerce) quickly unleashed 'Nigeria-McCarthyism'.[13] Repression of communists included denying them work in the public services and refusing to negotiate with renowned communist union leaders such as Nduka Eze. Communist literature was also banned.

This, however, did not stop the spread of communist ideas in Nigeria. The ranks of radical and revolutionary socialists continued to grow. New entrants that would play important roles in shaping the labour movement for decades entered the terrain in this period. Wahab Goodluck and Samuel U. Bassey in the trade unions, and the indomitable Eskor Toyo, who at the time was a secondary school teacher in Lagos, joined at this time.

During this period, the basis was also being laid for a left intelligentsia. The first university in Nigeria was only established in 1948, and the National Union of Nigerian Students was formed in 1957. Trade unionists such as Mayirue Eyeneigi Kolagbodi went to further their education in the Eastern Bloc. Ola Oni (later of University of Ibadan fame), Baba Omojola and Tunji Otegbeye (the future head of the Socialist Workers and Farmers Party in the 1960s) all went to study in Britain.

RADICAL AND SOCIALIST FEMINISM

Nigerian socialist feminism grew strong very quickly, given that women in Nigeria traditionally were *not* subject to the traditional patriarchal status quo of lore (except in urban bastions of Islam in the North). In fact, as Ifi Amadiume[14] and Matera et al. show us, not only had outright matriarchies ruled in some Igbo areas in the East such as Arochukwu, but where they did not exist (as in the West), there existed parallel power structures with markets, market shrines, market deities, ranks and political associations *for women*, along with those for the men.[15] Only in the 1920s–30s did the British manage to put an end to women's political power with the role they gave to warrant chiefs (and those were exclusively *men*). The Ogu Umunwaanyi, a social and political revolt against the loss of female agency, took place in 1929. Women in Nigeria were thus traditionally *freer* than women in the traditional European, or Middle Eastern cultures.

The radical feminist movement was born in 1946, at the intersection of market women and elite representatives of the educated class such as Fun-milayo Ransome-Kuti and later Margaret Ekpo. Ransome-Kuti, who played a role in the Soviet-backed international women's movement as well as West-ern-backed movements (!), would later die as a result of the military storming the compound of his son, world-famous singer Fela Kuti. In the early 1980s, Women in Nigeria was established as a platform to fight for women's liber-ation as an integral element of the working-class struggle for emancipation (Bene Madunagu), Ifeoma Okoye published many of her novels, Gambo Sawaba was active in the North, and Molara Ogundipe-Leslie (also known as Omolara Ogundipe) established African-centred feminism that she des-ignated 'Stiwanism' (Social Transformation in Africa Including Women) in her book *Re-Creating Ourselves: African Women and Critical Transfor-mations*, contributing to an unified socialist feminist theory with Marxian underpinnings.[16] Amina Mama today focuses on the toxic masculinity of US security plans on Africa.

Thus, contrary to the labour movement, the feminist socialist movement did *not* grow in the womb of the new wage employment economy.

THE NORTH AND SOCIALISM

Indirect rule and the internal spread of Islam characterised the North under colonialism. British Christian missions existed, but were discour-aged. Almost the same could be said for schools, which were few in number. The first prime minister of independent Nigeria, Abubakar Tafawa Balewa, from (domestic) slave lineage, was sent to school instead of his princes. The North was characterised by strong vestiges of feudal socio-economic systems. Equestrian elites of the North established a strong presence in federal Nigeria and its army.

Two important caveats have to follow here. The first is that Islam and Marxism have had a more nuanced relationship than is generally supposed (from Algeria to South Africa and Kyrgyzstan, including Nigeria). Second, there are Marxist thinkers who argue that the *par excellence* revolutionary class need not be an industrial working class under every social formation.

In the 1990s, the socialist thinker Claude Ake posited on this basis that revolution was not (yet) relevant for Africa,[17] which is a highly contentious position. Maoism and other Marxist schools have emphasised how, historically and contemporaneously, the peasantry may have revolutionary roles. In Northern Nigeria, after the British destruction of the indigenous Kano textile industry, there was almost no industrial working class. And today, the impact of years of neoliberalism has further taken its toll on the industrial working class that later emerged in the city.

The Marxian understanding of progress also, very pointedly, includes overcoming stubborn vestiges of feudal social and economic relations. In Nigeria, along with British-style common law, Sharia in the North (except Adamawa) and the 'law of the land' in general (feudal customary law) are valid sources of law: feudal relationships thus have legal sanction. The likes of those never existed in the United States, and they were abolished in 1789 in France, in 1917 in Russia, in 1949 in China, and in 1970 in India (when civil lists were discontinued in that country). *Nigeria has not had such a legal revolution up to this day, and progressives in the country have always fought for it.*

In fact, as early as 1946 came the Northern Elements Progressive Union with Mallam Aminu Kano at its helm (the party was in existence from 1946 to 1966). Kano was an aristocrat himself, but his party's cadre fought battles with the thugs of the Northern ruling party, the NPC, in the 1950s and 1960s. When the ban on parties was lifted, its successor became the People's Redemption Party (PRP) in 1978, with lapses the oldest extant party in Nigeria today. The party had some electoral successes and gained the governorships of Kaduna State (Abdulkadir Balarabe Musa, 1979–81) and Kano State (Abubakar Rimi, 1979–83). Balarabe Musa was impeached in 1981. Both fell out with the leadership of Aminu Kano due to the abolishment of the cattle tax (*jangali*) and personal tax (*haraji*). Rimi suspended the Emir of Kano in 1981, leading to riots in which his left-wing advisor Dr Bala Mohammed Bauchi was killed. Chinua Achebe was deputy president of the party in the early 1980s. With the Fourth Republic, the PRP was again free to operate under the leadership of Balarabe Musa until 2018 (while Rimi joined Babangida's and Abacha's anti-democratic administrations).[18]

In 1985, Eskor Toyo (a Polish-educated economics professor, but one with his own *sui generis* dialectical thought and version of Marxism-Leninism) called for every Nigerian Marxist to champion the cause of the PRP.[19] This was *against* the idea of one-party rule and the 'left wing major's coup' option that many Marxists preferred at the time. Finally, today's most important chronicler of neoliberalism in Nigeria, and Gramscian thinker, Usman Tar, hails from the North and lives and teaches in the North to this day.

Both feminist socialist strands and Northern Leftism prove the extent to which Nigerian leftism managed to fight exclusion on the basis of gender or regional or religious identity.

FLAG INDEPENDENCE AND THE TUMULTUOUS 1960S

We will now continue our chronological exploration of Nigeria's socialist (labour) trajectory. The union flag was lowered on 1 October 1960. Behind the raising of the green and white flag of the newly independent country Nigeria lay great dreams and deep contradictions. The working masses had high hopes of a better life under self-government. However, the new indigenous ruling class which negotiated independence was beset with internal contradictions that it could not overcome, leading to the demise of the First Republic in less than six years. The newly minted Nigerian administrative bourgeoisie demanded expatriate salaries as well as annual expatriate leave to Britain (!), university graduates earned £700 a year in a country where the average income was £29,[20] and the contractors and other comprador elements competed with feudalists and among themselves for the spoils of independence while rural people as well as the urban workers suffered.

On one hand, they reacted to the vast majority of Nigerians in much the same way that the British reacted in the past to all Nigerians. On the other hand, like warring brothers, they battled each other for the spoils of office, invoking ethno-regional identities shaped by the regionalist structure that the Macpherson constitution had instituted in 1951 as a framework for the negotiated flag independence. But no single group or coalition could dominate the national political and economic system, and this caused instability on grand scale.

After a precarious and short-lived unity as the second Trade Union Congress in 1959, the trade union movement was again split, with two simultaneous conferences in April 1960. The state threw its weight behind the moderate reformists whose conference was held in the northern city of Kano. The left at this point formed the Nigerian Trade Union Congress (NTUC), which would (at this point anyway) define itself as a communist trade union.

YOUTH AS A BAROMETER OF REVOLUTIONARY PRESSURES

The new Nigerian leaders 'had a morbid fear of communism and communist infiltration and subversion'[21] It thus maintained the stance of colonial masters against communists. However, left influence within the labour movement continued to grow with the development of the left-leaning trade unions. The students' movement equally became an arena for building its influence, particularly with the formation of the Nigerian Youth Congress (NYC). The first salvo of the popular struggle after independence came from these quarters of youth.

On 29 November 1960, over 1,000 students from the University College Ibadan stormed the parliament building in Lagos to protest the signing of the Anglo-Nigerian Defence pact ten days earlier. Six students were arrested, tried and discharged. More importantly, their action led to the demise of the pact, which would have allowed Britain to maintain military bases in the country.

A few months later, after Patrice Lumumba was killed on 17 January, students once again took up the gauntlet of leading street protests, organising a series of demonstrations in front of the Belgian and American embassies in Lagos. The gale of popular protests organised by the students continued throughout the early years of independence.

These included protests against the proposed Preventive Detention Law in 1963 and against the census manipulations of national population figures in 1962–63. These helped to raise the profile of the NYC, with its strong roots in the students' movement making it a veritable social force on the left.

However, these protests could not be equated to a challenge for power. Nor were they part of a broader strategic framework for such, which needed a party formation. The only left partisan body of any significance in the first two years after independence was granted was the Northern Elements Progressive Union. With an anti-feudalist populist ideology oriented towards the peasantry in the Northern region, it had a sizeable presence as opposition to the arch-conservative, aristocratic Northern People's Congress.

THE FOLLY OF 'ENTRYISM'

In 1962, Western Region leader Obafemi Awolowo and the circle around him leaned on the socialist left. Awo, as he was popularly called, was not new to socialist left circles. He had been elected at the July 1943 conference of the first Trade Union Congress as secretary and editor of *The Nigerian Worker*. Two years later, he formed an ethnic-based organisation of the Yoruba, Egbe Omo Oduduwa. It was this that metamorphosed into the Action Group (AG).

The party adopted a 'democratic socialist' ideology at its 1962 conference. Abdulraheem and Olukoshi aptly capture the futility of this deceptive fruit of left entryist work in the AG thus:

> The greatest legacy of the A.G. Leftists are the heaps of papers on proceedings of the annual summer schools in which party cadres were lectured on subjects as diverse as the meaning of dialectical materialism and the necessity of value politics. The Leftists were paper tigers in a party which was the vehicle of the rapidly rising Yoruba bourgeoisie.[22]

Marxists also carried out 'entryism', albeit to a limited extent during this period, in the National Council of Nigerian Citizens (NCNC), the Igbo (Eastern Nigerian) stronghold. The NCNC by this time was worse than a shadow of what it was in the 1940s, which had inspired its left wing, the Zikist movement named after its inspirational figure Nnamdi Azikiwe. It had become a party rooted in the Eastern Region, like the AG in the Western Region and Northern People's Congress in the Northern Region. Its adoption of 'pragmatic socialism' as its ideology was neither here nor there.

This would be decisive in many ways. Unlike in Ghana, where not only had radicalism defined the country's independence movement, but a range of subsequent governments were also informed by radical aims (even some putschists!), Zikist 'moderation' became a leitmotiv in Nigerian government and foreign policy for decades to come. Mokwugo Okoye's *A Letter to Dr. Nnamdi Azikiwe*'s opening passages are eternal:

> True Heresy
> Dear Dr. Azikiwe,
>
> I am obliged to address you openly since you have barred, by your recent Stalinist purge, the conventional channels of communication between us, and I am happy to do so on this first anniversary of my suspension from the Party executive. True heresy is not the pride of a saint or superman but a comrade's voice helping others, … your plot against us succeeded and when the judgement was announced, you will remember, a prominent townswoman of yours instinctively snapped out …. Even so, the unseconded motion was carried and the reactionaries, fearful of exposition for their evil deeds, jumped up in glee, one of them, a senior minister in the federal government, declaiming: 'That's right, now we can really

have time to plan operations, instead of everyday arguing with Okoye, Agwuna, and Nduka Eze.' Operation Chaos and Corruption, that is.[23]

The purge of radicals strengthened the party as a vehicle of ethnic politics.

What is clear, as Narasingha P. Sil points out,[24] is that the wave of protests and politicisation of labour in those early years of the republic did 'lend socialist rhetoric' to pronouncements of the major parties, such that even the conservative 'Nigerian People's Congress [NPC] made passing references to socialist doctrines', even though this, of course, was completely empty rhetoric.

LEFT UNIONISM AND PARTY FORMATIONS: FROM UNITY TO DIVISIONS

It was within this context that different factions of the left within the trade union movement initiated exploratory moves at founding a party in 1962. However, these factions were also at loggerheads within the Independent United Labour Congress (IULC).[25] They were centred around Wahab Goodluck and S.U. Bassey on one hand and Michael Imoudu and Amaefule Ikoro on the other.[26]

While the Imoudu-Ikoro group were all for forming a Revolutionary Socialist Labour Party, the Goodluck-Bassey group debated the formation of a national democratic front-type of labour party or the formation of a party 'based on scientific socialism'.[27]

The Socialist Workers and Farmers Party, which was formed in April 1963 as a Marxist-Leninist party, was the result of their tussle. However, the top leadership of the Nigeria Youth Congress (a factor in these confrontations) colluded with the Goodluck-Bassey faction of the IULC which reverted to be the Nigeria Trade Union Congress, in the process of party formation. This laid the basis for a split, resulting in the formation of the Imoudu-led Nigeria Labour Party (NLP) the following year.

Leading members of the NLP included trade unionists such as Michael Imoudu (Labour Leader Number One), Gogo Chu Nzeribe, Amaefule Ikoro and Mayirue Kolagbodi. Young activists such as Eskor Toyo, Baba Omojola and Ola Oni (who had only recently returned from the London School of Economics to teach at the University of Ibadan) also played leading roles in the party. While it might not have been clear at that point in time, the two major trends that would dominate the socialist movement for the next quarter of a century were thus established.

The 1964 general strike helped forge some level of unity at the trade union level, bringing together all tendencies. But this was not sufficient to help bridge the political divide. It might even have actually helped sharpen the commitment of the two factions of the left in the labour movement to go their different ways. The strike demonstrated workers' strength. Both the SWAFP, with the strong footing of the NTUC in the working class, and the NLP, which saw the presence of grand old Michael Imoudu as its leader, felt they were best suited to tap into this fount of power from below. But none eventually won the extent of benefit each felt it would win by building solo in the wake of the strike.

THE SWAFP, OPPORTUNISM AND STAGIST IDEOLOGY

The Socialist Workers and Farmers Party existed in a legal manner from 1963 to 1966, when coups resulted in the banning of all political parties. Edwin Madunagu pointed out the material opportunism of someone like Tunji Otegbeye, who became a monied man as a top party apparatchik, channelling Soviet resources, as well as acting as gatekeeper.[28]

Several leading figures of the party[29] did benefit materially from the party's ties with the Soviet Union, though not in terms of becoming monied men like Otegbeye, who appears to have held the money strings. They were able to send their children and wards as well as those of their supporters to the USSR and the Eastern Bloc, along with young cadres for further education.

But the more devastating shortcoming of the SWAFP with their consequent impact on the possible trajectory of the growth of the left in the 1960s was its being tied to the ideological apron strings of Eastern European 'scientific socialist' (i.e., Stalinist) orthodoxy regarding the strategy for communists to adopt in the Third World. Despite abandoning the idea of a national democratic front party, it remained stuck in the two-stagist perspective of a National Democratic Revolution as the immediate point of departure. This had a severe impact on its politics throughout its existence.

It was able to organise mass rallies in a number of cities and towns in the Western and Eastern Regions, in the South, towards the 1964–65 general elections. But soon afterwards, it ended up joining the United Progressives Grand Alliance of opposition bourgeois parties, and in a subordinate capacity. Justifying this, Otegbeye said, 'the party must learn the fine art of winning allies and supporting the forces which stand on progressive positions in local conflicts'.[30] Eventually, it came tenth out of eleven parties in the

1964–65 elections securing 0.4% of the 5,761,483 votes cast and no seat in parliament.

In contradistinction to the opportunistic (as well as unsuccessful) position of Otegbeye and the SWAFP, Eskor Toyo stressed contemporaneously that 'bourgeois democracy is limited by colonial and feudal survivals and by imperialism' and averred that the struggle of workers and peasants 'can and must lead at once to the building of socialism'.[31]

This is not to underestimate the extent of material reliance of the SWAFP (and NTUC) on the Soviet Union. The Patrice Lumumba Academy for Labour and Political Science which it established in 1964 along with its bi-weekly *Advance* newspaper received subventions from the Soviet Union. It also owned a restaurant, a print shop, a car garage, a hospital and a pharmaceutical shop.[32] There was thus an admixture of material and ideological opportunism which boded ill for building a genuine grassroots socialist movement.

'There was apparently some effort to establish a Trotskyist movement in Nigeria in the 1960s', according to records of the Second Congress after Reunification of the United Secretariat of the Fourth International in 1965,[33] but this did not take any identifiable root.

THREE COUPS, CIVIL WAR AND SOCIAL CHAUVINISM

The First Republic crumbled in the wake of an unsuccessful coup by radicalised army majors (Nzeogwu and other officers) on 15 January 1966. The top echelon of the army stepped in to salvage the day for the bosses' class after this ill-fated attempt. The SWAFP actually supported the military regime instituted by the generals!

In a statement it issued on the heels of the successful January coup, the party declared it 'a patriotic duty' for the masses to be educated that 'the passing away' of the first republic was 'to the best interest of the people'. And it was even more categorical on where the SWAFP stood with respect to the military regime when it said the 'SWAFP has offered its support and assistance to the new government'.[34]

While military vanguardism must no doubt be condemned as such in general, as some on the left did in the following decade, one could legitimately argue that such fawning might at least have been somewhat more excusable had the military government in question been that of majors who professed revolutionary intentions.[35] But for the General Ironsi-led regime of 1966 to have been so welcomed by a socialist party was indeed preposterous.

By July 1966 there was a counter-coup, this time by Northern officers. The unsuccessful first coup was perceived by many as an Igbo coup, and this would play into the hands of ethnic irredentists. There were pogroms against Igbo people in the Northern Region even before the counter-coup. Less than a year afterwards, the country was embroiled in a protracted civil war.

Most socialists in the federal republic, described as 'the federal Left' by Adulraheem and Olukoshi, supported 'their' respective bourgeoisies (federal/Northern and Yoruba versus Igbo). Similarly, on the amorphous Biafran left, most activists threw in their lot with 'their' bourgeoisie (Ikenna Nzimiro became a top Biafra ideologue).

However, there were mainly two tendencies on the federal left with respect to the Biafra War (1967–70) that was fought between federal Nigeria and Biafran (mostly ethnic Igbo) rebels, with over 2 million dead. The dominant line on the left, which the SWAFP was aligned with, was downright chauvinistic, accepting the propaganda of Igbo conspiracy to seize power. The second, which Eskor Toyo and a number of Marxists like S.G. Ikoku and Mokwugo Okoye also espoused, stood against Biafran secession, but drew attention to the war as an intra-bourgeois class war which brought working-class people hardship and pain.[36] A third tendency, represented by Peter Ayodele Curtis Joseph, appears to have attempted to create 'a united front of Marxists, Socialists and nationalists against the war'.[37] A former Biafran Marxist as well as Biafran ideologue anthropologist Ikenna Nzimiro would also join Toyo, Ikoku and Okoye in his own take on the war in retrospect.[38] Non-Marxist radical writer Wole Soyinka travelled to meet Biafran leader Ojukwu against federal advice in order to avert war (a move that led to his incarceration).

By this time, the Nigeria Labour Party had ceased to exist. Already split in 1965, with Ola Oni breaking away to form the Revolutionary Nigeria Labour Party after the NLP had gone back on its word to join an initial boycott of the general elections, the SWAFP continued a shadowy existence until around 1970 despite the general ban on political parties since 1966. With the Soviet Union supporting the federal government in prosecuting the civil war (miscalculating that it would woo Lagos, and also in order to avoid Balkanisation as in the Congo, thought to help the imperialist camp), Soviet cadres mobilised support for the military regime and its war, which then claimed over 2 million lives in Biafra. Egyptian pilots flew Soviet planes for the federal side in the war.

The size of Nigeria's working class continued to expand during the war period. A threefold increase in the number of workers employed in both the private and public sectors was witnessed between 1955 and 1968. The military issued decrees against strike actions as part of the supposedly collective efforts to 'go on with one Nigeria'. But there were quite a few wildcat strikes. The possible force of action a mobilised peasantry could bring to bear on popular politics was also driven home by the Agbekoya revolt of 1968, where 'middle-class elites (i.e. Nigeria's intermediate bourgeoisie within Ibadan Districts)' played a catalytic role.[39] Meanwhile, the socialist left was caught off guard and made no considerable inroads into the Yoruba peasantry.

THE TRADE UNIONS: A WAVE OF STRIKES, UNIFICATION EFFORTS AND THE GOVERNMENT'S FAILED INCORPORATION OF THE UNIONS IN THE 1970s

In 1970, the NTUC endeavoured to set up a new type of organisational structure. At the heart of this new framework were full-time 'cadres'. As resolved at the umbrella organisation's congressional convention, these cadres would be 'the frontline activists' of the movement, saddled with the 'dual responsibility' of being 'employed in the services of individual trade unions, while at the same time remaining loyal to the Congress, which paid their wages until they can ensure adequate payment of membership subscription to fund these – as well as the organisational costs of their work'.[40]

But there were two key developments that made this step towards institutionalising a left bureaucracy in the trade union movement a step towards economism. First was the fact that by then, the SWAFP had become history. As Madunagu pointed out in 1982, it could not go underground because it lacked both the mass base and a united, disciplined leadership.[41] Second, as Waterman points out, 1970 marked a new phase in the history of the trade union movement – a period of 'the revival of economic militancy'.[42]

The country suddenly became awash with oil revenue almost immediately after the civil war, joining the Organisation of the Petroleum Exporting Countries in 1971. Military head of state General Yakubu Gowon would be quoted in 1973 as saying, 'money is not our problem, but how to spend it'. But little of this money was available to working-class people, who had, of course, borne the brunt of belt-tightening during the civil war while war entrepreneurs became fabulously wealthy. Inflation made nonsense of the little the working people had, galloping away at 12–15% in these years.[43] Imports rose and more and more kinds of foodstuffs were imported, constituting an explosion in the cost of living. The 1970s was the time when

Nigeria's comprador 'lumpenbourgeoisie' (to use Andre Gunder Frank's expression) emerged with full force on the back of the oil money flood.

Waves of strikes for pay increases shook the world of work, and organising these to maintain relevance became the core of the tasks of the NTUC cadres – that, rather than providing political education. The four union centres constituted the United Committee of Central Labour Organisations to jointly present the trade unions' position to the government in their quest to win much-sought increments for workers. Pay rises were eventually realised at the end of 1974.

But this was not before the first step by the state aimed at redefining the context of trade unionism. For the first time after the demise of colonialism, a Trade Union Act was enacted as Decree No. 31 of 1973. The conditions for forming unions and federations were made more stringent. The number of persons who could form a union was increased from five to 50. The government felt the large number of unions contributed to unruly table banging, so to speak.

Subsequent to this decree, the two left federations, the NTUC and Labour Unity Front, and the nationalist Nigeria Workers' Congress took steps towards unification in December 1973. Some of their affiliated unions also started processes of merger. The real turning point towards trade union unity, however, came on 21 September 1974 with the Apena Cemetery Declaration. Leaders of all the four umbrella union centres, who were gathered for the burial of a former leader, signed this declaration, which committed them to forming one unitary and all-encompassing trade union centre. A steering committee was formed to drive this process and several meetings were held to constitute the leadership that would emerge.

The proposed leadership, with Wahab Goodluck nominated for president had an unwieldy National Executive Council of over 100 persons, but naturally there were still several leaders left out. Cutting across the deep divide between radical and moderate trade unionism, leaders who had been left out of the new, unified structure, united as 'democrats' against the 'Agege deal'. Like the house rat calling on the rat outside to come in and feast, they invited the military government to take action against the emerging mega-bureaucracy of trade union unity. And the federal state, as if it needed any prompting, seized on this opportunity.

The military junta led by General Murtala Mohammed that came to power in July 1975 immediately won goodwill with its radical steps taken ostensibly to curb corruption, instil discipline in society and support African national liberation struggles across the continent with the slogan 'Africa as the centrepiece' of its foreign policy.

Resting on such popularity, which would in turn contribute to military vanguardist illusions in some quarters of the left (e.g., by the journalist-activist Niyi Oniororo), it issued a 'New National Labour Policy' which rested on the so-called principles of 'limited intervention' and 'guided democracy' on 4 December 1975, a fortnight before the 18–19 December date fixed for the founding congress of the new and unified Nigeria Labour Congress, the name chosen for the new united centre. The NLC echoed with its name the first attempt at union unity a generation earlier, on 26 May 1950.

Based on the new policy of guided democracy, the newly formed NLC was actually banned right at birth (!) and a tribunal (the Adebiyi Tribunal) set up to look into trade unions' finances and practices. Based on its findings, eleven trade union leaders from all the four centres were banned for life from practising trade unionism because of their Marxist/Communist tendencies. The trade union movement was restructured (supposedly) along industrial lines, and a new amalgamated Nigeria Labour Congress was called into being on 28 February 1978.

Attempts to ensure the emergence of a malleable leadership for the new centre failed as Hassan Sunmonu, an associate of Wahab Goodluck, won against the government-supported candidate. Sunmonu would organise a general strike and contribute to political economy literature on Nigeria's plight well into the late twentieth century.

THE IVORY TOWER: A 'NEW LEFT' AND CONTINUITY OUTSIDE THE TRADE UNION LEFT

It could be said that the 1970s marked the coming into being of a truly left-wing intelligentsia in its fullness. While there were a handful of left-wing academics by the mid–late 1960s, these were few and far between. This changed in the 1970s. And the studentry, which had played important roles in the movement as a whole since the colonial period, became better entrenched to play catalytic roles in the struggle. Oil money built four dozen federal universities in Nigeria in the 1970s and 1980s. Student numbers swelled, and students were now a force to reckon with. Students demonstrated against injustice, and demonstrated often. The killing of Kunle Adepeju, an undergraduate student on a campus, on 1 February 1971 led to national outrage. This was the first time a university student was killed in the country's entire history. Within this context, the expansion of the university

system in the 1970s spurred the broadening of a radicalised students' movement's reach and power. Although this came at significant added cost to
the military as well, with 18 more students killed during the 1978 'Ali Must
Go' campaign (named after an education minister), the National Union of
Nigerian Students was banned as a result of organising this demonstration.

Before independence, there had been only one university in the country,
the University of Ibadan. Immediately after independence, each of the three
initial regions established universities. Together with the University of Benin
(established in 1970), these made up the first-generation universities in
the country. As part of the Third National Development Plan, seven new
universities were established across the country in 1975.[44] The impact of
students' demonstrations could now have greater impact across all the nooks
and crannies of the country.

It also meant much more room for expanding the cadre of a left intelligentsia. Several left academics, some trained in the USSR/Eastern Bloc,
others in the United States/Britain, returned back home. And with an
increasing number of those who had graduated from the first generation of
Nigerian universities, they all had a widened choice of schools where they
could, as the military government would later put it in 1978, 'teach what
they were not paid to teach' – along with what they were paid to teach as
well, of course.

These included revolutionary intellectuals who would be leading lights on
the left for the next four decades. Adam Mayer captures a sizeable number of
them in *Naija Marxisms*,[45] from the anthropologist Ikenna Nzimiro through
the economists Ola Oni and Bade Onimode, the historian Yusufu Bala
Usman and the belletrist Mokwugo Okoye to literary giants such as Festus
Iyayi and Ifeoma Okoye (both Marxists), and entire cohorts of literary critics
from Biodun Jeyifo and Chidi Amuta to today's leading critical criminolo-
gist, Biko Agozino, the celebrated cultural critic Olufemi Taiwo and Literary
critic Akin Adesokan (the latter cohort for many years in the United States).
A few more from the 1970s that could be added here would include Toye
Olorode, Idowu Awopetu, Dipo Fashina and Laoye Sanda. Radical and
revolutionary intellectuals such as Patrick Wilmot, Yusuf Bangura, Bjorn
Beckman and Ingrid Essien-Obot, to mention a few from other shores, were
also part of this emergent radical milieu in the Nigerian academe of the
1970s.

Not surprisingly, this period threw up the earliest, and some of the finest,
theoretical works of 'Naija Marxisms', as Adam Mayer captures, not least in
political economy, including through the platform of the *Review of African*

Political Economy. The left with roots in the academia were not merely academic. And their contribution to the movement was not simply one of theory.

A gradual radicalisation of the union in the ivory towers commenced early in this period. The hitherto largely conservative National Association of University Teachers (NAUT) went on strike for the first time ever in 1973. Its demands, as would be the demands of subsequent generations of university teachers' organisations, were threefold: enhanced remuneration, improved funding of tertiary education and meaningful university autonomy. But the consolidation of left influence on their union in the universities would come with the succession of the NAUT by the Academic Staff Union of Universities in 1978.

Their contribution to the movement was itself also not limited to radicalising their union. Rather, this was an outgrowth of the dynamics of several old and new forces of disparate left groups on different campuses and in different cities.

The old, which represented continuity, was the Ibadan-based circle around Ola Oni. It had established the National Academy of Arts, Science and Technology in 1970. It helped to constitute the Patriotic Youths Movement of Nigeria as a cadreship core within the National Union of Students in 1973 and published an ideological organ, *Theory and Practice*. But, like the then new groupings forming at other university towns such as Ife, Zaria, Lagos, Calabar and Benin, it still lacked any serious roots in the sociological working class.

It would appear, as some of its activists would aver, that this was because the trade union-based left shut it out of such space. This, however, amounts to failing to grasp a fact which the NTUC itself realised, as Waterman notes: 'that much of the Nigerian labour movement lay outside its [the NTUC's] confines',[46] and at a time that the ex-SWAFP cadre of the NTUC was more focused on addressing the rise of economic militancy.

Attempts to forge unity among the various atomised groups within and beyond the ivory tower gathered speed as the military's lifting of its ban on political activities in 1978 drew closer. The result, as Madunagu shows,[47] was still somewhat pathetic, with the revolutionary left collectively revealing that it 'constituted no threat whatsoever to the present social order', where it really mattered, despite the occasional electoral successes of radicals (Abubakar Rimi and Balarabe Musa became governors in the North in the democratic period).

THE LEFT, BOURGEOIS DEMOCRATISATION
AND A POTPOURRI OF DISCONTENTS

While the debate on 'military vanguardism' took on an engaged theoretical pace until the mid-1980s, the practice of some sections on the left reflected illusions in social transformation from above being introduced by the men in khaki, with the General Murtala Mohammed-led junta. This contributed to his image as a nationalist hero in the six months of his rule. When General Olusegun Obasanjo, Mohammed's successor after the latter's assassination, reaffirmed the commitment of the military to lift the ban on political activities and return to the barracks, there appeared to be renewed urgency for unity and collective partisan organisation on the left.

The Movement for Popular Democracy, a radical platform, was formed in 1976, and with Baba Omojola playing a mercurial role, it mobilised for the first All-Nigeria Socialist Conference in Zaria in 1977. The broad spectrum of the radical and revolutionary left participated in this historic meeting. 'The conference resolved that a socialist party should be formed, and that this party should be open and as inclusive as possible.'[48]

But when the ban on politics was lifted, two parties were formed. These were the Socialist Working Peoples Party (SWPP) led by Dapo Fatogun, the alter-ego of Wahab Goodluck and the Socialist Party of Workers, Farmers and Youths (SPWFY) led by Ola Oni. Essentially, this was along the lines of the SWAFP and NLP/Revolutionary Nigerian. Labour Party of the earlier decade.

As part of its aim of stabilising the political system in the interest of the bosses' class (who by this time were the triumphant 'lumpenbourgeoisie' – the educated middle class and the salaried managerial class were both on the path of being effectively destroyed), the military had introduced the politics of registration for electoral participation in the Second Republic. With this, it ensured neither of the two radical parties got registered.

Some on the left, not having learned the lessons of the First Republic (which they appeared to have washed off their backs like ducks), took on entryism in the Unity Party of Nigeria, a reincarnation of the Action Group. The former firebrand Zikist and trade unionist Nduka Eze pitched his tent with the bourgeois National People's Party as well. He joined a faction of the party to form the Great Nigeria People's Party.

While the SWPP and SPWFY continued to exist despite not being registered, their influence on the popular masses was non-existent. In Eskor Toyo's 'Open Letter to the Nigerian Left', written before the 31 December

1983 coup d'état, but published only in April 1985 (well after Muhammadu Buhari's coup), he presented a thought-provoking argument for the revolutionary left to work in the People's Redemption Party, the party of Northern-based anti-feudalists, but also that of Chinua Achebe, who was vice-president of the party at one point.

Noting that the 'Marxists' (meaning the anti-PRP 'hard core Marxist-Leninist faction' that dreamed either of scientific socialism or a socialist army major taking power) 'who sit in their armchairs to attack the PRP' were 'merely criticising the bourgeoisie, not mobilising the people against the bourgeois establishment', when 'the time for merely criticising the bourgeoisie in Nigeria' was far gone, he could draw attention to the folly of those who merely wait for the 'class struggle' and 'revolution'.[49]

The *Open Letter* reads thus:

The Marxists who sit in their armchairs to attack the PRP are not right. Of all the different 'lines' for Marxists in Nigeria, the most correct for the present phase is joining and working in the PRP. There are a number of reasons for this. First, the 'Marxists' are not doing politics at all who are not in the PRP. They are merely criticising the bourgeoisie, not *mobilising the people* against the bourgeois establishment. The time for merely criticising the bourgeoisie in Nigeria is past. One has to find a platform for going into action. Bala Mohammed through *significant* action became more a threat to the bourgeois establishment than all the criticising Marxists put together. This is why reaction killed him *in political action*. For Nigerians it is better to think of the death of Bala Mohammed and its whole significance than to celebrate the death of Marx and Lenin.[50]

In the North, the revolutionary, democratic anti-feudalists were waging direct class war on the feudal–capitalist alliance. In 1981 came the oil glut, leading the desperation of the masses to turn in the direction of revolution with added force.

Madunagu repeatedly warned of fascism at this time – by which he meant the rule of the 'lumpenbourgeoisie' in military garb – as a solution to the revolutionary pressures. The military governments of both Buhari and Babangida unleashed hitherto unprecedented fiscal austerity and economic suffering on a historically unique scale on Nigeria, as well as successfully containing revolutionary pressures with brute force, repression, thuggery and ethnicism.

Eskor Toyo's *Open Letter* remains a particularly insightful classic as a guide, on how *not* to make a tragedy of the past that has persisted as farce. Democracy in 1999–2000 would bring a system of militarised quasi-democracy (two elected presidents, Obasanjo and Buhari, had been military heads of state in their youth in the 1970s and 1980s!), but the twenty-first century's democracy is thus only in name, where freedoms have regularly been curtailed.

THE REVOLUTIONARY MOMENTUM SINCE 2018

The world has changed since the Great Recession of 2007–9. The status quo's hegemony or apparent legitimacy was truly fractured. Through the 2010s, security challenges have turned Nigeria into what many call a failed state, a failing state or a 'successful failing state'. Nigeria's capitalism is in effect still led by a 'lumpenbourgeoisie' that is structurally comprador, even contractor, amid deindustrialisation and agro-decline, while the country has become a major oil producer. Commodities rule the economy. But by 2021, even Aliko Dangote (the Nigerian commodity magnate and the richest man in Africa) is setting up shop in Manhattan, and the Nigerian capitalist class has been busy setting up exit strategies on an individual basis with efforts directed at emigration.

Beyond Nigeria, mass movements spread across the world were bursting out as revolts (Burkina Faso and Sudan), and in the Middle East and North Africa region, revolutions threw hitherto invincible dictators into the trashcan of history.

The 'Occupy Nigeria' uprising in January 2012 was part of that moment of global rising, as Baba Aye points out.[51] But the tragedy of the radical movement is that unlike the situation in many other countries, this did not translate into organisation to take efforts forward for deepening popular struggle in an anti-systemic manner. Four years after 'Occupy Nigeria', you could still put all self-avowed revolutionaries in the country into a *molue* (long bus) and still have to *pe 'ro s'oko* (call in passengers to fill empty seats).

The revolutionary alternative manifested finally in 2018, when the African Action Congress (AAC) was registered as a political party by Nigeria's Independent National Electoral Commission. From its radical roots, it set itself apart as a platform for the struggle of the popular masses within and beyond the electoral sphere of politics. It has flourished unapologetically into a party for revolution. It has inspired tens of thousands of young working-class and professional/middle-class people across the length and breadth of the country, and indeed globally among the Nigerian diaspora. This movement's alliance with revolutionary socialist groups gave birth to the Coalition for Revolution and the launch of its #RevolutionNow campaign, with Omoyele Sowore, National Chair of the AAC, at its helm. Sowore was detained by the state security service on the eve of the launch of the campaign. Mass outcry led to his release four months later, but his movement was restricted to the Federal Capital Territory Abuja until mid-2022, when he secured the AAC ticket to run for president again. His passport still remains with the state, and as of mid 2022, he is barred from leaving the country.

The mission of our generation, rising from the obscurity of neoliberalism, is global revolution – to build a better and more just world. We must not betray it. Working-class people, united and determined, cannot be defeated!

NOTES

1. Wogu Ananaba, *The Trade Union Movement in Nigeria*, Benin City: Ethiope Publishing Corporation, 1970, 1–4.
2. B. Oluwide, *Imoudu: A Biography. Political History of Nigeria 1939–1950*. Lagos: West African Economic Consultants and Social Research, 1993, 48.
3. T. Fashoyin, *Industrial Relations in Nigeria*, Lagos: Longman, 1980, 20.
4. A.G. Hopkins, 'The Lagos Strike of 1897: An Exploration in Nigerian Labour History', *Past and Present*, 35, 1966, 133–155.
5. Fashoyin, *Industrial Relations in Nigeria*, 22.
6. Ibid., 23.
7. Ibid., 24.
8. E.O. Egboh, 'Trade Union Education in Nigeria (1940–1964)', *African Studies Review*, 14(1), 1971, 83.
9. E.E.G. Iweriebor, *Radical Politics in Nigeria, 1945–1950: The Significance of the Zikist Movement*, Zaria: Ahmadu Bello University Press, 1996, 17.
10. G. Olusanya, *The Second World War and Politics in Nigeria, 1939–1953*, London: Evans Brothers, 1973.
11. This later became the National Council of Nigerian Citizens.
12. T. Abdulraheem and A. Olukoshi, 'The Left in Nigerian Politics and the Struggle for Socialism: 1945–1985', *Review of African Political Economy*, 13(37), 1986, 64–80.
13. H.I. Tijani, *Britain, Leftist Nationalists, and the Transfer of Power in Nigeria, 1945–1965*, London: Routledge, 2005.
14. Ifi Amadiume, *African Matriarchal Foundations: The Case of Igbo Societies*, London: Karnak House, 1987.
15. Marc Matera, Misty L. Bastian and Susan Kingsley Kent, *The Women's War of 1929: Gender and Colonial Violence in Colonial Nigeria*, London: Palgrave Macmillan, 2013.

16. Molara Ogundipe-Leslie, *Re-Creating Ourselves: African Women and Critical Transformations*, Trenton/Asmara: Africa World Press, 1994.
17. Claude Ake, *Democracy and Development in Africa*, Washington, DC: Brookings Institution, 1996.
18. Andrew Agbese, 'Falalu Bello Set to Emerge PRP National Chairman', *Daily Trust* (Nigeria), 2 September 2018, https://www.dailytrust.com.ng/falalu-bello-set-to-emerge-prp-national-chairman-268562.html.
19. Eskor Toyo, 'An Open Letter to the Nigerian Left (Before the Coup)', *Review of African Political Economy*, 12(32), 85–89.
20. Ruth First, *The Barrel of a Gun: Political Power in Africa and the Coup d'État*, London: Penguin, 1970, 106.
21. O.J.B. Ojo, 'Nigerian–Soviet Relations: Retrospect and Prospect', *African Studies Review*, 19(2), 1976, 43.
22. Abdulraheem and Olukoshi, 'The Left in Nigerian Politics and the Struggle for Socialism: 1945–1985', 69.
23. Mokwugo Okoye, *A Letter to Dr. Nnamdi Azikiwe: A Dissent Remembered*, Enugu: Fourth Dimension Publishing, 1979, 40–42.
24. Narasimha P. Sil, 'Nigerian Intellectuals and Socialism: Retrospect and Prospect', *Journal of Modern African Studies*, 31(3), 1993, 361–385.
25. By 1961, the federal government, in a move at incorporation, had tried to unite the reformist Trade Union Congress of Nigeria and the radical NTUC. This resulted in the formation of the United Labour Congress of Nigeria. No sooner was this done than the two sides of the trade union split once again. The reformists retained the name, while the left took up the name Independent United Labour Congress. Factional infighting resulted in a split by 1962–63, with the majority reverting back to the NTUC name while the other faction became the Labour Unity Front.
26. R.F. Melson, *Marxists in the Nigerian Labour Movement: A Case Study in the Failure of Ideology*, doctoral dissertation, Boston, MA: Massachusetts Institute of Technology, 1967.
27. Tunji Otegbeye, *The Turbulent Decade: An Autobiographical Prelude to 'The Tempest, the Restoration and the Crown'*, Lagos: Vision Link Nigeria, 1999.
28. E. Madunagu, *Problems of Socialism: The Nigerian Challenge*, London: Zed Books, 1982, 4.
29. Despite Tunji Otegbeye being the Secretary General, persons like Wahab Goodluck, S.U. Bassey and the journalist Dapo Fatogun would more aptly fall into this category.
30. Tunji Otegbeye, *Ideological Conflicts in Nigerian Politics*, Lagos: SWAFP Press, 1964, 22–23.
31. Eskor Toyo, *Crisis in the Nigerian Youths Congress*, Lagos: Nigeria Labour Party Publications, 1964, 9.
32. M.A. Tokunboh, *Labour Movement in Nigeria: Past and Present*, Lagos: Lantern Books, 1985, 73.
33. R.J. Alexander, *International Trotskyism, 1929–1985: A Documented Analysis of the Movement*, Durham, NC: Duke University Press, 1991, 116.
34. A. Langa, 'Nigeria: Behind the Coup', *African Communist*, second quarter, 1966.

35. A. Ademoyega, *Why We struck: The Story of the First Nigerian Coup*, Lagos: Evans Brothers, 1981.
36. Abdulraheem and Olukoshi, 'The Left in Nigerian Politics and the Struggle for Socialism: 1945–1985', 71.
37. Edwin Madunagu and Biodun Jeyifo, *Understanding Nigeria and the New Imperialism: Essays 2000–2006*, Calabar: Clear Lines, 2006, 340.
38. Ikenna Nzimiro, *Nigerian Civil War: A Study in Class Conflict*, Enugu: Frontline Publishing, 1982.
39. T. Adeniran, 'The Dynamics of Peasant Revolt: A Conceptual Analysis of the Agbekoya Parapo Uprising in the Western State of Nigeria', *Journal of Black Studies*, 4(4), 1974, 368.
40. Cited in P. Waterman, 'Communist Theory in the Nigerian Trade Union Movement', *Politics & Society*, 3(3), 1973, 283–312, at 290.
41. Madunagu, *Problems of Socialism*, 4.
42. Waterman, 'Communist Theory in the Nigerian Trade Union Movement', 285.
43. T.A. Johnson, 'Nigerians Awaiting a Pay-Rise Decision', *New York Times*, 22 December 1974, https://www.nytimes.com/1974/12/22/archives/nigerians-awaiting-a-payrise-decision.html.
44. Four universities were initially proposed in the plan; see J. Otonko, 'University Education in Nigeria: History, Successes, Failures and the Way Forward', *International Journal of Technology and Inclusive Education*, 1(2), 2012, 44–48, at 45.
45. Adam Mayer, *Naija Marxisms: Revolutionary Thought in Nigeria*, London: Pluto Press, 2016.
46. Waterman, 'Communist Theory in the Nigerian Trade Union Movement', 291.
47. Madunagu, *Problems of Socialism*.
48. Madunagu and Biodun, *Understanding Nigeria and the New Imperialism*, 72.
49. Toyo, 'An Open Letter to the Nigerian Left (Before the Coup)'.
50. Ibid., 85. For details of Bala Mohammed Bauchi's death, see the section 'The North and Socialism'.
51. Baba Aye, *Era of Crisis and Revolts*, Ibadan: Solaf Publishers, 2012.

6

The Movement for Justice in Africa and Democratisation in Liberia

George Klay Kieh, Jr

INTRODUCTION

The framing vision that anchored the creation of the Liberian state was fraught with contradictions, and this has led to a seemingly unending cycle of crises and conflicts in the evolution of the social formation.[1] As the Liberian historian C.E. Zamba Liberty observed: 'It may be accurately said that Liberia was conceived in controversy and developed in controversy. Today, it still seems to be engulfed in controversy.'[2] The overarching contradiction in Liberia's founding vision was the desire by the repatriated Africans from the United States(variously referred to as 'Americo-Liberians', settlers, and incorrectly as Congos),[3] who established the Liberian state, to create an exclusionary social formation for them and their descendants in a multi-ethno-communal environment. That is, prior to the arrival of the repatriated Africans from the United States beginning in 1822, the area which was then known as the Grain Coast was occupied by various African ethnic groups that had migrated from other areas on the African continent, including the central, eastern and northern regions.[4]

Significantly, in quest of the Africans repatriated from the United States to implement their vision of the Liberian state, which they declared a sovereign and independent entity on 26 July 1847, they created a constitutional order under which citizenship, for example, was denied to the members of the various indigenous African ethnic groups who constituted the majority of the population[5] (however, partial citizenship was granted to the members of the various indigenous ethnic groups in 1907, and full citizenship was granted in 1947). The emergent apartheid-like Liberian state pursued various anti-democratic policies against the majority groups, including forcing them to perform labour for the state and pay taxes.[6] In response, the various African ethnic groups resisted in various ways, including armed struggle.[7]

The final phase of Liberia's incorporation into the world capitalist system accentuated the importance of classes and their schisms. However, the ethno-communal current which had been at the vortex of the democratic struggles in Liberia since the country's founding remained, although in a secondary role.[8] This was because the ethno-communal current had not reached its logical conclusion.[9] This meant that the Africans repatriated from the United States were the dominant ethno-communal stock in the emergent local ruling class that included Liberians from the other cultural streams, including the African ethnic groups. Importantly, several individuals and political organisations, especially opposition political parties, emerged to oppose the excesses of the liberal democratic peripheral capitalist state and its various regimes. However, none of these groups was broad-based.

Against this background, the Movement for Justice in Africa (MOJA) emerged in 1973 as the first broad-based national social movement, amid efforts by the new Tolbert regime to liberalise the peripheral capitalist state that had assumed an authoritarian complexion in 1955. In this vein, this chapter has two major interrelated purposes. First, the chapter will examine the nature and dynamics of MOJA's struggle to democratise the Liberian state. Second, it will interrogate the impact and results of MOJA's democratisation efforts.

CONCEPTUAL ISSUES: DEMOCRATISATION

Democratisation is defined as the process of empowering citizens so that they can exercise their cultural, economic, environmental, political, religious and social rights and freedoms.[10] In other words, the process of democratisation is a multidimensional phenomenon that encompasses the broad spectrum of issues related to human security.[11] Importantly, democratisation transcends the holding of elections. It is fundamentally about the structural transformation of a country's political economy and the attendant power relations, among other considerations.

THE TRAVAILS OF THE LIBERIAN STATE: BACKGROUND

The sine qua non for examining MOJA's struggle for democratisation is understanding the evolution of the Liberian state. This is because the Liberian state is the generator of the contradictions, crises and conflicts that made MOJA's struggle for democratisation imperative. The Liberian state evolved in two major phases: settler (1822–1926) and peripheral capitalist (1926–present).[12] The settler phase had two major sub-phases: colonial (1822–39) and commonwealth (1839–47). The colonial sub-phase of the settler state commenced in 1822 with the arrival of the repatriated Africans from the United States, under the control of the American Colonization Society (ACS). The ACS, which was organised in the United States in 1816, consisted of some of the prominent members of the American ruling class such as Henry Clay, former Speaker of the House of Representatives, and Bushrod Washington, Associate Justice of the United States Supreme Court. The constraints of its marginal role in the 'international division of power', as well as major domestic challenges forced the US government to outsource the project for the repatriation of free black slaves to Africa to the ACS. The ACS ruled Liberia as a classical colonial power: it established a colonial bureaucracy and a political economy that were based on cultural hubris, economic exploitation and marginalisation, and political suppression of members of the African ethnic groups who were occupying the Grain Coast prior to the arrival of the repatriated Africans.[13] Several of the African ethnic groups resisted the colonial practices of the ACS, and this led to a number of conflicts, including wars between the ACS on the one hand and the various African ethnic groups on the other.[14] During the commonwealth era, the ACS transferred authority over the conduct of the day-to-day affairs of the commonwealth (which replaced the colony as the new administrative unit) to the light-skinned section of the repatriated African stock. Under the caste-cum-class system that anchored the political economy, skin pigmentation and ancestral origins were the major determinants of an individual's relationship to the means of production and the state. The repatriated African stock were divided into two major sections: light-skinned and dark-skinned.[15] On 26 July 1847, the repatriated Africans from the United States declared Liberia an independent state.

By 1926, Liberia's incorporation into the world capitalist system was completed by the introduction of wage labour, which was brought about by the entry of the Firestone Plantations Company, an American-based corporation, into the rubber sector of the Liberian economy as the first metropolitan-based business to invest in the country. This development fundamentally transformed the social structure of the political economy: Class overtook ethnicity as the major determinant of an individual's relationship to the major means of production and the state. However, ethnicity remained a major dimension of the social structure because it had not run its course. In sum, the emergent local wing of the ruling class was composed of individuals from across the country's ethno-communal divide, with the repatriated Africans as the dominant stock. The governance system remained liberal democratic, although apartheid-like. This was evidenced by the fact that the members of the African ethnic groups who constituted the overwhelming majority of the population had partial citizenship. By 1955, the Tubman regime transformed the governance system from a liberal democracy to an authoritarian one dominated by the ruling True Whig Party as the de facto single party in the country.

However, in 1971, William R. Tolbert, Jr, who had served as the country's vice-president for 19 years, succeeded President Tubman, the quintessential autocrat, who died in office. When Tolbert assumed the Liberian presidency, the country was facing multidimensional crises of underdevelopment. For example, politically, the country was under the stranglehold of authoritarianism. In this vein, being cognisant of the dissatisfaction of repression-weary Liberians, the Tolbert regime decided to liberalise the 'political space' by, among other measures, allowing Liberians to exercise their constitutional rights of freedom of assembly, freedom of association, freedom of the press and freedom of speech. Economically, there were class inequities. For example, about 4% of the population controlled about 60% of the national wealth.[16] Similarly, about 4% of the population controlled about 60% of the income.[17] In addition, the unemployment rate stood at about 40%.[18] Socially, the infant mortality rate was about 22 per 1,000 live births.[19] Life expectancy was about 45 years.[20] Further, the illiteracy rate stood at about 79.2%.[21] This meant that less than 20% of the population was literate.

THE MOVEMENT FOR JUSTICE IN AFRICA'S INTERVENTION IN THE STRUGGLE FOR DEMOCRATISATION AND DEMOCRACY IN LIBERIA

Origins

The Movement for Justice in Africa was set up in 1973 by a group of Liberian intellectuals who had returned home from pursuing graduate studies in the United States.[22] The founders of MOJA included Togba Nah Tipoteh (President), Dew Tuan-Wleh Mayson (Chair of the Propaganda Committee) and Amos C. Sawyer (Chair of the Membership and Recruitment Committee). Ideologically, Tipoteh was wedded to left-wing populism. As for Mayson and Sawyer, there was an interesting dichotomy between their theory and praxis:

on the one hand, in their writings (they co-authored several major publications) they employed a Marxist analytical framework. However, on the other hand, in practice they demonstrated a commitment to a liberal ideology, particularly Sawyer. MOJA was organised amid two major currents: domestic (Liberia) and regional (Africa). In the case of the former, Liberia had experienced a change in leadership: President William R. Tolbert, Jr replaced President Tubman, after the latter's death in 1971. Tubman left a legacy of authoritarianism, and what Robert Clower et al. refer to as 'growth without development'.[23] The confluence of repression fatigue and the human needs deficit forced the emergent Tolbert regime to consider undertaking political and socio-economic reforms. In the political realm, for example, the regime undertook a policy of political liberalisation that was designed to 'open the political space' so that Liberians could enjoy their constitutionally guaranteed political rights, including the freedoms of assembly, association, the press and speech. This is the domestic context that provided propitious conditions for MOJA's establishment.

At the regional (African continent) level, Africa was in the midst of the liberation struggles in Southern Africa (Angola, Mozambique, South Africa and Zimbabwe) and West Africa (Cape Verde and Guinea-Bissau). Initially, MOJA focused its attention on the liberation struggles that were ongoing on the African continent. This included the undertaking of a mass public education campaign in Liberia that was designed to educate the populace about these liberation struggles, especially within a pan-African crucible. In addition, MOJA sought to expand its ambit of forging pan-African solidarity around the liberation struggles by forging ties with the various liberation movements, as well as seeking to establish MOJA chapters on the African continent. One of the resultant effects was the establishment of a MOJA chapter in Gambia. Interestingly, President Tolbert of Liberia joined MOJA during this phase of the organisation's development because he professed to be committed to the liberation of Africa from colonialism and apartheid.

However, the Tolbert regime's political liberalisation campaign was short-lived, as evidenced by the government's resorting to the authoritarian past. The shift was occasioned by two major factors. One was that the 'opening of the political space' led to, among other developments, the emergence of the labour and student movements. These mass-based movements began to advocate for meaningful changes in Liberia's political economy beyond the form-driven nature of liberal democracy. The other was that both the pressures and militancy of the labour and student movements sent shock waves through the Liberian ruling class: the members of the ruling class were fearful that political liberalisation was posing a threat to their stranglehold on power. Hence, the Tolbert regime jettisoned its political reform agenda and reverted to the Tubman era's authoritarian proclivities. The crux of the liberal democratic retrenchment found expression in the 'closing of the political space'. For example, like the Tubman regime, the exercise of the constitutionally guaranteed freedoms of assembly, association, the press speech was criminalised.[24] Criticising the government led to arrest and imprisonment.[25] Importantly, the return to authoritarianism and the continuing crises of socio-economic development led MOJA to shift its focus from the liberation struggles in Africa to domestic issues in Liberia. However, MOJA remained involved in the liberation struggles that were taking place on the African continent. Interestingly, the shift in the locus of MOJA's struggle led to President Tolbert withdrawing his membership from the organisation.

Ideology

MOJA subscribed to a left-wing populist ideology.[26] The crux of this ideology was what Daniel Albertazzi and Duncan McDonnell generally refer to as the effort to 'combine left-wing politics with populist rhetoric and themes'.[27] In terms of left-wing politics, for example, MOJA argued that the locus of the political and socio-economic crises in Liberia was structural. However, MOJA blamed the ruling elites, not the peripheral capitalist mode of production and its associated relations of production for the structural problems. In other words, elite pathologies were responsible for the structural crises in the country's political economy. The implicit derivative was that the changing of the country's governing elites was the panacea for the crises of underdevelopment. As for populist rhetoric, MOJA developed various anti-elite and anti-establishment expressions in the Liberian version of pidgin English. The most widely used one was 'Monkey work, and baboon draw', which translates as the masses were working hard to generate revenues for the state, and the ruling elites and their relations were cornering the bulk of the returns. As Tiawan Gongloe observed:

> MOJA used [Liberia's] staple food, rice, as a symbol for advocating for a fair distribution of wealth, and general improvement in the social and economic conditions in the country, and the rights of all Liberians to participate in political activities and decisions affecting Liberia on an equal basis.[28]

However, an appreciable number of members of MOJA, including from the student movement, subscribed to Marxism.[29] The crux of their argument was that the crises of underdevelopment in Liberia were caused by peripheral capitalism. Hence, the elites, who were members of the ruling class, were operating based on the tenets of capitalism. Therefore, the solution to the country's crises of underdevelopment was the transformation of the peripheral capitalist authoritarian state and its political economy.

Organisational Structure

MOJA's organisational structure consisted of the congress, the steering committee and standing committees.[30] The congress comprised the general membership of the organisation and was the highest decision-making body. The congress held its first meeting in 1980, almost seven years after the organisation was established. The major decision made at that congress was the formation of a political party. However, the 12 April 1980 military coup, especially the decision of MOJA's leadership to suspend the activities of the organisation, delayed the implementation of the decision to set up a political party. After the military regime lifted the ban on political activities in 1984 as part of the transition to civilian rule, MOJA organised the Liberian People's Party (LPP). But fearful of the LPP's popularity and the potential adverse effects on his presidential ambitions, Master-Sergeant Samuel Doe, the military leader, banned the LPP from participating in the ensuing 1985 national elections for president and being members of the legislature.[31] The steering committee consisted of the President (who simultaneously served as chair of the Strategy Committee), Vice-president and the Chairs of the Membership and Recruitment and Information and Propaganda Committees. There were three standing committees: Strategy, Membership and Recruitment, and Information and Propaganda.

Interestingly, as a national social movement, MOJA did not have structures in the various regions of Liberia. As a social movement, MOJA's focus was on educating and mobilising the Liberian populace against the country's authoritarian system of governance. Hence, the members of MOJA in Monrovia, the capital city region where the movement was headquartered as well as members in the regions outside of the capital city did not have formal local structures through which to participate in the activities of the movement. Accordingly, the members in the capital city region participated through the national structures. On the other hand, the members outside the capital city region organised various informal structures as the vehicles for facilitating their participation in MOJA's activities.

Social Base

MOJA's social base consisted of three major sections: the intelligentsia, the labour movement and the general populace. In terms of the intelligentsia, this included instructors at the University of Liberia, Cuttington University and various secondary, junior high and elementary schools throughout the country, students and technocrats, including from the public sector.[32]

Another section consisted of members from the labour movement spanning the broad spectrum of the economy – from the agricultural to the maritime sectors. In terms of the agricultural sector, the members came from the Firestone Plantations Company and the Liberian Agriculture Company. In the mining sector, the members were workers from the Bong Mining Company and the Liberian American Swedish Mining Company (LAMCO). The members from the maritime sector were mainly dock workers.

In addition, MOJA drew its members from the broad spectrum of the Liberian society, including people from divergent ethnic, regional, religious, class and professional backgrounds. This included the rank and file of the country's civil service, army, police, and security establishments

The Major Instruments in the Struggle for Democratisation

MOJA employed several major instruments as the vehicles for waging its democratisation campaign in Liberia. A major instrument was cadre training. MOJA organised and conducted various cycles of cadre training for its members, especially those from the student movement and among the general populace. The training focused on various subjects, including political philosophy, socio-economic and political systems such as communalism, feudalism, capitalism, socialism and communism, as well as authoritarianism, totalitarianism and democracy. The overarching purpose was to enable members to acquire the knowledge base that was indispensable to understanding the crises of underdevelopment in Liberia and the resulting struggle for democratisation. In turn, the cadres went to their various communities and organisations to help educate and develop political consciousness.

Another major instrument was the development of mass consciousness.[33] This included the holding of monthly mass meetings in Monrovia, the capital city region, and the publication of a monthly newsletter. The mass meetings focused on various domestic political and socio-economic issues, as well as the national liberation struggles in Africa. Thus, they were designed to help educate the citizenry, as well as help develop political consciousness. Similarly, the monthly newsletter *Gwei Fei Kpei* ('Struggle Continues' in the Kpelle language, one of the African languages spoken in Liberia) covered a variety of political and socio-economic issues. It was written in simple English to enable Liberians who were not well versed in the English language to read it. It, too, was designed to help educate the citizenry and build mass political consciousness.

In addition, MOJA forged links with major societal forces in Liberia, including the student and labour movements, that were also engaged in the struggle for democratisation in the country, In the student movement, MOJA formed an alliance with the Liberian National Student Union (LINSU), the umbrella organisation for the student governments at the University of Liberia, Cuttington University and the various secondary schools in the country. Similarly, MOJA built alliances with the workers' unions at the Bong Mining Company, LAMCO and in the maritime sectors. The centre-piece of these alliances was collective engagement in various pro-democracy activities. For example, some members of MOJA collaborated with the Progressive Alliance of Liberia, a centrist-populist national social movement in Liberia, and LINSU in organising the 14 April 1979 mass demonstration (as a movement, MOJA did not officially endorse the mass demonstration).[34] Briefly, the mass action was designed to protest against the seemingly unending crises of underdevelopment in the country, especially socio-economic malaise for the country's subaltern classes. Using the Tolbert regime's decision to increase the price of rice, the country's staple food, as the trigger, MOJA and its allies mobilised Liberians, who staged a massive demonstration in the capital city.

Further, realising that a large segment of the country's population, especially adults, was illiterate (in terms of the English language, in 1975 the rate of illiteracy in Liberia was about 79%),[35] MOJA established an adult literacy programme for some of its members, who in turn conducted adult literacy classes throughout the country. Essentially, the adult literacy programme was designed to educate an important segment of the population in the English language, including its application. This was important because English is the official language in the country, so the business of government and the private sector was conducted in English. Hence, understanding the English language and being able to apply it were quite useful tools in educating the masses and building their political consciousness. However, MOJA did not develop literacy programmes to promote African languages.

Moreover, MOJA worked with the labour movement, especially the workers' unions at the Bong Mining Company and LAMCO, in the development of their negotiating and bargaining skills.[36] This included lessons in the capital accumulation process of the shareholders of these metropolitan-based multinational corporations that were generating millions of dollars, but were recalcitrant in the face of workers' demands for higher wages and better working and living conditions. In turn, these workers' unions used both the knowledge and skills during their contract negotiation processes with the managements of these multinational corporations.

Also, MOJA used the 'Sawyer for Mayor Campaign' as a major tool in its struggle for democratisation in Liberia: In 1978, the late Amos Sawyer, a founding member of MOJA and a member of the movement's Steering Committee and Chair of the Membership and Recruitment Committee, launched an independent campaign for the mayoralty of Monrovia, the country's capital city.[37] The 'Sawyer for Mayor Campaign' had two major objectives. One was to challenge the ruling True Whig Party's stranglehold on political power in the country: beginning in 1955 after the Tubman regime's crackdown on the political opposition, including the outlawing of opposition political parties, Liberia became a de facto one-party state.[38] The other objective was to make the 'property clause' a frontier issue in the struggle for democratisation: under the country's 1847 Constitution, only citizens who owned property (real estate) were eligible to run for public offices and to vote. This provision underscored the class character of the constitution, especially the privileging of the members of propertied class, while simultaneously disenfranchising the members of the non-propertied classes who constituted the majority of the country's population. Importantly, the 'Sawyer for Mayor Campaign' received massive support from the citizens of Monrovia.[39] Interestingly, fearful that Sawyer was poised to defeat the candidate of the ruling True Whig Party, President Tolbert postponed the mayoral election.[40] However, MOJA reaped two major dividends from the 'Sawyer for Mayor Campaign'. A key one was that it enhanced the movement's mass political conscientisation campaign, which was one of the major linchpins of its democratisation strategies. The other was the elimination of the 'property clause' as a pre-requisite for voting from the subsequent 1986 Constitution.

MOJA also issued position statements on various national issues in furtherance of its mass political conscientisation and education strategies. For example, in 1975 MOJA issued a statement condemning the visit of South

African Prime Minister John Vorster to Liberia.[41] Vorster's visit was part of the strategy of the apartheid South African regime and the US government (the apartheid system's principal international patron) of wooing African states to establish relations with apartheid South Africa. MOJA's statement, among other things, educated the Liberian populace about the venalities of the apartheid system in South Africa, drew parallels between the apartheid system and the multidimensional crises of underdevelopment in Liberia, and conscientised and galvanised Liberians to oppose any effort by the Tolbert regime to establish relations with the apartheid state.

ASSESSING MOJA'S IMPACT ON THE STRUGGLE FOR DEMOCRATISATION AND DEMOCRACY IN LIBERIA

What was MOJA's impact on the struggle for democratisation in Liberia? This question will be addressed by discussing MOJA's successes and challenges in waging its struggle for democratisation in Liberia. The 'balance sheet' of MOJA's democratisation promotion struggles in Liberia indicates positives and negatives, and this section will examine some of these.

Successes

Training of cadres was one of MOJA's greatest impacts on the struggle for democratisation in Liberia. This was reflected in three major ways. One was that the MOJA cadres played pivotal roles in the movement's efforts to develop the political consciousness of Liberians by engaging in various activities at the grassroots and organisational levels. For example, MOJA cadres conducted teaching and training sessions about the crises of underdevelopment in Liberia in various communities across Liberia. Similarly, MOJA cadres undertook teaching and training activities in various civic and other organisations that were intended to develop the political consciousness of the members of the organisations. In some cases, MOJA cadres also occupied leadership positions in these organisations. Another was that after MOJA prematurely suspended its activities after the 12 April 1980 military coup, MOJA cadres in the student and labour movements as well as other community-based and civic organisations filled the vanguard role that was vacated by MOJA. For example, MOJA cadres in the student movement provided checks on the Doe military regime by, among other actions, criticising its anti-people, anti-democracy and anti-development policies such as the International Monetary Fund's structural adjustment programme and its catastrophic effects on human material well-being. In 1982, angered by the pro-democracy activities of the student movement, the Doe military regime arrested and imprisoned several leaders from LINSU.[42] Subsequently, the student leaders were charged with treason, tried by the military tribunal and sentenced to death by firing squad.[43] However, an avalanche of domestic and international pressure forced the Doe regime to release them.[44]

MOJA made invaluable contributions to the development of mass political consciousness in Liberia by educating Liberians about the nature of the multidimensional crises of underdevelopment in the country. This included Liberians from the broad ethnic, regional, class, gender and educational spectrum. MOJA's capacity to tailor its messaging to the specificities of the various sectors of Liberian society contributed to the effectiveness of the political conscientisation campaign. For example, MOJA crafted both its written and oral communications in ways that enabled even Liberians who were not well versed in the English language to understand them. In addition, MOJA's mass conscientisation campaign enabled Liberians to apply the lessons they learned about various issues. MOJA also inculcated in Liberians the importance of exercising their constitutionally guaranteed political and civil rights, including the freedoms of assembly, association, the press and speech.

Another major contribution of MOJA to the struggle for democratisation in Liberia was the eventual removal of the 'property clause' from the country's constitution as a major eligibility requirement for voting. MOJA's impact in this area found expression in Liberia's 1986 Constitution. The major result was the expansion of participation in the electoral process by enabling the majority of Liberians to exercise their right to vote. Accordingly, since 1997, Liberians, irrespective of their class status, have had the right to vote.

Challenges

However, MOJA's contributions to the struggle for democratisation in Liberia were constrained by several major factors. One revolved around the limits of MOJA's variant of left-wing populism. MOJA's diagnosis of the multidimensional crises of underdevelopment located the motor forces in elite pathologies. That is, elite pathologies were blamed for problems such as mass abject poverty and authoritarianism. On the contrary, the peripheral capitalist mode of production and its relations of production are responsible for Liberia's crises of underdevelopment, including mass abject poverty, inequalities in wealth and income, and authoritarianism. Structurally, Liberia's political economy, as Magdalene David argues, straddles 'not one but two levels of articulation: between the world capitalist economic system and the peripheral social formation as a whole, and within the social formation'.[45] Accordingly, the Liberian peripheral capitalist state serves the world capitalist economic system by serving as an enclave for the production of primary products such as iron ore, rubber, gold, diamond and timber that are used to feed the industrial manufacturing complexes of the advanced capitalist and other developed states. Domestically, the peripheral capitalist Liberian state reproduces the structures and processes of ruling-class domination. The emergent portrait of the peripheral Liberian capitalist state includes its character and mission. In the case of its character, it has been described variously as 'criminalised', 'exploitative' and 'negligent', among other epithets.[46] A particular dimension of the state's character was, and is, dominant at each historical juncture, while the others are present, but dormant.[47] Similarly, the mission of the peripheral capitalist Liberian state is twofold. One is to provide an enabling environment in which metropolitan-based multinational corporations and other businesses from the United States and various European advanced capitalist states can engage in the predatory accumulation of capital through the exploitation of labour.[48] The other is the creation of propitious conditions for state managers, who constitute a major section of the ruling class, to engage in the primitive accumulation of capital through the use of various illegal means, including bribery, extortion, the stealing of public funds, and various fraudulent procurement schemes.[49]

Another challenge that adversely affected MOJA's struggle for democratisation was political timidity on the part of the movement's leadership. At the crux of this orientation was the insistence on avoiding confrontation with the Liberian government. Hence, for example, MOJA did not organise mass actions such as demonstrations. In fact, as has been discussed, the MOJA leadership did not officially endorse the 12 April 1979 mass demonstration. Instead, it was some rank-and-file members of MOJA who were leaders in the student movement, especially the Liberian National Student Union, the University of Liberia Student Union and the ruling Student Unification Party, who forged an alliance with the Progressive Alliance of Liberia (PAL) in organising the mass action. Another case was MOJA's leadership's opposition to the movement organising a political party to contest state power. Even after some MOJA members pressured the leadership to do so and the first national congress approved the action, the decision was not implemented until three years later – albeit after MOJA had lost its status as the leading social movement in Liberia due to the leadership's decision to suspend the movement's political activities after the 12 April 1980 military coup. In sum, the political timidity of MOJA's leadership presented a paradox: on the one hand the movement wanted to wage a struggle to democratise Liberia, but on the other it was unwilling to take mass action, including confrontation with the Tolbert regime, in this quest. Undoubtedly, the political timidity of MOJA's leadership contributed to the emergence of the PAL as an alternative social movement. Essentially, PAL had a liberal ideological orientation. This was because the PAL leadership, among others, believed that the movement had to establish a political party that would compete with the ruling True Whig Party for state power, and this was the best pathway for implementing the movement's vision of democracy in Liberia. In addition, the PAL leadership viewed mass action as a potent weapon in the struggle in Liberia (although some of PAL's mass actions such as the 'midnight demonstration' in 1980 were misguided and adventuristic).

Further, the MOJA leadership misdiagnosed the 12 April 1980 military coup, hence it prematurely embraced it. For example, one of the leaders of MOJA declared that the 'coup represented the end of the revolution'.[50] Briefly, the coup was not a revolutionary one, for two major reasons. One was that the coup was organised by the US Central Intelligence Agency because the American government was concerned about the Tolbert regime's policy of establishing diplomatic relations with the Soviet Union and other socialist states.[51] In the context of the Cold War, the United States repeatedly demonstrated a sense of paranoia whenever one of its client states sought to pursue the semblance of an independent foreign policy. The other factor was that the non-commissioned officers of the Armed Forces of Liberia who implemented the American planned coup hailed from the lumpen tier of the hoi polloi. Thus, as they quickly demonstrated on assuming state power, they began imitating the ways of the members of the ruling class, including their consumption patterns – expensive cars etc. Nevertheless, almost all of the leaders of MOJA and some members took positions in the military regime headed by Master-Sergeant Samuel K. Doe. Among them were Togba Nah Tipoteh, Minister of Planning and Economic Affairs, H. Boima Fahnbulleh, Jr., Minister of Education (and later Minister of Foreign Affairs) and Dew Tuan-Wleh Mayson, Chair of the National Investment Commission (and later Ambassador to France). In addition, the MOJA leadership suspended the movement's activities. This was because the MOJA leadership wrongly assumed that the coup-makers and the resulting military regime would set into motion the democratisation of the country. On the contrary, the coup-makers were simply interested in inheriting power and engaging in the primitive accumulation of wealth through their positions in the military regime. The latter action dealt a major blow to MOJA by depriving the movement of its organisational framework that was imperative for continuing the struggle for democratisation in Liberia even in the era of military rule. In sum, this action halted MOJA's struggle for democratisation in Liberia, and contributed to the ultimate erosion of the movement's status as the pre-eminent social movement in the country.

After barely a year, the US government, through its Ambassador to Liberia, William Swing, who was teleguiding the decisions of the People's Redemption Council, the ruling military junta, began to pursue a campaign to purge those in the government who were deemed either 'socialists' (principally the members of MOJA), and 'socialist sympathisers' (some leaders and members of the ruling military council).[52] Phase one of the purge revolved around accusing Major-General Thomas Weh Syen, the Vice Head of State and Vice Chair of the ruling People's Redemption Council (PRC), and five other members of the ruling military council (the so-called "socialist sympathisers') of plotting to overthrow the Doe regime.[53] General Weh Syen and the others were arrested, tried by the military tribunal and found guilty, and subsequently executed by firing squad.[54] In addition, Togba Nah Tipoteh (President of MOJA and the Minister of Planning and Economic Affairs) was also accused as a co-conspirator in the coup plot.[55] Fortunately, Tipoteh was out of Liberia on official business at the time.[56] Thus, he did not return to Liberia, but went into exile from 1981 to the mid-1990s, after the end of the first civil war.[57] The second phase of the purge targeted H. Boima Fahnbulleh, a leader of MOJA who was then serving as Foreign Minister in the military regime: he was dismissed from his position, and also went into exile.[58]

As has been discussed, the misdiagnosis of the coup, the resulting embrace of the military regime, and the subsequent suspension of MOJA's activities undermined the movement's capacity to mobilise its members as well as the Liberian citizenry in opposing the PRC for establishing a militarised form of authoritarianism. In addition, with the President of MOJA and other leaders and members of the movement in exile, MOJA gradually became moribund, thereby undermining its status as the country's pre-eminent social and pro-democracy movement.

However, in 1984, after the lifting of the ban on political activities by the military regime as part of the transition to civilian rule scheduled to occur in 1986, the Liberian People's Party was established. The establishment of

LPP was the by-product of the decision made by the First National Congress of MOJA to set up a political party. However, still fearful of MOJA and its potential impact on derailing his presidential ambitions (Doe established the National Democratic Party of Liberia as the political vehicle through which he sought to realise his ambition to become the 'civilian president' of Liberia), head of state Doe instructed the Elections Commission to erect obstacles for the legal registration of LPP. Among the obstacles (although applicable to all political parties) was the requirement that each aspiring political party provide proof of a bank account with a minimum balance of $150,000.00. In addition, proof was required for the possession of real estate valued at a minimum of $50,000.00. To Doe's chagrin, the LPP met the registration requirements, and hence became a legally registered political party. Doe responded with two major actions. First, in August 1984, his regime arrested and imprisoned the late Amos Sawyer, the Organising National Chair of the LPP, and LPP members George Klay Kieh, Jr, Tom Kamara and Nippy Manneh, and accused them of conspiring with some members of the ruling PRC led by Vice Head of State and Vice Chair Major-General J. Nicholas Podier to overthrow the Doe regime.[59] This led to an upsurge of domestic and global pressure on the Doe regime to release the members of the LPP. For example, on 22 August 1984, the students of the University of Liberia staged a massive demonstration on the institution's main campus in the capital city. In response, Doe gave his infamous 'move or be removed order' to the military, which led to a contingent of soldiers storming the campus of the university, engaging in beatings and committing of rape and murder. About two months after the mayhem, the Doe regime released the members of LPP, along with General Podier and the other imprisoned member of the PRC.

A few months prior to the 1985 presidential and legislative election, Doe prohibited the LPP and the United People's Party, the political arm of PAL, from participating in the election. Subsequently, Doe was declared the winner of the fraud-plagued presidential election. This was followed by an abortive military coup led by General Thomas Quiwonkpa, the former Commanding General of the Armed Forces of Liberia and fourth highest-ranking member of the ruling PRC. In January 1986, Doe was inaugurated as the new President of Liberia. However, about three years later, Liberia was plunged into its first civil war, which ended in 1997 with the election of Charles Taylor, the leader of the National Patriotic Front of Liberia, the main rebel group. Doe was killed in September 1990 by the Prince Johnson-led Independent National Patriotic Front of Liberia, one of the rebel groups.

CONCLUSION

MOJA made several major contributions to the struggle for democratisation in Liberia, including the development of mass political consciousness, the building of a corps of cadres and the expansion of suffrage by leading the efforts to remove property ownership as a major pre-requisite for voting. For example, MOJA cadres played pivotal roles in the pro-democracy crusade, as evidenced by their contributions to the labour and student movements and various civic organisations, including community-based ones. In addition, MOJA's adult literacy programme played a key role in helping to address illiteracy, and the resulting development of an informed citizenry.

However, MOJA's struggle for democratisation in Liberia was hampered by several major factors. A key one revolved around the inherent limitations of MOJA's left-wing populist ideology and its focus on elite pathologies as the motor forces for the multidimensional crises of underdevelopment in Liberia. However, the reality was, and is, that peripheral capitalism is the principal culprit for the legacy of authoritarianism and mass socio-economic malaise in Liberia. Another impediment was the political timidity of MOJA's leadership, as demonstrated by its fear of organising mass action and confronting the Tolbert regime when it was necessary. In addition, the MOJA leadership made a catastrophic error by embracing the 12 April 1980 military coup, including the assumption of various positions in the military government by several leaders and members of MOJA. MOJA also suspended its activities, thereby halting the tremendous momentum the movement had gathered over seven years. Cumulatively, the embracing of the military regime, the taking up of positions in the military regime, the suspension of MOJA's activities, and the effects of the purges that witnessed the ouster of MOJA leaders and members from the military regime eroded MOJA's status as the most prominent social and pro-democracy movement in Liberia. The suspension of MOJA's activities also deprived the movement of a contingency plan for organising and confronting militarised authoritarianism and the continued human needs deficit.

NOTES

1. For a sample of the studies that have been conducted on the various crises and conflicts, including civil wars, in Liberia, see: Jeremy Levitt, *The Evolution of Deadly Conflict in Liberia*, Durham, NC: Carolina Academic Press, 2005; George Klay Kieh, Jr, *The First Liberian Civil War: The Crises of Underdevelopment*, New York: Peter Lang, 2008.

2. C.E. Zamba Liberty, *Growth of the Liberian State: An Analysis of Its Historiography*, Northridge, CA: New World African Press, 2002, vii.
3. See: Amos Sawyer, *The Emergence of Autocracy in Liberia: Tragedy and Challenge*, San Francisco, CA: Institute for Intercultural Studies, 1992; Kieh, *The First Liberian Civil War*.
4. Ibid.
5. Ibid.
6. Ibid.
7. Levitt, *The Evolution of Deadly Conflict in Liberia*.
8. Kieh, *The First Liberian Civil War*; George Klay Kieh, Jr, *Liberia's State Failure, Collapse and Reconstitution*, Cherry Hill, NJ: Africana Homestead Legacy Press, 2012.
9. Ibid.
10. See George Klay Kieh, Jr, 'The Travails of Democracy in Liberia', in Said Ademujobi (ed.), *National Democratic Reforms in Africa*, New York: Palgrave Macmillan, 2015, 75–99.
11. Ibid.
12. For a comprehensive discussion of the historical development of the Liberian state, see: Liberty, *Growth of the Liberian State*; Amos Beyan, *The American Colonization Society and the Creation of the Liberian State: A Historical Perspective, 1822–1900*, Lanham, MD: University Press of America, 1991; Sawyer, *The Emergence of Autocracy in Liberia*; Kieh, *The First Liberian Civil War*; Kieh, *Liberia's State Failure*.
13. For a discussion of the pre-colonial or pre-settler era, see: D. Elwood Dunn and S. Byron Tarr, *Liberia: A Polity in Transition*, Methuen, NJ: Scarecrow Press, 1988; Sawyer, *The Emergence of Autocracy in Liberia*.
14. Levitt, *The Evolution of Deadly Conflict in Liberia*.
15. See Carl Patrick Burrowes, *The Settler Ruling Class Thesis: A Reconsideration. Occasional Paper*, Chicago, IL, 1982.
16. See Movement for Justice in Africa, *The Situation in Our Country: MOJA's Proposal for Change*, Monrovia: Movement for Justice in Africa, 1980.
17. See Ministry of Planning and Economic Affairs, Liberia, *Economic Survey of Liberia, 1970*, Monrovia: Liberia: Government Printing Office, 1971.
18. Ibid.
19. Ibid.
20. Ibid.
21. Ibid.
22. See: Felix Gerdes, *Civil War and State Formation: The Political Economy of War and Peace in Liberia*, Frankfurt: Campus Verlag, 2013; Togba Nah Tipoteh, *Bite and Blow*, Accra: Publish Wiz, 2016.
23. For a detailed discussion of authoritarianism during the Tubman regime, see: Tuan Wreh, *The Love of Liberty Brought Us Here*, New York: C. Hurst, 1976; Sawyer, *The Emergence of Autocracy in Liberia*. And for a comprehensive discussion of socio-economic development during the Tubman regime, see Robert Clower et al., *Growth without Development: An Economic Survey of Liberia*, Evanston, IL: Northwestern University Press, 1966. The overarching conclusion

of the study was that although Liberia experienced unprecedented economic growth (the second highest in the world during the 1960s) as the result of the influx of metropolitan-based capital, it did not translate into improving the material conditions of Liberia's subaltern classes.

24. Sawyer, *The Emergence of Autocracy in Liberia*.

25. Ibid.

26. See: Leon Dash, 'Liberian Elite Facing Rare Political Test', *The Washington Post*, 28 February 1980; Neil Hahn, *Two Centuries of U.S. Military Operations in Liberia*, Maxwell Air Force Base, Montgomery, AL: Air University Press, 2020.

27. Daniel Albertazzi and Duncan McDonnell, *Twenty-First Century Populism*, London: Palgrave Macmillan, 2008, 123.

28. Tiawan Gongloe, 'The Struggle for Rights and Rice: 75th Birthday of Dr. Togba Nah Tipoteh', *Front Page Africa*, 2 September 2016.

29. See Hahn, *Two Centuries of U.S. Military Operations in Liberia*.

30. See: H. Boima Fahnbulleh (ed.), *Voices of Protest: Liberia on Edge, 1974–1980*, Boca Raton, FL: Universal Publishers, 2004; Tipoteh, *Bite and Blow*.

31. Sawyer, *The Emergence of Autocracy in Liberia*; Kieh, *The First Liberian Civil War*.

32. See: Fahnbulleh, *Voices of Protest*; John Peter Pham, 'A Nation Long Forlorn: Liberia's Journey from Civil War to Civil Society', *International Journal of Not-For-Profit Law*, 7(1), 2004, https://www.icnl.org/resources/research/ijnl/lazarus-rising-civil-society-and-sierra-leones-return-from-the-grave; Hahn, *Two Centuries of U.S. Military Operations in Liberia*.

33. Fanbulleh, *Voices of Protest*; Hahn, *Two Centuries of U.S. Military Operations in Liberia*.

34. Sawyer, *The Emergence of Autocracy in Liberia*; Kieh, *The First Liberian Civil War*; Kieh, *Liberia's State Failure, Collapse and Reconstitution*.

35. See Ministry of Planning and Economic Affairs, Liberia, *Economic Survey of Liberia, 1975*, Monrovia: Government Printing Office, 1976.

36. See: Fahnbulleh, *Voices of Protest*; Tipoteh, *Bite and Blow*.

37. See: Leon Dash, 'Liberian Elite Facing Rare Political Test', *The Washington Post*, 28 February 1980; Alfred P.B. Kiadii, 'The Rice and Rights Riot: Social Struggle and the Quest for the Alternative Society in Liberia', *Modern Ghana*, 28 April 2019, 1–5.

38. See Wreh, *The Love of Liberty Brought Us Here*; Sawyer, *The Emergence of Autocracy in Liberia*; Kieh, *The First Liberian Civil War*.

39. See: Dash, 'Liberian Elite Facing Rare Political Test'; Kiadii, 'The Rice and Rights Riot'; Jimmy Kandeh, *Coups from Below: Armed Subalterns and State Power in West Africa*, New York: Palgrave, 2004.

40. See: Sawyer, *The Emergence of Autocracy in Liberia*; Kieh, *The First Liberian Civil War*.

41. Movement for Justice in Africa, 'MOJA Condemns the Visit of Apartheid South African Prime Minister John Vorster to Liberia', Monrovia, 1975.

42. See Yekutiel Gershoni, *Liberia under Samuel Doe, 1980–1985: The Politics of Personal Rule*, Lanham, MD: Lexington Books, 2022.

43. Ibid.

44. Ibid.
45. Magdalene David, 'The Love of Liberty Brought Us Here: An Analysis of the Development of the Settler State in 19th Century Liberia', *Review of African Political Economy*, 11(31), 1984, 58.
46. See: Kieh, *The First Liberian State*; Kieh, *Liberia's State Failure, Collapse and Reconstitution*.
47. See Pita Agbese's excellent discussion of the general character of the African state, which is applicable to the Liberian peripheral capitalist state: Pita Agbese, 'The State in Africa: A Political Economy', in George Klay Kieh, Jr (ed.), *Beyond State Failure and Collapse: Making the State Relevant in Africa*, Lanham, MD: Lexington Books, 2007, 33–48.
48. See George Klay Kieh, Jr, 'Capital Accumulation in Liberia's Rubber and Iron Ore Sector', in Emmanuel Oritsejafor and Allan Cooper (eds), *Africa and the Global System of Accumulation*, London: Routledge, 2021, 54–69.
49. Ibid.
50. See Liberia Data Project, *Cultural, Demographic,, Economic, Environmental, Geographic, Political, Religious, Security and Social Data on Liberia*, Cypress, TX: Liberia Data Project, 2022.
51. The late Mrs Victoria Tolbert, the wife of the late President Tolbert, who was an eyewitness to the 12 April 1980 military coup, discussed the US role in implementation of the coup that led to the assassination of her husband, in her book Victoria Tolbert, *Lifted Up: The Victoria Tolbert Story*, St. Paul, MN: Macalester Park Publishing, 1996. See also: Dunn and Tarr, *Liberia: A Polity in Transition*; Hahn, *Two Centuries of U.S. Military Operations in Liberia*.
52. See Liberia Data Project, *Cultural, Demographic, Economic, Environmental, Geographic, Political, Religious, Security and Social Data on Liberia*.
53. Ibid.
54. Ibid.
55. See J. Kpanneh Doe and Siahyonkrohn Naynseor, 'Coups and Building Tyrants', *The Perspective*, 17 April 2001, 1–2.
56. Ibid.
57. Ibid.
58. See Liberia Data Project, *Cultural, Demographic, Economic, Environmental, Geographic, Political, Religious, Security and Social Data on Liberia*.
59. See: Amos Sawyer, *Effective Immediately: Dictatorship in Liberia, 1980-1986 – a Personal Perspective, Working Papers*, Bremen: Liberian Working Group, 1987; Sawyer, *The Emergence of Autocracy in Liberia*; George Klay Kieh, Jr, 'Neo-Colonialism: American Foreign Policy and the First Liberian Civil War', *Journal of Pan African Studies*, 5(1), 2012, 164–184; Gershoni, *Liberia under Samuel Doe, 1980-1985*.

7

The FROLINAT and the Saharan Footprint on an African Revolution: The Case of the Chadian North

Tilman Musch, Moussa Bicharra Ahmed
and Djiddi Allahi Mahamat

In one of his writings on anti-systemic movements, Wallerstein distinguished four different types in 2002: movements that emerged from 'multiple Maoisms', greens that nowadays express themselves mainly in the form of political parties, human rights activists, and finally, those who oppose globalisation.[1] These four anti-systemic movements followed what was initially considered anti-systemic, namely movements based, in particular, on socialist thought. According to Wallerstein, there is a continuity from the 1968 revolutions in Europe to these current movements. The former was in fact triggered by two particular factors, one of which was opposition to the hegemonies of both the United States and the Soviet Union, and the other the disillusionment in regard to traditional anti-systemic movements which have come to power.[2] In this chapter, we propose an analysis of the Chadian revolution led by Front de Liberation Nationale du Tchad (FROLINAT, National Liberation Front of Chad) as truly anti-systemic because, from the beginning, it did not associate itself with any current universal ideology. While Wallerstein points to a certain continuity in the anti-systemic struggle leading from the socialist movements in history to the protest movements in the present, passing through 1968, we believe that the Chadian revolution received its dynamism from the fact that it bypassed these large anti-systemic movements. With a particularly strong emphasis on the struggle against neo-colonialism and thanks to its local anchorage, the revolution led by the FROLINAT can be characterised as anti-systemic in its very essence.

In 1979, the FROLINAT conquered N'Djamena, and the French-backed regime of General Félix Malloum with his prime minister Hissène Habré[3] came to an end. Thereupon, the eleven politico-military tendencies of the

FROLINAT formed the Gouvernement d'union nationale de transition (Transitional Government of National Union). The Seconde armée (Second Army), which will be in the focus of this chapter, is one of these tendencies that all contributed to the liberation of N'Djamena.[4] We have chosen to focus only on the Second Army and the period before 1979 because we wish to emphasise a part of the Saharan geographical space. In this chapter, we will therefore first look at where the FROLINAT drew its revolutionary motivation from in general, and then focus more specifically on the revolution in the Chadian Borkou-Ennedi-Tibesti (BET) and its characteristics as a properly Saharan revolution which can be considered as anti-systemic in its own right.

THE FROLINAT – A DISTINCTLY *AFRICAN* REVOLUTIONARY MOVEMENT

On 19 January 1962, the Chadian president at the time, François Tombalbaye, dissolved all Chadian political parties, with the exception of his own, the PPT/RDA (Parti progressiste tchadien/Rassemblement démocratique africain, Chadian Progressive Party/African Democratic Rally), which was henceforth the sole party. A government reshuffle followed, creating discontent among a number of political leaders who were arrested. At the same time, a constitutional court was created in Fort-Lamy (today N'Djamena), which handed down death and life sentences for opposition politicians. Faced with this arbitrary justice, a crowd demonstrated on 16 September 1963 in Fort-Lamy and demanded the release of the arrested politicians. During this demonstration, a shot was fired from the window of a nearby building, killing a 'white' man (probably of European origin). Thereupon, Tombalbaye, certainly backed by the French side, allowed troops to open fire on the crowd, causing the death of more than 100 people, according to the organisers of the demonstration, and 19 according to the authorities.[5] In its 'Déclaration remise à Radio-Ghana' ('Statement delivered to Radio-Ghana'), Ibrahima Abatcha, the future founder of the FROLINAT, declared on this occasion:

> The imperialist army of the Gaullist neo-colonialist community, responding to the call of its valet, the dictator Tambal, fired on the outraged demonstrators who were heading towards strategic points of the city, killing about 100 people and wounding about 400.

Abatcha came to the conclusion that 'against Tombalbaye a united national liberation front is an imperative national necessity' – the future FROLINAT.[6]

In 1962, Ibrahima Abatcha was sent by his party, the Union nationale tchadienne (Chadian National Union, also dissolved in 1962), to Ghana, whose president at the time was Kwame Nkrumah. The objective of Abatcha's mission was to explain the situation in Chad to the Ghanaian president and to make contact with other countries that might be favourable to the cause of the Chadian opposition, such as Egypt or the Soviet Union. His journey enabled this young revolutionary, who had always had a particular admiration for the progressive leaders of an independent Africa, such as Patrice Lumumba (Congo), Ahmed Sékou Touré (Guinea), Modibo Keita (Mali) and Gamal Abdel Nasser (Egypt), to make his first contacts with the international community.

From Ghana, Abatcha went to Algeria and then to Egypt, where he met Chadian students at the Al-Azhar University in 1964. The commitment of the progressive faction of the students was to be a driving force for the creation of the FROLINAT, because Abatcha succeeded, thanks to the help of an Egyptian diplomat who authorised him to establish contact with the North Korean Embassy in Cairo, in having seven of these students sent to North Korea for training in 1965. These students were to become the first intellectual cadres of the FROLINAT. Another group of Chadian students in Egypt abandoned their studies in favour of armed protest and returned to Chadian terrain to begin the liberation struggle.

On 22 June 1966, the FROLINAT was founded in Nyala, Sudan. The choice of Sudan as the starting point for this movement was not without reason. Not only was the FROLINAT in this former British colony beyond the reach of France and its neo-colonies, but also the populations living on the Chad–Sudan border are still very much linked to each other by culture and history, since colonisation had arbitrarily carved out a more or less homogeneous space by assigning it to different countries. The fact that the Chadian revolution was thus born in an 'exile' that was not really an exile is significant for a revolution that was to take place practically without the support of the great 'progressive' powers of the time, such as the Soviet Union or the Arab countries.[7]

A second important point is that the revolution triggered by the FROLINAT was part of a deeply local and African context: it was the advent of several peasant revolts or rebellions that took place in Chad in the years preceding the official creation of the liberation movement. The best-known example is the Mangalmé revolt in Moubi country in the Guéra in 1965, where a peasant insurrection rose up against excessive taxes and succeeded in killing a number of regime officials. However, it was quickly suppressed.[8] Ibrahima Abatcha's revolutionary organisation was 'grafted', as Buijtenhuijs puts it, 'onto this conjuncture of peasant insurrections and violence in the border regions'. However, these armed protests 'often went unnoticed at the time', thus 'the beginnings of the armed struggle are ... difficult to describe'.[9]

However, despite the strength and dynamism of the violent peasant protest, 'an armed movement without an ideology cannot claim to be revolutionary', as a FROLINAT manifesto of June 1970 puts it.[10] Yet, already on 22 June 1966, the FROLINAT had adopted an eight-point political programme.[11] This programme called for (here abbreviated): (1) the struggle 'by all means to overthrow the neo-colonialist and dictatorial regime that France has imposed'; (2) the evacuation of 'all foreign bases and troops', which constituted 'a great and permanent danger not only to the external and internal security' of Chad, 'but also a permanent threat and danger to other African brother countries'; (3) a 'progressive democracy by promulgating freedom of the press, speech, assembly, belief, movement, association, etc.'; (4) a 'radical agrarian reform', support for the peasants and a policy of price stabilisation; (5) an increase in workers' wages, the abolition of 'all arbitrary taxes and fines', work for the unemployed, 'equality of the sexes', 'free care for the sick'; (6) the encouragement and protection of 'small and medium-sized traders from big foreign firms' as well as the abolition of the 'economic monopoly of the imperialist countries, especially France'; (7) the building of a 'democratic, progressive culture and education with a national character', as well as (8) the acceptance of both Arabic and French as national languages.

This programme, according to Buijtenhuijs, corresponds to the phase of the national liberation struggle in Mao Zedong's scheme, 'insofar as it alludes to a fairly wide range of social categories'.[12] In his commentary on this programme, Buijtenhuijs notes an 'absence of any regionalist or religious references' (except for the demand to accept Arabic as a national language and the refusal to establish relations with Israel and South Africa) and stresses the fact that it clearly stands against neo-colonialism, an 'important dimension if one wants to understand the Chadian revolution'.[13] Conceiving a national revolution as a struggle against neo-colonialism contributes considerably to its 'African character', because it is particularly on this continent that policies of imperialist domination as (neo-)colonial networks and dependencies were and still are taking their toll.

According to Buijtenhuijs, in the FROLINAT's programme as well as in a large number of its publications, four dominant ideological themes are to be noted: the anti-imperialist revolutionary theme, the radical-syndical-ist reformist theme, the regionalist-northernist theme and the Arab-Muslim theme. However, 'the reality is different', and 'the whole of its publications, although numerous, do not allow us to identify a really coherent ideology'.[14] Buijtenhuijs's judgement can be linked to a comment by Dr Abba Siddick, who was one of the FROLINAT's main ideologists and its secretary general, but who was also one of the most controversial figures within the movement itself. In an interview for *Tricontinental*, Siddick states:

> What drove people to take up arms to fight was not so much the lowering of the standard of living and the curtailment of freedoms, but rather the realization that the situation was morally unbearable, and was entirely made up of vexations and humiliations. This *subjective factor* was the catalyst that threw people into the armed struggle; there have to be *objective* motivations. These are the economic, social and cultural conditions. Any revolution that does not overcome the subjective factors is con-demned to die.[15]

Buijtenhuijs also relates this comment to a survey carried out in 1969–70 on the reasons for joining the FROLINAT. According to this survey, 64.5% of FROLINAT's recruits joined because of humiliation, bullying etc., 15% because of injustice, 20% because of despoilment, and only 0.5% for political reasons.[16] The lack of political or ideological conviction among most of the supporters, which seems to be a shortcoming of a revolutionary movement for Siddick (and also for Buijtenhuijs), can nevertheless be seen as a guaran-tee of the rooting of a revolution at the local level. And isn't the motivation to redress an experienced humiliation equivalent to the conviction that one has to fight a humiliating system? Yet combating a humiliating system implies that those who revolt have a certain vision of an alternative for which they are fighting.

The lack of ideological conviction deplored by Siddick and noted by Bui-jtenhuijs (if there really was a lack) may also have been conditioned by another fact: the FROLINAT's revolution had to be enacted practically with-out any outside help, and thus also without one of the big 'progressive' actors, such as the Soviet Union, which provided, in similar contexts, a ready-made ideology. Indeed, 'the Frolinat received virtually no moral or material sup-port from countries belonging to the socialist bloc, apart from the limited but effective support to Ibrahima Abatcha from North Korea in 1966'.[17]

Moreover, despite the efforts of Dr Siddick and Mohammed El-Baghalani, both of whom worked to bring the FROLINAT closer to Arab or Middle Eastern countries, the latter never went further than giving 'moral support as a lip service ... and no material help came from this side, except from the Palestinians'. Thus, the only allies of the FROLINAT were Algeria, Sudan and Libya.[18] However, Algeria and Sudan retreated from 1971 onwards. The rebel leader and future president Goukouni Weddeye[19] commented in this regard: 'It must be said that the only country that helped the revolution at that time was Libya.'[20] However, even Gaddafi's Libya was wary of many of the FROLINAT's supporters for ideological reasons, and the events of the following years leading to a war with Libya showed the incompatibility of the political visions of both sides.[21]

Can the FROLINAT revolution be characterised as a properly 'African' or even 'Chadian' revolution? Three main features that caused the armed protest characterised the FROLINAT's political programme point in this direction. First, the FROLINAT's struggle was apparently grafted onto a heterogeneous peasant rebellion, and this peasant element played a very important role in the field and in the protests. Second, the emphasis placed on the struggle against neo-colonialism by the intellectuals of the FROLINAT and the revolt of the 'simple' peasants against a humiliating (and, in fact, neo-colonial) situation allow this protest to be seen within the framework of a struggle for African emancipation. And finally, the absence of significant external support not only deprived the Chadian revolution of a universal ideological imprint, but at the same time opened up the space for the evolution of a properly African or Chadian revolution. Such an ideology of the field found expression in the words of a FROLINAT militant given to Buijtenhuijs in 1974: 'The Chadian is not the man who forgets the past. The people of Chad defends the historical truth, his right to exist, his culture, his determined efforts against the abandonment his original language ....'[22]

A *SAHARAN* REVOLUTION

Observers agree that one of the turning points in favour of the revolution in Chad was the involvement of the large Saharan region of Borkou-Ennedi-Tibesti and its mostly nomadic population, despite the fact that the programmatic speeches of the FROLINAT seem to have forgotten to mention the herders.[23] The Tibesti and its inhabitants played a decisive role in the struggle, despite their small numbers, and one of them, Goukouni Weddeye, later became President of Chad (1979–82). The importance of the BET for the revolution despite its small population and high illiteracy rate may allow us to question notions such as 'integration of the masses' or 'intelligentsia' which are usually used in revolutionary discourse. The revolution of the BET's inhabitants was instead characterised by particular features that will be the focus of our considerations later in this chapter.

In 1968, more than two years after the start of the armed struggle of the FROLINAT against the Chadian state, the Tubu of the Tibesti and with them, successively, the other populations of the BET, got involved.[24] The two major events that historians describe as having triggered the revolt in the Tibesti were, once again, events that cannot be situated within an ideological framework, being rather linked to the local conditions and the humiliations experienced. The first was a quarrel at a dance in Bardai that resulted in the death of members of the Chadian army and was followed by brutal repression of the Tubu by the governmental authorities:

During the night of 2nd to 3rd September, in Bardai, a quarrel during a dance between civilians and soldiers resulted in the death of an ANT [Armée nationale tchadienne, Chadian National Army] soldier; three others were injured. Sanctions were immediately taken by the sub-prefect … The town was surrounded by the forces of order. The population, without distinction of age or sex, was gathered together and taken to the prison yard. Everyone was ordered to strip naked; people were beaten with rifles, whips and bayonets. In the afternoon of the 3rd [September], at around 6 p.m., Battalion Chief Odingar Noé [prefect of the BET] ordered the release of the women and children, but left all the men in prison. On the 4th, after his departure, Second Lieutenant Rodaï … proceeded to interrogate the prisoners. One of the men, Issa Aramini, dies; another, Idriss Barkimi, whose arm is badly bruised, has to be amputated a few days later in Fort-Lamy. Mahamat Guedamimi, shot in the head, is hospitalized in Bardai; he will never recover all his faculties.[25]

The second event of even greater significance occurred in December 1966: the *derde*, the supreme authority of the Tubu, went into exile in Libya, soon followed by a thousand locals. He was threatened by the prefect of the Tibesti (a character described as particularly brutal by witnesses of the time) because he refused to carry out an administrative decision that went completely against both Tubu's customs and environmental conditions: areas that had been recognised as barren since time immemorial had to be cultivated by locals.[26]

These two events triggered the revolt in the Tibesti. The first shot in the BET was fired in Aouzou on 5 March 1968 by Tubu nomadic guards who, on the same day, took over the garrison of the town.[27] What was initially presented as a simple mutiny later led to the creation of the second army of the FROLINAT, and the revolution spread over the entire terrain of the BET in the years to come. Buijtenhuijs writes: 'It was indeed an uprising in the whole Tibesti inspired by the *derde*.'[28] The rebels took on the company and defeated the reinforcements sent. Subsequently, there were ambushes and fights.[29] The reactions of the retreating government forces were brutal. For example, on 7 August 1968, they set fire to the palm groves of Aouzou.

Following this, a French military intervention started in April 1969. It succeeded in clearing Aouzou without fighting on 6 September 1968.[30] However, this intervention lasted from 1969 to 1971, longer than expected, because the Tubu, despite their inferior firepower, put up a fierce and deadly resistance:

It is this general uprising in the Tibesti that explains why the first French military intervention was prolonged beyond the recapture of Aouzou, at the beginning of September; it was also necessary to clear the posts of Bardai and Zouar besieged by the Teda insurgents.[31]

The toll of the French military intervention on the whole of Chad in general and on the BET in particular was heavy:

The human damage caused by the intervention of the French legionnaires in the Chadian conflict was immense. Villages and palm groves were devastated and burnt all over the BET. At the time, legionnaires were fighting together with Chadian forces. Who was doing what, we didn't know. We blamed all this damage on the French forces, as they were leading the operations. Innocent civilians were killed in several battles in Borkou, Ennedi and Tibesti.[32]

Nevertheless, neither the French nor the Chadian government military managed to completely drive out the rebels, who had developed their own tactics:

But we kept our own ground: if one day they flushed us out here, the next day they didn't stay, they left ... and we came to reclaim our bases. ...

When these [foreign] forces withdrew, we came to make our own law with our revolutionary committees.[33]

Despite its small numbers (it is said that there were 200 Tubu Teda at the beginning of the rebellion in 1968, with 'heterogeneous firearms from the Second World War, the Italian army and AfrikaKorps'), the Tubu rebellion proved to be extremely effective, which is due to the nature of the Tibesti as guerrilla terrain par excellence, but also to the endurance and age-old experience of the Tubu in particular, and of the Saharans in general, in matters of warfare.[34] Indeed, 'the Frolinat adopted it as a technique of armed struggle, to make the adversary run, to disperse him over the whole territory and to proceed, in this dispersion, to attacks by small combat groups'.[35] This strategy was successful, especially in the BET. Buijtenhuijs concludes:

> 75 per cent of the French losses were due to the actions of the second army in the BET. As the strength of this army was only about a quarter of the total strength of the FROLINAT armed forces, the disproportion becomes even more significant.[36]

Moreover, in the years to come, the fighters of the BET would constitute the main force in the conquest of N'Djamena. This fact calls for reflection on the reasons for the combativeness of the Tubu, who became 'contemporary nomads having conquered a state'.[37]

Where is the key to this military performance of the Tubu despite the low firepower of their weapons compared to those of the French Army at the beginning of the uprising? Some elements of an answer to this question are given by Jean Chapelle. This officer of the French camel infantry and Prefect of the BET from 1958 to 1961 characterises the Tubu in his 1982 monograph *Nomades noirs du Sahara* ('Black Nomads of the Sahara') as experienced and enduring warriors, as experts of the terrain, and as being always ready to defend their own honour and that of their people. However, one may ask whether these reasons can explain everything. What role did beliefs or ideologies play in the Tubu's revolutionary struggle?

In this respect, Goukouni emphasises that the inhabitants of the Tibesti were fighting for local issues, as seems to have been the case for many FROLINAT combatants outside the BET too. The majority of the Tubu had been rather apolitical:

Since there were no political leaders who had a broad view .... We tried to explain to them. They were vaguely told that people were fighting in eastern Chad. But what is the idea of the FROLINAT, how far it extends, nobody had any idea.[38]

Moreover, the political consequences of their struggle, both nationally and internationally, seemed hard to imagine for those fighting on the ground:

The camp leaders and fighters thought that once they had liberated the camps of Zouar and Bardai, peace would be established in the region. They did not imagine the consequences that would follow. They did not even think that the French would intervene on behalf of the Chadian government to fight them.[39]

Despite the absence of political leaders with a broad view deplored by Goukouni Weddeye, there is at least one exception: Mahamat Ali Taher, who, according to Buijtenhuijs, 'played a leading role in triggering the BET insurrection'. For Buijtenhuijs:

Taher, all things considered, did for the BET what Ibrahima Abatcha did for the Centre-Est: recruiting fighters from outside and then returning to the field where the revolt was already rumbling and where the conditions for armed struggle were met.[40]

Mahamat Ali Taher led, until his death in 1979, the Second Army of the FROLINAT that fought in the BET and 'sought to make the influence of the FROLINAT penetrate more deeply among the 700 to 800 Tubu warriors who, under the command of Goukouni, were organized into a second army towards the end of 1969'.[41] In this context, Goukouni explains:

The arrival in the Tibesti of Mahamat Ali Taher, whom the Tubu nicknamed 'Abadi' (which means uncle), is very important. The rebellion was born thanks to him. He had a certain military notion that allowed him to galvanize the fighters while reciting some verses from the Koran. At the time, whether we like it or not, we should tell the truth, we had to base ourselves a lot on Islam. You had to talk a lot to attract adherents, otherwise it was difficult. Someone other than Mahamat could not have done it. ... Initially, the FROLINAT did not have such a position. It even had a

totally different position. Its political program was clear: it had no connection with religion.[42]

The relationship to religion could have contributed, in the Tibesti, to the
'indigenisation' of this revolution. Thus, the latter could fit into conceptions
of a specifically 'African' or 'Chadian' revolution whose local features we
have already traced above.

However, given the quasi-absence of an ideological imprint and the fact
that the main causes of the armed protest were local, one might ask whether
the term 'revolution' is appropriate. Buijtenhuijs reflects on this issue, basing
himself on a description of daily life given by Thierry Desjardins. The latter,
a reporter for the French newspaper *Le Figaro* who went to Chad in order
to meet the hostages during the Claustre affair,[43] describes everyday life in
Gouro, a town on the eastern edge of the Tibesti massif, in the mid-1970s,
as follows:

> For years now, they have been living completely on their own, forgotten
> by the world, in this sort of independent Tubu nation; as a state, they
> have this revolution going on, as an economy, everything is done by
> barter: a little manioc, semolina, against a goat, against a camel; some-
> times a Libyan trafficker arrives here, and they exchange what they have
> against a piece of cloth or electric batteries or a transistor. For the rest,
> they live happily and freely with nothing; the kids grow up, leave with the
> herds, sometimes become soldiers of the revolution, return to the 'city', get
> married, leave again.[44]

To this description of an autonomous state organisation we can add another
one provided by Catherine Brandilly in 1984. On 18 February 1978, the
FROLINAT had taken the town of Faya, and the whole of the BET was
now under its control.[45] Despite the difficulty of the situation, daily life was
almost 'normal' in Faya in 1979:

> What is immediately apparent in the city is that life seems to be quite
> normal despite the latent war situation and the constant threat of attack
> (especially from the air). The sandy streets, shaded by palm trees and
> acacias, are clean and busy. There are many women in the market,
> buying and selling. Despite the scarcity, there are some imported goods
> (green tea, sugar, oil, syrup, cloths ...) and local products (dates, vege-
> tables, basketry ...). The striking contrast that this spectacle offers with

the market of Sebha, left only a few days before and where one does not meet a single woman, is more effective than learned speeches in making us understand at what level the incompatibility between the two cultures lies ... At a time when Radio France Internationale is broadcasting information gleaned from N'Djamena, and when it is reporting on the chaos that the FROLINAT is supposed to spread in its wake, the commissioner responsible for education remarks, not without humour, that the secondary school in Faya is functioning on a daily basis while the one in N'Djamena is closed due to disputes between General Malloum and his Prime Minister Hissène Habré.[46]

According to Buijtenhuijs, Desjardins' expression of a 'state-like revolution' is not exaggerated. In fact, there was an administration that could act openly and freely, and thus assumed 'most of the tasks of a legally constituted government'.[47] This state and this revolution were, moreover, endowed with a 'people's army' or 'popular militias', because 'in the regions controlled by the C.C.F.A.N. [Conseil de commandement des forces armées du nord (Northern Armed Forces Command Council)], all able-bodied men are obviously armed' — a fact that can be explained by, among other things, the warrior past of many Saharan peoples, in particular the Tubu.[48] Being involved in an egalitarian way with one's own weapon in a popular protest becomes the essence of a rebellion turned into revolution, despite the absence of a concise ideology. Or, as the words of a 1974 FROLINAT fighter express it: 'Your freedom is at the end of the gun barrel.'[49]

Another particular feature of the Tubu's revolution is the profoundly egalitarian character of the revolution in the BET. In this respect, Goukouni himself always remained modest and close to the simple people. In relation to his early days as a fighter at the Moursou front, an emblematic place[50] in the revolution in Tibesti, he explains:

As soon as I arrived at the front in Moursou, I joined as a simple fighter. Like any other combatant, I went on patrol with my companions; I stood guard as a sentry when it was my turn; I did the chores of preparing food and tea; I went to fetch wood or water, etc..[51]

This egalitarian character, once again, does not seem to stem from any revolutionary doctrine advocating the emancipation of the lower classes, but rather from the individualistic character of the Tubu and, by extension, of many Saharan peoples. The Tubu, recalcitrant towards any domination or

rule, have indeed often been described as strongly egalitarian and individualistic, even 'anarchic' and refusing any hierarchy.[52]

In summary, the features that could qualify the revolt in the BET as a truly
Saharan revolution are its egalitarian character, its deep-rootedness in the
local context, the quasi-state self-administration of the liberated areas, and
the fusion of the notions of 'combatant' and 'citizen', given that the armed
struggle was led by almost everyone (women also fought in the ranks of the
FROLINAT).

CONCLUSION: THE REFUSAL OF THE SYSTEM

Can the Tubu revolution be described as anti-systemic in the pure sense
of the term? To answer this question, one needs to return to a notion or
concept that seems to be dear to so many authors who have described the
Tubu: that of anarchy or disorder.[53] For these authors, it seems that this term
can describe best a reality where individuals are deeply attached to their own
freedom and where a society, very recalcitrant towards ideas of personal,
state, or other hierarchies, refuses any kind of system.

However, do authors who adopt this concept not presuppose, in an
overly normative approach, that their own realities may serve as a reference,
whereas there should be no reference at all? What system could the Tubu
fighters have accepted at a time when all the existing systems had more or
less discredited themselves, either by their lack of interest in the FROLINAT
revolution (socialist countries) or by their neo-colonial hegemony (France,
United States, 'the West' in general)? For Wallerstein, quoted in our introduction, the idea of disillusionment plays an important role in the evolution
of anti-systemic movements. Perhaps there was never this disillusionment
during the FROLINAT revolution because, from the beginning, it was
more or less left to itself and its strength was drawn from particularly local
dynamics. In brief, one could thus say that the Chadian revolution was on
the one hand anti-systemic because it stood against a neo-colonial system,
but beyond this, it was non-systemic because it was not part of the major
ideologies and prevalent systems, drawing its particular character and
dynamism from local factors.

NOTES

1. Immanuel Wallerstein, 'New Revolts against the System', *New Left Review*, 18,
    2002, 29–39, at 34–35.
2. Ibid., 33.

3. Hissène Habré, a Tubu from Borkou, studied political science in France and returned to Chad in 1971. After having visited the *derde* and the rebels around Goukouni, he took over the leadership of the Second Army at the latter's suggestion (Robert Buijtenhuijs, *Le Frolinat et les révoltes populaires du Tchad, 1965–1976*, New York: Mouton Publishers, 1978, 271–275, at 243–245). On 29 August 1978, Habré was appointed prime minister by then-President Félix Malloum. He was president of Chad from 1982 to 1990.

4. Even the 'Saharan part' of the FROLINAT's history is multifaceted. For a broader view, interested readers wishing to familiarise themselves with more detailed perspectives (which would go beyond the limits of this chapter) can have a look at the memoirs of three prominent FROLINAT personalities published in recent years: Adoum Togoï Abbo, *Mémoires sur le FROLINAT, ses déchirements internes et les relations tchado-libyennes de 1971 à 2003, 2ième edition*, N'Djamena: Yagabi, 2017; Goukouni Weddeye, *Combattant, une vie pour le Tchad*, Paris: Espaces & Signes, 2019; Oki Dagache, *Ma contribution à l'histoire du FROLINAT*, N'Djamena: Éditions CIM, 2020. It should also be emphasised that there were other opposition movements like the Mouvement démocratique de la rénovation du Tchad (Democratic Movement for the Renovation of Chad) founded by Dr Outel Bono, who was assassinated in Paris on 26 August 1973. In a communiqué of 10 June 1974, the FROLINAT stressed that there had been attempts by the N'Djamena administration to accuse the FROLINAT of the murder of Outel Bono. According to the same communiqué, the administration itself had armed the killer, and in cooperation with the French secret service, had created a 'veritable organisation of murderers'. See: FROLINAT, CP 049, 'Qui a tué le Dr Bono?'

5. Christian Bouquet, *Tchad: genèse d'un conflit*, Paris: L'Harmattan, 1985, 124.

6. Buijtenhuijs, *Le Frolinat et les révoltes populaires du Tchad, 1965–1976*, 468–469.

7. Laurent Correau, *Weddeye, Goukouni: témoignage pour l'histoire du Tchad*. Entretiens avec RFI. 2008, https://issuu.com/vincentroux/docs/goukouni_weddeye, 45.

8. Buijtenhuijs, *Le Frolinat et les révoltes populaires du Tchad*, 103–110.

9. Ibid., pp. 130, 103.

10. Ibid., 346.

11. Anonymous, *Tchad: une néo-colonie*, Paris: Éditions Git-le-Cœur, 1992, 156–157; Abbo, *Mémoires sur le FROLINAT, ses déchirements internes et les relations tchado-libyennes de 1971 à 2003*, 33–38.

12. Buijtenhuijs, *Le Frolinat et les révoltes populaires du Tchad, 1965–1976*, 124–125.

13. Indeed, Chad's geostrategic position at the 'centre' of Africa, the presence of French capitalists in the country, as well as France's important interests in Niger (uranium) and the Central African Republic (diamonds) and promising indications of hydrocarbons, tungsten, wolfram, and uranium in Chad itself are among the reasons why France sought to maintain Chad in a situation of neo-colonial dependence. In addition, there were the strong presence of Israel (instructors, bases, training) and the interests of the United States in Chad; see Anonymous, *Tchad*, 74–77.

14. Buijtenhuijs, *Le Frolinat et les révoltes populaires du Tchad, 1965–1976*, 345–375.

15. 'Le fond d'une lutte', interview for *Tricontinental*, in 'Tchad: lutte armée au cœur de l'Afrique', 1971, cited in Buijtenhuijs, *Le Frolinat et les révoltes populaires du Tchad, 1965–1976*, 380.

16. Ibid., 379.

17. Ibid., 237.

18 Ibid., 330–331.

19. Goukouni Weddeye was the son of a supreme chief of the Tubu, the *derde*. At that time, Weddeye Kichidemi held the office of *derde*, and was forced into exile in Libya to escape the intimidation of the local Chadian authorities. In 1979, Goukouni became the leader of the Second Army of the FROLINAT, present in Borkou, Ennedi and Tibesti. He was President of Chad from 1979 to 1982.

20. Correau, *Weddeye, Goukouni*, 45.

21. On the ideological differences between the Libyan and Chadian revolutions, Goukouni explains: 'It is clear, Libya was a young revolution, it wants to help the progressive opposition against a dictatorial regime ... Abba Siddick was an executive, a former minister in the Chadian government, a career doctor, an intellectual who was in France and who at one point made contact with Libya ... The derde, for his part, was a feudal ... with the young Libyan revolution, it didn't work. That's why Libya helped Abba Siddick. We, the others, we were simple fighters, soldiers ... He was the secretary general of the FROLINAT. So it was normal for them to take a position in favor of Abba Siddick'; ibid., 46.

22. Buijtenhuijs, *Le Frolinat et les révoltes populaires du Tchad, 1965–1976*, 479–488.

23. Ibid., 406.

24. The Tubu are a Saharan group living in the north-east of Niger, the north of Chad, the south of Libya and the north-west of Sudan. They are constituted of several sub-groups. One of them is the Teda, living in particular in and around the Tibesti, but also in the south of Libya and the north-west of Niger. For some speakers, 'Tubu' refers to the whole group, for others exclusively to the Teda. In the latter case, the terms 'Dazagada' or 'Gorane' are used to designate Tubu who are not Teda.

25. This is an extract from a report by Captain Pierre Galopin of 2 May 1968 (Anonymous, *Tchad: une néo-colonie*, Paris: Éditions Git-le-Cœur, 1992, 63–66). We have opted for this description because this French soldier, who probably worked for Tombalbaye and his secret services, cannot be suspected of defending the cause of the Tubu. Other actors, such as Goukouni and Adoum Togoi 'consider it to be true in its broadest sense' (Buijtenhuijs, Ibid, 146). Galopin was finally condemned to death and executed by Tubu fighters during the Claustre affair. He was blamed for having worked to divide the Tubu in favour of the Chadian regime and the French neo-colonial policy: 'He was the architect of this division, which has been extremely damaging to us'; Correau, *Weddeye, Goukouni*, 60.

26. Bouquet, *Tchad*, 133; Buijtenhuijs, *Le Frolinat et les révoltes populaires du Tchad, 1965–1976*, 147–149.

27. Weddeye, *Combattant, une vie pour le Tchad*, 49–51.

28. Buijtenhuijs, *Le Frolinat et les révoltes populaires du Tchad, 1965–1976*, 152–154.

29. A long list of them can be found in Anonymous, *Chad*, 73.

30. Buijtenhuijs, *Le Frolinat et les révoltes populaires du Tchad, 1965–1976*, 73 and 152–154.
31. Anonymous, *Tchad*, 79.
32. Correau, *Weddeye*, 36. See also: 'It is a record of horror and barbarity that France will leave in Chad. The FROLINAT still denounces the crimes of the French military on the civilian population, especially the elderly, women and children. It is the systematic murder of a people whose only "crime" is to have said "no" to the conditions of slavery, to have wanted to live and work in dignity'; press release 36, 14 November 1970, cited in Buijtenhuijs, *Le Frolinat et les révoltes populaires du Tchad, 1965–1976*, 236.
33. Ibid., 8.
34 Ibid.; Jean Chapelle, *Nomades noirs du Sahara: les Toubous*, Paris: L'Harmattan, 1982, 17–19, at 41–43.
35. Anonymous, *Tchad*, 147.
36. Buijtenhuijs, *Le Frolinat et les révoltes populaires du Tchad, 1965–1976*, 215.
37. Robert Buijtenhuijs, 'The Chadian Tubu: Contemporary Nomads Who Conquered a State', *Africa*, 71(1), 2001, 149–161.
38. Correau, *Weddeye, Goukouni*, 21.
39. Ibid., 29.
40. Buijtenhuijs, *Le Frolinat et les révoltes populaires du Tchad, 1965–1976*, 161.
41. Bouquet, *Tchad*, 134–135.
42. Correau, Ibid, 25.
43. On 21 April 1974, Habré had the German doctor Christoph Staewen and the French Françoise Claustre and Marc Combe kidnapped. This was apparently intended to attract international attention to the rebels' struggle and to obtain a ransom, which Habré considered compensation for the population of the BET for the destruction caused during the French military intervention. While Staewen was released after less than two months through a diplomatic intervention by the German government of the time, the Claustre affair became a highly political dispute that lasted into 1977.
44. Thierry Desjardins, *Avec les otages du Tchad*, Paris: Presses de la cité, 1975, 174.
45. Buijtenhuijs, Ibid, 12.
46. Monique Brandilly, 'Le Tchad face nord 1978–1979', *Politique africaine*, 16, 1984, 45–65, at 48–50.
47. Desjardins, *Avec les otages du Tchad*.
48. Buijtenhuijs, Ibid, 291.
49. Ibid., 488.
50. In April–May 1969, French AD4 fighter-bombers bombed the Teda insurgents in the Moursou Pass as part of the French military intervention in Chad ordered by de Gaulle. In this context, Goukouni raises questions about the ingratitude of French foreign policy: 'Does he [de Gaulle] know that his AD4 fighter-bombers are dropping tons of bombs at Moursou on the children and grandchildren of numerous leaders and camel infantrymen who participated in the liberation of El Gatrun and Murzuk during the Second World War, thus making it possible for the Colonne Leclerc to cross this very pass of Moursou and take the long road that would lead them to the liberation of Paris?'; Weddeye, *Combattant*,

THE FROLINAT IN THE CHADIAN NORTH • 157

une vie pour le Tchad, 84. In 1942, the Leclerc army had gathered in Zouar, not far from Moursou. In the same year, it advanced into the Fezzan, where German and Italian troops were stationed, and defeated them. This military achievement was only possible with the help of Teda guides and camel infantrymen who took part in the fighting and led the French Army over the Moursou Pass into Libya.

51. Correau, Ibid, 28–29.
52. Chapelle, Ibid, 1962.
53. Catherine Baroin, *Anarchie et cohésion sociale chez les Toubou: les Daza Kécherda (Niger)*, Paris: Cambridge University Press and Maison des sciences de l'homme, 1985; Judith Scheele, 'The Values of "Anarchy": Moral Autonomy among Tubu-Speakers in Northern Chad', *Journal of the Royal Anthropological Institute*, 21, 2015, 32–48; Julien Brachet and Judith Scheele, *The Value of Disorder: Autonomy, Prosperity, and Plunder in the Chadian Sahara*, Cambridge: Cambridge University Press, 2019.

8

Brazzaville: Crossroads of the Revolutionary Left in Central Africa in the 1960s and 1970s

Héloïse Kiriakou and Matt Swagler

INTRODUCTION

During the 1960s and 1970s, Congo-Brazzaville was the crossroads of the revolutionary left in Central Africa. In August 1963, a general strike and popular rebellion in the capital city overthrew the country's first government, leading to the establishment of a second republic that soon adopted a programme of 'scientific socialism'. Within a few short months, this small country of just over 850,000 people upset the geopolitical status quo in Central Africa. As the only socialist regime in the region (until the independence of Angola in 1975), Congo soon became a rear base for several African liberation movements and hosted internationalist networks that shaped the country's revolutionary process.

Congo's revolution was only possible in the urban setting of Brazzaville. The city had long been important in Central African politics, as the capital of the four federated colonies of Afrique equatoriale française (EAF, French Equatorial Africa) beginning in 1910, and then of Free France during the Second World War (1940–42). In the decade preceding independence from France in 1960, emerging Congolese politicians jostled for the allegiance of Brazzaville's African residents and its influential European businessmen.[1] But Brazzaville was also a changing city: the population had nearly doubled between 1955 and 1963 (to about 150,000 people), as young adults from rural areas arrived in search of education and work.[2]

Following formal independence, the country's first president, Fulbert Youlou, and many of his ministers had become increasingly unpopular in Brazzaville. Their visibly lavish lifestyles and apparent disregard for the city's large unemployed population engendered resentment.[3] At the same time, radical trade unionists and students who challenged Youlou's unwillingness to break from colonial institutions became the victims of anti-communist repression. His proposal to establish a single-party state under his leadership further provoked great anger in the city, temporarily uniting Marxist and Catholic trade union leaders. Brazzaville was home to the majority of Congo's approximately 70,000 waged workers, and on 13 August 1963 union leaders jointly launched a strike and several rallies in Brazzaville. Though the city was a centre for working-class organisation, one-third of the working-age population were unemployed.[4] Soon thousands of young men joined the protests, attacking multiple sites of power (the city's jail, the national assembly and the radio station). They later occupied the forecourt of the presidential palace, demanding the resignation of President Youlou and his unpopular ministers, which they obtained on 15 August.

But early supporters of the revolution had been united by a rejection of the status quo, not by a shared vision of the future. A period of transition then began whereby new actors from civil society, particularly youth organisations, began to shape the direction of the transitional 'revolutionary' government. While maintaining dialogue with the newly installed administration, youth organisation leaders simultaneously forced their elders to negotiate the direction of the transition. Describing life under Youlou as 'incomplete' independence, they instead demanded 'true' or 'real' independence. This entailed the establishment of a single party committed to implementing 'scientific socialism', the expulsion of French troops (who remained in Congo after independence), the nationalisation and secularisation of education (which remained largely in the hands of missionaries) and the construction of a network of industrial, agricultural and commercial state enterprises to shift economic power away from foreign companies.

Not only did the 1963 uprising depose nearly all of the city's former political elites and reorient national politics, it simultaneously put the young nation's capital at the centre of a regional struggle against colonialism and neocolonialism. For the young intellectuals who led Congolese youth organisations, the revolution was never simply about national independence. One of their first demands was for the new government to open diplomatic relationships with self-declared communist nations like China and Cuba, as well as left-leaning nationalist regimes, including those in Algeria and Egypt. At the same time, youth leaders began inviting anti-colonial and leftist exiles from across Central Africa to come to Congo, both to escape repression and to contribute to the country's revolution. Thus, following the 1963 uprising, Brazzaville became critical to the survival of leftist movements from Cameroon, the Democratic Republic of Congo (DRC) and Angola, all of which set up headquarters in the new revolutionary city.

By hosting delegations from anti-colonial movements and different socialist countries, Brazzaville became a cosmopolitan city, and a crossroads for Marxist, Third World and Pan Africanist ideologies – much like Algiers, Conakry, Dar es Salaam and Accra.[5] As in each of those cities, international and regional politics were shaped within Brazzaville's urban space. On the one hand, each of these urban capitals was a site of official state power – and exiles often had privileged access to state officials. Yet on the other hand, expatriate militants were integrated into Brazzaville's social life: they often lived in the African, working-class neighbourhoods of the city, their children attended public schools, and they conducted training alongside Congolese soldiers and youth militants.

This chapter thus makes three interconnected claims. First, the 'revolution' in Brazzaville in 1963 provided refuge for many struggling anti-colonial and revolutionary groups in Central Africa. The leadership of the Movimento Popular de Libertação de Angola (MPLA, People's Movement for the Liberation of Angola), for example, was able to rebound from near annihilation by taking up residence in Brazzaville, eventually winning in the struggle over Angola's independence. Second, as Brazzaville became a home for revolutionaries from across the region, they worked alongside Congolese youth organisations to move Congolese politics towards a greater association with Third World Marxism. For example, exiles from Central Africa played a crucial role in the political education of Brazzaville's young activists, who then used the language they learned to call for the adoption of socialist policies. Third, the interplay of local and expatriate militants had the cumulative effect of altering the Cold War dynamics of Central Africa. As the United States and United Kingdom left Brazzaville in response to Congo's socialist turn, Cuban, Chinese and Soviet representatives moved in, finally gaining a foothold in a region of otherwise hostile regimes.

YOUTH IN A CHANGED CITY

The 1963 uprising created an opening for Congolese politics to move in entirely new directions. In the wake of the government's collapse, Congo's three electoral parties were disbanded and nearly all former national assembly deputies were barred from positions in the new government. The lone exception was Alphonse Massamba-Débat, a schoolteacher-turned-minister whom trade union leaders asked to head up a provisional government composed mostly of young technocrats who had been working in different ministries. Buoyed by support from the same youthful urban population that had flooded the streets in August of 1963, Massamba-Débat immediately began talking about a 'revolution' taking place in the Congo. But his first task was to assert the authority of the provisional government in the face of opposition from partisans of the former president, Fulbert Youlou. While Youlou's supporters had seemingly melted away during the protests in 1963, almost immediately afterward they began to rally outside the camp where he was being held under house arrest.

At the same time, Brazzaville became a political laboratory for a small group of about a dozen students and recent graduates who coalesced with the aim of organising the 'youth' in defence of the revolution. This informal organisation, the Groupe de Mpila, was drawn from among Congo's tiny population of young adults who had access to upper secondary schooling or university education abroad. A majority of the city's population was likely under 20 years old, but was cut through with ethnic, political, religious, gender and class differences.[6] As Congo did not yet have a university that could become a focal point of student organising, the Groupe de Mpila focused on the urban neighbourhoods where they lived. Some had already participated in existing youth and student organisations that pre-dated the 1963 uprising, either in Congo or while attending university in France. Many were versed in Marxist and Third World theories and followed debates within the Cold War left. They positioned themselves as self-appointed leaders of the 'youth' – a category they linked not to age, but to one's relationship to the revolution.

The day after the collapse of the old government, youth leaders created what they called the *quartiers jeunesses* ('youth neighbourhoods') to structure their activities at the local level. They used the networks of existing youth organisations to form nuclei of activists in different neighbourhoods. Many of the first recruits were the young, largely underemployed men who had been so visible during the uprising. The self-appointed youth leaders of the Groupe de Mpila sought to instil in them a sense of political power. Worried about looting and protests from Youlou's supporters, the *quartiers jeunesses* granted themselves the authority to police and surveille urban space. They set up checkpoints on the main roads to control traffic at night in search of possible weapons or suspicious individuals, and even eavesdropped at bars for pro-Youlou chatter. This made thousands of young adults, mostly men in their teens and twenties, unavoidable as new figures of unofficial authority.

The patrols provided them with a political role they had not previously been allowed.

Omnipresent in Brazzaville's neighbourhoods, these new youth militants were indispensable for President Massamba-Débat, whose legitimacy depended on their support. This came sharply into view in February 1964 when the *quartiers jeunesses* turned back an attempt by Youlou's supporters to free him.[7] As different youth leaders organised themselves under the umbrella of a national youth council they further sought to define the political meaning of 'youth' through mass meetings, demonstrations and a newspaper, *Dipanda*, ('independence' in Lingala). The omnipresence of young people in the city and their political weight in the management of the various crises in 1964 enabled youth leaders to put pressure on Massamba-Débat to accept the creation of a single 'revolutionary' party with a youth section, the Jeunesse du Mouvement national de la révolution (JMNR, Youth of the National Movement of the Revolution). The youth leaders who pushed for the creation of the JMNR hoped to use it to further solidify the connection between their calls for socialism and the 'youth' in opposition to other young intellectuals – Catholic youth leaders in particular – whom they deemed reactionary.

The creation of an official youth section of the single party allowed young intellectuals around the Groupe de Mpila to gain influential positions within the new government.[8] Now acting as party youth leaders, they successfully pushed the regime to adopt 'scientific socialism' as official doctrine. As described in JMNR speeches and the pages of *Dipanda*, socialism would be introduced through government intervention in the economy. State industries would be created in order to facilitate capital accumulation for the benefit of the nation. The state would then direct resources toward expanded economic and social development projects. Such a vision of socialism directed 'from above' was common in the Third World at the time, drawing inspiration from Stalin's Soviet Union and Mao's China. Like those models, Congo's revolution involved little popular decision-making, but expected cooperation from the public to carry out the decisions made by the government.

This model of state-directed socialism provided young intellectuals with a special role to play. As JMNR president André Hombessa proclaimed in 1965:

[In Congo] we saw the classic revolutionary process completely upended. Whereas until now the working class has always played the role of the vanguard, a unique phenomenon in this revolutionary process, in our country this role is played by the youth.[9]

Notable in Hombessa's statement is the sense that the youth were far more reliable guardians of the revolution than Congo's working class. After the revolution, the fragile truce between the trade unions quickly fell apart. The dominant Catholic federation leaders were resistant to the socialist direction of the revolution and quickly found their autonomy being constrained by the new government. Thus, despite the centrality of Congolese workers to the original uprising, their momentum was quickly lost.

Chapters of the JMNR quickly spread to all the districts of Brazzaville, unlike the party itself, which remained mostly a body of government officials restricted to the city centre and the Ministry of Information. Chapters of the JMNR took over the management of social, cultural and educational issues at the neighbourhood level: organisation of literacy courses, musical groups and community clean-ups, and the construction of public works, including schools and wells. Thus, the militants of the youth section of the ruling party were able to supplant the action of the government at the local level and propose their vision of the revolution – a demand President Massamba-Débat was not able to refuse. Consequently, their proposals to expel French troops from Congo, nationalise and secularise the education system and construct national industries were all adopted by the national assembly in 1964 and 1965.

BRAZZAVILLE: EPICENTRE OF THE AFRICAN REVOLUTION

As much as youth leaders were concerned with national policies, they simultaneously conceived of the revolution as part of a struggle against colonialism and neocolonialism that was being fought across Central Africa. In part, this regional and international perspective developed from young Congolese intellectuals' ideas about Third World and Marxist solidarity. In an environment of Cold War belligerency, they also believed that the revolution's survival was at stake. Youth leaders understood Congo's new government to be surrounded by threats. To the southeast lay the Angolan enclave of Cabinda, occupied by Portuguese troops attempting to violently suppress anti-colonial agitation. To the north lay Gabon (under Léon M'ba) and Cameroon (under Ahmadou Ahidjo), two hostile regimes propped up by French military intervention. But most threatening to Brazzaville's young revolutionaries were a succession of antagonistic governments across the

Congo River in the Democratic Republic of Congo following the murder of the DRC's first prime minister, Patrice Lumumba.

Congo-Brazzaville existed in the shadow of the DRC, a former Belgian colony, which was nearly seven times larger with 16 times as many people in 1963. Moreover, Brazzaville lay just across the Congo River from its neighbour's large capital city of Léopoldville (now Kinshasa). Thus, the new revolutionaries in Brazzaville paid careful attention to what took place on the other side.[10] The death of Lumumba had radicalised many Congolese youth and student leaders in Brazzaville.[11] Lumumba's assassination was carried out in Katanga, a region of the DRC that had seceded under the leadership of Moïse Tshombe, who was backed by Belgian forces attempting to maintain their control over the region's mineral wealth. The secession, along with revelations that the Belgian and United States governments had assisted Tshombe's troops in seizing and killing Lumumba, raised fears of neocolonialism across the region.[12]

When Tshombe became prime minister of the DRC in 1964, he was seen as a genuine threat to the socialist experiment underway in Brazzaville.[13] To make matters worse, Youlou and Tshombe had been close allies. Among supporters of Brazzaville's new government, fears abounded that Youlou's supporters would try to restore the former president by using Kinshasa as a base for organising an armed attack. Multiple covers of *Dipanda* portrayed Tshombe with fangs and clawed hands, working in collaboration with the United States to steal the wealth of Congo-Brazzaville. Such fears were well founded. In 1964, Youlou escaped house arrest and got to Kinshasa with Tshombe's support and the aid of the French military. The following year, Youlou's supporters launched an unsuccessful coup attempt from Kinshasa against the government in Brazzaville.[14]

In the midst of a hostile geopolitical environment, youth leaders saw Brazzaville as a socialist citadel that needed to be defended at all costs as an organising centre for aggressively spreading the revolution beyond the nation's borders. The *quartier jeunesse* patrols in the city and along the banks of the Congo River were thus intended to detect threats from pro-Youlou partisans that might be coming from outside the country as much as from inside the city. At the same time, Congolese youth leaders believed that Brazzaville (and by extension the revolution) would be more secure if they fostered new allies coming from abroad. In 1964, Tshombe expelled all Congolese originating on the Brazzaville side of the river (and Malians) from Kinshasa. Youth organisations in Brazzaville deployed their energy to organise the reception of the refugees, temporary lodging in classrooms and gymnasiums, and the distribution of food. From their perspective, the survival of the revolution depended upon this sort of humanitarian solidarity, but also on solidarity with like-minded peers outside the country. As JMNR leader André Hombessa proclaimed to a gathering of young militants in 1967, 'the national revolution is inseparable from the global revolutionary movement.'[15] Acting on this principle, Congolese youth leaders moved quickly to turn Brazzaville into a centre for anti-colonial and revolutionary movements in the region, along with representatives from socialist countries.

EVERYDAY INTERNATIONALISM

The first beneficiary of Congo's revolutionary solidarity was the Angolan anti-colonial party, the People's Movement for the Liberation of Angola. Under pressure from youth organisations, Massamba-Débat met with MPLA leader Agostinho Neto just two months after the fall of Youlou.[16] Previously, the MPLA leadership had been based across the Congo River in Kinshasa, but following the murder of Lumumba and the change in government, the Angolans were arrested and expelled. When the Organization of African Unity officially backed the MPLA's rival, the Frente Nacional de Libertação de Angola (National Front for the Liberation of Angola), the future of the MPLA looked bleak. But after meeting with MPLA representatives, Massamba-Débat agreed to allow the organisation to move its headquarters to Brazzaville, which it did in 1964.

The new Congolese government's willingness to host the MPLA proved fateful for the history of the region. Youth leader Claude-Ernest Ndalla served as a guide to Ernesto Che Guevara when he stopped in Brazzaville in January 1965 on his way to support 'Lumumbist' rebels in the eastern DRC. Ndalla showcased the achievements of the Congolese revolution and the favourable reception given to leftists from across Central Africa, including the militants of the MPLA. During Guevara's press conference in Brazzaville, he insisted on the exceptional solidarity of Congolese militants and pushed the Cuban government to offer military support to the exiled movements in Brazzaville.[17] From that point onward, Cuba lent 30 years of diplomatic and military backing to the MPLA (and Neto's faction within it), ultimately propelling the organisation into power in Angola and helping to secure the independence of neighbouring Namibia in 1991. As historian Piero Gleijeses has argued, the revolution in Brazzaville saved the MPLA at a crucial moment in its early history and set it on a path towards victory in Angola.[18]

But while Massamba-Débat showed a willingness to host the Angolans, he was far more reticent to support leftist opposition groups from neighbouring Cameroon, Gabon and the DRC. Even if the leaders of those countries were hostile to the socialist orientation of the revolution in Congo, unlike Portuguese-occupied Angola they were independent African governments. Massamba-Débat and his foreign minister, Charles Ganao, were caught in a bind. Youth leaders demanded that Massamba-Débat criticise the 'reactionary' policies of those countries' national leaders and support opposition forces instead. But the new government in Brazzaville desperately needed to establish diplomatic relations with these same neighbouring states, as Congo's economy was still largely based on its colonial role as a centre of regional trade.[19]

To get around opposition from Massamba-Débat and Ganao, youth leaders invited political exiles to come to Congo in their capacity as representatives of the ruling party's youth section. This was how Congo became a refuge for militants from the Union of the Peoples of Cameroon (UPC). In the early 1950s, the UPC had been the first anti-colonial organisation in Francophone West Africa to call for complete independence, but had been decimated by brutal campaigns of repression, first carried out under French rule and then under Cameroon's first president, Ahmadou Ahidjo. By 1963, the UPC's attempt to foment a rebellion against Ahidjo's government had reached its nadir. UPC militants had initially taken refuge in Ghana, Guinea and Egypt. But by 1963 each of these countries had sought to secure diplomatic relationships with Ahidjo, and to appease him, they pushed the UPC exiles out.

As with the MPLA, the revolution in Congo offered a lifeline to the beleaguered UPC. Although Massamba-Débat's government never officially granted the UPC refuge, Congolese youth leaders were able to bring a group of 185 UPC militants to Brazzaville under the sponsorship of the MPLA. Once in the Congo, the UPC created an official leadership committee in exile.[20] Youth activists similarly hosted some members of the Conseil de libération nationale (CNL, National Liberation Council) from the DRC, a grouping of formerly pro-Lumumba political leaders and an assortment of other opponents of the government in Kinshasa. These oppositionists often moved back and forth between the two Congos, much to the chagrin of Brazzaville's diplomats, who were trying to smooth relations across the river.[21] Within a year of the fall of Youlou, youth leaders in Congo had succeeded in establishing Brazzaville as a hub for left-wing opposition groups in Central Africa – often in spite of the desires of the new government.

As crucial as the revolution in Congo was for reviving the hopes of these political exiles, their actions also encouraged local youth militants to see Brazzaville as the centre of a regional struggle, not just a local or even national one. In Brazzaville, Angolan exiles and Congolese youth militants began to develop close relationships. The MPLA militants were housed in a camp nicknamed Angola libre ('Free Angola') in the working-class district of Bacongo. There they lived with and had daily exchanges with Congolese youth militants. As many MPLA exiles were originally from northern Angola, they spoke Kikongo, a language also spoken in Brazzaville. All mostly in their twenties and early thirties, they became frequent speakers at youth organisation events in Brazzaville, and MPLA communiqués were regularly printed in the independent youth newspaper *Dipanda*.[22] Claude-Ernest Ndalla, one of *Dipanda*'s editors, further used his influence at the national radio station to secure a regular programme for the Angolan exiles in 1964.[23] By doing so, Ndalla integrated them, at least symbolically, into the infrastructure of the revolutionary government and its media.[24]

Some expatriates in Brazzaville played a long-term role in providing political education to local youth militants, particularly Osendé Afana of the Cameroonian UPC and Abdoulaye Yerodia from the CNL of the neighbouring Congo. Having been forced into exile, Afana had come to Brazzaville after the revolution along with his UPC comrade René Jacques N'gouo Woungly-Massaga. Both held PhDs (Afana in economics and Woungly-Massaga in mathematics) and were considered intellectual assets to the revolution. But more important than their academic credentials, they were prized for their knowledge about global politics and political theory. Having moved in the left-wing circles of African students in France, they were familiar with the work of Third World and Marxist thinkers. This included Marx, Lenin, Mao, Fanon, Stalin and even Trotsky – each studied for their theoretical insights, but also for political and military strategy.

They were joined by one of the CNL activists, Abdoulaye Yerodia, who had been born in Kinshasa, but had moved to Brazzaville with his father before independence. Yerodia and Afana gave Sunday presentations for Congolese youth organisations at the Ministry of Information, and both went on to play a formative role in the creation of the Institut de formation idéologique (Ideological Training Institute), a school of political education created in 1964.[25] Their role at the institute was to educate different neighbourhood and village JMNR (youth) leaders so that those local leaders could then lead political education in their local chapters.

The internationalism of the Congolese revolution also extended to the activities of Congolese youth abroad. In the dormitories of the University of Paris, Congolese students promoted the revolution to French and foreign activists who also resided there. The Congolese musician and poet Franklin Boukaka met several activists while travelling and recording in Paris – the couple Ambroise and Maïté L'Hénoret, Paule Fioux and Bernard Boissay – who later came to Brazzaville to participate in the revolution. These foreign supporters served as ambassadors for the Congolese revolution abroad. They were thus granted a privileged political position by the authorities in Brazzaville, who did not hesitate to use the era's romantic image of youth to legitimise their regime.[26]

REORIENTING CENTRAL AFRICA IN THE COLD WAR

The exiled leaders from Cameroon, Congo-Léopoldville and Angola had varied relationships to the international communist movement. Nevertheless, in the context of the Cold War, their presence in Brazzaville, coupled with the revolutionary regime's new openness toward communist countries, made it more difficult for Massamba-Débat and youth leaders to proclaim 'nonalignment' as their foreign policy. There were two major results, the first of which was the United States government's decision to break diplomatic ties with Brazzaville. Congo's youth militants were publicly hostile to the US government, which they saw as a neocolonial force in the world. The JMNR regularly hosted North Vietnamese or National Liberation Front delegations during the war in Vietnam.[27] They were also critical of racism in the United States, and *Dipanda* published photos of police brutality against African Americans and printed translated interviews with Malcolm X.[28] Facing this animosity from the ruling party's youth section, the US government ended diplomatic relations with Congo-Brazzaville in 1965, settling into a friendlier relationship with the new regime of Joseph Mobutu across the river in Kinshasa.[29] For youth leaders, the departure of the US embassy was a victory, and the United Kingdom soon followed suit.

The changing international relationships in Brazzaville were indicative of a broader shift taking place in Central Africa's Cold War politics. As the US and the UK departed Brazzaville, the Congolese government welcomed Chinese and Soviet embassies and cooperation agreements, which included a direct meeting between Mao Zedong and Massamba-Débat in 1964.

This Chinese and Soviet interest reflected their desire to gain a foothold in Central Africa, but also to keep an eye on the activities of Cuban trainers now working in Brazzaville with Angolan and Cameroonian exiles. Through new connections with China, Cuba and the Soviet Union, communist literature flowed into local youth organisations – none more memorable to former leaders than the sudden ubiquity of *Quotations from Chairman Mao Tse-Tung* ('The Little Red Book').[30]

It had barely taken a year for the tiny city of Brazzaville to become the primary meeting place for leftist expatriates from across West Central Africa and representatives from the communist world. But the inadvertent beneficiaries of these new arrivals were local Congolese youth leaders like Ndalla, who gained in three ways. First, they felt emboldened that their revolution had been recognised by none other than Che Guevara and Mao Zedong, two icons of the Third World and communist movements. Second, as documented above, they drew on the intellectual resources these new relationships offered in the form of political training and literature. Finally, and most crucially, they gained access to arms and military training. As the next section explores, it was this last resource – weapons – that had the biggest impact on the future of the revolution.

FOREIGN REVOLUTIONARIES' INVOLVEMENT IN CONGOLESE AFFAIRS

In order to understand how important internationalist networks became in Congo, it is necessary to examine the role they played in the upheavals of political life in Brazzaville. As noted earlier, foreign interference was extremely frequent in the 1960s, usually in the form of attempted coups d'état supported by Moïse Tshombe and later Joseph Mobutu (Sese Seko) from Kinshasa. Both officially welcomed many opponents of the revolutionary regime in Brazzaville, including former president Youlou and former army officer Pierre Kinganga. Youth leaders in Brazzaville feared these outside threats, but were equally concerned about the possibility of an internal military coup. In response, they sought to arm their own supporters. While the *quartiers jeunesses* and similar vigilance patrols had been one of the key ways for youth leaders to secure influence over the city's daily political life in 1963–64, these groups were initially unarmed. But the arrival of Cubans, sent to arm and train MPLA exiles in Brazzaville, presented an opportunity to change this.

Youth leaders once again asserted their independent influence by convincing the Cubans to help train Congolese youth in the same camps as the MPLA. Integrated into these tightly knit camps, the resulting armed force, the Civil Defence, numbered 1,345 young militants by 1968. Created by youth leaders as a way to counter the threat of a military coup, the Civil Defence was under the direct command of the JMNR (youth) leaders – not Congo's army generals. This move elevated the power of youth in the city and laid the groundwork for a conflict with the military. In 1968, those tensions came to a head when Massamba-Débat was ousted from power in favour of a young army captain, Marien Ngouabi. In the aftermath, the Cuban embassy in Brazzaville offered to exfiltrate Massamba-Débat to Havana, though he refused.

The ascendancy of Ngouabi paved the way for the disbanding of youth militias and independent youth organisations in the early 1970s – but it did not mark the end of internationalist networks in Congo. One poignant example concerned the failed coup d'état of Ange Diawara in February 1972. Diawara was a former youth leader and had been head of the now disbanded Civil Defence. Having served as Minister of Agriculture early in Ngouabi's administration, he embodied the left wing of the new ruling party. In open conflict with Ngouabi over the direction of the revolution, and seeing that the situation within the party was increasingly unfavourable to him, Diawara opted for a coup de force to overthrow the regime. With the help of several officers, cadres and activists from youth organisations, during the night of 21–22 February 1972 he attempted to take control of various strategic points in Brazzaville: the army's headquarters, the barracks of various regiments, the radio station and the presidency. But his plan failed, and most of his companions were arrested in Brazzaville. He and a few others were able to take refuge in the province of Goma Tsé-Tsé, south of the capital, while waiting to reorganise their movement.[31]

During this extremely difficult moment for the left wing of the former youth leadership, a small group of French Marxist development workers stationed in Brazzaville intervened. Several of them had privileged links to Diawara's companions and had already participated in actions challenging Ngouabi's regime, such as organising a conference in 1971 to reform the educational system in the Congo. The assassination of three activists close to Diawara in the aftermath of the failed uprising of 1972 (including the musician Franklin Boukaka) led many of the foreign development workers to join the resistance. With the help of student activists, they clandestinely distributed leaflets in Brazzaville, made their vehicles available, and delivered messages and food to the fugitives hunkered down in Goma Tsé-Tsé.

When five of the French workers were ultimately arrested, one of them, Paule Fioux, opted to remain in prison to be tried with her Congolese companions, against the advice of the French ambassador.[32] In April 1973, Diawara and fellow conspirators Jean-Baptiste Ikoko, Jean-Claude Bakekolo and Jean-Pierre Olouka were savagely murdered by Congolese troops. President Ngouabi likely also wanted to make examples of the Congolese prisoners in jail with Fioux. But by refusing a separate negotiation, Fioux correctly presumed that her visibility as a white development worker would prevent Ngouabi from carrying out executions or other severe treatments of the Congolese activists she was jailed with.

The presence of Fioux, like that of Cuban military trainers and activists from Cameroon, Angola and the DRC discussed above, bolstered the influence of young Congolese leftists in the 1960s and early 1970s. At the same time, expatriates impacted the direction of the revolution in Congo through their influence on youth leaders – pushing them towards a deeper engagement with Marxist ideas and Cold War networks, militarising youth organisations, and providing them with a sense of Brazzaville's global importance. Having been hounded from nearby countries, exiled Central African leftists also benefited from the revolution in Congo, which provided them with access to military equipment, training and a supportive intellectual community. Brazzaville served as a model and testing ground for movements such as the MPLA, which relied heavily on Cuban assistance to take power in Angola in November 1975. In this way, Brazzaville's urban neighbourhoods not only became a political laboratory for Congolese youth, but also the centre of an experiment in global solidarity that connected anti-colonialists and socialists from across Central Africa to allies as far away as Cuba and Vietnam.

SELECT BIBLIOGRAPHY

For an English-language introduction to the Congolese revolution, see Héloïse Kiriakou and Matt Swagler (2016), 'Autonomous Youth Organizations' Conquest of Political Power in Congo-Brazzaville, 1963–1968', in Françoise Blum, Pierre Guidi and Ophélie Rillon (eds), *Etudiants africains en mouvement: contribution à une histoire des années 68*, Paris: Publications de la Sorbonne, 57–76.

In French, the 1990 account by Rémy Boutet (Bazenguissa-Ganga) of the fall of Youlou remains crucial: *Les 'trois glorieuses', ou, la chute de Fulbert Youlou*, Dakar: Editions Chaka.

For an extensive political history of the post-1963 period, see Congolese historian and diplomat Jérôme Ollandet (2012), *L'expérience congolaise du socialisme de Massamba-Débat à Marien N'Gouabi*, Paris: L'Harmattan. Héloïse Kiriakou details how the revolution was experienced in one of Brazzaville's most important African neighbourhoods in her 2021 chapter 'Bacongo: une histoire du socialisme (1963–1968)', in Françoise Blum et al. (eds), *Socialismes en Afrique*, Paris: Éditions de la Maison des sciences et de l'homme. In contrast, Françoise Blum places the Congolese revolution in comparative African perspective in her 2014 volume *Révolutions africaines: Congo-Brazzaville, Sénégal, Madagascar, années 1960–1970*, Rennes: Presses Universitaires de Rennes.

NOTES

1. Florence Bernault, *Démocraties ambigües en Afrique centrale: Congo-Brazzaville, Gabon, 1940–1965*, Paris: Karthala, 1996.
2. For population estimates, see *Lettre de Brazzaville*, 7 May 1963, reprinted in *Revue de la presse*, 14 May 1963, carton PR58, National Archives of Congo-Brazzaville (ANCB). See also: Rémy Boutet, *Les 'trois glorieuses', ou, la chute de Fulbert Youlou*, Dakar: Editions Chaka, 1990, 71; Phyllis Martin, *Leisure and Society in Colonial Brazzaville*, New York: Cambridge University Press, 1995, 28.
3. See, for example, *Lettre de Brazzaville*, 7 May 1963, reprinted in *Revue de la presse*, 14 May 1963, carton 58, PR, ANCB.
4. International Bank for Reconstruction and Development, International Development Association, 'The Economy of the Republic of Congo (Brazzaville)', 15 February 1965.
5. See, for example: Françoise Blum et al. (eds), *Socialismes en Afrique*, Paris: Éditions de la Maison des sciences de l'homme, 2021; Andrew Ivaska, *Cultured States: Youth, Gender, and Modern Style in 1960s Dar es Salaam*, Durham, NC: Duke University Press, 2011; George Roberts, *Revolutionary State-Making in Dar Es Salaam: African Liberation and the Global Cold War, 1961–1974*, Cambridge: Cambridge University Press, 2021; Elaine Mokhtefi, *Algiers, Third World Capital*, London: Verso, 2011. Jeffrey S. Ahlman, 'Road to Ghana: Nkrumah, Southern Africa and the Eclipse of a Decolonizing Africa', *Kronos*, 37, 2011, 23–40.
6. Based on demographic estimates in Virginia Thompson and Richard Adloff, 'Supplement', in *The Politics of Congo-Brazzaville*, Stanford, CA: Hoover Institution Press, 1973, 217.
7. Bulletin particulier de renseignements, Objet: Manifestation du 7 février 1964 à Brazzaville, carton GR 10 T 647, Deuxième bureau, Armée de terre, Service historique de la défense, France.
8. For example, Groupe de Mpila participants Pascal Lissouba and Ambroise Noumazalay became the country's next two prime ministers. At the age of just 23, Martin Mberi was elected to the national assembly and sat on the commission that drafted the new constitution. Claude-Ernest Ndalla, who edited *Dipanda* with Mberi, became the head of national radio and television.

9. 'Nouvelles nationales, n.1. Ouverture solennelle de la première réunion du Comité central de la JMNR,' Agence congolaise d'information (ACI), 10 September 1965, carton 25, Brazzaville ambassade (BA), Diplomatic Archives, Nantes, France (CADN).

10. Migration between the two countries was also common, and people shared several common languages across the border, including Kituba, Lingala and French.

11. Lecas Atondi Momondjo, interview with Matt Swagler, 13 October 2012; Ange Edouard Pongui, interview with Matt Swagler, 27 November 2012.

12. Congolese youth leaders also feared the presence of the French army, whose base in Brazzaville was one of the most important installations in the region, thus leading to calls to expel the French military, which took place in 1965.

13. Note d'information, 'Objet: a/s de la situation politique au Congo-Léopoldville', 16 October 1965, Série B, ANCB.

14. Note d'information, 'Objet: a/s de la situation politique au Congo Léopoldville', 13 October 1965, Série B, ANCB; Note d'information, 'Objet: a/s de la normalisation des relations entre Léopoldville et Brazzaville', 9 November 1965, and ACI, 'Nouvelles nationales, ouverture du deuxième congrès de la J.M.N.R.', 20 July 1967, both in carton 25, BA, CADN.

15. 'L'Anniversaire de la J.M.N.R. à Brazzaville', 13 February 1967, carton 25, AFP 17, BA, CADN.

16. Ndalla, interview with Matt Swagler, 19 October 2012.

17. Jihan El Tahri, *Cuba: An African Odyssey* (documentary film), 2007. Guevara also met with CNL leaders in Brazzaville.

18. Piero Gleijeses, *Conflicting Missions: Havana, Washington, and Africa, 1959–1976*, Chapel Hill, NC: University of North Carolina Press, 2002, 82.

19. This was cause of tension between Ganao and the editors of the paper *Dipanda*, specifically Martin Mberi and Claude-Ernest Ndalla. See Telegram 900-901 from French embassy in Brazzaville (no name) to French Ministère des affaires étrangères, 2 December 1963, carton 8, BA, CADN.

20. Note de renseignements, 'Objet: a/s de Mr. Joseph Ngakou, ressortissant camerounais, militant de l'UPC', 7 September 1967, carton 9, PR, ANCB.

21. Relations between JMNR militants (the youth section of the ruling party) and CNL exiles in Brazzaville could be contentious, with each accusing the other of criminal activity. See Note d'information, 'a/s C.N.L. Lumumba (Comité national de libération)', 15 October 1965, carton 25, BA, CADN; Note d'information, 'Objet: a/s de la J.M.N.R., section fluviale', 15 October 1965, Série B Congo politique, ANCB.

22. See for example, *Dipanda*, 23 July 1967; as well as 'Note de renseignements, n. 128 du 28 April 1964, 'Objet: Journée mondiale de la Jeunesse contre le colonialisme', and 'Commemoration de la Journée mondiale du colonialisme', ACI, 25 April 1966, both in carton 25, BA, CADN.

23. See, for example, Note de renseignements, n. 128, 'Objet: Journée mondiale de la Jeunesse contre le colonialisme', 28 April 1964; 'Commemoration de la Journée mondiale du colonialisme, ACI, 25 April 1966, both in carton 25, BA, CADN.

24. Ndalla, interview with Matt Swagler, 19 October 2012. See also *Dipanda*, 4 February 1966.
25. Matt Swagler, interviews with José Maboungou, 9 October 2012, Claude-Ernest Ndalla, 18 October 2012, Paul Nzete, 23 October 2012, and Martin Mberi, 19 November 2012; Jérôme Ollandet, *L'expérience congolaise du socialisme de Massamba-Débat à Marien N'Gouabi*, Paris: L'Harmattan, 2012, 47; 'L'éducation politique des militants du M.N.R., de la J.M.N.R.', ACI, 16 November 1964, carton 25, BA, CADN.
26. But these different foreign actors sometimes took opposing sides in conflicts *within* Congolese politics and did not always defend the government in place.
27. Vietnamese delegations were often present at major JMNR events. See 'Message of Solidarity to Vietnamese youth' from the Comité centrale of the JMNR Brazzaville, ACI Flash, 17 April 1967, carton 25, BA CADN. The message was greeted with five minutes of spontaneous applause before JMNR members stood up to sing 'The Internationale'.
28. See, for example, *Dipanda*, 12 September 1964. A contingent of exiled Black Panther Party activists would later visit Brazzaville in 1971. See Matthew Swagler, 'Panthers in Congo', *Africa Is a Country*, 5 July 2022.
29. Diplomatic relations between the United States and Congo-Brazzaville did not resume until 1977.
30. In addition, *Dipanda* often ran profiles of Mao and the Cultural Revolution. Later, in Brazzaville, it was possible to get the Chinese newspaper *Pékin Information*; see, for example, 'Entrevue du président Mao et du président Ngouabi' ('Interview between Chairman Mao and Chairman Ngouabi'), *Pékin Information*, 31, 6 August 1973, in the private collection of Paule Fioux, La contemporaine, Nanterre.
31. While in hiding, Diawara and his companions circulated an analysis of the situation in Congo (and their failed uprising). See Ange Diawara et al., *Autocritique du M22*, Paris: L'Harmattan, 2011.
32. Paule Fioux, *Foudres d'Afrique: les impostures d'une révolution*, Paris: L'Harmattan, 2017.

9

May 1972 in Madagascar:
A Student Movement Causing the
Fall of the 'Father of Independence'

Irène Rabenoro

Half a century ago, twelve years after Madagascar's independence, a student movement caused the fall of the 'father of independence' on 13 May 1972. The collapse of President Tsiranana's regime started when the Forces républicaines de sécurité (FRS, Republican Security Forces) shot at the crowd standing quietly with bare hands in front of the town hall of Antananarivo.[1] The FRS were a fairly small but well-armed group of paramilitary police which was set up in 1966 by André Resampa, the Minister of the Interior at the time, and trained by some Israeli instructors.[2] Not only students on strike, but also all kinds of people, including the students' parents and Zatovo Ory Asa Mitolona (ZOAM, unemployed young activists) gathered there, hoping to get some news about the 374 or so students who had been arrested during the night of 12–13 May 1972.[3] Some journalists, unionists and doctors were also arrested, but according to one of them, Rémy Ralibera, this was only on the morning of Sunday 14 May.[4] All were sent to the convict island of Nosy Lava, off the north-western coast of Madagascar's mainland.

Philibert Tsiranana was called the 'father of independence' because he was the president of the First Malagasy Republic. He is still considered as such despite his fall in 1972. Recently, on 14 October 2020, current president Andry Rajoelina paid tribute to Tsiranana, the symbol of independence.[5] Yet, it took students only 20 days to overthrow the 'father of independence' on 13 May 1972. Despite his poor health, Tsiranana was a candidate for the presidential elections for the third time and had been re-elected three months before, on 30 January 1972, with 99.7% of the votes.

What made it all possible? How is it that students, who were mostly secondary school pupils, came to cause the collapse of the First Republic? This chapter will try to respond to this question. However, it should be noted that this study is limited to facts occurring in 1972 in the capital city, Antananarivo, as not enough information could be collected about what happened in the provinces. Nevertheless, it is interesting to note that secondary school pupils went on strike not only in Antananarivo, but also in some small towns, according to Frédéric Randriamamonjy: Fianarantsoa and Antsirabe from 29 April 1972 onward, Ambalavao from 2 May onward, Toamasina, Mananjary, Ifanadiana and Ambohimahasoa from 3 May onward, and Mahajanga, Ambatolampy and Ambositra from 4 May onward.[6] Pupils in Faradofay (now Taolagnaro) and Antsiranana also started their strike on 8 May, while those in Toliara joined in on 9 May 1972.[7]

Also, the period under survey extends from Monday 24 April 1972, the first day of students' strike, to Saturday 13 May 1972, the day when the FRS forces fired on the crowd gathered in the city centre on the Avenue of Independence.

We will begin with an overview of the background of these events, then attempt to account for the fall of the First Republic. For this purpose, a survey on the events will be carried out: what actually happened and who did what.

BACKGROUND OF THE 1972 EVENTS

For Asinome Harimino Elisé, the demands made in May 1972 simply reflected the Malagasy people's aspirations as expressed during the Journées nationales de la planification du développement (National Days on Development Planning) organised on 19–24 April 1971[8] by the government at Ankorondrano Antananarivo.[9] With regard to education, the objectives of the fundamental educational reform proposed were twofold: to adapt training to the country's socioeconomic conditions and to constantly improve education quality in order to limit dropouts. According to Henri Rahaingoson, who thinks Malagasisation and democratisation of education were the core of the whole May 1972 movement, these National Days on Development Planning served as a springboard for popular claims.[10]

These two viewpoints suggest that May 1972 was the outcome of Malagasy people's aspirations, which were based on debates held at a national level in the previous year.

Moreover, two well-known members of the Strike Committee, which was the highest body of the movement, contend that May 1972 was not a spontaneous movement. According to Michel Rambelo (called 'Michou lahy', 'Michou the man') and Micheline Ravololonarisoa (called 'Michou vavy',

'Michou the woman'), it had been conceived and organised by a group of students to which they belonged.[11]

So far, educational issues have been identified as the causes of May 1972. Yet there are other factors that have to be taken into consideration, starting with the socioeconomic background which is usually thought to cause revolutions. Regarding the socioeconomic background of May 1972, views vary. Mervyn Brown asserts that the economic situation was fairly good: 'The steady economic progress was recognized when in 1970 UNCTAD [the United Nations Conference on Trade and Development] removed Madagascar from the list of the world's poorest countries.' However, he noted that 'the standard of living of the peasant, unlike the town-dweller, actually declined'.[12]

However, Elisé shows in a recently published article that living conditions were not so good for most Malagasy people. He states that in 1967, only 8% of job applications were fulfilled, which means that unemployment was a serious issue. He further points out social inequalities due to great differences in salaries and an increase in the cost of living.[13] Although we cannot tell whether socioeconomic difficulties were one of the students' motivations for going on strike, on the whole, even disadvantaged people now think they had a much better life in 1972 than in the later decades.

As regards the linguistic and cultural background of May 1972, it is characterised by the dominance of the French language and culture. French was the only medium of instruction. This is probably the reason why many families sent their children to the Centre culturel Albert Camus (Albert Camus Cultural Centre), a French government body, to practise their French, broaden their knowledge of French culture and develop their reading skills by borrowing books.

As far as the Malagasy language is concerned, being the sole national language, it was and remains the language that unites all Malagasy people, the language of everyday communication, the language of the poor and of the uneducated. It was also used in religious contexts. For instance, when Malagasy was not taught in *lycées* (this was after independence), it was in Sunday schools in protestant churches that the opportunity to learn to read and write in Malagasy was provided.

Probably due to the dominance of the French language and culture, the Association théâtrale et artistique de l'Université de Madagascar (ATAUM, Artistic and Theatre Association of the University of Madagascar) staged a play titled *Iza moa aho?* ('Who am I?') in 1971, showing students' search for identity.

Apart from French culture, Malagasy urban youth were also attracted by American culture, especially the hippy movement. Counterculture around the notions of love, justice, peace and freedom influenced some young Malagasy people, especially in the capital city, thus shaking the establishment to a certain extent. Some adopted the Afro hairstyle, while others had long hair. But very few seemed to be aware of the anti-Vietnam war and anti-nuclear armament protests in the US and Europe. Many more enjoyed Bob Dylan, Jimi Hendrix and the like.

In university circles as well as in *lycées*, very few students had heard about May 1968 in France or were interested in the event, according to Constant Raveloson, one of the May 1972 movement leaders. Nevertheless, Jean-Claude Rabeherifara, for instance, stated that for the famous poster *Ndao* ('Come') he designed and which was displayed on many walls and on the windscreens of most taxis in Antananarivo, he was inspired by the French May 1968 posters.[14]

As mentioned earlier, Malagasisation and democratisation of education were probably the favourite topics of May 1972. Indeed, the Syndicat des enseignants et chercheurs de l'enseignement supérieur (SECES, Union of Higher Education Teachers and Researchers), the only trade union of Malagasy universities' teaching and research staff, held a seminar on the Malagasisation and democratisation of the university shortly before the May events, on 12–15 February 1972. As early as April 1968, the Fédération des associations des étudiants de Madagascar (FAEM, Federation of Students' Associations in Madagascar) had held a congress in Antsirabe on the themes of Malagasisation and democratisation of education. FAEM had earlier held a congress on the topic 'Bilingualism and national culture' in April 1967. University students proved to be very much concerned with social, cultural and political matters, as we can see from the congress held by FAEM in Toamasina in 1969 on the theme 'University and Society'.

In any case, as pointed out by Michel Rambelo and Micheline Ravololonarisoa, the university was a place for exchanges and debates, whether formal or informal.[15] Such activities tended to develop students' analytical skills and critical thinking. Students were keen on reading works by economist Samir Amin, Marxist philosopher and sociologist Herbert Marcuse, agronomist René Dumont and publications such as the Third World-oriented Africasia, despite its being censored by the Malagasy authorities.[16]

Censorship was not unusual, and that is why, for example, the then Secretary General of SECES, Ignace Rakoto, told me he had to put pillows around the radio when listening to the communist station Radio Peking at night, fearing some FRS forces patrolling nearby might hear.[17]

With regard to the political background of May 1972, there are aspects of 1971 that are inevitably mentioned as causes of the 1972 events. One is the university students' strike in April 1971. The Faculty of Medicine and the Faculty of Law and Economics were at the centre of the strike. Students questioned the system of studies and examinations which had been devised in Paris. The authorities decided to close the university, and a committee was set up to deal with the issue, but nothing came out of it. Due to a meeting of the Association des universités partiellement ou entièrement de langue française (Association of Fully or Partly French-Speaking Universities), the university had to be reopened and activities resumed. There was also a short strike of the *classe de 3e* (fourth year of secondary school) *lycée* students in April 1971 against the competitive examination for admission to the next form, the *classe de 2nde*, but it was not important enough to be commented upon.

Two other aspects to be taken into account are far more serious. The first is the insurrection of the peasants in the south of Madagascar on 1 April 1971 led by Monja Jaona in the poorest part of the country which has always suffered from the lack of water. Monja Jaona is a historical figure of the 1947 national liberation struggle against the French colonisers. He was the leader of Madagasikara otronin'ny Malagasy (MONIMA, Madagascar for the Malagasy), an opposition party which was mainly based in the south.

Although famine raged between July 1968 and January 1969, the local authorities continued to demand that the population pay taxes.[18] Many such actions, viewed as unfair, led Monja Jaona to prepare for a rebellion.

The rebels attacked prisons, administrative offices, *gendarmes* (paramilitary police), barracks etc. Repression by the *gendarmes* and by local authorities is reported to have been fierce – many rebels were tortured and/ or killed – in a situation where the rebels only had knives and truncheons. The death toll is not known for sure, but according to the estimates of the catholic newspaper *Lumière*, there were between 800 and 1,000 dead.[19] Monja Jaona declared he was fully responsible for everything that had happened.

Although information about this insurrection was scarce, people in the capital city were aware something wrong was going on in the political sphere. Such a feeling was confirmed with the arrest of the would-be successor of President Tsiranana, Second Vice-President André Resampa, on 1 June 1971. Resampa was accused of preparing a coup with the help of some foreign powers. The United States was implicitly suspected. He was assigned to remain in Sainte-Marie Island off the eastern coast of Madagascar, and was released only a year later, in June 1972, by the Ramanantsoa government.

There was another political prisoner, Régis Rakotonirina, who worked for the then Office de la recherche scientifique et technique outre-mer (Overseas Technical and Scientific Research Office) in close collaboration with French researcher Gérard Roy. Both were supposed to be arrested on the charge of preparing a Maoist plot aiming to overthrow the regime, but in the end only Rakotonirina was actually arrested in October 1971. Gérard Roy had gone home to France on regular leave.[20] Like all political prisoners, Régis Rakotonirina was released in June 1972.

With regard to political parties, two of them were conspicuous in the capital city: President Tsiranana's Parti social démocrate (PSD, social democratic party) on the one hand, and on the other the Antokon'ny kongresin'ny fahaleovantenan'i Madagasikara (AKFM, Madagascar's Independence Congress Party), led by the mayor of the capital, Richard Andriamanjato. The AKFM, which was close to the former USSR, was the official opposition party until its leader declared he agreed with 80% of the PSD's policies.

According to André Rasolo, the PSD was more of an instrument of power and patronage than a political organisation.[21] It was at the same time a parallel administration, a political police force and an inevitable path for careerists, offering advantages connected to political power. It was therefore popular neither with urban people nor those in rural areas who suffered from the PSD's abuse of power and the members who wielded this power.

Madagascar's independence was also challenged by important French presence. First, there were two French military bases: one at Ivato, a dozen kilometres away from the capital city, and the other one in Antsiranana, in the north of Madagascar. In addition, some Frenchmen occupied important positions: Eugène Lechat was Minister of Public Works, Paul Roulleau was President Tsiranana's Chief of Staff, and General Bocchino was the Chief of Military Staff. The rector of the University of Madagascar was French, and so were all deans of faculties and most lecturers. Principals of *lycées* and many *lycée* teachers were also French, and so was the teaching staff of many other state schools. The French were still a highly visible physical presence.

This overview shows that 1971 was a turbulent and violent year politically and socially. While enabling representatives to express their opinions and aspirations at the National Days on Development Planning, Tsiranana's regime had become violent, and he was regarded by many as a dictator.[22]

Therefore, the president's image as the 'father of independence' was inevitably seriously damaged.

Before focusing on the three decisive weeks of 24 April–13 May 1972, we must examine what happened between January and April 1972 to give an accurate sense of the dynamics of the events.

WHAT HAPPENED BETWEEN JANUARY AND APRIL 1972

Midwifery students and students of the School of Medicine – different from the Faculty of Medicine of the University of Madagascar – went on strike on 22 January 1972, demanding better living conditions. On request of the government, the students decided to suspend their strike so as not to disturb the presidential elections which were held on 30 January 1972.

On 4 February 1972, the Minister of Cultural Affairs told strikers that due to the lack of doctors in rural areas, the School of Medicine had to go on training students who would later work in rural areas. On 29 February, the Association des étudiants en médecine et pharmacie (AEMP, Association of Medical and Pharmacy Students) issued a communiqué with the same content as the Strike Committee had promulgated on 27 January: the same rights for the Malagasy population to access the same health care provided by doctors holding the same degrees, and consequently, the same rights for the Malagasy youth to access the same medical training.

On 11 March, the authorities decided to temporarily close the School of Medicine as they considered it to be a threat to public order.

On 14 March, the FAEM, Association des étudiants d'origine malgache (AEOM, Association of Students of Malagasy Origin), based in France, SECES and Syndicat de l'enseignement secondaire public (SEMPA, Union of Public Secondary School Teachers) issued a joint statement in which they affirmed their solidarity with the AEMP and appealed to the Malagasy people to do the same.

On 31 March, the authorities announced that in order to be readmitted to the school, students would have to present a letter signed by their parents on 10 April. On the same day, a joint statement issued by the AEOM, FAEM, SECES, SEMPA and Syndicat national des instituteurs publics de Madagascar (SNIPUMA, National Union of Public Primary School Teachers in Madagascar) denounced what they called illegal, unfair and dictatorial measures taken by the authorities against the School of Medicine students.

On 8 April, the government decided to postpone the deadline for the letter signed by parents to 12 April 1972, but on that day, the AEMP restated its demands and declared the continuation of the strike.

On 19 April, the government decreed the dissolution of the AEMP on the grounds that it might disturb public order and opinion. On Sunday 23 April, at a meeting of representatives of *lycées* and other schools, the decision was made to conduct a solidarity strike with the students of Befelatanana (the location of the School of Medicine). Pamphlets were drafted and duplicated and distributed on the following day.

Thus, on Monday 24 April 1972, secondary school students were quite surprised to receive and read pamphlets in French and in Malagasy.[23] One of the pamphlets was bilingual. It was titled in Malagasy *Miady na ho faty* and in French *Lutte ou crève* ('Fight or die'). This was a real surprise for their readers, as talking about dying unless you fight was quite shocking. The pamphlet addressed quite a few questions: it criticised the age limit for entering secondary school, it demanded the transformation of secondary schools into schools which were to comprise an upper level (*lycées*), it carried information about the School of Medicine students who were prevented from expressing their demands, it told about private school students who wished the *pré-Bac* (examination preceding the one at the end of secondary education) to be abandoned, it mentioned that primary school as well as secondary school students were victims of frequent changes in the curricula and of having to buy textbooks although their parents' salaries were not high enough.[24] The pamphlet ended with a call for dialogue with the authorities and condemned top-down decisions.

The second pamphlet was in Malagasy and was titled *Henoy!* ('Listen!'). It was much shorter, and it took up the main ideas of the former pamphlet. Both pamphlets were signed 'Strike Committee'.

University students were already on strike. As for *lycée* students, they went on strike with these messages in their minds. They seem to have been receptive, since they continued the strike over the following days and weeks. A pamphlet in Malagasy distributed on the second day of the strike, Tuesday 25 April, incited students to refuse being considered as children and to take their future in their own hands. In the afternoon, students marched to the Ambohijavoto garden in the city centre although the government radio station – the only one at the time – had warned against all demonstrations and gatherings. They did not stay long. They sang the national anthem and dispersed.

As for SEMPA, it appealed to parents and the people to support the students around the following points: the impossibility for the people's children to access state schools (secondary schools and the university), no freedom of expression, as proved by the dissolution of the AEMP, and the mismatch between education and the country's needs.

On the morning of Wednesday 26 April, university and secondary school students rallied again in the Ambohijatovo garden, which they called the *Jardin de la grève* ('Strikers' Garden'). Firefighters gently hosed them down, and the rally ended quietly. In the afternoon, as the Minister of Cultural Affairs, Laurent Botokeky, had invited the strikers to meet him at the Alarobia stadium, a couple of kilometres away from the city centre, many thousands of students marched to the stadium. Most of them were teenagers between the ages of 12 and 19. No dialogue was possible: whereas the minister referred to the students' initial demands, those demands consisted of the Malagasisation of education and the cancellation of the cooperation agreements with France. Micheline Ravololonarisoa and Hubert Ramaroson (nicknamed 'Ralay') were the minister's main interlocutors.

All observers agree that students were quiet, non-violent, did not cause any damage and were astonishingly disciplined. Rémy Ralibera admired the leaders of these strikes and demonstrations in May 1972, whom he called the 'guys' of Rakotonirina Manandafy and Germain Rakotonirainy. Indeed, Manandafy and Germain had trained a number of young men so well to ensure order and discipline in rallies and that they were real specialists of more or less improvised mass organisations.[25] He went on to relate that at the students' rallies at Ankatso on the university campus in the last week of April 1972, thousands of students followed the direction of a few students who were in charge of keeping order. The person in charge of keeping order Willy Razafinjatovo,[26] was nicknamed *Maître Olala* ('Master Oh La La') due to his frequent use of this interjection which made young students laugh. Students listened to speeches in silence, they sang as a choir, they chanted slogans etc.

On 27 April 1972, the strike continued in schools and on the university campus. Minister of Home Affairs Barthélémy Johasy again stressed that it was in the students' interest to resume classes. On Friday 28 April, the strike continued in schools and on the campus. In the afternoon, thousands of strikers gathered on the campus. The SECES read a statement in which it approved of the university and secondary education students' strike.

On Saturday 29 April, a Permanent Council of the strikers, which was the deliberative body of the movement, was set up on the campus. It consisted of two delegates per school or faculty. As one of the successive chairmen of the Permanent Council, Ramidison Avonelina, recalls that 110 secondary schools and the university faculties were represented on the council.[27] A Strike Committee with a dozen representatives elected by the Permanent Council was also set up. As stated previously, the Strike Committee was at the top of the hierarchy of the movement.

From the morning of Tuesday 2 May 1972, all students, according to the school or faculty they belonged to, were distributed in the classrooms and lecture rooms of the university. They held what was called *loabary an-dasy* ('seminars') and discussed a common theme – the new educational system – based on pamphlets that were distributed.

Every morning, a chairperson and two secretaries were elected in each meeting room. Decisions made or ideas proposed in relation to the questions raised in the pamphlet(s) were transmitted to the Studies Committee, which would draft one or several pamphlets for the next day based on the reports it received. From the afternoon of Tuesday 2 May onward, all the students gathered at the Ankatso Stadium on the campus. They listened to messages of support from the provinces (Toliara, Ambositra, Antsirabe, Miarinarivo etc.), strike-related poems (notably by Ondatin-droy) and to singers, some of whom became famous, such as the Mahaleo.[28]

SEMPA appealed to all teachers to suspend their courses in that afternoon of 2 May. It declared that it shared the students' demands on Malagasisation and democratisation of education as they were in the people's interests. On Thursday 4 May, thousands of students' parents went to the campus to listen to the students' explanations about the strike. They brought their moral and financial support for the strikers. On Friday 5 May, a pamphlet in French signed by the Strike Committee was distributed. It contained an appeal to organise seminars in each school and faculty with a view to holding a national congress. Another pamphlet, also signed by the Strike Committee, demanded cancellation of the cooperation agreements with France. After visiting the provinces, the President of the Republic took some rest at Ranomafana, which is known for its healing thermal springs, about 400 kilometres southeast of Antananarivo. He stayed there until Saturday 13 May.

On the morning of Saturday 6 May, thousands of students marched in Antananarivo in memory of a 17-year-old student, Modeste Randrianarisoa, who was reported to have died in police custody in Ambalavao, about 460 kilometres south of Antananarivo. On Sunday 7 May, a mass for the student was held on the campus.

On Monday 8 May, the Minister of Home Affairs formally denied the death of a student due to police beatings. On Tuesday 9 May, the political bureau of the PSD issued a statement condemning the strike and launching an anti-strike offensive. Then, on Thursday 11 May, President Tsiranana announced from Ranomafana[29] that there would be changes in the government, and that as soon as the Constitution was revised, a prime minister would be appointed and form a new government. The strikers' Permanent Council made the decision to ask the workers and the unemployed to voice their opinions about the new educational system, called *sekoly vaovao* ('new school').

In a pamphlet distributed on that day, the AEOM, FAEM, SECES, SEMPA and SNIPUMA invited workers to a meeting with students on the university campus at 2:30 p.m. on Saturday 13 May in order to discuss education issues and all the other problems that oppressed everyone. These unions and associations of university students and teachers at all levels of education, along with workers from the private sector and civil servants, joined in the students' movement from 13 May onward, when violence came from the government's security forces.

On Friday 12 May, the PSD political bureau declared on the media that the students' strike actually aimed to overthrow the regime, since their demands were no longer related only to education, but concerned the cooperation agreements, Malagasisation of education etc.

On that same day, the authorities closed the campus in order to prevent students from holding seminars and rallies. The government pointed to communists, especially French Maoist teachers, who were alleged to be behind the student strikers. Actually, according to some of the leaders of the movement (Jean-Claude Rabeherifara, Victor Ramanantsoa, Michel Rambelo, Jean Constant Raveloson and Micheline Ravololonarisoa), no-one actually claimed to be Maoist or Trotskyist etc.

A pamphlet issued by all the organisations except for SNIPUMA, which had signed the 11 May one, indicated a change in the venue of the meeting of students with workers. Instead of the campus, which was the usual venue for the students, the location had been changed to the Avenue of Independence in the city centre, in front of the town hall, at 2 p.m. This pamphlet is likely to have caused panic among the authorities and led them to make the decision to repress the movement since the movement's participants, who so far had been limited to people in the world of education, now extended to workers.[30]

On the night of 12–13 May, about 374 people were arrested on the campus, many of them during the Permanent Council's meeting.[31] Not all were members of the Permanent Council. A few other people were also arrested on 13 and 14 May, but outside the campus. Among them were journalists

Rémy Ralibera (of the *Lakroa* newspaper), Georges Rasamizanany (of the *Andry-Pilier* newspaper), physicians Janvier Ratsarazaka and Manan'Ignace Rakotomalala, and union or Scout leaders such as Odon Rafenoarisoa.

On Saturday 13 May, the Minister of Home Affairs announced on the national radio that the leaders of the strike had been arrested, that the strike was over, and that classes would resume in the provinces on Monday 15 May. In the morning, students marched to the city centre. Many other people joined in, including the ZOAM, everyone quietly waiting for some news about those who had been sent to Nosy Lava. At about 10:30 a.m., the FRS launched tear gas to disperse the crowd, and then opened fire on them. Whereas the *Lumière* newspaper reported 19 dead among the demonstrators and seven among the FRS, Rémi Rahajarizafy, in his book *Mey 1972*, gave the figures of 31 dead on 13 May, plus five ordinary citizens and three FRS on 15 May, totalling 39 dead.[32] According to a document titled *Fifandraisan'ny Mpitolona eto Antananarivo* ('Liaison of Activists in Antananarivo'), there were 36 dead and 144 wounded. Victor Ramanantsoa, a member of the Strike Committee,[33] said that many of the victims were from the ZOAM,[34] as they were more daring in facing the FRS.

At 1 p.m., President Tsiranana arrived in Antananarivo by helicopter. Demonstrators took away the sign reading 'Place Philibert TSIRANANA' ('Philibert Tsiranana Square') in front of the town hall and put in its place a sign which read 'Place du 13 Mai 1972' ('13 May 1972 Square'). At 2:30 p.m., a state of emergency was declared. At 7:30 p.m., President Tsiranana made a memorable address on the national radio. He said the youth were being fooled, 'trapped' by communist politicians, and that many had died – which was a pity – but that many more could be killed, and he imitated the sound of a machine gun, '*tssak tssak!*'

From then on, the regime was bound to collapse. No government in Madagascar can stand against the population's reaction to a regime that opens fire on its people. On 18 May 1972, President Tsiranana lost control of power and gave full powers to General Gabriel Ramanantsoa to set up a new government. Tsiranana eventually quit power after a referendum held on 8 October 1972.

CONCLUSIONS

In trying to establish the reasons why the First Republic collapsed after 20 days of a student strike, we should consider that the PSD regime was weak due to Tsiranana's poor health. Moreover, staying too long in power – twelve years – had prevented the post-independence government from being fully aware of the challenges to be faced. Thus, the education-related issues – those of the School of Medicine and of the university – could have been addressed properly as early as 1971. However, we have to also consider the immense strength of the student movement and the support of other trade unions and workers.

When thinking of 13 May itself, it is clear that only the FRS defended Tsiranana. The *gendarmes* were there, but they did not move decisively against the protests. Solidarity within the government was not evident. The French government could have helped, considering the French military base was nearby at Ivato, but they seem to have let Tsiranana down.[35]

There is another point which contributed to the fall of the First Republic: President Tsiranana's lack of credibility due to his unbelievable victory at the presidential election with 99.7% of the votes. Since national unity, tensions between the Merina (the ethnic group in the region of the capital) and the so-called *côtiers* ('coastals', of whom the president was one) have always been thought to be a threat to peace, so it is interesting to note what happened in Mahajanga. Although it was the main town of the province where President Tsiranana came from, five students were reported dead on 13 May 1972 due to the clashes between strikers and security forces.

Regarding the university students and the main leaders of the May 1972 movement, fighting for more justice, especially in the field of education, was their main purpose. Success in studies meant the chance of a more successful life, having opportunities for good living conditions. That is why what is now called equitable and inclusive education (in pursuit of United Nations Sustainable Development Goal 4) was viewed as worth struggling for.

Students did not rely on political parties, especially on the official opposition, the AKFM.

The messages the leaders conveyed to the mass of students were simple and easy to grasp as political vocabulary based on Malagasy roots had already been built and used in the pro-MONIMA's newspaper *Andry-Pilier*. According to investigations that have been carried out recently, half a century later, only 16.4% of 1972's political vocabulary is unknown by current university students.[36] This may mean that the 1972 values are more or less integrated into Malagasy society, or at least in the capital city.

Also, being able to enter classrooms and lecture rooms at the university was quite exciting for secondary school students, and holding discussions in Malagasy about 'serious' matters – what was wrong with the educational system and how to improve it – was thrilling. Indeed, both secondary school students and university ones were free to take the floor and express their ideas and points of view, and even to handle a meeting with about 50–150 participants, depending on the size of the room. It is interesting to note that although it was a relief not to have to speak French as in class, no anti-French feeling could be sensed.

But what makes May 1972 unique is that none of its leaders obviously thought of deriving personal benefit from the movement. None became a minister nor became suddenly rich, at least in 1972. When the leaders refuse to be coopted, this impacts positively on the movement as a whole. Activists believed in what they were doing, they wanted to do good, they fought for social justice, and they regarded their behaviour as patriotic. Seeking real independence may not have been part of their schemes.

There is another important point that needs to be addressed: the importance of quality education. May 1972 may not have occurred without the movement leaders, especially university students and young lecturers like Rakotonirina Manandafy, who were engaged in political and social activism and had been educated in the country.

The movement could be so well organised because some of the student leaders were active in cultural, religious, social or political associations (for instance, the AKFM or the MONIMA youth organisation). They seem to have learnt a lot about organisation, leadership and management in the associations they belonged to.

The movement had a great sense of responsibility handling so many young student strikers. There was self-respect and mutual respect between old and young, males and females, educated and uneducated (the ZOAM), well-off and disadavantaged.

On 12 May 2022, by the end of the study day on 13 May 1972 held at the Faculty of Arts and Humanities of the University of Antananarivo, discussions started to become difficult around the idea that Madagascar's *descente aux enfers* ('descent into hell') had apparently started in 1972. But this is quite another matter that will have to be explored elsewhere. The student movement, and allied unions and groups, had proved that they were a radical and counter-hegemonic force that political parties and the state would have to contend with.

NOTES

1. This was confirmed by the then Minister of Health: 'Mal préparées à faire face aux émeutes citadines, les FRS ont tiré sur la foule des manifestants devant

l'Hôtel de Ville d'Antananarivo. Cet épisode sanglant est à la source de la chute du régime Tsiranana' ('As they were not well prepared to face urban riots, the FRS shot at the crowd of demonstrators in front of the town hall. This bloody episode caused the fall of Tsiranana's regime'); quoted in Césaire Rabenoro, *Les relations extérieures de Madagascar de 1960 à 1972*, Paris: L'Harmattan, 1986, 111.

2. Robert Archer, *Madagascar depuis 1972: la marche d'une révolution*, Paris: L'Harmattan, 2021, 49. In 1972, André Resampa, accused by Tsiranana of plotting a coup with the Americans, was in exile in Sainte-Marie Island.

3. Those arrested in the night of 12–13 May on the university campus were mostly students. According to Article 1 of Decree No. 72-147 issued on 18 May 1972, 374 individuals convicted of having participated in subversive actions were assigned to fixed residence in the convict island of Nosy Lava. However, this figure is not accurate as some who had been arrested are not on the list and some others who had not been arrested are. On the whole, the figures provided in this chapter are not always reliable.

4. Rémy Ralibera, *Souvenirs et témoignages malgaches: de la colonisation à la IIIe République*, Antananarivo: Foi et justice, 2007, 129–130.

5. 'Célébration du 62ème anniversaire de la Première République Malagasy: honneur au père de l'indépendance, le Président Philibert Tsiranana', https://www.presidence.gov.mg/actualites/informations/politiques/1030-celebration-du-62eme-anniversaire-de-la-premiere-republique-malagasy-honneur-au-pere-de-l-independance-le-president-philibert-tsiranana.html. Accessed 17 May 2022.

6. Frédéric Randriamamonjy, *Tantaran'i Madagasikara 1895–2022*, Antananarivo: Trano Printy Fiangonana Loterana Malagasy, 2006, 290.

7. Ibid., 294.

8. *Journées nationales de la planification du développement (19–24 avril 1971): rapport final de synthèse*, Antananarivo: Centre d'information et de documentation scientifique et technique, 1971.

9. Asinome Harimino Elisé, 'Assises nationales d'avril 1971 à Ankorondrano: pour la réforme et le (re)décollage du pays', *Politika*, 26, 2022, 38. A development charter was drafted based on participants' ideas at national level. The charter includes three basic objectives: overall improvement of Malagasy people's living conditions, real economic independence and equal access to national resources.

10. Henri Rahaingoson, 'Malgachisation et démocratisation de l'enseignement: tronc commun à toutes les aspirations de "mai 72"', 13 mai 1972 histoire d'une révolution', *Revue de l'Océan Indien*, special issue, May 2012, 58.

11. Michel Rambelo and Micheline Ravololonarisoa, 'Nous étions conscients du caractère néocolonial des rapports entre Madagascar et la France' , *Politika*, 26, 2022, 27. Special thanks to Micheline Ravololonarisoa and Michel Rambelo for answering my questions.

12. Mervyn Brown, *A History of Madagascar*, Ipswich: Ipswich Book Company, 1995, 305–306.

13. Asinome Harimino Elisé, 'Les clivages socio-économiques ou le bilan désastreux du régime Tsiranana', *Politika*, 26, 2022, 62.

14. Jean-Claude Rabeherifara, 'L'affiche "Ndao", une expression combative dans le contexte du reflux soixante-douzard', *Politika*, 26, 2022, 43.

15. Rambelo and Ravololonarisoa, 'Nous étions conscients du caractère néocolonial des rapports entre Madagascar et la France', 28.

16. René Dumont published a widely read book at the time: *L'Afrique noire est mal partie*, Paris, Éditions du Seuil, 2012 (1962).

17. Ignace Rakoto then lived in a small flat near the AKFM *Andry-Pilier* opposition newspaper in Andravoahangy Ambony, Antananarivo. He was one of those who gathered around *Andry-Pilier* since 1971.

18. Françoise Raison-Jourde and Gérard Roy, *Paysans, intellectuels et populisme à Madagascar: de Monja Jaona à Ratsimandrava (1960–1975)*, Paris: Karthala, 2010, 229. This book is the most comprehensive one regarding the 1971 insurrection.

19. Ibid., 240.

20. Raison-Jourde and Roy, *Paysans, intellectuels et populisme à Madagascar*, 277–289.

21. André Rasolo, 'Autour de mai 1972: la question du pouvoir', *Cahiers des sciences sociales*, 1, 1984, 11. Last accessed 10 Feb 2022.

22. In order to have an idea of the way President Tsiranana handled national affairs, see an account by a German advisor to the Ministry of Planning of a visit the president made to the south in March 1972 in Gaspard Dünkelsbühler, *Ombre et lumière à Madagascar: une révolution à Tananarive vue et racontée par un Allemand (1971–1973)*, Paris: Karthala, 2012, 205–213.

23. About pamphlets, see Irène Rabenoro, *Le vocabulaire politique malgache pendant les évènements de mai 1972*, doctoral thesis, Paris: University of Paris 7-Denis Diderot, December 1995, Volume IV, 'Appendices'. See also see Irène Rabenoro, '*Sekoly vaovao*: de l'espoir d'une "école nouvelle" en mai 1972 à Madagascar', in Françoise Blum, Pierre Guidi and Ophélie Rillon (eds), *Etudiants africains en mouvements: contribution à une histoire des années 1968*, Paris: Publications de la Sorbonne, 2016, 93–205.

24. Some works on May 1972 provide inaccurate information about *lycée* students, whom they regard as privileged. Actually, *lycée* students were privileged in the sense that they were lucky enough to get quality education, but many of them were far from being socially privileged. As my memory may not serve me well, I looked at three class photos taken when I was in primary and secondary education at Lycée Jules Ferry and at Lycée Galliéni, where there were non-Malagasy pupils (French, Indian-born, Comorian etc.). In the three classes, only two to five Malagasy pupils came from privileged families, the other 20–27 Malagasy pupils' parents were mid- or low-ranking civil servants, small traders, clerks etc. This sort of inaccuracy is probably recurrent because some Malagasy informants of foreign authors have biased views. Such is the case with Robert Archer's *Madagascar depuis 1972: la marche d'une révolution*, Paris: L'Harmattan, 2021: 'la grève fut coordonnée par les filles et les fils de la bourgeoisie Merina' ('the strike was coordinated by the sons and daughters of the Merina bourgeoisie'), ibid., 58. Only a handful of strike leaders came from a privileged background.

25. Ralibera, *Souvenirs et témoignages malgaches*, 136.

26. Willy Razafinjatovo later became a barrister and defended many victims of the failing rule of law. See Rahaingoson, 'Malgachisation et démocratisation de l'enseignement', 61. He died on 25 January 2022, a few months before the celebration of the 50th anniversary of May 1972.

27. This is from a discussion I had with Ramidison Avonelina (nicknamed 'Midy') on 9 December 2021. Avonelina was a student of Malagasy Letters at the Faculty of Arts and Humanities in 1972. He chaired the students' association of the Ankatso halls of residence. He later carried out further studies and became a civil administrator. He was Prefect of Imerina, the region where the capital city is located. Until recently, he was a member of the Komitin'ny fampihavanana malagasy (Committee in Charge of Malagasy Reconciliation), whose mandate has not been renewed by the current regime.

28. Mahaleo was a group of seven young men (only two are still alive) who were about 18 years old in 1972. Their first songs became famous in 1972. For them, the values they discovered in 1972 rallies and adopted included unity in action, solidarity, mutual assistance, discipline, listening to the others, debating, sharing, taking root in history and culture, humility, loyalty, freedom of expression, and cultural and intellectual freedom. See Jean-Aimé A. Raveloson, 'Mahaleo: de soixante-douzards à stars', *Politika*, 26, 2022, 47.

29. Due to his poor health, the president was taking a rest in this spa resort, although the political situation in the capital city was quite a matter of concern.

30. Irène Rabenoro, 'Les deux tracts à l'origine du 13 mai 1972', *Politika*, 26, 2022, 7.

31. Again, available figures are not accurate. Some people who are on the list of those sent to the convict island of Nosy Lava had not actually been arrested, whereas some others who are not on the list were. See Decree No. 72-147 of 18 May 1972, reporting Decree No. 72-137 of 13 May 1972 assigning to fixed residence some individuals who were arrested on the charge of participating in subversive actions.

32. Rémi Rahajarizafy, *Mey 1972*, Antananarivo: Librairie mixte, 1982.

33. I would like to thank those who were willing to speak as witnesses of May 1972 at the University of Antananarivo on 13 May 2022 as they provided some precious information. They are Noel Andrianaivojaona, Ramidison Avonelina, Victor Ramanantsoa, Henri Ranaivoharisoa, Gilbert Randriamora, Jaonimanana Randrianasolo, Aimé Rapelanoro Rabenja and Jean Constant Raveloson.

34. The ZOAM being unemployed and for the most part uneducated, after the May 1972 movement they were provided with jobs as far as possible. In 1972, Gérard Rajaonson was the one who most often held meetings on the university campus with them.

35. According to Françoise Blum, the French Ambassador was totally against a French military intervention; Françoise Blum, 'Mai 1972: la révolution malgache', *Le maitron*, 14 November 2014, https://maitron.fr/spip.php?article167384.

36. Irène Rabenoro, 'Madagascar 50 ans après: les étudiants face aux néologismes et aux formules du terroir de mai-1972', paper delivered at Institut national des langues et civilisations orientales study day, University of Paris, 13 April 2022, www.inalco.fr/sites/default/files/asset/document/programme_7_0_0.pdf.

10
Southern Sudanese Radical Projects, *c.* 1963–83

Nicki Kindersley

There is a strong tradition of revolutionary leftist politics in Sudan, not least in the deep history of unionised industrial labour and the Sudan Communist Party (SCP), and the left's role in successive popular revolutions in the 1960s and 1980s. The SCP was established in 1946, and was commonly held to be one of the strongest communist parties in Africa, playing a significant role in expanding civil and political rights for the majority in Sudan.[1] This leftist politics has been part of the recent uprising that overthrew the 30-year rule of Omer el-Bashir, as protesters drew on old tactics, revolutionary memories and leftist cultures of poetry, art, songs and imagery.[2]

This chapter does not survey Sudanese communist and trade unionist left politics. Most research on the left in Sudan has focused on these union-isms and communisms in urban and otherwise industrialised spaces, such as the cities and railways of Khartoum and Atbara. These histories are subjects of old and resurgent research.[3] Instead, this chapter focuses on the southern regions of Sudan, what is now South Sudan after independence in 2011. South Sudan's diverse geographies and communities have been subjected to successive generations of brutal exploitation, violent government and strategic underdevelopment from at least the arrival of slave raiders and traders in the mid-1800s.[4] The Sudanese state as it evolved under the Turkiyya, Mahdiyya and then Anglo-Egyptian Condominium has worked to concentrate power and wealth at the riverain centre around Khartoum and the fertile Gezira farming belt to its south. Since Sudan's independence in 1956, successive governments and military regimes have used top-down projects of 'national unity' on the one hand and violent repression on the other to control surrounding regions. Continued peripheral conflict worked to continue under-education and underdevelopment and maintain a cheap migrant labour supply to the centre.

This centralisation of economic development and resources created a small but powerful working class at the centre of Sudan. Increasingly strong unions and groups engaged in revolutionary politics since the 1920s including the Black Block and the White Flag League, which attempted a revolution in 1924.[5] However, for the rural majority, revolutionary language focused on fighting colonial exploitation based on more localised histories of resistance to oppression. Most political researchers since the 1960s have generally agreed there was little to no reach for African Marxisms or socialist ideas in these generally rural economies of mostly independent pastoral farmers and small landholders.[6] In Foreign Office papers in London, political analysts agreed with relief that there was no communist threat in South Sudan, even while southern Sudanese armed fighters began regional rebellion by 1963.

This assumed urban–rural divide is part of why southern migrant workers, students, civil servants and politicians are generally on the margins of histories of left politics in Sudan. There are three other main reasons for a continued lack of intellectual histories or histories of political thought from the left in South Sudan. Firstly, southern Sudan's specific historical trajectory through histories of colonialism and 'separate development' policies have encouraged both political activists and historians to focus on southern struggles against colonisation by British then northern Sudanese violent governments, set in terms of racism, slavery and biblically framed demands for independence.[7] This regional representational politics restricted the field of possibilities for political rhetoric and action.[8]

Secondly, historians most often look for radical and leftist politics in organised parties, student movements and unionised work, but there is very little of any of these activities in the south and other Sudanese peripheries because of their long histories of limited waged labour, party politics and educational systems, and the disruptions of repeated conflicts. Of course, people in these peripheries have engaged in local and global conversations about exploitation, marginalisation, and societal revolution for political and economic equality and equity – what historians and locals might consider leftist political debate – but there are still few studies of the small but existing history of labour, party political and educational organising and strikes in South Sudan.[9]

Thirdly, South Sudanese political theorising has been understood by many national and international historians as generally elite, instrumentalist and extraverted. Socialist and radical political rhetoric during 1960s coups and southern civil war (c. 1963–72), in the 1970s under President Nimeiry's Sudan Socialist Union, and in the 1980s and 1990s by the Sudan

People's Liberation Army in the south during the second civil war (1983–2005) are all often understood as a tactical means of securing funding and political access for various other ends. Since the end of the second Sudanese civil war in 2005, the secession of South Sudan and renewed southern civil war from 2013, contemporary political research has focused on the failure of the neoliberal state-building project, with many, especially international researchers, implying a continued lack of political theory in South Sudan beyond a politics of the belly.[10]

As such, there seems to be little point to the study of socialist political ideology or leftist thought in South Sudan. Discussion of the lack of leftist politics in South Sudan usually focuses on two men as exemplars of the three problems outlined above: Joseph and John Garang (no relation). Both are dead, and supposedly their ideologies died with them. Joseph Ukel Garang, born in 1932, is an example of the migrant southern student and later politician in Khartoum, who, in adopting Khartoumite communist activism, alienated himself from his southern community.[11] John Garang de Mabior, born in 1945, is a contrasting example of another migrant student who moved towards the left during higher education and became the leader of the main South Sudanese armed movement for southern liberation in the 1980s and 1990s.[12]

John and Joseph had, at least on paper, two possibly competing revolutionary leftist proposals for Sudan, and particularly for its poor and marginalised black peripheries. Their writings and speeches both focused on total revolution in Sudan, a change of political system that would rebuild a political system based on equality, economic redistribution, devolution of power, and socialist recognition and support for Sudan's diverse cultures. John Garang framed this (somewhat loosely) as the idea of a 'New Sudan'. But they are both remembered differently. A South Sudanese rebel in 1966 emphasised that 'The only southern Communist is Joseph Ukel.'[13] He was apparently politically isolated towards the end of his life, and is rarely referenced today. And most accounts hold John Garang's socialist leanings as purely instrumentalist, using the opportunistic language of Ethiopian-style Marxism (statist, centralised and USSR-friendly) to seek patronage for his new rebel group built on Ethiopian borders in 1983. This was widely believed to be pure ideological gloss, used by an essentially authoritarian military commander, and discarded quickly after the fall of Mengistu in 1991.[14]

This chapter looks beyond the two Garangs and seeks to explore their context. It surveys recent and older research that examines political philosophy and leftist politics in these Sudanese peripheries, as well as archival evidence from Durham's Sudan Archives, the Comboni Mission archives in Rome, the South Sudan National Archives in Juba and the author's 'Learning Lessons from Educational Histories' research project with Professor Yosa Wawa of the University of Juba. The chapter seeks to reconsider whether and how we can write intellectual histories of political radicalism and leftist movements in South Sudan.

The chapter is split into three short sections: a survey of the existing evidence for leftist political organisation over the 1960s and 1970s, in first the civil then military spaces, and then an enquiry into what might consti-tute the revolutionary left outside this sphere of students, unions, parties and armed groups. This brief chapter raises three questions: one concep-tual, one methodological, and one for the academic community as a whole. Firstly, what is the 'revolutionary left', particularly in political spaces where Marx and Mao had very little reach? How do we write radical histories of political thought beyond self-identified, literate and organising leftists and student activists? What are the historical consequences of a methodological focus on textual, literate political cultures? Finally, the endeavour of seeking leftist histories raises a final question: why might we want to study the rev-olutionary left now, in our current political moment in South Sudan and globally, and what implications does this have for historians?

UNIVERSITY, UNION AND GRADUATE POLITICAL PROJECTS

In the last decade, historians have turned their attention towards southern histories of political thought. Most work has focused on what are commonly considered key spaces of political organisation: industrial sites (for example, the Nzara Agricultural Scheme in what is now south-west South Sudan), formal secondary schools, churches and universities, and exile and regional diaspora and refugee spaces.[15] This is partly because these spaces only opened up with the formalisation of state rule in these Sudanese peripheries in the 1930s (after decades of brutal 'pacification', including mass burning of villages in some areas).[16] With this formalisation came major agricul-tural projects and some mission-led educational institutions established to produce the clerks, officers and translators needed for colonial rule. This meant that there was an extremely small student, teacher, civil service and industrial worker class that emerged unevenly across the south, depend-ing on location over the 1930s to the 1970s. Education for South Sudanese people in particular only really expanded beyond a few thousand men during the second civil war in the 1980s. Otherwise, the other space where

collective organisation was possible was the military, and this is where revolutionary action has repeatedly come from in Sudan's wider peripheries,
including the south, in mutinies, uprisings and rebel movements.

Highly mobile student and graduate workers – often moving between
village homes and southern towns and Khartoum – built networks of political organisation and information. The first engagements many southern
school students had with international political theory (i.e., beyond the
political theory of their own villages and communities) was through the
'wall newspapers' students made and posted in the half-dozen secondary
schools and vocational training institutes that made up education beyond
basic primary schools. These single-page, hand-made newspapers reflected
political committees, discussion groups and parties organised within
student communities and boarding houses. These wall newspapers included
The Spark at Rumbek senior secondary,[17] *The Observer* at the University of
Khartoum, and the weekly *The Negro*, which drew on writings and speeches
by Nkrumah and Azikiwe that were in circulation among the student body.[18]
These were more radical than the newsletters produced by the mission
schoolteachers, but these newsletters included student and alumni letters
and debates by correspondence on local administration and politics.[19]

African and international political ideas, news, theory and texts spread
through these schools. Pio Yukwan, a local priest and teacher in Malakal,
wrote in his diary that he found 'a good deal of beliefs' in different doctrines, international and African socialisms, Negritude, and communism
at the schools in his catchment, although he was not sure how far people
understood these discourses. He records conversations with visiting colleagues and migrant workers through the 1960s in which they discussed the
spread of 'communist ideas' at various mission schools and public universities.[20] Hilary Logali, an early southern student and politician, notes that he
read Marxist texts and *Time* magazine while at the University of Khartoum
in the 1950s, and that 'we raked Stalin's treatise on the "National Question"',
looking for useful arguments to deploy for the cause of southern independence. He notes in his unpublished autobiography that 'From all these [*sic*]
leftist literature, we learnt a lot in organisational skill particularly the cell
system, which I put to full use in our underground movement.'[21]

We know that, at least in print, southern politics and leftist ideas were
being spread and discussed through various magazines and news sheets.
These included *The Light* magazine, published by the Malakal American
Presbyterian Mission and managed by Mading de Garang, who later became
a key propagandist for the 1963–72 southern rebel movement; *The Vigilant*,

the mouthpiece of the Southern Front party, and *The Explorer* and *The Voice of Southern Sudan*, the newspapers of the Sudan African National Union, which did occasionally reach southern towns,[22] along with the Sudanese Communist Party English-language news sheet *The Southerner*, run and partly written by Joseph Garang.[23]

There are two problems with researching this textual history of political thought, though; firstly, these wall newspapers were ephemeral and (appear to) have not survived, other than via some notes in the South Sudan National Archives security files.[24] Secondly, these texts were secondary to the oral debates and discussions that (still) make up political discourse in Sudan's majority-rural regions. These discussions depended on these small but highly mobile student-teacher and state worker communities, for example policemen, military servicemen, and migrant labourers on holiday from postings. University students and graduates would work as teachers during holidays and while unemployed at their old schools.[25] A good example is Othwon Dak, who worked as a teacher after he graduated from secondary school at Rumbek in 1958, while moving through the universities of Khartoum and Makerere from 1959 to 1967 and running student organisations; he is credited with 'introducing socialism' to Rumbek secondary school, which earned him the nickname 'the Red prince'.[26]

The 1950s and 1960s saw a boom in southern and Darfuri student organisation, and Sudan Communist Party outreach into these regions. Some Marxist northern Sudanese teachers held informal classes near Rumbek secondary school, attended by Othwon Dak, Mading de Garang, Oliver Albino and Joseph Garang, with apparently heated debates on southern secession, anti-colonialism and the place of Marxist theory within these issues.[27] In the other direction, travelling students would visit the few southern politicians and MPs working in Khartoum during this period, primarily supporting the most militant voices (such as Ezbon Mondiri and Saturnino Lohure, both of whom became key rebel figures by 1965).[28]

By the mid-1960s, though, as civil war in the south grew and disparate guerrilla groups began to formulate a rebel front, the political space closed. In 1965, as the civil war escalated sharply, teachers, students and literate workers were targeted in massacres across towns in the south, including in a massacre at a wedding in Wau, where 76 people – including civil servants and local politicians – were killed. This shifted the political centre to Khartoum and into exile spaces in East Africa, as martial law forced students and teachers to flee.[29]

MILITARY INTELLECTUAL HISTORIES

The spread and debate of internationalised leftist political discourse cannot be disentangled from the growth of a peripheral literate class through the 1950s, 1960s and 1970s. But at the same time, many of these (mostly) men's less literate colleagues and family members in military and agricultural work – most people living in the southern region of Sudan – were investing in more local revolutionary organisation. This was a growing insurgency spreading over the 1960s following the army mutiny at Torit in 1955, leading to the formation of guerrilla groups in the early 1960s and the fragmented but powerful Anya-Nya rebellion by 1963. These 'classes' were not separate: many young students, teachers and civil servants joined the rebellion throughout the 1960s.[30] Groups of guerrillas had transistor radios, and listened to Kenyan and Zanzibari independence broadcasts, discussions of the Cuban Missile Crisis, and the Voice of Germany; Saturnino Lohure had books on Che Guevara.[31]

The various factions of the first civil war rebels did not have a coherent political ideology beyond what Meredith Terretta has usefully called a 'hybridised village nationalism' that blended local debates over freedom with an imagined collective future of a nation.[32] Clement Janda, then a young teenage Scout for an Anya-Nya band near Yei in the late 1960s, explains that rebel resistance was put in more specifically local terms during meetings and recruitment drives: built on local histories of exploitation, domination and enslavement, long memories of violent racism, and nursed anger against the current generation of 'Arab' northern elites who continued this history. As Clement said, it 'didn't look very homogeneous. I wouldn't relate the Southern Sudanese liberation movement to Pan-Africanism. The anti-slavery attitude was part of it, a reaction to the Arab slaving past. It was an awakening to the impact of white domination.'[33]

Some rebels did use some of the language and tactics of this global revolutionary left to frame their demands and plans, even if these never came to fruition. For example, in 1963 the Anya-Nya declared that their two main programmes were a liberation war against Arab Imperialism and a war for political education in the south, explicitly echoing the Sudan Communist Party's contemporary rhetoric and educational work.[34] From conversations with several old rebels and school-age Scouts and teen supporters, Anya-Nya rebel factions did organise 'political officers' to 'enlighten, indoctrinate and instil in the minds of the masses not only the causes of our struggle but make them politically conscious' and to fight against the tactical underdevelopment of the south as 'a huge illiterate island for the Arab Imperialists to rule ruthlessly'.[35] The 1966 manifesto of the Anya-Nya political faction the Azania Liberation Front demanded that Sudan pay 'in full all cost of reparations for all Southern Public Religions and private institutions destroyed by the Neo Arab–colonialistic armies'.[36]

However, any radical political education or radical intellectual work in the southern war ran up against a series of problems: local smallholders and communities who did not necessarily frame their political theory in terms of class and imperialism, but in the discourse of racial repression and slavery, the immediate necessities of organising practical unity, funding and fighting, and the search for international recognition and support.

These were a longstanding problem, and by the 1960s the literate classes of the southern Sudanese provinces were essentially trapped into representing themselves as the leaders of a coherent 'Southern' community, in collective opposition against the spectre of the 'Arab North' of Sudan. In the 1940s and 1950s, this had been a way of gaining access to political space in Sudan, justifying the role of this tiny cadre of educated elites in national and international politics. As Justin Willis puts it, these 'men who found themselves becoming politicians ... were repeatedly drawn into the task of representing a generic community of southerners'.[37] This was also useful in international politics: these men used this 'Southern' collective as a way to speak as representatives of a united and distinct black African constituency fighting colonial oppression. They drew on black African nationalist language (for example, the subtitle of the magazine *Voice of Southern Sudan* from 1963 to 1965 was 'Negritude and Progress') and referred to Pan-Africanist struggles for liberation and national independence.[38]

But in asserting this de facto, apparently pre-existing, southern political community, these spokesmen fought against further debate or the multiplication of southern parties and factions, arguing that this was a 'watering down' and a 'multiplication of the southern voice in order to complicate the search for a solution of the southern problem'.[39] For example, the creation by Joseph Garang of the Southern Democratic Party (the SDP, a wing of the SCP) in 1966, calling for regional autonomy, but also greater democracy and less isolation of the southern political movement, was deeply criticised as divisive.[40] At the time, Garang argued for building a southern anti-imperialism that would eventually be in line with a northern mass democratic movement, and saw pro-Western separatist groups as reactionary, focused only on opposition to 'Arab' north and without a clear conception (or discussion) of a political future that would solve the uneven economic development at the heart of frustrations with the marginalisation and exploitation of Sudan's colonialists and neo-colonialists.[41] The SDP came second in two of the three southern seats it contested in the 1968 election, but struggled to find popular support and was fought by other southern leaders.[42] In demanding collective action as 'Southerners' in a black African nationalist liberation struggle, in Willis's words, these men 'came to exclude other possibilities, both larger and smaller than "the south" ... and effectively rebuffed attempts by some in Sudan's northern provinces to create a wider constituency of the marginal.'[43]

Any wider discussion of more radical possibilities for structural reform rather than regional independence was finally overtaken by the rise of the military leadership of the Anya-Nya rebels by 1969 – uniting the disparate guerrilla groups, but generally stopping political organisation or debate – and by the coup in Khartoum the same year, installing the military dictatorship of Jaffar Nimeiry and the single-party state built around the Sudan Socialist Union. Nimeiry allied Sudan with the growing power of the Arab socialist bloc, finding funding for the Sudanese military the same year.[44] This compounded the pressure on the Anya-Nya rebels to dispense with any leftist language or political arguments, although John Howell (a researcher at the time) stated that 'I have found no southerner who has regarded anti-communism as anything other than a tactical ploy.'[45] Howell noted that it was 'convenient to be anti-Communist' from 1969 onwards, recording rebel leaders' ambitious letters and approaches to Western embassies in East Africa claiming to offer 'a base in the Nile to defeat Communism in the continent of Africa.'[46] For Israel, this was convenient. Between 1969 and 1971, the Israeli government supported the Anya-Nya with training, funding and propaganda assistance, aiming (as Yotam Gidron details) to 'delegitimize Arab nations and their Soviet supporters and draw attention away from anti-Israeli and pro-Palestinian propaganda in the years following the Six-Day War of 1967'.[47] As in the second civil war (1983–2005), this first war of liberation in Sudan appeared to quickly close down revolutionary leftist strategies and possibilities in favour of gaining international funds and support for more authoritarian and practical military action, based on an asserted 'Southern' unity as black African nationalists fighting for a moderate, liberal independence as a new nation.

POPULAR REVOLUTIONARY DISCOURSE

Studying the discourse and discussion of global, black and African radical political thought on people within South Sudan is therefore extremely difficult, even when focusing on the political thought and personal histories of the comparatively elite and urban literati. These students, civil servants, teachers and journalists, political activists and guerrilla fighters are often the leftists we recognise (in ourselves, possibly) – we can trace them, and they organised, on paper and in text, and they use a recognisable language of international socialism and global political thought.

Because there are so few of these students, teachers, politicians and civil servants from Sudan's black peripheries by the late 1960s, it is easy to over-extrapolate from these individuals' diverse, wide-ranging intellectual careers, and possibly to infer too much from their travels to, for example, the University of Dar es Salaam's radical 1960s campus. It would be very possible, for instance, to examine the politically diverse career of the poet and politician Sirr Anai Kelueljang (1943–1999), who learnt about the Moral Rearmament movement while at school in Rumbek and travelled to India to meet Rajmohan Gandhi, and to London for a journalism degree. Sirr was one of the founders of the revolutionary National Action Movement in 1978, which aimed to organise an armed struggle against the Khartoum government for southern liberation.[48] Sirr's career would contrast with his slightly younger colleague Arop Madut Arop, who studied journalism in East Germany in 1972, taught English across Sudan while working as a journalist, and was involved in another rebellion-building movement, the African Liberation Front, from 1982 onwards.

Beyond these literati, even southern Sudanese political activists complained that most peripheral residents were 'preoccupied with daily survival strategies and occupational concerns, and were often oblivious to larger political issues', and this seems perfectly reasonable in light of the challenges of day-to-day survival and social organisation.[49] This meant that South Sudanese students and graduate workers were confident that they were the only people who could be politically representative of this uneducated, illiterate, rural and apparently intellectually isolated constituency. As Gordon Muortat asserted in 1966:

> it is the educated people who understand the wrongs committed against the South and it is they who can point out and speak against the sufferings of the Southern people. It is they who are the eyes of the illiterate masses in seeing that their political rights are secured and preserved.[50]

In the same vein, Howell observed what he called a 'large gulf between the educated elite and the great majority', with even urban migrant workers 'largely ignored by the politicians' – therefore both a real and a constructed gulf.[51]

Stepping away from these minority graduate personal histories, though, historians may be able to trace wider political discussions, if international historians in particular listen to southern linguistic and oral historical gene-alogies. There is a wider field of local revolutionary ideas of economic justice and societal reform on the basis of wider black repression and shared histo-ries of struggle within oral historical space. This includes songs against the Mahdiyya's invading and enslaving armies, and systems of self-organisation among ex-slave, ex-army and seasonal labourer communities, who devel-oped and maintained patterns of self-organisation, mutual aid and social support, and built political education and discussion within these practical associations.[52] Many of the survivors of the White Flag League's attempted revolution in 1924 formed al Kutla al Sawda ('the Black Block') particularly across migrant black worker communities in growing cities in the 1930s and 1940s, and many also joined the Communist Party.[53]

This 'underground politics' – whether practical or conceptual – had long been the normal form of political expression for southern and other mar-ginalised groups in Sudan, rather than political parties. Violent protests organised by southern and otherwise non-Arab residents in cities through the 1950s and 1960s – including the extreme violence of the Black Sunday protests on 6 December 1964 – challenge this common South Sudanese political elite idea of the supposedly politically 'unconscious' masses. According to archival discussions, these demonstrations and protests were not instigated or coordinated by upper-class leaders.[54] Outside major polit-ical parties like the Communists, there were other more short-lived but localised groups that were not only the preserve of students and gradu-ates, including the Pan-African Socialist Society, Democratic Front and the African Thought and Cultural Society.[55] These groups built social solidar-ity: they 'paid the poll tax of an impoverished member, helped at times of bereavement, arranged funerals and mourning parties and so on', and financed poetry and song-writing that criticised political and economic injustices.[56]

But there is very little historical record of these radical projects and imag-inaries from the peripheries, or histories of political thought written from oral histories and song records over the nineteenth and twentieth centuries. From new song recordings and archival work, there were, of course, much broader discussions about shared economic wealth, equitable labour and welfare systems, ending racist exploitation and regional inequality, and the overthrow and total reformation of a consistently violent and predatory state.

CONCLUSION

This chapter has sketched out a few of the circles in which leftist black and international ideas circulated and were propagated within South Sudanese intellectual space, especially over the mid-twentieth century. This history is a fertile field of new historical research, using hidden archives, oral histories, unpublished memoirs, missionary records and the newly formed South Sudan National Archives. Historians of South Sudan are moving towards writing histories of political thought that look at wider circuits and repercussions of intellectual history that echo rather than follow dominant global discourses or do entirely their own radical work.[57]

This work will take us beyond a focus on textual sources and literate, literary actors, and beyond the structures of Cold War geopolitics and theory, towards linguistic histories and creative oral cultures that spell out other radical political theories and social organisation on their own terms. Everyday intellectuals in these spaces were often organising not as political or labour actors, but as social, artistic or welfare groups, using community languages, school-building or neighbourhood organising as their terrain, and researching these radical discussions requires finding and listening to songs, poetry, associational and mutual welfare social histories, and conceptual work in Sudanese languages.

It is possible that this move towards radical histories of political thought reflects a need for revolutionary possibilities in South Sudan and more widely. This has implications for the safety and position of South Sudanese historians. It also has implications for the responsibilities of non-South Sudanese and especially white Western academics: towards our colleagues, for our subjects of study, and for our own political engagements in South Sudan and in our own contexts.

SELECT BIBLIOGRAPHY

Abbas, Philip (1973), 'Growth of Black Political Consciousness in Northern Sudan', *Africa Today*, 20(3), 29–43.
Sikainga, Ahmad Alawad (2002), *'City of Steel and Fire': A Social History of Atbara, Sudan's Railway Town, 1906–1984*, Portsmouth, NH: Heinemann.

Vezzadini, Elena (2013), 'Spies, Secrets, and a Story Waiting to Be (Re)Told: Memories of the 1924 Revolution and the Racialization of Sudanese History', *Northeast African Studies*, 13(2), 53–92.

NOTES

1. Yoshiko Kurita, 'The Sudanese Communist Movement', *Oxford Research Encyclopedia of African History*, Oxford: Oxford University Press, 2019.
2. 'Leftist Leanings and the Enlivening of Revolutionary Memory: Interview with Elena Vezzadini', *Noria*, 2019, https://noria-research.com/cultures-of-the-left-and-revolutionary-memory-in-sudan/.
3. Ahmad Alawad Sikainga, *'City of Steel and Fire': A Social History of Atbara, Sudan's Railway Town, 1906–1984*, Social History of Africa, Portsmouth, NH: Heinemann, 2002; Ahmad A. Sikainga, 'Organized Labor in Contemporary Sudan: The Story of the Railway Workers of Atbara', *South Atlantic Quarterly*, 109(1), 2010, 31–51; Mohamad Said Al Gaddal, 'The Sudanese Communist Party and Liberal Democracy: 1946–69', in Mahmood Mamdani and Ernest Wamba-dia-Wamba (eds), *African Studies in Social Movements and Democracy*, Dakar: Codesria, 1995, 69–98; Ahmad Alawad Sikainga, *Organized Labor and Social Change in Contemporary Sudan*, Middle East Papers, 74, Durham: University of Durham, Centre for Middle Eastern and Islamic Studies, 2003; Elena Vezzadini, *The 1924 Revolution: Hegemony, Resistance, and Nationalism in the Colonial Sudan*, Bergen: University of Bergen, 2008; Elena Vezzadini, 'Nationalism by Telegrams: Political Writings and Anti-Colonial Resistance in Sudan, 1920–1924', *International Journal of African Historical Studies*, 46(1), 2013, 27–59; Elena Vezzadini, '"An Uphill Job Demanding Limitless Patience": The Establishment of Trade Unions and the Conflicts of Development in Sudan, 1946–1952', *International Development Policy*, 8, 2017, 81–108; W.J. Berridge, *Civil Uprisings in Modern Sudan: The 'Khartoum Springs' of 1964 and 1985*, London: Bloomsbury Publishing, 2015; Abdel Ghaffar M. Ahmed and Mustafa Abdel Rahman, 'Small Urban Centres: Vanguards of Exploitation. Two Cases from Sudan', *Africa*, 49, special issue 03, 1979, 258–271; Sondra Hale, *The Changing Ethnic Identity of Nubians in an Urban Milieu: Khartoum, Sudan*, Ann Arbor, MI: University Microfilms International, 1982; El-Wathig Kameir, 'Nuer Migrants in the Building Industry in Khartoum: A Case of the Concentration and Circulation of Labour', in Valdo Pons (ed.), *Urbanization and Urban Life in the Sudan*, Hull: University of Hull, Department of Sociology and Social Anthropology, 1980, 449–476.
4. Douglas H. Johnson, 'Sudanese Military Slavery from the Eighteenth to the Twentieth Century', in Léonie J. Archer (ed.), *Slavery and Other Forms of Unfree Labour*, London: Routledge, 1988, 142–156; Jok Madut Jok, *Sudan: Race, Religion and Violence*, Oxford: Oneworld, 2005; Benaiah Yongo-Bure, 'The Underdevelopment of the Southern Sudan since Independence', in M.W. Daly and A.A. Sikainga (eds), *Civil War in the Sudan*, London: British Academic Press, 1993, 51–77.

5. Elena Vezzadini, 'Spies, Secrets, and a Story Waiting to Be (Re)Told: Memories of the 1924 Revolution and the Racialization of Sudanese History', *Northeast African Studies*, 13(2), 2013, 53–92; Vezzadini, *The 1924 Revolution*; Christopher Gallien Tounsel, '"God Will Crown Us": The Construction of Religious Nationalism in Southern Sudan, 1898–2011', unpublished PhD thesis, Ann Arbor, MI: University of Michigan, 2015, 190; Abdel Ghaffar M. Ahmed, *Sudanese Trade in Black Ivory: Opening Old Wounds*, Occasional Paper 31, Cape Town: Centre for Advanced Studies of African Society, 2007; Stanislaus Abdullahi Paysama, *Autobiography: How a Slave Became a Minister*, Khartoum, 1990, 70.

6. John Young, 'John Garang's Legacy to the Peace Process, the SPLM/A & the South', *Review of African Political Economy*, 32(106), 2005, 535–548, at 538.

7. Tounsel, '"God Will Crown Us"'; Jok Madut Jok, *Breaking Sudan: The Search for Peace*, Oxford: Oneworld, 2017; Lam Akol, *Southern Sudan: Colonialism, Resistance, and Autonomy*, Trenton, NJ: Red Sea Press, 2007; Øystein H. Rolandsen and Cherry Leonardi, 'Discourses of Violence in the Transition from Colonialism to Independence in Southern Sudan, 1955–1960', *Journal of Eastern African Studies*, 8(4), 2014, 609–625.

8. Justin Willis, 'The Southern Problem: Representing Sudan's Southern Provinces to c. 1970', *Journal of African History*, 56(2), 2015, 281–300.

9. There is new research on strike actions through the 1970s in progress by Professor Yosa Wawa, University of Juba, forthcoming.

10. Alan Boswell et al., *The Security Arena in South Sudan: A Political Marketplace Study*, London: LSE Conflict Research Programme, 2019; A. de Waal, *JSRP Policy Brief 2: A Political Marketplace Analysis of South Sudan's Peace*, London: LSE Justice and Security Research Programme, 2016.

11. Joseph Ukel Garang was born in 1932, and became a socialist in 1949 as a secondary school student in Rumbek town. He joined the Sudan Communist Party in the early 1950s, and went to the University of Khartoum to become the first South Sudanese law graduate in Sudan. At university, he joined the Socialist Students Group and organised an anti-imperialist student conference in the southern town of Wau in 1955. Joseph joined the SCP's Political Bureau and Central Executive Committee, organising political education in the south while working as a lawyer defending political detainees. In 1965, he revived the English-language SCP daily paper *Advance* in Khartoum. In 1969, he was appointed a government minister, and soon after became Minister for Southern Affairs, writing a government declaration in 1969 recognising the cultural identity and autonomy of the southern provinces. Joseph was a prolific publisher, founding and editing the *Nile Mirror* newspaper, and writing in *African Communist*. He was executed on 28 July 1971 by President Nimeiri after a failed communist coup attempt.

12. John Garang de Mabior was born in 1945 and educated in Tanzania during the southern civil wars in the 1960s. He gained a scholarship at Iowa State University for a BA in Economics in 1969, and then became a research associate at the University of Dar es Salaam during 1969–70. This is when John apparently became a socialist Pan-Africanist, inspired by Dr Walter Rodney and his co-student Yoweri Museveni (now President of Uganda). John returned to the civil war

as a guerrilla captain in 1970, and after peace in 1972 he joined the Sudan armed forces as a captain, gaining a Diploma in Military Science from Fort Benning in the US during 1974–75, then going to Iowa State University for his MA and PhD during 1977–81. John returned to Khartoum and joined the Military Research Institute as well as lecturing in the Department of Rural Economy at the University of Khartoum until 1983; that year, he rebelled, founding the Sudan People's Liberation Movement and Army after a mutiny in the southern garrison town of Bor, writing a manifesto that was explicitly socialist and revolutionary. He died in a helicopter crash in 2005, weeks after signing a peace deal.

13. L. Baroco to Joseph Oduho, 22 May 1966, Comboni, A/104/9/30.

14. Young, 'John Garang's Legacy to the Peace Process, the SPLM/A & the South', 538–539.

15. Jesse A. Zink, *Christianity and Catastrophe in South Sudan: Civil War, Migration, and the Rise of Dinka Anglicanism*, Waco, TX: Baylor University Press, 2018; Christopher Gallien Tounsel and Christopher Tounsel, 'Khartoum Goliath: SPLM/SPLA Update and Martial Theology during the Second Sudanese Civil War', *Journal of Africana Religions*, 4(2), 2016, 129–153; Christopher Tounsel, *Chosen Peoples: Christianity and Political Imagination in South Sudan*, Durham, NC: Duke University Press, 2021; Christopher Tounsel, '"Render to Caesar": Missionary Thought and the Sudanese State, 1946–1964', *Social Sciences and Missions*, 31(3–4), 2018, 341–374; Rebecca Glade, '"Shama Will Not Dance": University of Khartoum Politics, 1964–69', *Africa*, 89(S1), 2019, 109–126; Sebabatso Manoeli, 'Narrative Battles: Competing Discourses and Diplomacies of Sudan's "Southern Problem", 1961–1991', PhD thesis, Oxford: University of Oxford, 2017.

16. Lilian Passmore Sanderson and Neville Sanderson, *Education, Religion & Politics in Southern Sudan 1899–1964*, Sudan Studies Series 4, London: Ithaca Press, 1981; Cherry Leonardi, *Dealing with Government in South Sudan: Histories of Chiefship, Community & State*, Martlesham: Boydell & Brewer, 2013.

17. J. Howell, 'Political Leadership and Organisation in the Southern Sudan', unpublished PhD thesis, Reading: University of Reading, 1978, 142.

18. Hilary Logali, 'Autobiography', 201–202, Sudan Archives, Durham University, 890.1–2.

19. Tounsel, '"God Will Crown Us"', 175–178.

20. 'Diary of Mons. Pio Yukwan', 1964, 1–2, 96, Comboni, A/107/6.

21. Logali, 'Autobiography', 38 and 50. While the organising power and effectiveness of these 'cells' in Khartoum and southern towns is arguable, the cell system of spreading information is a common theme in histories of southern underground organising from the 1950s to 2000s; Nicki Kindersley, 'The Fifth Column? South Sudanese Political Organisation in Khartoum, 1969–2015', PhD thesis, Durham: Durham University, 2016.

22. Tounsel, *Chosen Peoples*, 176–177.

23. Tounsel, '"God Will Crown Us"', 176–177; Howell, 'Political Leadership and Organisation in the Southern Sudan', 150, footnote 1; Joseph U. Garang, *The Dilemma of the Southern Intellectual: Is It Justified?*, Khartoum: Ministry for Southern Affairs, 1971, Middle East Documentation Unit, 17/3/GEN/278.

24. See, for example, the file HEC 36.G.1, South Sudan National Archive, Juba.
25. 'Diary of Mons. Pio Yukwan', 16a.
26. Entry for 'Othwon Dak 1934–2002', in Kuyok Abol Kuyok, *South Sudan: The Notable Firsts*, Bloomington, IN: AuthorHouse, 2015.
27. Howell, 'Political Leadership and Organisation in the Southern Sudan', 142.
28. Ibid., 143.
29. Logali, 'Autobiography', 51.
30. 'Diary of Mons. Pio Yukwan', 33a.
31. Tounsel, '"God Will Crown Us"', 267.
32. Meredith Terretta, '"God of Independence, God of Peace": Village Politics and Nationalism in the Maquis of Cameroon, 1957–71', *Journal of African History*, 46(01), 2005, 75–101, at 77.
33. Interview with Clement Janda, Arua, 6 March 2017.
34. Severino Fuli Boki Tombe Ga'le, *Shaping a Free Southern Sudan: Memoirs of Our Struggle, 1934–1985*, Limuru: Loa Catholic Parish Council, 2002, 237; Anya-Nya Declaration, 31 July 1963.
35. Fuli Boki Tombe Ga'le, *Shaping a Free Southern Sudan*, 238.
36. George Akumbek Kwanai, 'The Azania Liberation Front (ALF) Manifesto', 1966, Comboni, A/107/2/94.
37. Willis, 'The Southern Problem', 284.
38. Yotam Gidron, '"One People, One Struggle": Anya-Nya Propaganda and the Israeli Mossad in Southern Sudan, 1969–1971', *Journal of Eastern African Studies*, 12(3), 2018, 428–453, at 432.
39. 'The Sudan Communist Party in Disguise', *The Vigilant*, 239, 12 December 1966, Sudan Archives, Durham University.
40. 'Garang and Group Form a New Party', *The Vigilant*, 238, 11 December 1966, Sudan Archives, Durham University.
41. Howell, 'Political Leadership and Organisation in the Southern Sudan', 173 and 279; Tarcisio Ahmed (a teacher) and Wilson Ariamba (a lawyer) were widely suspected of being communists while working with Joseph Garang in the Ministry of Southern Affairs from 1969; Ezbon Mondiri was accused of leftist sympathies after visiting Tanzania; Joseph Oduho, 'The New Regime', 1969, Comboni, A/104/30/20; 'The Struggle and Its Progress: The Political Leaders', 1967, Comboni, A/104/6/4.
42. Howell, 'Political Leadership and Organisation in the Southern Sudan', 230.
43. Willis, 'The Southern Problem', 284.
44. Gidron, '"One People, One Struggle"', 437.
45. Howell, 'Political Leadership and Organisation in the Southern Sudan', 287.
46. Ibid., 286.
47. Gidron, '"One People, One Struggle"', 429.
48. Entry for 'Sirr Anai Kelueljang 1943–1999', in Kuyok, *South Sudan*.
49. Sikainga, 'Organized Labor in Contemporary Sudan', 15.
50. 'Mourtat [*sic*] Addresses', *The Vigilant*, 24 February 1966, TNA FO 371.190417 VS1015.24.
51. Howell, 'Political Leadership and Organisation in the Southern Sudan', 89 and 146.

52. Sikainga, *Organized Labor and Social Change in Contemporary Sudan*, 7–8.

53. Vezzadini, *The 1924 Revolution*; Yoshiko Kurita, *The Sudanese Diaspora in Politics: Félix Dar Fur, Dusé Muhammad 'Ali 'Abd al-Latif*, London: Kegan Paul, 2003, 192.

54. Howell, 'Political Leadership and Organisation in the Southern Sudan', 79. Bona Malwal, 'Report of the Secretariat to the General Meeting of the Southern Front on 6 February 1965,' Comboni, A/90/8/10.

55. Philip Abbas, 'Growth of Black Political Consciousness in Northern Sudan', *Africa Today*, 20(3), 1973, 29–43, at 36. See also Foreign and Commonwealth Office note, 30 October 1979, TNA FCO 93.2126, and memo from Youth Advisor to Director of Ministry for Southern Affairs, Khartoum, n.d. c. 1969, SSNA MSA 10.A.3/39.

56. Abbas, 'Growth of Black Political Consciousness in Northern Sudan', 36; Howell, 'Political Leadership and Organisation in the Southern Sudan', 256.

57. In Saul Dubow's words, to start 'recognising multiple family resemblances than strict lineages or rigorous intellectual traditions'; Saul Dubow, 'Uncovering the Historic Strands of Egalitarian Liberalism in South Africa', *Theoria*, 61(140), 2014, 7–24, at 8.

11

Communists of Katwe: Pan-African Marxism and the Uganda People's Congress, *c.* 1960–*c.* 1964

Adrian Browne

This chapter constitutes an initial effort to reinsert the revolutionary left as a political tendency within the history of Uganda. It focuses on the beginnings of this movement in the couple of years either side of Uganda's independence from Britain in 1962.[1] The left faction of the Uganda People's Congress (UPC) rose to prominence in this period under the young firebrand General Secretary John Kakonge. But the left's ascent within the UPC proved short-lived, reaching its zenith just before the party's 3rd Annual Delegates' Conference in Gulu in late April 1964. In his bid to be re-elected at the conference, Kakonge found himself dramatically outmanoeuvred and defeated by pro-Western barrister Grace Ibingira, leader of the UPC right and newly named Minister of State. The UPC Executive Committee, operating with Prime Minister Obote's approval, had manipulated the party's internal organisation and reprinted membership cards to rig the election. The immediate circumstances and details of this setback for the left, cast in retrospect as either narrow escape or fateful closure and anti-democratic precedent, have been frequently recounted in both the scholarship and popular memory.[2] But the left itself has been subject to little study by historians. Its wider history comes slightly more into focus in works by Akiiki Mujaju on the party's Youth League (UPC-YL) and Jack Edgar Taylor on the early post-colonial urban politics of race and respectability.[3] The source of the increasing 'ideological sharpness' that Mujaju notes among the UPC left in these years remains unexplored, however. The ideological commitments, international connections, and social bases that shaped the UPC left's rise lie at the margins of these accounts centring on the succession of early direct actions and protests that brought activists to public attention and infamy.

This chapter comprises an internal history of the early UPC left, supplemented by a series of short biographical profiles covering activists' lives up to early 1964. It examines the forces and ideas that pushed Kakonge to the left – and over the line of austere post-colonial social democratic permissibility – in the years immediately preceding the 1964 Gulu Conference. Using declassified UK, US and Czech official archival sources, this chapter identifies the formative milieux, sites of political education, seedbeds of struggle and ideological currents that shaped several important leftist militants long neglected in the historiography of post-colonial Africa.

KAKONGE AND THE UPC LEFT, *c.* 1960–*c.* 1962

At the time of Uganda's independence from Britain in October 1962, circumstances for the revolutionary left were unpropitious even by East African standards. The country exhibited a small industrial proletariat organised by a labour movement that had been institutionalised largely by the late colonial government. The Uganda Trade Union Congress (TUC) functioned to a considerable extent as a client of the International Confederation of Free Trade Unions, the labour bureaucracy through which Western governments channelled funds and propaganda. Uganda's politics reflected the conservative proclivities of not only these Cold War anti-communist institutions, but also Christian missions and mission schools, Makerere University College, and the centralised and hierarchical African historical kingdoms in the south, particularly Buganda, the political and economic core. Potential countervailing political forces threatened advance elsewhere in the country, particularly in the ethnically heterogeneous east, namely Bugisu, Bukedi and Teso districts. These areas had tended to resent pre-colonial Buganda's expansionary designs, and later struggled against the colonial state and European and South Asian traders, with conflict centred on cotton and coffee. The UPC, as the anti-colonial political party with the most serious anti-monarchist credentials, gained strong support in this part of the country. But in 1962, UPC found itself involved in an unstable and unnatural coalition with Kabaka Yekka, the party of Buganda separatism, conservatism and feudalism.[4] Far left politics' lack of expression was partly a matter of the UPC leadership's need to contend with Uganda's various well-resourced anti-communist bulwarks.

Questionable leftist commitment within the UPC also posed a challenge. Contrary to many later readings, there is little evidence that General Secretary John Kakonge, who had been elected to this office in 1960 shortly after returning from India, brought a Marxist orientation with him. Kakonge had been to a significant extent a product of the political patronage and tutelage of Indian Prime Minister Jawaharlal Nehru, with whom he had close contact in his early to mid-twenties in Delhi. Kakonge had mainly imbibed Nehruvian notions such as the 'socialistic pattern of society' and the 'socialist co-operative commonwealth'. These non-Marxist concepts, advanced by India's National Congress Party, were redolent of the British Fabian tradition.[5] Kakonge's Indian-educated post-1960 appointees within the UPC bureaucracy exhibited similar politics.[6]

Two years on, the figurehead of the Ugandan left still adopted an equivocal stance on capitalism. Kakonge developed many links with Marxist socialists from supportive regimes, including the Czechoslovakian government, which he visited in 1961; however, he showed little evidence of ideological alignment. His decision to accept a directorship in a corporation owned by a Ugandan Indian business magnate in mid-1962 drew heavy criticism even from some towards the right of the UPC who were proponents of the Africanisation of the bourgeoisie.[7] In a pamphlet produced to mark national independence, Kakonge appeared to disparage ideology altogether, claiming that 'the justifiably impatient African masses will not listen to any political philosophy nor economic theory'.[8] Although the right of the party encouraged Obote to work against him from 1962 onwards, Kakonge's professed politics was much in line with those of the UPC prime minister, whose policy offering on the eve of independence included, at most, some sort of welfare state, couched in quite defensive terms.

PAN-AFRICAN MARXISM, POLITICAL PEDAGOGY AND PECKHAM, 1960–63

This ambiguity contrasted sharply with the ideological assuredness of an influential section among Ugandans based in the UK in 1962. Represented officially by the Uganda Association (UGASSO), with considerable engagement also with the London branch of the UPC, Ugandans constituted an increasingly significant feature in the African student landscape at the metropole, making up the largest contingent from Britain's east and central African territories at a moment when African student numbers in the UK swelled, reaching an estimated 7,400 in 1959–60.[9] Students from Buganda had dominated the community of Ugandan exiles for most of the 1950s. But around the turn of the 1960s, the status quo was challenged by students from elsewhere in Uganda. This insurgent movement was led by easterners, such as Boloki Chango Machyo w'Obanda from Bukedi and Dani Wadada Nabudere from Bugisu.[10]

A new leftist political current in African London surfaced strongly from 1960 onwards. Communists and fellow travellers quickly sought to take control of the executive of relatively new umbrella body, the Committee of African Organisations (CAO), whose founding affiliates in 1958 had included UGASSO and the Uganda National Congress, one of the UPC's progenitors. Africans in the UK generally grew more favourable to the Communist Party of Great Britain (CPGB) as the 1960s approached. Long an unwanted presence in the metropolitan anti-colonial Movement for Colonial Freedom, the CPGB energetically involved itself in campaigns against racial violence and discrimination in west London, apartheid in South Africa, and Western imperialism and neo-colonialism in Congo.[11] From 1960 onwards, the CAO received support from the embassies of China and the Soviet Union as well as the increasingly radicalised Ghanaian President Kwame Nkrumah.[12] The CPGB's Africanists grew close to the ideologues of Nkrumah's Convention People's Party (CPP) who were in the early 1960s publicly embracing a form of Marxism-Leninism.[13]

London's Ugandan students were profoundly shaped, and proceeded to influence, the key events and institutions of the era. Hitherto mainstream African nationalists were propelled leftward by the crisis in Congo, which spilled over the border with a Uganda whose own independence loomed.[14] Between the East and the West, the choice was clear for a growing number of these neophyte Pan-African Marxists. Under Machyo's chairmanship, UGASSO issued a statement in mid-1961 denouncing efforts by some of their countrymen and the West to make propaganda of the return of disgruntled students from behind the Iron Curtain.[15] Machyo served on the communist-controlled CAO executive as treasurer from 1960 and chairman a couple of years later;[16] in these capacities he had 'frequent contact' with CPGB and communist embassies, according to the British Security Service.[17] Nabudere, meanwhile, went further still in his connection to the CPGB.

Militant Profile: Dani Wadada Nabudere

Born in 1932, Nabudere was, like his older comrade Machyo, the son of a colonial chief. He attended an African-run school that developed a reputation as a nationalist breeding ground. Nabudere's older brother, Erieza W. Mashate, was deeply involved with the UNC and went on to be a feature of the UPC right at regional level in the 1960s. Nabudere spent almost a decade rising through the African ranks of the Post Office before leaving for the UK in 1959 on a district government scholarship. He was admitted in January 1960 to train as a barrister at Lincoln's Inn. Nabudere was, as he later recalled, so untaxed by his legal studies that he spent a lot of time reading Marxist literature at the library in the British Museum, as well as finding time to take leading roles in UGASSO, the CAO, the Africana Study Group (ASG) and his student union.[18] With his political engagement 'no longer restricted to African, let alone Ugandan issues', as he later recalled, Nabudere became not only a Marxist, but also an active member of the CPGB – one of very few eastern Africans to do so.[19] In 1962, Nabudere was living in Peckham, where the local CPGB branch was the largest in London's south-east. He was 'holding classes in Marxism' for other East African students in March 1963 while serving as President of the East African Students Association, as one British official reported.[20]

The Ugandan leftists first propagandised through established channels. Machyo's output in journals like *Ugasso* and the CAO's *United Africa* started to evince his interest in political economy, warning against neocolonialism. Rejecting Marcus Garvey's vision for 'black capitalists', Machyo championed the Pan-African socialism of Black American sociologist (and recent Communist Part of the USA applicant) W.E.B. Du Bois.[21] *Ugasso*'s editorial committee, which included Nabudere, directed readers to suggested recommended reading such as titles by Otto Kuusinen, Secretary of the Central Committee of the Communist Party of the Soviet Union, and Jack Woddis, one of the CPGB's Africa specialists. At home, *Uganda Argus* also frequently printed letters written by the exiles and the socialist resolutions issued by UGASSO, whose president in 1962–63 was Nabudere.[22]

Leftist commandeering of UGASSO and its publications created resentment among their political opponents. An escape from these constraints was offered in 1962 by Nabudere and Machyo's new leftist organisation, the Ntu Study Group (NSG), taking its name from the Bantu language stem meaning 'human' or 'life'. Based at CAO's Nkrumah-funded Africa Unity House in Kensington, the group offered the formalised political education that was central to associational life in these self-consciously intellectual exilic circles;[23] CAO affiliates included, for example, the Zanzibar Study Group, led by the young communist Salim Said Rashid, and Ghana's National Association of Socialist Student Organisations Study Group, the CPP's educational wing. The NSG soon renamed itself the Africana Study Group, but retained *Ntu* as the title for a new quarterly journal, first issued in the early months of 1962. In the ASG, Nabudere and Machyo were joined by other eastern Ugandans, but also westerners, such as Edward Rugumayo, who later took over as editor of *Ntu* as he remained in London to work as a science teacher after graduating.[24]

The ideological orientations and general political affiliations of the ASG were clear from the outset.[25] The mission of the ASG, by the middle of 1962, was to align the Ugandan exiles with Pan-African scientific socialism. *Ntu* increasingly in 1962–63 ran topical pieces approvingly citing, or reproduced from, magazines produced by Nkrumah's Bureau of African Affairs, including *The Spark*. The ASG identified and relentlessly critiqued threats to this socialist vision. Like those of the CPGB, the ASG's intellectuals from late 1962 reserved particular hostility for the concept of 'African socialism' and the 'neocolonial' institution of the European Common Market, to which the UK's Conservative government had applied for membership.[26] In London in March 1963, the ASG, represented by Machyo, combined these attacks in a paper given at the All-Nations Trade and Economic Discussion Conference, organised by the Forward Britain Movement, a Eurosceptic campaign group created jointly by a Labour Party member and a trade unionist. The ASG asserted that there was 'no such thing' as African socialism. There was only one course of action: 'Africa will have to adopt the universalist socialist principles' and 'the major means of production, exchange and distribution will be publicly owned by the people', it continued. '[T]he economy shall be Africanised, planned and co-ordinated on a continental scale.'[27]

RACIAL NATIONALISM, CLASS AND IDEOLOGY IN THE UPC LEFT, 1962–63

New leftist forces were also emerging and building power in Uganda in the months around independence. The leading figures were school-leavers, aged between their mid-twenties and mid-thirties. These activists fought principally for control of the UPC-YL. Other factions controlled that organisation in 1963, with the single strongest sub-group, Makerere students, tending to see themselves as non-aligned, non-leftist nationalists.[28] Nevertheless, leftist school-leavers holding important UPC-YL positions included: Raiti Omongin, National Organiser; Jonah Waswa, Chairman of Buganda Region; S.B. Mangeni Aurrah, Vice-Secretary of Buganda Region; Peter Kinuka, a committee member; and J. Saul Kisolo-Makanya, Organiser for Bugisu. Leftists also featured as officeholders in the UPC: ex-journalist Silvano Kwamya Baguma was Deputy National Organiser and later became Financial Secretary; Charles W.A. Onyutta was Assistant Organising Secretary as well as self-styled 'Chargé d'Affaires in the Congo'; Charles Wellington Sabatanda-Mutanda was Assistant Secretary in the Research and Information Bureau; Lonny Ong'weng Obbo was Regional Secretary in Bukedi; David Livingstone O. Ojepa was a Teso District Councillor; and Jackson Maumbe Mukhwana was a Mbale Municipality Councillor. Some, like Natolo Masaba, simultaneously held offices for the party and its youth wing, serving as both Bugisu Organiser and UPC-YL committee member.

A smaller group of university graduates gave the left respectability in the hierarchies of social status of postcolonial Uganda. Kakonge's South Asian-educated allies featured most heavily among the earliest crop: Calcutta-trained Francis Xavier Wadada Musani served as UPC Publicity Secretary from 1961; Jaberi Bidandi-Sali returned from university in Pakistan to work as Party Mobiliser in 1962; and the same year, the Delhi graduate Ally Muwabe Kirunda-Kivejinja became Secretary of the UPC's Research and Information Bureau. For a time, there was even participation from a UK-educated Makerere College man: economics lecturer Semei Nyanzi, an Edinburgh University graduate who, as well as being a member of the East African Central Legislative Assembly, 'successfully combined the prestige of being one of the few Africans of the Makerere faculty with close contact and association with both the left wing and the leadership of the UPC'.[29]

Extraordinary ethnic diversity characterised this early Ugandan left. East-erners made up the largest contingent: Musani was Gisu, Kirunda-Kivejinja was Soga, Ong'weng Obbo was Dhola, Aurrah and Mugala were both Samia, Omongin was Adhola and Ojepa was Iteso. The western region was rep-resented by Kinuka, who was Nkore, and Baguma, who was Tooro. The northern region, Obote's domain, featured through Nyanzi, who was Acholi, and Onyutta, who was Alur. Even the Ganda community were represented in the form of Bidandi Ssali, Sabatanda-Mutanda and Musoke; indeed, the Buganda branch of the UPC had long been perhaps the most radical in the country. These Ganda men had strong ties with Abbasi Kibazo, one of the leaders of the Bawejjere ('Common Men') Association, a left populist UPC affiliate organisation in Buganda.[30] For good measure, the left also included militant activists and trade unionists from Kenya, such as Felix Bukachi.

In terms of social bases, the UPC left was an exclusively male and largely urban, although reasonably diverse, phenomenon comprising younger teachers, clerks and industrial workers. The left's interest in workers mani-fested most explicitly through participation in a splinter labour centre called the Uganda Federation of Labour (UFL). The UFL had emerged in 1961 in the industrial town of Jinja out of a split in the TUC, but the rivalry was not initially ideological in nature.[31] After existing largely in name initially, the UFL had once again been revitalised by the left in 1962, with several key UPC-YL figures serving as UFL executive officers. Moreover, Obote's ruling clique at the centre of the UPC for a time actively supported the UFL in a bid to undercut the position of the TUC.[32] In the months immediately following independence in 1962, the UFL attracted leaders with strong roots in the trade union movement. The work of Organising Secretary A.H.W. Mugalla, the General Secretary of the Textile Workers Union, centred on the Nyanza Textile Industries Ltd factory in Jinja, where he had considerable support in the view of Special Branch. The latter worried that similar influence was exercised in Teso district in the 'leftist' Amalgamated Transport and General Workers' Union (ATGWU) by Ojepa, the UFL's National Treasurer.[33] The UFL also developed a power base in Kampala through its Secretary General Bukachi and President Nyanzi, both influential officeholders within the Makerere Employee Union. In early 1963, the overlapping UFL and the UPC-YL left leadership combined forces in a series of illegal strikes in businesses in Kampala and Soroti.

The left in Uganda began to forge connections to international Pan-African and communist networks. Like their UK-based leftist compatriots, the Uganda-based left was aligned with the radical 'Casablanca group' of African states which strove towards continent-wide political integration; the UFL accordingly joined and received funding from the Ghana-based All-African Trade Union Federation (AATUF). Links were also growing with the communist world: connected by figures like Machyo in London, British communists in the Movement for Colonial Freedom (MCF) had long played a supporting role to the UFL, and key figures on the UPC left went on study tours to China as guests of the All-China Federation of Trade Unions or the China Committee of the All-African Peoples' Solidarity Organisation.

A key unresolved issue remained the ideological circumspection and incoherence that characterised the UPC left's politics. Activists certainly did not exhibit a Marxist orientation. If anything, the rhetoric and political stunts often reflected a racial economic nationalism – or 'nationalist socialism', as Mujaju labels it.[34] UFL leaders incessantly lambasted the TUC as an agent of 'neo-colonialism' and condemned 'hostile alien exploiters'.[35] The left did not, however, express much concern for the means of production's ownership, as long as it was African. The UPC left's 'generally anti-imperialist position' left a great deal unspecified.[36]

There was only so far that the leading leftists' spectacular protests and vigilantism could take them. As the UFL began to itself pose a growing challenge to the newly independent government in early 1963 through a series of wildcat strikes, the TUC's relations with the government improved.[37] The

TUC was strengthened later in the year by the jailing of influential UFL figures such as Omongin and Aurrah for their involvement in strikes and other protests. With funding drying up from their unimpressed Ghanaian funders, the UFL disbanded.[38] As the left attempted to push Kakonge into a more confrontational stance, American officials saw in him someone worth offering an inducement in the form of an all-expenses-paid trip to the US. He was a figure who had 'learned from experience to temper idealism with practical considerations', as one US diplomat put it.[39]

Militant Profile: Raiti Omongin

Omongin's life is shrouded in mystery despite his reputation as 'perhaps the most articulate and most consistent radical socialists the League or even the UPC itself ever produced'.[40] Born in 1936 or 1937, he hailed from Bukedi near the Kenyan border and had spent part of his life in Kenya. He came to prominence in his mid-twenties as Northern and Eastern Region Organiser of the UPC Youth Wing, sitting on the party's Central Executive Committee as a youth representative from 1960. Omongin was closely associated with Kenyan comrades on either side of the border.[41] He came to national notoriety in 1963 when he called for the banning of the 'neo-colonialist' Western-backed ICFTU's Labour College, the TUC, and any trade union unaffiliated to the Ghana-spearheaded AATUF.[42] Three days after his early release from prison late that year for leading an illegal strike, Omongin was again arrested, this time for assaulting and unlawfully imprisoning the director and manager of the *Uganda Argus*. Fined and jailed for two years in January 1964, he was released on the prime minister's orders in June the same year.[43] In mid-1963 Omongin and his comrade Ojepa visited North Korea and China, where they were hosted by the All-China Federation of Trade Unions.[44] Increasingly influenced by Marxism, Leninism and Maoism, Omongin considered himself 'a communist', as his one-time comrade Yoweri Museveni later recalled.[45]

Militant Profile: David Livingston O. Ojepa

A self-described 'true son of Africa', Ojepa was from Kumi in Teso district.[46] He was elected UPC Teso region Organising Secretary and appointed National Assistant Organising Secretary for the party in 1962.[47] According to US officials monitoring the Uganda labour movement, Ojepa had made his name as an official in the Lango district branch of the Amalgamated Transport and General Workers' Union.[48] He began to build international socialist connections when he travelled to Yugoslavia in September 1962 to attend a trade union

conference.[49] Ojepa was later President of Teso ATGWU, a Teso District Councillor, and UFL's Vice President and National Treasurer. In these roles, he found
himself in frequent controversy which reached new heights during a series of
strikes in Soroti in January 1963.[50] Along with his fellow eastern Omongin, he
visited China and North Korea a few months later. Rarely out of the spotlight,
Ojepa was sentenced in early 1964 to nine months' imprisonment for assaulting
an Asian bar owner during an argument over the payment of drinks, but was
released after just a couple of months.[51]

'WHAT ONE MIGHT CALL DOCTRINAIRE POLITICS':[52] SCIENTIFIC SOCIALISM IN KATWE, 1963–64

The last few months of 1963 witnessed a shift in the left's orientation and trajectory as key figures increasingly articulated and disseminated a clear and
confident ideological position and political strategy. Omongin emerged as
a committed Marxist, railing against the 'bourgeoisie' and using the court-
room to brandish North Korean propaganda and publicise his intention to
'smash completely once and for all capitalist exploitation'.[53] Kirunda-Kivejinja was also now 'pretty close to being a Communist', British diplomats
feared.[54] Kakonge, appointed government Director of Planning in June
1963, transformed from 'at least maintaining the public appearance of a
nationalist, non-aligned radical political leader' to serving as 'an unqual-
ified and outright apologist for the Bloc line', as the US Embassy saw it.[55]
Kakonge began advocating publicly for scientific socialism, echoing the line
of the CPGB and ASG.[56] In December 1963, the UFL was dissolved by its
Central Executive, with a view to forming a new organisation that would
take seriously the education of workers.[57] The questions of party democracy, ideology and strategy were debated among the key figures of the UPC
left in March 1964 at a seminar on 'the problem of party organisation', led by
Kisolo Makanya of the Bugisu District UPC-YL.[58] This was the trial run for
Kakonge's speech on socialism and internal party democracy at the fateful
April 1964 Gulu conference where he was to announce it is 'high time we
directed our minds to IDEOLOGY'.[59]

The flows of new ideas and resources that were profoundly shaping
the emerging left partly emanated from foreign socialist organisations
and governments now active in Kampala. The Soviet Union and China
increasingly openly and rancorously vied for influence, with embassies
distributing literature, films and funding to individual activists and
politicians, some famously close to one side (e.g., Omongin and China), but

most opting for a less discriminating approach to communist patronage. The UPC left's main Soviet contacts arrived in April 1963 to prepare the ground for the ambassador arriving from his previous posting in London.[60] Through these connections, in 1963 the Soviet Union hosted first Kakonge, leading a delegation that joined the celebrations in the Soviet Union for the anniversary of the October Revolution, followed by a hand-picked group of activists who undertook an eight-month 'study tour' to learn 'political economy, scientific socialism, party organization'.[61] Chinese, Ghanaian and, according to rumour, Soviet support were all involved in the September 1963 revival and rebranding of a defunct title *African Pilot* as a leftist newspaper, printed in the Kampala's Katwe neighbourhood and co-owned by Kirunda-Kivejinja, fresh from a tour of communist Asia, and a couple of his South Asian-educated comrades.[62] With the ideological assault from the left gathering pace in early 1964, this 'more and more left wing' title was disapprovingly discussed by Uganda Police Special Branch, and approvingly cited by the CPGB's *Marxism Today*.[63]

But the chief impetus for the refutation of African socialism came from the Ugandan exiles in London. These activist-intellectuals' Marxist-oriented theory had a profound effect on their comrades in and around Kampala over the six to twelve months that followed independence, owing to a steady stream of propaganda in the form of letters via the pages of the *Uganda Argus*, copies of *Ntu* and articles compiled and republished under the Lumumba Memorial Publications imprint, dedicated 'to all the toiling masses of Africa'.[64] Until late 1964, Machyo remained away from Uganda. But he could scarcely have been more involved, being one of the most prolific contributors of letters to the editor in the history of the *Argus*, the main UK contact for Eastern Bloc scholarships, and a consummate networker across Europe and beyond.[65]

Returning exiles were perhaps even more important assets to this political shift among the left in Kampala. Nabudere returned in July 1963, and soon became 'known for his keenness' in the UPC-YL.[66] His influence in terms of leftist networks and ideas belied his lack of a formal role. Strikingly, all the while, he was employed on year-long pupillage in one of the key institutions of the UPC right wing, a law firm run by Lameck Lubowa and Grace Ibingira, fellow London-trained barristers, who were serving as government ministers in Obote's cabinet.[67] Nabudere was reported by British intelligence to have 'retained his contacts with British communists' who visited Uganda after his return and 'appeared to be well acquainted' with UPC-YL members.[68] Like a younger, more radical version of the 'fellow-travelling'

British barristers Dennis Pritt and John Platts-Mills, Nabudere represented UPC-YL figures at their trials for assaulting the *Argus* newspaper editor in late 1963;[69] and when Omongin appealed his conviction at the start of 1964, it was Platts-Mills who Nabudere enlisted to help.[70] Nabudere's contribution extended far beyond legal contacts and skills, however. Before going into private practice as a lawyer in Mbale in late 1964, he built up the connections between Kampala and the emerging Bugisu District UPC-YL, many of whom he had known much earlier in life. The only Ugandan who had received training in Marxist-Leninist political technologies, he focused the interest of the left on political education, socialist theory and the party form. When Information Minister Adoko Nekyon, one of Obote's relatives, charged that Kakonge's speech to the Gulu conference in April 1964 exhibited 'communist leanings', it was Nabudere who demanded Nekyon identify the offending 'communist' content.[71]

Militant Profile: Natolo Masaba

Masaba was a famous non-conformist who was born in about 1931 and lived for most of his life 20 miles from Mbale Town in Manyiga County of Bugisu, where he was a peasant farmer. A flamboyant character, Masaba had received junior secondary schooling and worked briefly as a clerk before being sentenced to five years' imprisonment in 1957 for robbery with violence. After his release, he was elected a county councillor and co-ordinated campaigns of 'systematic non-cooperation' with the central and local governments' efforts to conduct censuses and tax collection.[72] In the early 1960s, Masaba abandoned his Christian name George and turned up to a meeting with Obote wearing a goat skin and carrying an envelope full of the ashes of a burned effigy of the British Chairman of the Commission of Inquiry into a district boundary dispute.[73] Increasingly involved in the UPC-YL, his activities in Mbale were closely followed by Special Branch.[74] Masaba was among five youth wingers who travelled several months later for an extended course of political education in the Soviet Union. He returned to Bugisu district espousing 'a picturesque variety of folk communism' and describing his experience as 'a voyage to an extraterrestrial paradise', in the words of one disapproving political scientist.[75]

CONCLUSION

This chapter has examined the forms of political organisation, education and ideology that made the UPC left a potent force in April 1964, one that the right crushed by resorting to anti-democratic means. It did so by bringing into the frame not only the long-forgotten school-leaver militants of Katwe in Kampala, but also the activist-intellectuals – and the journals, associations and study circles – of London at the turn of the 1960s, who together shaped the history of decolonisation and the Cold War in Uganda. As such, this chapter de-centres the figure of UPC General Secretary Kakonge, instead focusing on those who were to carry the mantle long after his co-option and neutralisation in 1965–66.

SELECT BIBLIOGRAPHY

Browne, Adrian J. (2022), 'Liberation Ethnology: District Decolonisation, Knowledge Production, and the Neoliberal Revolution in Uganda', in Katherine Bruce-Lockhart, Jonathon L. Earle, Nakanyike B. Musisi and Edgar C. Taylor (eds), *Decolonising State and Society in Uganda: The Politics of Knowledge and Public Life*, Woodbridge: Boydell & Brewer, 295–316.

Mujaju, Akiiki Bomera (1972), 'Youth Action and Political Development in Uganda', unpublished PhD thesis, New York: Columbia University.

Mujaju, Akiiki Bomera (1973), 'The Demise of the UPCYL and the Rise of NUYO', *African Review*, 3(2), 291–307.

Nabudere, D.W. (1980), *Imperialism and Revolution in Uganda*, Dar es Salaam: Onyx Press.

Serra, G., and Gerits, F. (2019), 'The Politics of Socialist Education in Ghana: The Kwame Nkrumah Ideological Institute, 1961–66', *Journal of African History*, 60(3), 407–428.

Taylor, Edgar Curtis (2019), 'Affective Registers of Postcolonial Crisis: The Kampala Tank Hill Party', *Africa*, 89(3), 541–561.

Young, W. Crawford (1977), 'Bugisu', in Joel Barkan (ed.), *Uganda District Government and Politics 1947–1967*, Madison, WI: African Studies Program, University of Wisconsin-Madison, 89–112.

NOTES

1. For another early approach, from a different angle, see Adrian J. Browne, 'Liberation Ethnology: District Decolonisation, Knowledge Production, and the Neoliberal Revolution in Uganda', in Katherine Bruce-Lockhart, Jonathon L. Earle, Nakanyike B. Musisi and Edgar C. Taylor (eds), *Decolonising State and Society in Uganda: The Politics of Knowledge and Public Life*, Woodbridge: Boydell & Brewer, 2022, 295–316.

2. 'Postcard from Gulu 1964: Obote's UPC Ghosts', *The East African*, 13 December 2014.

3. Akiiki Bomera Mujaju, 'The Demise of the UPCYL and the Rise of NUYO', *African Review*, 3(2), 1973, 291–307; Edgar Curtis Taylor, 'Affective Registers of Postcolonial Crisis: The Kampala Tank Hill Party', *Africa*, 89(3), 2019, 541–561.

4. Notes on a meeting with A. Milton Obote, 11 October 1961, SOAS, MCF 10/147.

5. A.M. Kirunda-Kivejinja, *Uganda: The Crisis of Confidence*, Kampala: Progressive Publishing House, 1995, 17
6. 'Why Just Indians?', *Uganda Argus*, 5 January 1962.
7. 'Kakonge Talks of "Trap"', *Uganda Argus*, 27 June 1962.
8. *UPC Independence Souvenir, 9th October 1962*, Kampala, 1962.
9. 'African Students in Britain', *The Times*, 31 October 1960.
10. 'Uganda Association Censures Lukiko', *Uganda Argus*, 1 July 1958.
11. Report No.4, 10 November 1959, Special Branch, Scotland Yard, 1. UKNA, HO 325/9.
12. LASCAR recorded 5 September 1959, UKNA, KV 2/3985; MI5, 'A Study of the External Threats Bearing on the Internal Security of Commonwealth Territories in Africa', n.d. [*c.* April/May 1960], UKNA, DO 119/1211.
13. For more about this phenomenon in Ghana, see G. Serra and F. Gerits, 'The Politics of Socialist Education in Ghana: The Kwame Nkrumah Ideological Institute, 1961–66', *Journal of African History*, 60(3), 2019, 407–428.
14. Dani W. Nabudere, 'Patrice Lumumba and the Congo', *Ugasso*, 3(2), 1961, 18–21; Dani Nabudere, letter to the editor, *Uganda Argus*, 31 March 1961; B. Chango Machyo, 'Christianity and Afrikan Nationalism', *The Cemian*, 9(2), 1960, 21–24.
15. Uganda Monthly Intelligence Report for the month ending 31 May 1961, UKNA, CO 822/2064.
16. Extract from T/C on Committee of African Orgs, 27 April 1960, UKNA, KV 2/3697.
17. RJW to J. Bourn, 17 May 1963; RJW to Welser, 21 June 1963, UKNA, FCO 168/986; LASCAR Reid, Gollan and Pillay, 12 December 1962, UKNA, KV 2/3986, f. 414a.
18. Jibrin Ibrahim, 'Dan Wadada Nabudere and the Search for Peace', *Daily Trust*, 14 November 2011; Dan Nabudere, 'Report on the Liverpool Council', *GLIM*, 31, 1962, 43.
19. Dani W. Nabudere, *African Social Scientists' Reflections Part 2: Law, the Social Sciences and the Crisis of Relevance*, Nairobi: Heinrich Böll Foundation, 2001, 81.
20. Hart to Wallace, 2 April 1973, UKNA, FCO 31/1583.
21. B. Chango Machyo, 'An Example for Uganda: The Co-Operative Movement in Denmark', *Ugasso*, 3(2), 1961, 18–21; B. Chango Machyo, 'The New Danger', *The United Africa*, September 1961, 4–5; Chango Machyo, 'Pan-Africanism', February 1962, ICS 141/28.
22. 'Uganda Should Send Students to Russia', *Uganda Argus*, 25 April 1962; 'Federation Is the "Only Safeguard" – Students', *Uganda Argus*, 12 June 1962; 'Students Reject Cash Rise', *Uganda Argus*, 5 October 1962; S.A. Ocero, letter to the editor, *Uganda Argus*, 23 November 1962; 'Students Opposed to TV Plan', *Uganda Argus*, 9 April 1963.
23. Communist Party of Great Britain, *28th National Congress: Report of the Executive Committee from January 1961 to December 1962*, London, 1963.
24. E.B. Rugumayo, 'The Place of Youth in Today's African Society', *Ntu*, 1(4), 1962, 4–9.

25. 'Editorial', *Ntu*, 1(1), 1962, 1–5; B. Chango Machyo, *Land Ownership and Economic Progress*, London: Dunbar Press/Lumumba Memorial Publications, 1963.

26. B.C. Machyo, 'Land Titles & Economic Progress', *Ntu*, 1(1), 1962, 17–32, at 19; D. Wadada Nabudere, 'Book Reviews', *Ntu*, 1(4), 1962, 17; 'Editorial: There Is Only One Socialist System', *Ntu*, 2(1), 1963, 1–3; 'Editorial: Africa's Need for an Ideology', *Ntu*, 2(2), 1963, 1–2; Vera Pillay, 'The Common Market', *Ntu*, 1(4), 1962, 9–16.

27. B. Chango Machyo, *Africa in World Trade*, London: Africana Study Group, 1963, 11–15.

28. Amembassy Kampala to Department of State, 28 May 1963, NARA, RG59, Box 4078, SNF 1963, POL 15-1

29. Amembassy Kampala (W. Kennedy Cromwell) to Department of State, 21 July 1963, NARA, SNF 1963, Box 4078, POL Uganda.

30. 'MPs' Pay Rise Brings Protest from UPC – Youth Wings Plan to Demonstrate', *Uganda Argus*, 22 June 1963.

31. J.J. Barya, 'Law, State and Working Class Organisation in Uganda: 1962–1987', unpublished PhD thesis, Warwick: University of Warwick, 1990, 107.

32. J.M. Luande (President of UTUC) to E.K. Welsh, 19 March 1963, IISH, ICFTU, 4618.

33. Security Intelligence Report, Eastern Region, for the month of February 1963', Jinja District Archive, JLOS, Box 8, file 18; Deming (Amembassy Kampala) to Department of State, 27 May 1964, NARA, SNF, 1963, E Uganda.

34. Akiiki Bomera Mujaju, 'Youth Action and Political Development in Uganda', unpublished PhD thesis, New York: Columbia University, 1972, 148–185.

35. S.K. Baguma, 'Press Release', 26 November 1963, in A.M. Kirunda-Kivejinja, *Uganda: The Crisis of Confidence*, Kampala: Progressive Publishing House, 1995, 309.

36. D.W. Nabudere, *Imperialism and Revolution in Uganda*, Dar es Salaam: Onyx Press, 1980, 255.

37. 'Union Man Lashes Out at the U.D.C.', *Uganda Argus*, 3 January 1963; 'Youth Wing and Band for T.U.C.', *Uganda Argus*, 1 April 1963.

38. Amembassy (Dennis A. Flinn, Charge d'Affaires) to State Department, 10 December 1963, ARA, RG 59, Box 3599, SNF 1963, LAB-LABOUR & MANPOWER – Uganda.

39. W. Kennedy Cromwell to Raymond J. Barrett, 15 May 1963, NARA, RG 59, Entry A1 3110H, Box 6, Records relating to Uganda, 1959–1964, POL 12.

40. Mujaju, 'Youth Action and Political Development in Uganda', 128.

41. 'Youths' Evidence Is Heard', *Uganda Argus*, 21 January 1964.

42. 'Abolish College', *Uganda Argus*, 2 February 1963; 'Discipline This Man – Mr. Luande', *Uganda Argus*, 12 February 1963; 'Wasuda Attacks "Suggestions"' and 'Luande is an "Agent of Neo-Colonialism"', *Uganda Argus*, 8 February 1963.

43. *Uganda Argus*, 30 January 1964; Amembassy Kampala (Flinn) to Department of State, 12 February 1964, NARA, RG 59, Box 2773, SNF 1964–1966, POL 29 Arrests.; 'State Criticised in Youth Wing Case', *Uganda Argus*, 8 May 1964.

44. 'Uganda Men in China', *Uganda Argus*, 13 May 1963.

45. Yoweri Museveni, *Sowing the Mustard Seed: The Struggle for Freedom and Democracy in Uganda*, Oxford: Macmillan, 1997, 54.
46. Letter to the editor, *Uganda Argus*, 11 August 1961.
47. 'Teso U.P.C. Officials', *Uganda Argus*, 10 February 1962.
48. Amembassy (Dennis A. Flinn) to Department of State, 11 August 1963, NARA, RG 59, SNF 1963, LAB – LAB & MANPOWER Uganda 1963.
49. 'U.P.C. official for Yugoslavia', *Uganda Argus*, 28 August 1962; 'Mr. Ojepa replies to criticism', *Uganda Argus*, 4 September 1962.
50. 'Soroti Union "Vital"', *Uganda Argus*, 12 March 1962; 'Assembly Man Replies to U.P.C.', *Uganda Argus*, 29 September 1962; '"No Confidence in Appointments Board of Teso"', *Uganda Argus*, 4 January 1963; 'U.P.C. Move Attacked by Union', *Uganda Argus*, 3 September 1962; 'Premier Appeals to Strikers', *Uganda Argus*, 18 January 1963.
51. 'Jailed for Bar Attack', *Uganda Argus*, 6 January 1964.
52. 'Prime Minister's Press Release', 7 January 1964, UKNA, DO 213/57.
53. 'Common Man and "Bourgeois"', *Uganda Argus*, 16 August 1963; *Uganda Argus*, 30 January 1964; Amembassy Kampala (Flinn) to Department of State, 12 February 1964, NARA, RG59, Box 2773, SNF 1964-1966, POL 29.
54. Reith to Duke, 30 April 1964, UKNA, DO 168/58.
55. Amembassy Kampala to Department of State, 12 January 1964, NARA, SNF 1963, Box 776, E Uganda.
56. Amembassy Kampala to Department of State, 4 May 1963, SNF 1963 59.250.5.20.4 4077 POL Uganda. A February 1964 seminar paper by Kakonge was published in April 1964 as John Kakonge, 'Scientific Socialism in Africa', *East Africa Journal*, 1(1), 1964, 6–9.
57. 'The End of U.F.L.', *Uganda Argus*, 5 December 1963.
58. 'Youths Pledge Support', *Uganda Argus*, 5 March 1964.
59. J. Kakonge, 'Fundamental Basis of the Uganda Peoples' Congress', in A.M. Kirunda-Kivejinja, *Uganda: The Crisis of Confidence*, Kampala: Progressive Publishing House, 1995, 310–322, at 319.
60. Kampala to Department of State, 5 September 1964, NARA, SNF 1963, BOX 776 E Uganda.
61. 'UPC Youth for Russia', *Uganda Argus*, 1 November 1963.
62. Nalle, 'Sino-Soviet Activities in Uganda', n.d. but 1965, NARA, RG 59, Entry 5235, Box 36, LOT67D34; Kirunda Kivejinja, Bidandi Ssali and Kintu Musoke, *The Sapoba Legacy: A Story of Ideals and Idealism in Ugandan Politics and Family Life*, Kampala: Menha Publishers, 2014, 145.
63. 'Monthly Intelligence Appreciation for the Period Ending 14th February, 1964', 15 February 1964, Kabarole District Archive, Box 385, folder 2; 'Editorial Comments', *Marxism Today*, 8(6), 1964, 161–165, at 162.
64. B. Chango Machyo, *Land Ownership and Economic Progress*, London: Dunbar Press, 1963.
65. Chango Machyo, letter to the editor, *Uganda Argus*, 29 June 1963; J.C. Edmonds, 'Dr Martin Aliker', 25 July 1963, UKNA, FO 1110/1737.
66. Akiiki Mujaju, 'Youth Action and Political Development in Uganda', unpublished PhD thesis, New York: Columbia University, 1972, 140.

67. Dani W. Nabudere, *African Social Scientists' Reflections, Part 2: Law, the Social Sciences and the Crisis of Relevance*, Nairobi: Heinrich Böll Foundation, 2001, 81.

68. Hart to Wallace, 2 April 1973, UKNA, FCO 31/1583; 'Monthly Intelligence Appreciation (for the period ending 18th March, 1964), 19 March 1964, KDA 385/2.

69. 'No Bail for U.P.C. youths', *Uganda Argus*, 25 November 1963; 'Youths Remain in Custody', *Uganda Argus*, 6 December 1963.

70. John Platts-Mills, *Muck, Silk and Socialism: Recollections of a Left-Wing Queen's Counsel*, Wedmore: Paper Publishing, 2001, 394–395.

71. Nabudere, *Imperialism and Revolution in Uganda*, 256.

72. 'Security Intelligence Report, Eastern Region, for the Month of February 1963', Jinja District Archive, JLOS, Box 8, file 18; W. Crawford Young, 'Bugisu', in Joel Barkan (ed.), *Uganda District Government and Politics 1947–1967*, Madison, WI: African Studies Program, University of Wisconsin-Madison, 1977, 89–112, at 105.

73. 'Mr. Masaba Sees Premier', *Uganda Argus*, 22 November 1962.

74. 'Security Intelligence Report, Eastern Region, for the Month of April 1963', Jinja District Archive, JLOS, Box 8, file 18.

75. Crawford Young, 'Bugisu'.

12

Challenging 'African Socialism' through Marxism-Leninism: The University Students African Revolutionary Front in Tanzania

Patrick Norberg

INTRODUCTION

During the tumultuous era of decolonisation, Tanzania[1] became a focal point of left-wing organising in Sub-Saharan Africa, leading Mazrui[2] to call the international fixation with the country 'Tanzaphilia'. This enchantment was derived from Tanzania's openly left-wing and anti-imperialist leadership during whose rule Dar es Salaam became a 'hub for a transnational, global 1960s left'.[3] The existence of this broad left and the development of Tanzania's socialist project did not proceed without internal contradictions, confrontations, and eventually irreconcilable conflict. The Tanzanian left was never a cohesive whole, but was fractured into two lefts which co-existed during the early post-independence period.[4] The first left was the national liberation movement transfigured into a state-led socialist project, espousing progressive ideals, but delivering them in a top-down manner. The second left was composed of a relatively small number of Marxist radicals who arose as the chief critics of the socialist project, but were largely constrained to campus territory. The foremost group of the critical left was the University Students' African Revolutionary Front (USARF) which existed at the University of Dar es Salaam[5] (UDSM) from 1967 to 1970. Despite their short-lived existence, USARF's activities at a strategic moment in Tanzania's history allowed it to wield significant political influence. USARF had a complicated relationship with the Tanzanian state, as it was supportive of the socialist ideals the state propounded, but critical of the utopian nature of the *Ujamaa*[6] project itself. USARF's self-declared ideological position was

Marxist-Leninist, which provided it with the space to criticise the state's theoretical idealism and limited implementation of socialist policies.

This chapter provides an event-driven and theoretically informed account of USARF's development into a left opposition group to the *Ujamaa* project. Most importantly, it highlights the role of the Marxism-Leninism which formed USARF's organisational basis and positioned it outside Tanzania's one-party structure – a space it used to put forward a historical materialist and class-based critique of *Ujamaa*. This chapter draws heavily on largely unknown publications of USARF (including its journals *Cheche* and *Majimaji*), supported by an interview with a leading member of USARF, Georgios Hadjivayanis, as well as the memoirs of other members of the group. The argument is further supported by publications from Nyerere and his critics, and by secondary literature on the development of socialism in Tanzania. First, it will provide a brief historical outline of Tanzania's development to illustrate the political situation which fuelled the country's shift towards socialism. This will be followed by a section providing an event-driven analysis of USARF's formation and its engagements with the Tanzanian state. Finally, it will focus on the disagreements between USARF and the representatives of the *Ujamaa* project.

POST-INDEPENDENCE TANZANIA

Tanzania became independent in 1961, as the national liberation movement spearheaded by the Tanganyika African National Union (TANU) forced the departure of the British. TANU was a petty bourgeois-led movement whose claimed concern was the maintenance of inter-class and racial unity, which led to its decision to transform Tanzania into a one-party state.[7] However, the state's pro-capitalist approach to post-independence economic development led to an increase in inequality while failing to raise living standards for the majority. This created significant social tensions, culminating in the Dar Mutiny of 1964,[8] when the Tanganyika Rifles overtook the government and were suppressed by the British army brought in as a last resort by President Julius Nyerere. While Nyerere's popularity and authority among Tanzanians remained undisputed, the mutiny led to a crackdown on trade unions and civil society organisations.

Although the crackdown consolidated TANU's position, it did little to suppress the underlying class conflict in Tanzanian society. This found expression in a generational conflict in the National Service Crisis of 1966. In response to the mutiny, the state created the National Service to serve as a political and paramilitary organisation for the nation's youth with the purpose of cultivating patriotism. Its harsh conditions made it extremely unpopular, leading the state to make it compulsory for all university graduates. This provoked a protracted confrontation between students and bureaucratic elites. The conflict, in essence a struggle within the petty bourgeoisie, where two generations were fighting over access to the same limited privileged positions on the Tanzanian job market, was important for two reasons. Firstly, UDSM served as a symbolic achievement of TANU's rule, as education was the highest social expense for the Tanzanian state.[9] Secondly, TANU's entire governance agenda had been built on the rhetorical justification of a self-sufficient future, and the youth occupied the centre ground as both the agents and beneficiaries of this transformation.[10] After mass demonstrations, the crisis of 1966 culminated in the expulsion of 338 students from UDSM, and finally 'forced the emergent comprador bourgeoisie to awaken to reality' of postcolonial inequality.[11] Nyerere's response was the Arusha Declaration.

THE ARUSHA DECLARATION

The Arusha Declaration was unveiled in 1967 as a party document[12] that set out TANU's vision of *Ujamaa* and articulated its core ideas of socialism, self-reliance and democracy. The underlying sentiment of the Declaration was its idealist conceptualisation of socialism which viewed it as 'a way of life'.[13] Socialism was defined as fidelity towards a set of egalitarian principles rather than a specific organisation of the relations of production. This idealist socialism was presented as arising from pre-colonial Tanzania, or as Nyerere put it, 'we, in Africa, have no more need of being "converted" to socialism than we have of being "taught" democracy. Both are rooted in our own past – in the traditional society which produced us.'[14] This is linked to the concept of self-reliance as an alternative foundation for development following the failure of the previous capital-dependent model during 1961–67. Namely, as reliance on foreign direct investment in extractive sectors proved insufficient to fund industrialisation, the focus shifted to individual effort with the hope that it could be aggregated upward. The notion of bottom-up unity was predicted in the vision of *Ujamaa* as a form of non-confrontational socialism, where cooperation between classes overruled antagonism.[15]

The Declaration was immediately followed by a spree of nationalisations, from banks to import–export houses, and the later implementation of a leadership code (*Mwongozo*) which sought to limit wealth accumulation among the political elite. The crucial question of rural development was addressed with a large-scale villagisation policy that sought to reorganise the countryside into *Ujamaa* villages – units of collective economic and social reproduction. Grassroots movements sprung up across the country in response to Nyerere's socialist policies.[16] One such instance took place at the campus of the UDSM, where the Declaration unleashed energies that had been gradually building up since the foundation of the university.

RADICALISATION AT THE UNIVERSITY OF DAR ES SALAAM

Prior to 1967, the UDSM had been run based on the Western model of higher education, with strictly defined disciplines and with the majority of faculty coming from Western countries. This was soon challenged by a group of radical expatriate academics called the Group of Nine.[17] The group's critique challenged the isolationism of the university and sought to reorient its work towards a critical engagement with the socio-political situation in Tanzania.[18] Exploiting the space opened by the Arusha Declaration, the group managed to create a Common Course compulsory for all students that provided an interdisciplinary exploration of progressive theories. It was this process which established Marxism-Leninism as an important stream of thought within the university.[19] It is important to note that the mainstreaming of Marxism in Tanzanian academia only became possible due to the influx of international scholars with socialist sympathies who were drawn to Nyerere's African revolution.[20] And even though these international scholars came from very different backgrounds, such as the Guyanese Rodney and the Italian Arrighi, the formation of a progressive grouping at the UDSM was made possible by their allegiance to Marxism.[21]

It was in these ideologically charged conditions that USARF was founded to take up Nyerere's call to continue the debate on socialism.[22] In the spirit of Nyerere's promulgation that 'the youth should always be on his left',[23] USARF sought to promote radical left-wing ideas to transform East African campuses from spaces of reaction to hotbeds of revolution. The importance of USARF went beyond student politics, as the UDSM had a uniquely influential role in the political affairs of Tanzanian society.[24] Due to Tanzania's colonial legacy, there was no tradition of student radicalism at the UDSM, which meant that students tended to view themselves as the elite-in-waiting. As a result, the number of militants joining USARF was relatively low, ranging from 40 to 100 from a student population of around 1,600.[25] The only political organisation on campus which preceded it was the TANU

Youth League (TYL), which served to promote *Ujamaa*'s ideas among the youth, but it lacked radicalism and was only open to Tanzanian nationals.[26] Welcoming non-Tanzanian members became a unique recruitment point for USARF, as it had members from all races, religions and regions of Tanzania, in addition to comrades from Uganda, Kenya, Malawi and other African states.[27]

USARF needed to carve out a space for its existence to distance itself from *Ujamaa*, a space which, while contingent on the goodwill of the state, nevertheless granted it sufficient autonomy to function as left opposition to Nyerere. This was necessary because TANU's one-party state increasingly dominated civil society organisation, developing a proclivity to curb critical thinking in favour of the party line.[28] Moreover, party organisations functioned as vehicles for individual ambition and career aspirations. USARF therefore embraced the theoretical framework of Marxism-Leninism as 'scientific' socialism which could be counterposed to the idealism of the *Ujamaa* project – turning them into the left opposition: supportive of *Ujamaa*'s aims, but acutely aware of the limitations of its methods.

USARF rapidly became a political and ideological force on campus. Its foundational activities were concerned with self-education and the development of revolutionary theory through ideological classes.[29] Oriented around the Leninist maxim that 'there can be no revolutionary party without a revolutionary theory', the classes sought to develop human resources for Tanzania's socialist development. Importantly, USARF's Marxism-Leninism was creative and non-dogmatic, strongly grounded in a dialectical materialist outlook, but sufficiently inclusive to engage with a variety of left-wing ideas. Despite USARF's view of Marxism-Leninism as a 'scientific' methodology, it was not beholden to a positivist or a specifically sectarian perspective, instead identifying with the ruthless critique found in the works of both Marx and Lenin. The curriculum included earlier authors such as Marx, Engels and Lenin, as well as later ones ranging from Nkrumah and Fanon to Baran and Sweezy. These classes were attended and conducted by leading academics such as Rodney and Saul, who were associate members of USARF.[30] While UDSM had a well-stocked library,[31] USARF also had extensive access to Marxist classics from the Soviet, Chinese and North Korean embassies,[32] and obtained modern publications from the Monthly Review Press. A key activity was organising seminars and public lectures by visiting academics and activists such as Stokely Carmichael and C.L.R. James. The ideological undercurrent of these events was always Marxist, as can be seen from the celebrations organised by USARF, such as Karl Marx, Che Guevara and Mao Zedong days.[33]

Aware of its class position and the limitations of campus-based activism, USARF sought to form connections with the workers and peasants of Tanzania. Avid readers of Amílcar Cabral's 'The Weapon of Theory',[34] USARF's romanticised vision of political activism was the notion of committing class suicide. In pursuit of this, it organised monthly visits to *Ujamaa* villages, which included 'labouring with the masses' and engaging in reciprocal political dialogue.[35] While these activities do not amount to radical left-wing organising, they illustrate USARF's commitment to the *Ujamaa* notion of self-reliance, allied to a view of society as class-divided.

THE FOUNDING OF *CHECHE*

The most important moment in USARF's development was the founding of its journal *Cheche,* which took its name from Lenin's *Iskra* and Nkrumah's *Spark* and served to promote revolutionary ideas.[36] Despite being a cyclostyled magazine produced with next to no resources, *Cheche* was the first dedicated space for the discussion of Tanzania in a Marxist framework. In the first issue, the chairmen of USARF and TYL[37] set out the magazine's primary focus in no uncertain terms:

> Let no one misunderstand, lest they consider this to be an advocation of the deceptive, superficial, idealist and historically retrogressive theories – the so-called 'African Socialisms' that have sprouted up everywhere in Africa. No! Socialism is one; scientific and international.[38]

There were 293 copies printed of the first issue, and demand far exceeded the available resources. Copies were sold to students and circulated to African liberation movements in Dar, and embassies of both socialist and capitalist nations, and sent abroad to Kenya, Uganda, America, Sweden, Germany and the United Kingdom.[39] Benefiting from the extensive academic freedom permitted by Nyerere's rule, the first issue of *Cheche* featured articles on 'Why We Should Take Up Rifles' by Yoweri Museveni and a denunciation of the UDSM's educational model by Issa Shivji in 'The Educated Barbarians'. There was an overwhelmingly positive reaction among progressive elements in Tanzania. Perhaps most importantly, *Cheche* was enthusiastically embraced by Tanzania's struggling secondary school students, among whom radical tendencies were developing.[40] On the other hand, the official reaction, encompassing the political establishment and mainstream media, was entirely negative – it saw *Cheche* as embracing Leninist tendencies and promoting violence. From the outside, it was felt that USARF was turning the university into an institution for Marxist indoctrination, as academics from neighbouring Uganda's Makerere university published warnings of the communist threat at the UDSM.[41] Domestically, the Catholic Church had originally supported the *Ujamaa* project, but with USARF's rise to prominence, felt that it had been compromised by Marxist influences.[42]

An important controversy arose from the *Second Seminar of the East and Central African Youth* which was organised by TYL and had official state support. During the seminar, Rodney gave a presentation on the 'Ideology of the African Revolution', in which he denounced post-independence African governments as neo-colonial puppets.[43] As the lecture was reprinted in the state-owned *The Nationalist*, it was met by a strong rebuke titled 'Revolutionary Hot-Air', thought to originate from Nyerere himself.[44] The article attacked Rodney for his calls to overthrow African governments, and finished with a threat: 'those who insist upon indulging in such practices will have to accept the consequences of their indulgence'.[45] Consequently, USARF's reputation as being communist extremists alerted Nyerere sufficiently to organise a question-and-answer session on the UDSM campus which Hirji[46] describes as a 'milestone in the rising tensions between the state and campus radicals'. While USARF had prepared a set of critical questions for the occasion, it was clear from 'the atmosphere' that Nyerere had arrived with a mission to condemn the radicals, leading Saul to conclude that 'twice in recent months a cannon had been used to swat a fly – and a friendly fly at that!'[47]

NYERERE'S IDEALISM AND *UJAMAA*'S UTOPIANISM

The tension between nominally socialist aims and their failed implementation was a recurrent problem for national liberation movements in Africa.[48] Arrighi,[49] who was at the UDSM during 1966–69, saw *Ujamaa* as a nationalist movement without a real basis for genuine socialist development. USARF on the other hand, despite TANU's obvious shortcomings, saw the Arusha Declaration as the first step in Tanzania's break with capitalism. In the early post-Declaration period, it was common among Marxists in Tanzania to bargain with Nyerere in the hope of shifting his positions.[50] It was considered vital for USARF to challenge the weak grounding of *Ujamaa* on a theoretical level. But Nyerere was an idealist, and his intellectual background ranged from Christian humanism to the Fabian tradition.[51] He argued that 'human equality before God which is the basis of all the great religions of the world is also the basis of the political philosophy of socialism'.[52] That is, Nyerere promoted a moralistic understanding of socialism which was reliant on the individual dedication of TANU leaders at all levels of the state. This was especially important due to the nature of the one-party state, where the impetus for socialist development moved in a top-down manner. Similar to his view on building socialism, Nyerere saw capitalist exploitation as stemming from individual laziness and greed. Although the Declaration postulates a classless society as the aim of socialism, Nyerere failed to acknowledge economic structures or class relations as determinants of constructing *Ujamaa*. His approach to socialism can be seen as 'revolution by evolution',[53] a reformism which seeks to establish an exploitation-free society through gradual institutional development. Nyerere argued in *The Purpose of Man* that 'the important thing for us is the extent to which we succeed in preventing the exploitation of one man by another, and in spreading the concept of working together cooperatively for the common good instead of competitively for individual private gain'[54] – rejecting any fundamental contradiction between the interests of the poor and the powerful. Nyerere also saw capitalism as synonymous with colonialism, viewing capital accumulation as a creed imported from Britain, and thus something to be defeated with the correct nationalist attitude.

USARF identified these utopian tendencies as a key threat to building socialism in Tanzania, decrying the subjectivism at the heart of Nyerere's thinking which served to obfuscate the country's continued development of capitalist relations of production. The editorial for the second volume of *Cheche* argued that 'a realistic and clear theory is an indispensable guide to successful action' in order for 'the nature of class struggle and imperialist domination [to] be exposed'.[55] Criticising the lack of scientific analysis, USARF's aim was to warn Nyerere of the dangers of building socialism through bureaucratic means.[56]

While USARF did not question Nyerere's moral commitment, it criticised his lack of material analysis and his reluctance to engage with the concept of class. Even though Nyerere would frequently use the term 'class', USARF distinguished between a materialist understanding of class which focused on the antagonism between workers and capitalists and an idealist notion of class based on an individual's mindset. When Nyerere rejected materialist class analysis due to his hostility to Marxism-Leninism as a philosophy based on conflict and remained steadfast in his commitment to class unity,

Shivji retorted by asking, 'how can we talk about a "Tanzanian Revolution" without even knowing the friends and enemies of such a revolution?'[57]

There were nevertheless still signs of Nyerere's shift to the left, such as the nationalisation of *The Standard*, where he installed an openly pro-Soviet editor from South Africa, Frene Ginwala.[58] Under Ginwala, the paper took an explicitly Marxist line and provided extensive coverage of USARF's work as a homegrown Marxist-Leninist tendency. Having reached an agreement with Ginwala to publish a weekly column, *The Standard* became an important space for USARF's publications. During this period, Nyerere regularly invited USARF members to his private residence for meetings, as he wished to maintain communications with the 'true socialists'.[59] The meetings with Nyerere were cordial and saw him expressing general agreement with USARF's arguments. For example, USARF presented an argument that increased class stratification between the bureaucratic elite and the people resulted in an erosion of democratic accountability. Nyerere acknowledged the critique and made a gesture by amending the universities' bill to give greater representation to students. Hadjivayanis[60] argues that this followed a general pattern of appeasement on behalf of Nyerere, where he gave USARF small concessions to pacify it.

DISENGAGEMENT AND THE NEO-COLONIAL STATE

As enthusiasm around the Declaration waned and the limitations of TANU's reformism were becoming more apparent, the cautious support Marxists had lent to Nyerere started to flounder. The key shift within USARF's approach came with the publication of Shivji's 'The Silent Class Struggle' as a special issue of *Cheche*. Shivji's long-form essay, which later became the founding text of the Dar Debates,[61] served as an attempt to provide a materialist analysis of the post-Declaration economic developments. Shivji's paper pinpointed Nyerere's failure to challenge imperialism and his general misunderstanding of neo-colonialism as the main factors which hindered any substantial shift towards socialism in Tanzania. Despite Nyerere's progressive credentials, Shivji's paper showed how his nominally socialist policies in the post-Declaration period were leading to the entrenchment of neo-colonialism. Tanzania was locked into a state of underdevelopment due to its reliance on foreign capital with an interest in short-term profits from primary commodity production which failed to facilitate investment into industry and thus lead to an integrated economy.

The paper's focus was the post-Declaration nationalisations which had been undertaken in TANU's pursuit of self-reliance. In studying their impact, Shivji found that the newly deprived capitalists were brought back in through management contracts, the extractive nature of the economy remained unchanged, and a new stratum of economic bureaucracy was created to run the para-statal companies. In fact, many of the companies saw significant benefits from nationalisations in the form of secured profit rates and a more docile labour force.[62] Therefore, as the class structure remained unchanged, the exploitation of Tanzanian workers and peasants continued as well. Shivji argued that 'the fundamental and antagonistic contradiction … is between imperialism and the people',[63] and its local manifestation is the rise of a secondary contradiction between the people and the new economic bureaucracy. This bureaucratic element had been developing since Tanzania gained independence in 1961, and had captured the state through the nationalisation policy. This highlighted how, by not going far enough, the post-Declaration nationalisations strengthened the presence of neo-colonialism in Tanzania instead of weakening it.

USARF's perspective was influenced by Lenin's *Imperialism: The Highest Stage of Capitalism*, which led it to acknowledge international capital's regressive dominance of (post-)colonial elites. While this new social stratum was developed through political means, Shivji saw that due to the presence of enlightened leaders, the bureaucrats did not yet hold enough power to stamp out the progressive movement. Nevertheless, he saw TANU's mass party formation as insufficient to stop their rise, as it lacked both the theoretical tools to appreciate this danger and the political power to challenge it. Around this time Nyerere had declared that he did not think it necessary to expel non-socialist members from TANU – a nominally socialist party.[64] Therefore, Shivji saw the transformation of TANU into a vanguard party as the only possibility to continue Tanzania's progressive course, arguing that 'the supremacy of the Party manifested through the ultimate control by a committed vanguard is therefore a prerequisite for destroying the old social order and building of socialism'.[65] The vanguard's capacity to solve the secondary contradiction between the bureaucrats and the workers was contingent on resolving the primary contradiction – Tanzania needed to disengage from the global economy. The problem was that the exploitative tendencies of imperialism were not directly experienced by the workers and peasants, thus confrontation with imperialism was mediated by the petty bourgeois stratum.[66] The social base of the petty bourgeoisie was established within international capital, which had assigned them the role of maintaining the status quo. Therefore, if the bureaucrats building socialism were driven by imperatives posed by international corporations, Shivji argued that TANU was building 'socialism' through capitalist means.[67] By that point, Shivji's paper was the most aggressive position USARF had taken against TANU, dismissing *Ujamaa* as a petty bourgeois project, and effectively stating that it needed to be overcome. USARF had previously challenged post-colonial African leaders as 'Uncle Toms' who had only achieved 'paper' and 'briefcase' independence, but they had always distinguished Tanzania as an exception.[68] This was no longer the case. The publication of *The Silent Class Struggle* served as an acknowledgement that Nyerere could not be turned towards a Marxist-Leninist perspective, thus the way to pursue disengagement was vanguardist agitation. In this context, Rodney commented that 'Shivji's paper is itself a contribution to the silent class struggle.'[69]

Disengagement formed a central and radical part of USARF's platform. In the preface to Shivji's essay, USARF weighed up total isolation and decreasing economic dependency, viewing disengagement as a way to limit imperialist resource extraction. Museveni argued that 'the acid test of all the measures taken in Uganda, Zambia, Tanzania, etc. is whether they fundamentally alter our dependence on imperialist economies in all aspects'.[70] Underpinning USARF's demand for disengagement was the aim to see Tanzania align itself with the socialist states against imperial powers. This approach was vehemently rejected by Nyerere, as USARF had already found out when it brought up this idea at a private meeting.[71] Non-alignment formed the basis of Nyerere's foreign policy, which allowed him to maintain relative autonomy from both capitalist and state-socialist countries. USARF's critique of non-alignment, which argued for closer collaboration with the socialist world, challenged Nyerere to evaluate the primacy of 'African' within African Socialism.

THE INTERNATIONALISM OF MARXISM-LENINISM AND THE NATIONALISM OF *UJAMAA*

As has been highlighted above, Nyerere's understanding of socialism was based on the notion of rediscovering the egalitarian tendencies already present in Tanzania's past. However, he was also aware of the necessity to reinvent this pre-capitalist socialist tendency to fit the developmental needs of a post-colonial country. There was a tension between the logics of traditionalism and modernisation throughout the *Ujamaa* period, which came to the fore through the conflict between the internationalism embedded within socialist ideas and Nyerere's suspicion of anything 'foreign'.[72] For example, under Nyerere Tanzania opened the first and only drive-in cinema in the socialist world, but he also signed on to suppression of black American culture by banning soul music.[73] Thus, even though Nyerere was one of the most vocal advocates for Pan-Africanism in the twentieth century, his anti-colonial sentiments led him to a conservative distrust of foreign influences. Nowhere was this clearer than in Nyerere's attitude to Marxism-Leninism, which he considered unsuitable for his country, proclaiming: 'if Marx had been born in Tanzania, he would have written about growing cotton'.[74] Nyerere had a very derivative understanding of Marxism and was often stuck on dogmatic interpretations of Marxist ideas, such as equating them with the two-stage theory of revolution. In denouncing Marxism, Nyerere stated: 'there is no African Marx in this country. We are a bunch of pragmatists … We have no bible.'[75]

In this context, USARF members were the natural suspects in the eyes of the ruling party, as they were simultaneously a highly diverse and transnational group and argued for the relevance of Marxism-Leninism to Tanzania. TANU's rulebook, which prohibited non-Tanzanians from joining party organisations, had spurred the formation of USARF, as those left out found a political home there. In fact, the internationalism inherent in Marxism-Leninism was an important factor which attracted USARF members towards it, as it united the various national struggles across the world for a common cause. USARF entirely rejected Nyerere's notion of Marxism as foreign to Tanzania, arguing along Leninist lines that:

> our revolution must be made according to our local conditions and according to our analysis. This does not mean that we are chauvinists or racists. It in fact means that we understand the essence of Marxism: theory being determined by practice according to the concrete conditions.[76]

Hirji stated that 'capitalism was born, grew and matured essentially as an international mode of production and hence the class-divisions overflow national borders'.[77] Thus, USARF rejected the usefulness of methodological nationalism for socialist analysis, as it saw socialism as only viable as an internationalist project. USARF contested the meaning of Nyerere's Pan-Africanism, which it argued was neither well-defined nor consistent. Its critiques of African neo-colonial leaders were constantly met with strict condemnation by the state, highlighting how Nyerere's vision of Pan-Africanism was anti-colonial rather than socialist.

USARF's dedication to internationalism was most explicit in its support for anti-imperialist struggles across Africa. Benefiting from the radical scene in Dar es Salaam, USARF formed links with radical expatriates, socialist groupings and liberation movements.[78] It used various means to support these organisations, from hosting their events and fundraising for their causes to creating international linkages between left-wing movements. USARF was especially close to Frente de Libertação Moçambique (FRELIMO, Mozambique Liberation Front), which had many adherents of Marxism and subscribed to the analyses produced in *Cheche*. During this period, USARF members undertook a trip to the liberated areas of Mozambique, based on which they produced a pamphlet to counter reactionary propaganda against FRELIMO in Tanzania.[79] USARF saw militant liberation movements as central to overcoming imperialism. As Museveni put it: 'struggle, with armed struggle as its highest form is the only way to end exploitation'.[80]

Ivaska[81] argues that USARF's internationalist focus and transnational makeup were the reason for its sudden demise. On 9 November 1970, members of TYL were summoned to meet the vice chancellor of the university, who relayed to them an order from State House that both USARF and *Cheche* must cease immediately. The order, which came directly from Nyerere, offered two separate rationales: firstly, USARF did not represent any significant group within Tanzania and therefore should not meddle in the affairs of the country, and secondly, USARF was reliant on foreign ideologies and promoting 'Russian socialism', as its journal was named after Lenin's *Iskra*.[82] The extent to which these charges functioned as a pretext or represented actual concerns is up for speculation, but they clearly framed USARF as a foreign element. Hadjivayanis sees some legitimacy to this concern, arguing that as Nyerere had read Lenin, he was aware of how the spark had kindled in other countries, and thus sought to squash it before it spread in Tanzania.[83] When USARF was banned, the TYL was granted a monopoly on political activities on the UDSM campus which displaced non-Tanzanian radicals and pushed campus activism in a decidedly nationalist direction.[84]

Peter and Mvungi have argued that 'the death of USARF nipped in the bud the growth of a real revolutionary left in Tanzania'.[85] After graduating from the UDSM, the state posted USARF members across the country to prevent their organising collectively.[86] The banning of USARF followed a general slide into authoritarianism by the state, where the victims were largely the radical left and foreign elements. Ginwala was expelled from *The Standard* and the country in 1971, the following year a Kenyan student leader was removed from the UDSM by riot police and deported,[87] and most importantly, Nyerere went to great lengths to suppress the post-*Mwongozo* wave of wildcat strikes and workers' struggles.

While Nyerere tolerated it, USARF was allowed to thrive, but when he cracked down, USARF ceased to exist – foreshadowing a slide into a more authoritarian form of governance which eventually suffocated the civic energies behind the *Ujamaa* project. Nevertheless, Nyerere's earlier enlightened rule gave USARF more space to oppose his government than was allowed for most other left-wing movements across Africa.

CONCLUSION

Despite USARF's short-lived existence, the group was at the forefront of political developments in Tanzania as the chief critic of *Ujamaa*. Its embrace of Marxism-Leninism conditioned the form and direction of the group's activities, functioning as a focal point which drew together all progressive elements inside the UDSM. In this context, USARF had some affinity with the idea of vanguardism, seeing its members as petty bourgeois class traitors who would rise to lead the workers. Throughout its existence, USARF's actions on the outside of mainstream political structures were facilitated by Marxism-Leninism – that is, embracing a scientific form of socialism which could be opposed to the utopianism of African socialism allowed USARF to outflank *Ujamaa*, which sought to be the sole representation of progressive ideas in Tanzania.

By adopting a historically materialist reading of society, USARF was able to establish Marxist categories of abstraction, focusing on class struggle and relations of production, and thus to unmask the nominally socialist rhetoric of TANU. By seeking to expose the neo-colonial nature of African socialism, USARF was able to foresee many of the limitations of the Tanzanian path to socialism, some of which became fatal to the project itself. It exposed the myth of a 'classless Africa', laying bare the ruling class formation taking place within the one-party state, a danger which TANU itself acknowledged only after banning USARF. USARF's constant attacks on the economic bureaucracy subservient to the imperialist cause put Nyerere in a difficult position, as the *Ujamaa* project depended on the nominal unity of classes. In a speech to the Catholic bishops, Nyerere argued that he had to ban USARF due to its promotion of communism which went beyond the logic of *Ujamaa*,[88] highlighting that while Marxism-Leninism was USARF's driving force, it was also that which led to its demise. Nyerere saw USARF as a great threat precisely because there was no way to mediate the inherent conflict between his idealist socialism and the materialism of Marxism.

NOTES

1. The union between Tanganyika and Zanzibar forming Tanzania took place in 1964, but for simplicity I will refer to the country as Tanzania throughout.
2. Ali Mazrui, 'Tanzaphilia', *Transition*, 31, 1967, 20–26.
3. Andrew Ivaska, *Cultured States: Youth, Gender, and Modern Style in 1960s Dar Es Salaam*, Durham, NC: Duke University Press, 2011, 189.
4. Sabatho Nyamsenda, 'The Left in Tanzania: Agonising or Organising?', *Review of African Political Economy*, 45(158), 2018, 609–677.
5. Founded as a constituent college of the University of East Africa in 1961, it became a full university in 1970.
6. *Ujamaa*, a Swahili word which translates as 'familyhood', denotes the Tanzanian version of African socialism – a developmental project informed by a set of humanist and anti-capitalist principles.
7. Idrian N. Resnick, *The Long Transition: Building Socialism in Tanzania*, New York: Monthly Review Press, 1981.
8. Andrew Coulson, *Tanzania: A Political Economy*, 2nd edn, Oxford: Oxford University Press, 2013, 178.
9. Olivier Provini, 'The University of Dar Es Salaam: A Post-Nyerere Institution of Higher Education? Legacies, Continuities and Changes in an Institutional Space (1961–2010)', in Marie-Aude Fouéré (ed.), *Remembering Julius Nyerere in Tanzania: History, Legacy, Memories*, Dar es Salaam: Mkuki na Nyota, 2015, 5.
10. Ivaska, *Cultured States*.
11. Chris Peter and Sengondo Mvungi, 'The State and Student Struggles', in Issa G. Shivji (ed.), *The State and the Working People in Tanzania*, Dakar: Conseil pour le développement, 1986, 165.
12. The Arusha Declaration was written and pushed through by Nyerere himself as a left-wing intervention that was opposed by the reactionary elements in TANU.
13. TANU, 'The Arusha Declaration: Socialism and Self-Reliance', in Julius Nyerere, *Ujamaa: Essays on Socialism*, Dar es Salaam: Oxford University Press, 1974, 234.
14. Nyerere, *Ujamaa*, 12.
15. Julius Nyerere, *Freedom and Socialism/Uhuru na Ujamaa*, Dar es Salaam: Oxford University Press, 1968.
16. Coulson, *Tanzania*.
17. The Group of Nine included high-profile academics such as Walter Rodney, Terence Ranger, Giovanni Arrighi, Grant Kamenju and John Saul.
18. Mahmood Mamdani, 'The African University', *London Review of Books*, 19 July 2018.
19. Peter and Mvungi, 'The State and Student Struggles'.
20. Andrew Ivaska, 'Movement Youth in a Global Sixties Hub: The Everyday Lives of Transnational Activists in Postcolonial Dar Es Salaam', in Richard Jobs and

David Pomfret (eds), *Transnational Histories of Youth in the Twentieth Century*, London: Palgrave Macmillan, 2015, 188–210.

21. Immanuel Harisch, 'Walter Rodney's Dar Es Salaam Years', Master's thesis, Vienna: University of Vienna, 2018.

22. Issa Shivji, 'Rodney and Radicalism on the Hill 1966–1974', *MajiMaji*, 43, 1980, 29–39.

23. Yoweri Museveni, 'My Three Years in Tanzania', *Cheche*, 2, 1970, 12–15, at 14.

24. Ivaska, *Cultured States*.

25. John Saul, 'Radicalism and the Hill', *East Africa Journal*, 7(12), 1970, 27–30.

26. The national TYL was at that point engaged in a campaign to police women's dress code by fighting against mini-skirts.

27. Karim Hirji (ed.), *Cheche: Reminiscences of a Radical Magazine*, Dar es Salaam: Mkuki na Nyota, 2010.

28. George Hadjivayanis, interview with a member of USARF, *Conversation*, 15 August 2019.

29. Hirji, *Cheche*.

30. Rodney only thanks two people by name in the introduction to his seminal *How Europe Underdeveloped Africa* (London: Bogle-L'Ouverture Publications, 1970), Hirji and Mapolu, both of whom were USARF members.

31. Iconoclast, 'Nairobi Diary', *Cheche*, 2, 1970, 39–42.

32. Hadjivayanis, interview.

33. Ibid.

34. 'The Weapon of Theory' was an address given by Amílcar Cabral to the first *Tricontinental Conference*, which took place in Havana in January 1966; see https://www.marxists.org/subject/africa/cabral/1966/weapon-theory.htm.

35. Zakia Meghji, 'Sisterly Activism', in Hirji, *Cheche*, 77–82.

36. Shivji, 'Rodney and Radicalism on the Hill 1966–1974'.

37. At this point, TYL and USARF had a significant overlap in membership.

38. N. Kasihwaki and J. Kamala, 'Message from the Revolutionary Front and T.Y.L., University College', *Cheche*, 1, 1969, 3.

39. Hirji, *Cheche*.

40. Hadjivayanis, interview.

41. Grant Kamenju, 'In Defence of a Socialist Concept of Universities', in L. Cliffe and J. Saul (eds), *Socialism in Tanzania: Volume 2*, Dar es Salaam: East African Publishing House, 1973, 67–68.

42. Issa Shivji, 'Mwalimu and Marx in Contestation: Dialogue or Diatribe?', *Agrarian South: Journal of Political Economy*, 6(2), 2017, 188–220.

43. Hirji, *Cheche*.

44. John Saul, 'Book Review: Nyerere on Socialism', *Cheche*, 3, 1970, 40–42.

45. Ivaska, *Cultured States*, 158.

46. Hirji, *Cheche*, 41.

47. Saul, 'Radicalism and the Hill', 29.

48. David A. McDonald, 'Icon(oclastic): John S Saul Reflects on Southern African Liberation Struggles', *Journal of Contemporary African Studies*, 34(2), 2016), 300–308.

49. Giovanni Arrighi, 'The Winding Paths of Capital', *New Left Review*, 56, 2009, 61–94.
50. Cranford Pratt, 'Tanzania's Transition to Socialism: Reflections of a Democratic Socialist,' in Bismarck U. Mwansasu (ed.), *Towards Socialism in Tanzania*, Dar es Salaam: East African Publishing House, 1979, 193–237.
51. Shivji, 'Mwalimu and Marx in Contestation'.
52. Nyerere, *Ujamaa*, 79.
53. Mohamed Babu, *Babu: I Saw the Future and It Works: Essays Celebrating the Life of Comrade Abdulrahman Mohamed Babu, 1924–1996*, ed. Haroub Othman, London: E&D, 2001, 28.
54. Nyerere, *Ujamaa*, 102.
55. USARF, 'Editorial', *Cheche*, 1, 1969, 1–2.
56. Issa Shivji, 'The Silent Class Struggle', *Cheche*, special issue, August 1970.
57. Shivji, 'Class Struggle', 2.
58. Trevor Grundy, 'Frene Ginwala, the Lenin Supplement, and the Storm Drains of History', https://www.politicsweb.co.za/opinion/frene-ginwala-the-lenin-supplement-and-the-storm-d, 15 August 2017.
59. Hirji, *Cheche*, 56.
60. Hadjivayanis, interview.
61. The Dar Debates were a far-ranging discussion of global proportions in the 1970–80s which concerned the socialist experiments of less developed countries, particularly focusing on the pitfalls of neo-colonialism and ruling class formation. USARF's analysis of *Ujamaa* in Tanzania was foundational for these debates. See Yashpal Tandon (ed.), *University of Dar es Salaam Debate on Class, State and Imperialism*, Dar es Salaam: Tanzania Publishing House, 1982. See also next chapter in this volume 'Questions from the Dar es Salam Debates'.
62. A Namama, 'Does Nationalisation Help Stamp Out Exploitation?', *Cheche*, 3, 1970, 19–23.
63. Shivji, 'The Silent Class Struggle', 33.
64. John Saul, 'Who Is the Immediate Enemy?', in *The Silent Class Struggle*, Tanzanian Studies, 2, Dar es Salaam: Tanzania Publishing House, 1974, 69–78.
65. Shivji, 'The Silent Class Struggle', 37.
66. Walter Rodney, 'Some Implications of the Question of Disengagement from Imperialism', *MajiMaji*, 1, 1971, 3–8.
67. Shivji, 'The Silent Class Struggle', 38.
68. Yoweri Museveni, 'Why We Should Take up Rifles', *Cheche*, 1, 1969, 32–37, at 34.
69. Rodney, 'Some Implications of the Question of Disengagement from Imperialism', 66.
70. Yoweri Museveni, 'On "The Silent Class Struggle"', *Cheche*, 3, 1970, 35–39, at 37.
71. Hirji, *Cheche*.
72. Laura Fair, 'Drive-In Socialism: Debating Modernities and Development in Dar Es Salaam, Tanzania', *American Historical Review*, 118(4), 2013, 1,077–1,104.
73. Ivaska, 'Movement Youth in a Global Sixties Hub'.
74. Hadjivayanis, interview.
75. Pratt, 'Tanzania's Transition to Socialism', 237.
76. Museveni, 'Why We Should Take up Rifles'.

77. Karim Hirji, 'Salient Implications of the Silent Class Struggle', *Cheche*, 3, 1970, 23–35.
78. Hirji, *Cheche*.
79. USARF, 'Our Last Stand', in Hirji, *Cheche*, 207–212.
80. Museveni, 'Why We Should Take up Rifles', 35.
81. Ivaska, *Cultured States*.
82. Hirji, *Cheche*.
83. Hadjivayanis, interview.
84. Hirji, *Cheche*.
85. Peter and Mvungi, 'The State and Student Struggles', 180.
86. Hadjivayanis, interview.
87. Colin Legum, *Africa: The Year of the Students: – a Survey of Students Politics in Universities and Schools*, Africa Contemporary Record Current Affairs Series, London: Rex Collings, 1972.
88. Karim F. Hirji, 'The African University: A Critical Comment', *Pambazuka News*, https://www.pambazuka.org/education/african-university-critical-comment, 30 August 2018.

13
Questions from the
Dar es Salaam Debates[1]

Zeyad el Nabolsy

This chapter aims to revisit some of the key questions which were debated at the University of Dar es Salaam during the 1970s and 1980s. The University of Dar es Salaam was a hotbed of progressive politics during the period in question. Radial political economy was frequently taught and discussed by the students and professors at the university.[2] The ruling party, the Tanganyika African National Union (TANU), under the leadership of Julius Nyerere, was embarked on a project of building socialism, but this was not a Marxist project, rather it was informed by the theory of 'African Socialism' which was adhered to by Nyerere. Proponents of African Socialism claimed that because African societies were and are classless societies, a theory of social transformation which was centred on class struggle was inapplicable to such societies.[3] There were other proponents of African Socialism, but it was only in Tanzania that this theory was applied as a theory of socialist development. The proponents of African Socialism in Tanzania held that the situation there was exceptional compared to developments across the African continent in so far as communal forms had survived into the end of the colonial period. On this basis, the claim was made that such communal forms could provide an alternative basis for building a socialist society without the need for going through a stage of independent capitalist development.[4] This view might have appeared especially plausible when its proponents contrasted the case of Tanzania with the case of neighbouring Kenya, where a fairly strong class of rich peasants able to hire the labour of others emerged during the colonial period.[5]

CONTEXT: POLITICAL, ECONOMIC, AND SOCIAL
DEVELOPMENTS IN THE POST-INDEPENDENCE PERIOD

To contextualise the Dar es Salaam Debates, we will provide a brief overview of class struggles during the independence and post-independence periods.

During the struggle for independence, peasant mobilisation played a significant role in the movement which brought TANU to power.[6] However, the party's other significant base was to be found in the petty bourgeoisie, specifically the traders. It was traders who provided links between the intelligentsia (the leaders of the party) and its mass base (the peasantry).[7] Upon gaining independence in 1961, TANU's leadership attempted to attract foreign investment in order to develop the productive forces in Tanzania. However, such efforts failed due to various factors, including the underdevelopment of Tanzania's infrastructure and industrial sectors compared to its Kenyan neighbour as well as problems at the level of international relations. Nyerere and TANU's leadership discovered that Tanzania could not maintain an independent foreign policy without paying a significant price.[8] Thus, when Nyerere tried to maintain an independent foreign policy with respect to the German Democratic Republic and when he broke off relations with the UK over Rhodesia's unilateral declaration of independence, foreign capital fled the country. Between 1964 and 1965 about TZS 290 million left the country.[9]

TANU was also under pressure because of the slow pace of its 'Africanisation' policy, as evidenced by the army mutiny of 1964 as well as union agitation during the 1960s. It was clear that the leadership of TANU had to make important concessions to the professional classes comprising a part of the petty bourgeoisie in Tanzania. Yet this class, at least before 1967, was still unable to break the power of the commercial bourgeoisie (mostly Asian merchants who had attained a privileged position under the colonial state).[10] As the ruling party consolidated its grip on the state, it turned to suppressing labour strikes. The Trade Disputes (Settlement) Act of 1962 essentially banned strikes, and by 1964, all the trade unions were amalgamated into a single national union, the National Union of Tanganyika Workers.[11]

The Arusha Declaration and its attendant policies of nationalisation can be interpreted as driven by at least two main considerations: an attempt to redirect capital towards industrial enterprises and as a successful attempt by the elements of the petty bourgeoisie which controlled the state to break the power of the commercial bourgeoisie. The elements of the petty bourgeoisie which controlled the state also recognised the need to raise agricultural productivity in order to increase revenues, and to acquire the capital necessary for industrial investment. The villagisation programme aimed to concentrate the rural population in villages which would then be provided with more advanced machinery with the aim of increasing agricultural productivity, especially of cash crops for export. However, it was clear by the mid-1970s that this forced villagisation programme had failed, peasants had resisted attempts at relocation, and food production had decreased.[12] The villagisation programme also provided opportunities for rich peasants to develop greater contacts with the wing of the petty bourgeoisie which occupied local bureaucratic positions, and to use these contacts to redirect the process in their favour.[13] In general, it appears that by the mid-1970s the conservative wing of TANU was in the ascendency.[14] Nevertheless, we should be careful to not take these developments to imply that essentially nothing changed in the post-independence period, a view which has become increasingly popular among Western scholars of African history, but which does not seem to track the perceptions of the people who lived through the independence period, even those who fell out with TANU at some point.[15]

A METHODOLOGICAL NOTE ON THE PLACE OF MARXOLOGY IN THE DEBATES

Having provided a very condensed account of class struggles during this period, we now turn to analysing how Marxists living in Tanzania during this period assessed Nyerere's policies, and some of the internal debates which arose between them. Some of the prominent questions which were raised during the Dar es Salaam Debates were: (1) What is the nature of the ruling class in the neo-colonies? (2) What is the relationship between the attempt to build socialism and the national question, given the reality of imperialism? (3) What is the relationship between the base and the superstructure, and is there anything specific about this relationship under the condition of domination by foreign capital? (4) What is the nature of neo-colonialism, and how can it be combated?[16] I contend that all these questions are still pertinent today for African liberation struggles. I do not suggest that one can find all or even most of the answers to these questions by revisiting these debates. However, I do argue that reflection on these debates can help us refine our understanding of these questions today, and that by paying attention to the rich intellectual history of African Marxism, we can also avoid reinventing the wheel. To this end, I provide a brief exposition of some of the main themes of these debates. The list of participants in these debates includes some very famous names and some less famous names, and some of them later changed their views on the issues which are presented below. Hence, this account will restrict itself to considering their views in the 1970s and the 1980s. While this account is primarily expository, I will also point out inconsistencies in some of the views that were put forward. Furthermore, I should warn the reader that the debate itself was often characterised by appeals to authority, specifically to Marx and Lenin's authority. However, in my view, such appeals to authority seem to have been largely performative. By this I mean that the arguments presented by the various participants stand, for the most part, on their own. I have therefore chosen to excise such deferential appeals to authority. However, there were important moments in the debates where the appeal to the textual corpus of classical Marxism cannot be characterised as an instance of an illegitimate appeal to authority. This took place when the debate shifted from evaluating a specific explanation for a given phenomenon to evaluating whether the explanation offered was compatible with the basic theoretical commitments that Marx, Engels and Lenin held – i.e., the extent to which the explanation offered is compatible with Marxism. There are obvious parallels here to other kinds of debates – e.g., philosophers can appeal to Kant's texts in order to ascertain whether a specific explanation which presents itself as Kantian is in fact consistent with what Kant is committed to. There is no illegitimate appeal to authority in such cases, since the participants all present themselves as Kantians, or at least as interested in discerning whether the explanation offered is Kantian.

ON THE NATURE OF THE RULING CLASS IN THE NEO-COLONIES

It is obvious that Marxists in Tanzania had to clarify the nature of the ruling class in Tanzania in order to be able to justify taking any specific determinate stance towards Nyerere's project. One line of thinking, put forward by Peter Meyns and Issa Shivji, claimed that the ruling class in Tanzania under Nyerere was a bureaucratic bourgeoisie. As Meyns put it:

> the leading force in the development of class struggle in Tanzania since independence has been the bureaucratic bourgeoisie. Based on its alliance with the peasants and workers it has successfully reduced the influence and strength of the commercial bourgeoisie and consolidated its own.[17]

However, there was a conceptual problem here in thinking of the ruling class as the bureaucratic bourgeoisie, for strictly speaking, 'wealth is not a Marxist criterion of class'.[18] Babu put this point elegantly: 'A petty-bourgeois, say a successful auctioneer, may be wealthier than a small manufacturer but because of his position in production, i.e., appropriating no direct surplus value, the former will still remain a petty-bourgeois and the latter full bourgeois.'[19] That is, we cannot just point to a wealthy group of corrupt political elite and say that they are the ruling class simply because of their wealth. Rather, it is one's relationship to the means of production which serves to fix one's class identity, according to Marxist social theory. This was a point that M. Mamdani and H. Baghat made in response to Shivji.[20] Now, of course, this does not imply that wealth has nothing to do with class, for in most cases, the wealthiest members of society are those who control the means of production. Nevertheless, it means that the explanation of unequal wealth distribution must refer to different relationships to the means of production. What this implies is that saying that ruling class in Tanzania is the bureaucracy is to say that it controls the means of production. Nationalisation would be a necessary condition for this to take place:

> only when state power becomes, through nationalizations of means of production, not simply the agent of oppression, but also that of exploitation; and of a social group, because of its control over the state, exercises control over [the] means of production, only then can we identify the emergence of bureaucratic capital and thus of a bureaucratic bourgeoisie.[21]

As a conditional statement, this seems correct. And it leads to another conclusion, namely that while nationalisation is a necessary condition for the transition to socialism, it is not a sufficient condition, for it is also a necessary condition (at least in the Tanzanian context) for the rise of a bureaucratic bourgeoisie. In other words, nationalisation taken abstractly does not determine the nature of the development which is unfolding. Shivji, who believed that the ruling class in Tanzania was the bureaucratic bourgeoisie, thought that the nationalisations which took place in the aftermath of the Arusha Declaration in 1967 created the economic basis for the emergence of the bureaucratic bourgeoisie as a ruling class in the Marxist sense, and not just as a governing class:

> up until the Arusha Declaration, the 'bureaucratic bourgeoisie' cannot be said to have really become a *bourgeoisie*. Although the state played an important role in the economy, it was mostly a regulatory one. With the Arusha Declaration the state and state institutions (including the parastatals) became the dominant factor in the economy ... political power and control over property had now come to rest in the same class.[22]

However, there was a problem for Shivji here, for he also did not deny that foreign capital was still dominant – this was what he meant when he wrote that 'the "bureaucratic bourgeoisie" is a *dependent* bourgeoisie – dependent on the international bourgeoisie'.[23] Everything hinged on what he meant by 'dependent'. On the one hand, if it only meant that the bureaucratic bourgeoisie needed to enter into relations with foreign capital in order to reproduce itself, then every bourgeoisie (whether located in the core or the periphery) that has ever existed can be said to have been dependent in this sense, and as such the thesis is rather weak (but true). On the other hand, if he meant to say that it was dependent in the sense that it accumulated through service to an international bourgeoisie and that the latter was the primary owner and controller of the means of production in Tanzania, then he was wrong to say that the Tanzanian state was the dominant factor in the Tanzanian economy in the aftermath of the Arusha Declaration. And if the Tanzanian state was not the dominant factor in the Tanzanian economy, then the necessary condition for the rise of a bureaucratic bourgeoisie did not obtain.

If we emphasise the point about the Marxist criterion of class, then a new problem emerges: if it is true that the economies of states like Tanzania were dominated by foreign monopoly capital (and this is a minimal commitment for any Marxist version of the theory of imperialism) during the period in question, then it follows that there was a complicated problem in identifying the ruling class in the neo-colony. For if the ruling class of a given society is comprised of the wealthiest members of that society, then by definition this ruling class will be comprised of a group of people living in (or belonging to) that society. However, if the ruling class of a given society is comprised of the people who control the means of production of that society, then that group of people may or may not be members of that society (in the sense of living in that society). What this implies is that the ruling class of a given society might not be a part of that society. In fact, if African states in the post-independence period in the 1960s–1980s were neo-colonies, in the sense that their economic and political trajectory was controlled by forces that were external to those states, then the ruling class in those states did not exist (in the common spatiotemporal sense of that term) within those states. Indeed, this is the conclusion that Dan Nabudere arrived at:

> the political achievements of the neo-colony are brought under the control of the financial oligarchy [in the West] – a process that has never been disposed of. Under these circumstances, can there be any doubt that the economically dominant class in the neo-colony is the financial oligarchy of the imperialist countries, and that politics [in the long run] must reflect the base?[24]

This view was also stated by A.B. Kayonga and S.M. Magara: 'as the financial oligarchy dominate the state of their own countries, so do they also politically dominate the states of other countries where they are economically dominant'.[25] What this implies is that, strictly speaking, classical political philosophy and political theory in so far as they take the primary question to be how to regulate the relationship between citizens and the state (treated as a closed system) are misguided, and that they are inapplicable (without significant modifications) to neo-colonies.[26] If this is correct, then this by itself would be a significant result. Nevertheless, from the perspective of Marxist strategising, which is fundamentally centred around the notion of class struggle, the non-existence of an internal ruling class can lead to an impasse in terms of political action. After all, how could Tanzanian Marxists organise against an external ruling class?[27] Nabudere's claim also led to other significant problems, since it seemed to imply not only that the independence of the neo-colonies was compromised, but also that it was non-existent. This was the point Karim Hirji raised in his response to Nabudere: 'what independence implies is the establishment of a *separate* state and thus of a *separate* class controlling the state'.[28] But Hirji did not thereby claim that the means of production in the neo-colonies were primarily controlled by an internal ruling class. This is in turn entails that he thought that the political ruling class can be different from the economic ruling class. In other words, this was a claim about the 'relative autonomy' of the political. This relative autonomy was presented not as a function of internal causal factors, but as a result of the existence of inter-imperial rivalries, as well as the rivalry between the socialist camp and the imperialist camp in the context of the Cold War. Yash Tandon stated this point clearly: 'the contradictions between imperialist countries and between imperialist and socialist countries provide the basis for the relative autonomy of the dependent ruling classes in the neo-colonies'.[29] The question then becomes: is it possible to specify this relative autonomy in a manner that is consistent with historical materialism as a framework for socio-historical explanation? One prediction which seems to be entailed by the theory of historical materialism is that the relative autonomy of the political in such a situation cannot survive in the long run – i.e., control over state power without control over the means of production, which are left in the hands of foreign capital, will lead to either the overthrow of the class which only holds state power, or to its subordination in the long run. This also essentially explains the demise of the Bandung movement: in the long run, the economic must assert its primacy, good intentions (and bad intentions) notwithstanding. This is in fact what happened in Tanzania. At the end of the day, Nyerere had to concede and enter negotiations with the International Monetary Fund between 1981 and 1985, and Tanzania had to submit to 'structural adjustment'.[30]

FRIENDS AND ENEMIES IN THE NEO-COLONY

The debate about the specification of the nature of the ruling class in the neo-colonies is obviously important for understanding who the primary enemy is. For if one holds, as Nabudere did, that the ruling class in the neo-colonies was the ruling class of the imperialist countries, then this class will be marked as the number one enemy of the working class and the peasantry in the neo-colonies. This was exactly the conclusion that Nabudere arrived at: 'to us in Tanzania, Kenya, and Uganda, the principal enemy is imperialism'.[31] In Nabudere's view, there was, strictly speaking, no such thing as a national bourgeoisie in any African country in so far as there was no internal social group which accumulated surplus through ownership of the means of production, and which structured social, economic and political relations in those societies to suit its interests – i.e., there were no national capitalists. There was a governing class – i.e., the class whose members occupied political office – but the laws it passed and the changes it made in society were geared towards the interests of finance capital. This does not imply that it did not benefit from this relationship, but only that it was subordinated. In other words, if there was a clash of interests between its interests and the interests of finance capital (or the bearers thereof), its interests would have suffered, all else being equal. Of course, one can choose to define 'national bourgeoisie' in a different way. For example, Babu claimed that there are two segments of the national bourgeoisie in the neo-colony. The first segment is 'the small one which generates and accumulates capital without recourse to finance capital', and the second is 'the big bourgeoisie whose capital is part of imperialist finance capital'.[32] One way Nabudere could have responded to Babu's objection was to note that in political and social analysis, the bare fact of existence is not important, and that what is important is causal efficacy – i.e., if there is an element in the social system which exists, but which does not exert any significant causal influence on the rest of the elements in the system, then it can be safely ignored. After all, any model must simplify to be useful.

Nabudere thought that a segment of the petty bourgeoisie in the neo-colony had interests which were in contradiction with the interests of overseas finance capital, and he also believed that this segment might be persuaded to enter into an alliance with workers and peasants (and radical petty-bourgeois intellectuals) as part of the 'national democratic revolution':

> the petty-bourgeoisie is a product of imperialist domination. It cannot be disjointed from it but at the same time it has a contradiction with imperialism because of this oppression and domination. That is why, the national democratic revolution encompasses a wide body of the population of our countries.[33]

Here, Nabudere was clearly influenced by Mao's 'New Democracy' of 1940. According to Mao, the rise of a socialist power in the aftermath of the Bolshevik Revolution reconfigured the global order in such a manner that it was now possible to reconfigure the project of a bourgeois democratic revolution, which, in the classical Marxist account, was the first stage of a two-stage process which would lead to a socialist revolution in the colonies and semi-colonies; in the classical version of the theory, the first phase was a struggle against feudalism which would end with the rule of the bourgeoisie, against whom the struggle would be waged in the second phase. For Mao, in the semi-colonies there were segments of the bourgeoisie whose interests were opposed to the interests of the imperialist capitalists: 'China's national bourgeoisie has a revolutionary quality at certain periods and to a certain degree, because China is a colonial and semi-colonial country which is a victim of aggression.'[34] However, this oppressed bourgeoisie was also seen as dependent on imperialist capitalists, and to this extent, while it was thought that they may be induced to join a united front against imperialism, they were also viewed as unreliable allies, who could not be expected to lead the struggle for a national democratic revolution successfully:

> At the same time, however, being a bourgeois class in a colonial and semi-colonial country and so being extremely flabby economically and politically, the Chinese national bourgeoisie also has another quality, namely, a proneness to conciliation with the enemies of the revolution.[35]

Thus, they did have a role in the national democratic revolution, but only if they could be stripped of leadership and only if they were subordinated to a movement which was guided by proletarian ideology (and note that this is distinct from a movement lead by the proletariat, a distinction to which we will return below). But it was obvious that these segments of the bourgeoisie could not be induced to join any nationalist movement unless concessions were made to them. For Mao, these concessions necessitated recognising that the successful outcome of a national democratic revolution will bring about a state that is not under the dictatorship of the proletariat, but neither would it be under the dictatorship of the bourgeoisie – instead, it would be ruled by a coalition of different classes.[36] In this transitional phase, private property will not be abolished and there will be no socialising of agriculture, but the state will nationalise (with the aim of socialising) key strategic sectors. But why did Mao think that the path to capitalist development in the classical sense was blocked? First, he thought that the imperialist powers will struggle against attempts towards independence, regardless of whether such attempts aim at the imposition of an independent capitalist order or an independent socialist order – for example, it is not unreasonable to think that today, even if Cuba abandoned socialism and turned towards capitalism, while attempting to maintain its independence, the US would still exert tremendous pressure on it, as long as it refuses to be part of the American empire's 'backyard'. The second reason is closely tied to the first reason, namely the need for assistance from the socialist camp in order to fight off imperialism, and this in turn meant that there would be a demand that the country should not fall into the capitalist camp when it attained independence.[37] A third reason, which was especially salient in the case of Tanzania and other African countries, had to do with the non-existence of an independent national capitalist class that can restructure society on the basis of its interests while preventing systematic surplus drain. As Tandon put it in his defence of Nabudere: 'capital [in the neo-colonies] belongs to the imperialist bourgeoisie, the local [ruling?] classes which employ that capital, while unquestionably appropriating a part of the surplus value, are *objectively* only servicing agents of imperialist capital'.[38]

However, here we might suggest that while this is true of Tanzania and Uganda (to take two of the most discussed cases in these debates),[39] it is not clear that this is generalisable to places like India, or indeed, to take an African example, Egypt. This is a point made by J. Shao, but Shao went further than that and defended something close to Bill Warren's thesis when he wrote:

colonialism, the domination of the world by the capitalist mode of production, the international division of labour and development of the productive forces in the colonies are not incompatible. On the contrary, they provide conditions for the rapid development of the productive forces on a world scale.[40]

Warren's thesis was that 'the imperialist countries' policies and their overall impact on the Third World actually favour its industrialization; and that ties of dependence binding the Third World to the imperialist countries have been, and are being, markedly loosened'.[41] The problem with Warren's thesis as it was applied to African economies was that it failed to explain any of the significant empirical data. And when its proponents have looked at African economies during the colonial period, they have tended to invent forward and backward linkages where these do not exist.[42] Also, they have tended to discount the fact that in many places, including in parts of East Africa, levels of development were higher before the colonial period than during it.[43] Moreover, Warren assumed what he was supposed to argue for, namely that the proliferation of joint ventures in the former colonised countries implies the nationalisation of foreign capital, rather than the denationalisation of local capital.[44] For this is precisely the crux of the issue.[45]

If there is indeed no 'national bourgeoisie', and if exploitation is carried out by foreign capital or its local representatives (as providers of an intermediate service), then it would be a strategic mistake to identify the principal enemy as an internal enemy – the politically governing class or the office holding class. In fact, for both Nabudere and Tandon, it was not feasible to think of any democratic national revolution which did not bring a significant portion of the petty bourgeoisie to the side of the workers. If one believes this, then one will also believe that attacking 'the bureaucratic bourgeoisie' is liable to weaken the anti-imperialist movement, by attacking 'important sections of the anti-imperialist united front'.[46] Thus, the debate was really about the line which Marxists in Tanzania should take towards Nyerere's TANU – i.e., should they enter into an alliance with it, at least in its struggles against imperialism, or should they denounce it as the principal enemy? Supporters of the view that the main struggle should be carried out against the internal ruling class, claimed that the Nabudere-Tandon line was essentially a concession to the petty bourgeoisie, and that it would disarm the proletariat. This is the position which was taken up by Mamdani: 'so long as a specific imperialism does not physically invade Uganda ... the class struggles remains principally internal'.[47] Critics of the Nabudere-Tandon line also pointed out that since African intellectuals tend to be from the same petty bourgeois class as the governing class, they are often hesitant to criticise it or identify it as the enemy.[48] Of course, this cannot be an argument against the truth of the Nabudere-Tandon line, but it can be rhetorically powerful, and it can be deployed to show why this view was held (although the view itself would have to be refuted on independent grounds). However, in my view, it does appear that the Nabudere-Tandon line was simply the conclusion of a valid argument that starts from basic Marxist-Leninist premises:

1. In the era of imperialism, the means of production in at least some of the neo-colonies (including Tanzania and Uganda) are owned, for the most part, by foreign capital, and its bearers – i.e., the ruling class in the imperialist countries.
2. The group that owns most of the means of production in a given society is the ruling class of that society, even if it is not the governing class (i.e., does not hold political office).

The conclusion is that in the era of imperialism, the ruling class in at least some of the neo-colonies (including Tanzania and Uganda) is the ruling class of the imperialist countries.

This argument is, I submit, valid (i.e., if the two premises are true, then the conclusion must be true). The dispute about its soundness can be divided into an empirical dispute over the truth of the first premise and a theoretical or conceptual dispute regarding the truth of the second premise. One can accept the truth of the second premise while denying the truth of the first premise on empirical grounds, as Cranford Pratt did.[49] We clearly cannot resolve this dispute here, but I hope that I have contributed, in a very small way, towards its resolution through clarifying the issues at stake.

PEASANTS AND WORKERS IN THE NEO-COLONY

So far, we have been concerned with identifying the different contending positions regarding the characterisation of the ruling class in the neo-colony in general and Tanzania in particular. However, we will now turn towards a discussion of the relationship between the peasantry and the workers as it was conceived by some of the participants in the Dar es Salaam Debates. Nabudere, as has been pointed out above, envisioned a united national front that was to be led by the working class: 'only on the basis of a new democratic revolution [in the Maoist sense] in which the working class plays a leading role can imperialism be contested'.[50] There was an obvious problem with this proposal, namely the fact that because of the narrow industrial base which was inherited from the colonial period, there were not that many workers in Tanzania. In 1961, for example, there were only 411,538 wage earners in Tanzania,[51] the vast majority of whom were not employed in industry, which was practically non-existent. To this extent, the significance of the working class in Tanzania was derived more from the strategic location it occupied than from the number of its members. Their ability to carry out strikes that could paralyse the economic life of the country despite their small numbers was on full display during the 1950s, when they engaged in a series of strikes in support of the independence movement.[52] Moreover, most of the participants in the Dar es Salaam Debates believed that due to their greater exposure to certain facets of modern urban life, the proletariat were capable of articulating, with the help of radical intellectuals 'who have raised themselves to the level of comprehending theoretically the historical movement as a whole',[53] their opposition towards their exploitation in a more systematic and radical manner than the peasantry. Furthermore, at the level of political capacity, they also believed that the way workers are organised in factories, docks and plantations across different parts of the country allows them to act more effectively as a unified force. This claim goes back to at least Marx and Engels: 'this union [of workers] is helped on by the improved means of communication that are created by modern industry and that place the workers of different localities in contact with each other'.[54]

The peasantry vastly outnumbered the workers; however, they were seen as a great physical force, and not as a great revolutionary force per se. They shared this view with Amílcar Cabral, who adhered to this thesis on the grounds of his experiences in Guinea-Bissau:

> I shall confine myself to my own country, Guinea, where it must be said at once that the peasantry is not a revolutionary force – which may seem strange, particularly as we have based the whole of our armed liberation struggle on the peasantry. A distinction must be drawn between a physical force and a revolutionary force.[55]

Cabral's thought in general was clearly influential on some of the participants in the Dar es Salaam Debates, like Shivji.[56] On this specific issue, there seems to have been agreement by most of the participants that this distinction must be taken into consideration.

What this meant was that while any revolutionary movement had to recruit the peasantry, its ideological orientation could not be determined by the class instincts of the peasantry. Instead, its demands would have to be articulated as an elaboration and a rendering explicit of the demands inherent in the class instincts of the workers despite their numerical inferiority. For the participants in the Dar es Salaam Debates, the peasantry, because they were still petty commodity producers (even if only in a very formal sense), could not be expected to come to a socialist standpoint without being guided by a party led by proletarian ideology. Moreover, it was thought that the articulation of grievances by the peasantry often takes the form of emphasising unequal exchange – i.e., exploitation through price manipulation at the point of exchange. When this view of exploitation is extended to workers, there is a danger that one reverts to a pre-Marxist socialism which tended to view the exploitation of workers as happening at the point of exchange rather than at the point of production. We should not forget that there were Ricardian socialists before Marx, such as Thomas Hodgskin, John Gray and William Thompson, who attempted to understand the exploitation of workers as occurring at the point of exchange, and whose political proposals were adversely affected by this theoretical misunderstanding.[57]

The aforementioned characterisation of the peasantry becomes clearer when contrasted with the view of Fanon. In his *The Wretched of the Earth*, Fanon wrote:

the peasantry is systematically left out of most of the nationalist parties' propaganda. But it is obvious that in colonial countries only the peasantry is revolutionary. It has nothing to lose and everything to gain.[58]

The problem with this view is that even in the Algerian case, the resistance of the peasants and their revolts and attacks on the *colons*, which Fanon observed, did not lead to a general revolutionary war until the peasants were mobilised by leadership coming from the urban areas. This was acknowledged even by scholars who were sympathetic to Fanon's account.[59] One of those scholars, B. Marie Perinbam, attempted to defend Fanon by arguing that because the working class was so small in the African colonies, Fanon had no choice but to mark out the peasantry as the revolutionary class.[60] However, this argument is not convincing because it seems to conflate two issues: the necessity of drawing on the peasantry in any struggle that could have a reasonable chance of success, and the question of whether the peasantry is a revolutionary class. These are two distinct claims which should not be conflated. Moreover, the fact that there are peasant revolts and acts of resistance is not what is at issue, since the mere fact of revolt and resistance does not indicate any revolutionary tendency. For one could revolt against the existing situation because it has made it impossible to fulfil one's 'traditional role', and such a revolt could occur without being revolutionary in any way in so far as it does not involve rejections of 'traditional' norms and social relations, although it might be channelled by outside forces in a revolutionary direction.[61] Marxism, if it is anything at all, is a theory of revolution, not a theory of revolt or of everyday resistance.

For the participants of the Dar es Salaam Debates (and on this, there was agreement), Fanon conflated the fact that there could be no successful revolution in African countries without the mobilisation of the peasantry with the thesis that the peasantry is a revolutionary class. Shivji articulated the discontent with Fanon's claims in a representative manner: 'Fanon is completely confused on these issues. Unlike Lenin he had neither a grasp of the scientific theory nor experience in working class struggle. His was essentially a very radical petty bourgeois populist.'[62] It is not my aim here to defend or criticise Fanon on this point. However, I wish to indicate this divergence between the participants in the Dar es Salaam Debates and Fanon because it is not unfair to say that there have been attempts to depict Fanon as essentially representing all that is interesting about African anti-colonial Marxism. The uncritical worship of Fanon in some circles is, in my view, partially explained by referring to the fact that he is taken as the sole representative of African anti-colonial Marxism, and this in turn is explained by the fact that there is ignorance about the diversity of standpoints which were taken up by African Marxists in the aftermath of the struggles for national independence. This chapter has aimed to contribute towards remedying this situation by introducing readers to some of the key debates that occurred at Dar es Salaam during the 1970s and 1980s.

NOTES

1. I would like to express my thanks to the 'AT crew' – Max Ajl, Sina Rahmani and Louis Allday – for their insights about the past and present of imperialism. I would also like to thank Ajit Singh and Rogelio Scott for stimulating conversations about imperialism and leftist politics in the Global North. Parts of this chapter were presented at an International Studies Association Roundtable, and for this I thank Alina Sajed for the invitation, as well as the other presenters – Lisa Tilley, Bikrum Gill, Naeem Inayatullah and Quỳnh N. Phạm – for their helpful comments. It's good to know that not everybody worships 'agency'! I also wish to thank the editors of this volume for their comments on how to improve this chapter.
2. Ng'wanza Kamata, 'Samir Amin and Debates at the University of Dar es Salaam in the 1980s', *Agrarian South: Journal of Political Economy*, 9(1), 2020, 65.
3. P.F. Nursery-Bray, 'Tanzania: The Development Debate', *African Affairs*, 79(314), 1980, 55–56.
4. W. Rodney, 'Tanzanian Ujamaa and Scientific Socialism', *African Review*, 1(4), 1972, 61–76.

5. S.D. Mueller, 'The Historical Origins of Tanzania's Ruling Class', *Canadian Journal of African Studies/Revue canadienne des études africaines*, 15(3), 1981, 459–497.

6. J.S. Saul, 'African Peasants and Revolution', *Review of African Political Economy*, 1, 1974, 41–68.

7. Issa Shivji, *Class Struggles in Tanzania*, London: Heinemann, 1976, 57–58.

8. It is interesting to note that, at about the same time, Nasser in Egypt made a similar discovery.

9. Mueller, 'The Historical Origins of Tanzania's Ruling Class', 487.

10. Shivji, *Class Struggles in Tanzania*, 71.

11. D. Jackson, 'The Disappearance of Strikes in Tanzania: Incomes Policy and Industrial Democracy', *Journal of Modern African Studies*, 17(2), 1979, 219–251.

12. P.L. Raikes, 'Ujamaa and Rural Socialism', *Review of African Political Economy*, 3, 1975, 33–52.

13. Issa Shivji, 'Peasants and Class Alliances', *Review of African Political Economy*, 3, 1975, 10–18.

14. Saul, 'African Peasants and Revolution', 57.

15. E. Hunter, '"The History and Affairs of TANU": Intellectual History, Nationalism, and the Postcolonial State in Tanzania', *International Journal of African Historical Studies*, 45(3), 2012, 365–383.

16. A.M. Babu, 'Introduction', in Yash Tandon and A.M. Babu (eds), *University of Dar es Salaam Debate on Class, State and Imperialism*, Dar es Salaam: Tanzania Publishing House, 1982, 1–12.

17. Peter Meyns, 'Tanzania and the Struggle for National Independence and Socialism: Comments on Issa Shivji's *Tanzania: The Class Struggles Continues*', in Tandon and Babu, *University of Dar es Salaam Debate on Class, State and Imperialism*, 22.

18. Babu, 'Introduction', 3.

19. Ibid.

20. M. Mamdani and H. Bhagat, 'A Critique of Issa Shivji's Book *Class Struggles in Tanzania*', in Tandon and Babu, *University of Dar es Salaam Debate on Class, State and Imperialism*, 37.

21. Ibid., 39.

22. Issa Shivji, *Class Struggles in Tanzania*, 85.

23. Ibid.

24. D. Wadada Nabudere, 'Imperialism, State, Class and Race: A Critique of Issa Shivji's *Class Struggles in Tanzania*', in Tandon and Babu, *University of Dar es Salaam Debate on Class, State and Imperialism*,, 62.

25. A.B. Kayonga and S.M. Magara, 'Nabudere the "Kautskyite" and Hirji the "Marxist-Leninist"', in Tandon and Babu, *University of Dar es Salaam Debate on Class, State and Imperialism*, 79.

26. Olúfẹ́mi O. Táíwò, 'States Are Not Basic Structures: Against State-Centric Political Theory', *Philosophical Papers*, 48(1), 2019, 74.

27. Babu, 'Introduction', 5.

28. Karim Hirji, 'The "Marxism-Leninism" of Professor D. Wadada Nabudere', in Tandon and Babu, *University of Dar es Salaam Debate on Class, State and Imperialism*, 73.

29. Yash Tandon, 'Who Is the Ruling Class in the Semi-Colony?', in Tandon and Babu, *University of Dar es Salaam Debate on Class, State and Imperialism*, 53.

30. Godfrey Mwakikagile, *Tanzania under Mwalimu Nyerere: Reflections on an African Statesman*, Dar es Salaam: New Africa Press, 78–79.

31. D. Wadada Nabudere, 'A Caricature of Marxism-Leninism (a Reply to Karim Hirji)', in Tandon and Babu, *University of Dar es Salaam Debate on Class, State and Imperialism*, 89.

32. Babu, 'Introduction', 3.

33. D. Wadada Nabudere, 'ECHO Interviews Nabudere', in Tandon and Babu, *University of Dar es Salaam Debate on Class, State and Imperialism* 153.

34. Mao Tse-Tung, 'New Democracy', in *Selected Works of Mao Tse-Tung, Volume II*, Oxford: Pergamon Press, 1965, 348.

35. Ibid., 349.

36. Ibid., 350–351.

37. Ibid., 355.

38. Yash Tandon, 'Whose Capital and Whose State?', in Tandon and Babu, *University of Dar es Salaam Debate on Class, State and Imperialism*, 169.

39. The case of Kenya is different because a more or less mature bourgeoisie did develop there; see Mueller, 'The Historical Origins of Tanzania's Ruling Class', 459–463.

40. J. Shao, 'Theories of Underdevelopment and Imperialism: Charles Bettelheim or the Comedy of Errors', in Tandon and Babu, *University of Dar es Salaam Debate on Class, State and Imperialism*, 241.

41. Bill Warren, 'Imperialism and Capitalist Industrialization', *New Left Review*, 81, 1973, 4.

42. Thandika Mkandawire, 'Review of *The Development of Capitalism in Africa* by John Sender and Sheila Smith', *Africa Development/Afrique et développement*, 12(2), 1987, 167.

43. D. Slater, 'On Development Theory and the Warren Thesis: Arguments against the Predominance of Economism', *Environment and Planning D: Society and Space*, 5, 1987, 263–282.

44. Philip McMichael, James Petras and Robert Rhodes, 'Imperialism and the Contradictions of Development', *New Left Review*, 85, 1974, 90.

45. D. Wadada Nabudere, *The Political Economy of Imperialism: Its Theoretical and Polemical Treatment from Mercantilist to Multilateral Imperialism*, London: Zed Books, 1977, 164–184.

46. Omwony Ojwok, 'Who Is to Lead the Popular Anti-Imperialist African Revolution in Africa? (in Refutation of Issa G. Shivji's Petty-Bourgeois Neo-Marxist Line)', in Tandon and Babu, *University of Dar es Salaam Debate on Class, State and Imperialism*, 190.

47. Mahmood Mamdani, 'The Makerere Massacre', in Tandon and Babu, *University of Dar es Salaam Debate on Class, State and Imperialism*, 132.

48. Babu, 'Introduction', 6.

49. Cranford Pratt, 'Tanzania: The Development Debate – a Comment', *African Affairs*, 79(316), 1980, 345–346.
50. D. Wadada Nabudere, *Imperialism in East Africa, Volume 2: Imperialism and Integration*, London: Zed Books, 1982, 187.
51. Shivji, *Class Struggles in Tanzania*, 52.
52. Ibid.
53. Karl Marx and Friedrich Engels, *The Communist Manifesto*, London: Penguin, 2002, 231.
54. Ibid., 229–230.
55. Amílcar Cabral, 'Brief Analysis of the Social Structure in Guinea', in *Revolution in Guinea: Selected Texts by Amilcar Cabral*, trans. Richard Handyside, London: Love and Malcomson, 1974, 50.
56. Shivji, *Class Struggles in Tanzania*, 53.
57. Noel W. Thompson, *The People's Science: The Popular Political Economy of Exploitation and Crisis 1816–34*, Cambridge: Cambridge University Press, 1984, 82.
58. Frantz Fanon, *The Wretched of the Earth*, trans. Richard Philcox, New York: Grove Press, 2004, 23.
59. B. Marie Perinbam, 'Fanon and the Revolutionary Peasantry – the Algerian Case', *Journal of Modern African Studies*, 11(3), 1973, 438.
60. Ibid, 434.
61. The role of women in the struggle of independence in Guinea (Conakry) is an example of this; see Elizabeth Schmidt, *Mobilizing the Masses: Gender, Ethnicity, and Class in the Nationalist Movement in Guinea, 1939–1958*, Portsmouth, NH: Heinemann, 2005, 296.
62. Issa Shivji, 'ECHO Interviews Shivji', in Tandon and Babu, *University of Dar es Salaam Debate on Class, State and Imperialism*, 184.

14

The Road to Durban: Workers' Struggles, Student Movements, and the Resurgence of Resistance Politics in Namibia and South Africa

Heike Becker

INTRODUCTION

This chapter looks into connections between radical politics in Namibia and South Africa in the early 1970s. It demonstrates the significance of entwined histories of student and labour movements during the heyday of apartheid colonialism in South Africa and its colony, then known as 'South West Africa'. Today, the regional entanglements of radical politics in southern Africa are largely forgotten; at best they are told as footnotes of separate post-apartheid narratives of nationalist liberation struggles.

Early 1973 saw a massive wave of strikes in the South African port town of Durban which is often regarded as the turning point of anti-apartheid struggles. They heralded an upsurge of resistance that led to the Soweto revolt, the popular uprisings of the 1980s, and eventually the demise of the regime. This chapter tells the story of the period *preceding* the 1973 Durban strikes; I am particularly interested in the connections between ostensibly distinct southern African radical trajectories during the late 1960s and early 1970s. The significant links between the Namibian and the South African student and worker movements of the period between, roughly, 1968 and 1973 have not yet found much attention in the historiography of the southern African anti-apartheid struggles. This chapter endeavours to address this lacuna; it thereby draws particular attention to the Namibian contract workers' strike of 1971–72 and the transnational repercussions the strike had as 'a vital precedent to the Durban strikes'.[1]

THE DURBAN MOMENT

Between January and March 1973 almost 100,000 workers came out on strike in Durban and made their demands heard through songs and marches. Workers exercised the power of factory-based mass action. The strikes signalled the growth of militant non-racial trade unionism, and a revived spirit of rebellion in the country.

Notwithstanding the brutal repression of the 1960s, the resurgence of workers' action and the liberation movements could draw on sustained networks which had continued to exist in the underground and the fringes of legal activism. Links between young activists and intellectuals, who in different ways embodied South Africa's 1968 moment, were particularly significant, such as the political, intellectual and personal friendship between Steve Biko, the intellectual and activist leader of the radical 1970s Black Consciousness movement, and Richard ('Rick') Turner, a lecturer in political philosophy at the University of Natal and researcher into and organiser around labour issues. In the early 1970s, Biko and Turner were based in Durban, where they and other activists of the generation born in the 1940s influenced student politics and labour and community organising in creative, new ways. They signify the importance of the conversation between protagonists of increasingly radical Black Consciousness ideas, and new-left non-sectarian Marxist thought for the resurgence of resistance politics.

SOUTH AFRICA'S 1968 MOMENT:
STUDENT POLITICS IN BLACK AND WHITE

South African students took part in the global 1968 wave of uprisings, although this is today largely forgotten. Transgressive politics reinvented forms and ideologies of resistance, and echoing protests elsewhere in the 'Global 1968' movements, broke rules in a variety of ways, some related to explicitly oppositional politics against apartheid and racial capitalism, others more indirectly political in the spirit of 1960s counterculture.[2]

In the historiography of South African resistance politics, the decade between the mid-1960s and mid-1970s is usually regarded as marked by a silence of the graveyard, which ended only with the Soweto uprising of 16 June 1976. The mass revolt of high-schoolers, and also university students, which spread quickly across the country, is often considered the turning point after severe repression. Harsh repression accompanied the economic and political heyday of apartheid, from the suppression of anti-apartheid

264 • REVOLUTIONARY MOVEMENTS IN AFRICA

politics and emerging Pan-Africanism following the Sharpeville massacre of 21 March 1960 to the Rivonia trial in 1964, where Nelson Mandela and his comrades were sentenced to lifelong imprisonment.

Raymond Suttner, however, maintains that the African National Congress (ANC) underground, despite the harsh repression, remained present in people's homes and memories as a 'pattern of social and political activity that has affected interpersonal relations and modes of conduct in society'.[3] Suttner does not discuss the implications of student activism, but it has been highlighted by Julian Brown, who argues that the decade before the 16 June 1976 uprising was characterised by a student-led reinvention of the politics of protest in South Africa. Students became radicalised; their protests connected with those of workers. Significantly, other social groups began to adopt the experimental forms of protest first tried out by students. New alliances were forged, though they tended to be jagged. The emergence of the new opposition did not happen in a single explosion of protest in 1976, Brown shows, 'but rather through an unplanned series of experiments taking place over the course of a long decade'.[4]

Protests were driven by different groups of students. From 1959 onwards, when the infamously misnamed Extension of University Education Act was passed, South African students had been admitted to universities strictly along racial and ethnic lines. Student protests and forms of organising were necessarily affected by educational apartheid, which closed down the few earlier spaces of cross-racial interaction at the country's previously 'open' universities. Student organisations, even when they were dedicated to oppositional politics, reflected the ravages of segregation. Despite these constraints, complicated alliances emerged between different groups of students, and between students and other social groups.

Cape Town 1968: A Sit-In Occupation

One significant action was a sit-in occupation at the University of Cape Town (UCT), previously one of South Africa's few 'open' universities, now purged into an exclusively white institution. In 1968, Archie Mafeje, a black master's graduate (cum laude) of UCT and by then in the process of completing his PhD at the University of Cambridge, was appointed to a senior lecturer position in Social Anthropology. With strong support from his mentor and teacher, Monica Wilson, then the head of Social Anthropology at UCT, the university offered him the job, but then, after government pressure, rescinded the offer.

When the university failed to stand up against the regime's intervention, a mass meeting took place in August 1968. After rousing speeches from student leaders, most of the 1,000-strong audience marched out, and about 600 students occupied the university's administration building. UCT at the time had only about 6,000 students, so indeed a substantial proportion of the then almost entirely white student population took part.

Eventually, the occupiers – about 90 had stayed the course – gave up and left after one-and-a-half weeks, following violent attacks by right-wing students from the university of the Afrikaner apartheid elite, Stellenbosch University, and threats by police. A white anthropologist was appointed in Mafeje's place. South Africa's oldest university had caved in to the demands of the apartheid policy regarding university education.

Yet, for a brief period in August 1968, South African students had felt a liberating taste of '1968'. As one of the UCT activists later recalled: 'In one fell swoop we had thrown off our mental shackles. At last we were not just some isolated racist outpost of empire, but part of an international student movement.'[5]

Black Consciousness Ideology and the Formation of the South African Students Organisation

South Africa's campus rebellions had distinctive dimensions of the 1960s counterculture. At the same time, there were profound revolts against apartheid and institutional racism. The most significant new student movement was the South African Students' Organisation (SASO). SASO, founded in 1968, and the Black Consciousness ideology it embraced, were associated with Stephen Bantu ('Steve') Biko, who became SASO's first president in July 1969. Also in 1969, at Fort Hare, the until then fairly independent black institution for higher education, students boycotted the installation of the new rector, Johannes Marthinus de Wet, a member of the Afrikaner Broederbond (a male secret society of white Calvinist Afrikaner nationalists). The university was closed, and 23 students were not allowed to come back. The developments that led to the formation of SASO need to be understood in the politics of South Africa's 1968 moment and a reinvention of protest politics. Yet SASO's formation was also due to the complex relations of black students with the country's national student organisation, the National Union of South African Students (NUSAS). At issue was the fact that, notwithstanding its multiracial membership, NUSAS was essentially controlled by white students.

This white dominance in 'liberal' organisations was what Biko had in mind when he expressed his objection to 'the intellectual arrogance of white people that makes them believe that white leadership is *a sine qua non* in this country and that whites are divinely appointed pace-setters in progress'.[6] In 1970 Biko, wrote in the SASO newsletter: 'True to their image, the white liberals always knew what was good for the blacks and told them so'.[7]

The students concluded that in order to avoid domination by white 'liberals', black people had to organise independently. SASO thus offered membership to students of all 'Black' sections of the population, which included those who had experienced oppression as members of the 'African', 'Coloured' and 'Indian' apartheid categories.

Black Consciousness ideology was profoundly influenced by the SASO leadership's reading of Frantz Fanon, particularly the militant psychiatrist and political philosopher's *Black Skin, White Masks*. The African-American Black Power movement was also influential with their early focus on psychological empowerment, an idea they expressed by popularising the slogan 'black is beautiful'.

As early as 1971, the SASO leadership discussed proposals to start projects outside the academic environment. Thus included the formation of a Black Workers' Council (later renamed the Black Workers Project) and the Black People's Convention, a new political movement that would soon run alongside SASO. The activists started Black Community Programmes to reach out to townships and rural areas.

'Towards Participatory Democracy': Rick Turner's Anti-Capitalist Thinking

The protests initially confined to university politics increasingly embraced non-student concerns. In the aftermath of South Africa's 1968, radical anti-apartheid and increasingly 'new-left' white students at the University of the Witwatersrand (Wits) invited speakers to rediscover the history of resistance, which had been hidden through the repressive climate of the 1960s.[8] This was followed up with a campaign for the release of all political prisoners.[9]

Most important for the emergence of new alliances was the engagement of students, and some radical academics, with workers and other marginalised social groups. Initially they addressed labour conditions on university campuses, but soon the initiatives' focus broadened. In July 1971, a proposal was made at a NUSAS conference that wages and economic commissions be set up at all the historically 'English' liberal universities. The proposal called for students to research labour conditions and to support workers' demands, on and off campuses.

Rick Turner played a significant role in the nascent student–worker alliances. The active supporter of radical student movements had, for a short time, extraordinary impact on the emerging New Left in South Africa. His radical inputs were linked, in critical ways, to a radically different Marxist thinking, as well as his response to Black Consciousness ideology.

His experience with the French intellectual left during his doctoral studies at the Sorbonne in the 1960s had a profound impact on the young South African, which he shared with students and friends, first in Cape Town, and from 1970 in Durban. In 1968, while temporarily teaching at UCT, he had been heavily involved in the 'Free University' of alternative lectures that the student occupiers had run during the sit-in to protest the non-appointment of Mafeje.[10]

In 1970, Turner took up a position as a lecturer in Political Science at the University of Natal, where he became an extraordinary influence on a number of (white, predominantly male) students with anti-apartheid desires. A year later, this core group formed the first Student Wages Commission in Durban.

Turner's thinking drew from French leftist intellectual traditions. Sartre was a major influence, but he also incorporated Marxist perspectives; among others, he translated and taught Althusser's works. His most important publication was *The Eye of the Needle: Toward Participatory Democracy*, which was published in 1972. The book called for the development of a radical alternative in which not only was apartheid to be abolished, but the decentralisation of South African policy and economy was to be embraced, with the aim of eliminating hierarchy.

Capitalism was the basic cause of social inequality and conflict in South Africa, Turner argued,[11] though the South African 'capitalist human model' was profoundly culturalised and racialised.[12] The aim of participatory democracy was not only universal franchise, but also 'the replacement of private ownership of the means of production by workers' control in industry and agriculture'.[13]

Turner emphasised the necessity of utopian thinking, which he understood as the imagination of another possible South African society.[14] He further held that those fighting for liberation ought to 'prefigure the future. Organizations must be participatory rather than authoritarian. They must be areas in which people can experience human solidarity and learn to work with one another in harmony and in love.'[15]

In this spirit, Turner also appreciated Black Consciousness, although he cautioned that 'an assertion of the dignity of blackness is not enough'; this should be combined with the rejection of the values of capitalist society.[16] Furthermore, Turner called on South African whites to develop a critical 'White Consciousness' and rethink race as a social force. White South Africans had to understand that the existing South African society and their position in it was a result not of the 'triumph of white civilization', but of the 'bloody and ambiguous birth of a new technology'.[17] Turner's understanding of critical whiteness entailed a radical rejection of the entrenched paternalistic thinking among white South African liberalism. His critique built on a profoundly anti-authoritarian departure from the vanguardism of the South African left, especially the Communist Party with its close affinity to the Soviet Bloc.

Student Wages Commission

Rick Turner was an extraordinary teacher and popular with students who were already leaning towards anti-apartheid and anti-establishment thinking. He played a crucial role by helping them to develop an understanding of capitalist society and a commitment to involve themselves in opposing South African political economy and racialism.[18] Turner also gave extra-curricular lectures on social and political topics in communities across Durban, and spoke at protest meetings and other events to which he was invited by different organisations.[19]

Through his students, whom he had encouraged to get involved with the black working class as the key factor of change in his analysis, Turner played a crucial role in the formation of the first Student Wages Commission in Durban in 1971. Initially, the aim was to assist university auxiliary workers to advocate for better conditions of employment.[20]

Soon the students became involved in a broad array of activities to support black workers. They played an important role in the establishment of the General Factory Workers' Benefit Fund that attracted hundreds, later thousands, of workers into a kind of mutual social benefit association. Students visited workers in their hostels (worker compounds), wrote pamphlets and distributed them to workers. They established a newspaper, mostly written in isiZulu, called *Isisebenzi* ('The Worker').

The Wages Commission students encouraged hundreds of black workers to attend meetings of the Department of Labour's Wages Board, which set the wages of black workers for specific industries, and speak for themselves. Cole cites the observations of a dockworker leader, Morris Ndlovu:

'It was at that meeting [in July 1972] where we realised our power because we were talking for ourselves at that meeting.' Ndlovu credited the 'Wage Com' radicals for his participation: 'It is because I was actually encouraged by the students about organisation, that without unity and speaking with one voice we were not going to win.'[21]

A vocal though volatile alliance of activists, students and intellectuals of the South African 'new left' engaged a radical critique of multi-racial liberal anti-apartheid politics, such as the Liberal Party of South Africa, which had been founded in 1953. They assessed 'race' and its relation to class in apartheid society and explored different forms of Marxist and socialist critiques.[22] In Durban, their connections with workers were particularly strong, and eventually resulted in that turning point of January 1973.

Biko and Black Consciousness in Durban

The commonly used label of the 'Durban moment' suggested a convergence of the different radical movements, embodied by Turner and Biko, the two leading intellectual-activists. However, researchers and contemporaries of the Durban strikes differ regarding the role of the Black Consciousness activists. Labour historian Peter Cole, for instance, agrees that Biko offered a brilliant and radical critique of apartheid and the anti-apartheid movement. However, he maintains that those who embraced the Black Consciousness ideology were more concerned with communities than with factories. He maintained that 'when black consciousness student activists attempted to organize black workers, they had little success'. On the other hand, Cole claims that Black Consciousness adherents mostly rejected alliances with white radicals, 'though Biko and Rick Turner were on good terms'.[23]

However, Omar Badsha, at the time a union organiser and involved with underground networks and the resurrection of the Natal Indian Congress, remembers that Biko and others, especially among the 'Indian' Black Consciousness activists, as well as Turner, and Badsha himself, worked together in community mobilisation in the Phoenix settlement in Durban. Originally founded by Gandhi in the early 1900s, the settlement was a site of experiments in communal living, social and economic justice and nonviolent action. The community initiatives became more politically orientated with the emergence of young leaders in the early 1970s. Turner's biographer Kenniston argues that Biko and Turner did not view Black Consciousness and working-class activities as incompatible.[24] Both were involved in a Phoenix study group and mobilisation. The Black Consciousness movement may have had less of a role than the existing trade unions, and particularly unionists like Harriet Bolton, the General Secretary of the Garment Workers' Industrial Union in South Africa, the (white) radical students in the Wages Commission in the mobilisation of the massive Durban strikes of 1973, or indeed earlier labour action by dockworkers, as Cole has pointed out. But indications are that Biko and his associates in the Black Consciousness movement were indeed part of a significant stream of renewed political energy that characterised Durban in the early 1970s.

Omar Badsha remembers 1971–72 as a moment of extraordinary fluidity and convergence. He recalls, for instance, that some of his comrades in the underground Umkhonto we Sizwe (the ANC's armed wing) structures were also active in the Black Consciousness movement. There was also a meeting ground between the re-emerging Natal Indian Congress and the Black Consciousness movement through the involvement of 'Indian' Black Consciousness activists.

THE NAMIBIAN GENERAL STRIKE

The activists in Durban were part of a wider regional mobilisation in southern Africa. By the time of the Durban uprising, protest and labour action had already erupted into full public view in South Africa's colony. In Namibia, student protests occurred as early as August 1971, followed by the massive contract labour strike in December 1971 and January 1972. A careful look at the Namibian events and their ramifications in South Africa helps to understand the entangled history of southern African resistance politics.

When contract labourers in Namibia went on strike in 1971, this was not the first time black workers in the country had done so. Strikes were common in Namibian colonial history from as early as 1893, although, like in South Africa, black (African) workers were not allowed to unionise.[25] However, little was known in public about labour protests in Namibia until the 1971–72 strike. The authors of a comprehensive history of Namibian labour action point out that it was the strike of 1971–72 which:

the South African regime found impossible to conceal and which finally shook the outside world into an awareness of the plight of the black Namibian worker. It was a general strike in all but name, involving over 13,000 migrant workers and attracting unprecedented support from among the African population as a whole .... Above all the strike – the largest and longest in Namibia's history – demonstrated the potential power of the workers and their capacity to take sustained and organised action ....[26]

Despite its bitter-sweet endings, the Namibian general strike was an important turning point of the revival of radical resistance in the politics of southern Africa.

The Contract Labour System

In Namibia, labour was marked by a particularly rigid and oppressive system. Only men were recruited through the much-hated contract system known as *omutete wOkaholo* (literally 'to queue up for the [identity] disc'),[27] because of the copper or plastic bracelets with their identification number, which freshly recruited contract labourers had to place on their wrist after the mandatory medical examination – a thoroughly humiliating experience. At their workplaces, contract labourers were housed in single-sex compounds. The workday was scarcely limited; workers were required 'to render to the master his services at all fair and reasonable times'.[28] Contracts were running for long periods: workers did not see their families for 18 (later 12) months.

Women in the northern rural areas had to take care of agricultural production, and raise their families on their own. Contract labour was clearly a defining factor for the profound changes in the social structure and interpersonal relations in northern Namibia. However, it also allowed for contact across the tightly controlled divisions, and eventually became a primary factor in the emergence of Namibian nationalism.

It started in the 1950s. About 200 Owambo,[29] most of whom had deserted labour contracts on the Witwatersrand mines, lived under precarious, and in many cases illegal, circumstances in Cape Town. They were under imminent danger of being arrested and deported to Namibia if caught. The group formed a closely knit community which catered for the well-being, social security and recreational needs of its members.[30] Every Sunday, the men gathered at a barbershop in Somerset Road. From there, they would go to the Grand Parade in central Cape Town to listen to speeches by local anti-apartheid activists. Andimba Herman Toivo ya Toivo, who emerged as the leader of the group, became acquainted with members of the Cape Town left, including Jack Simons, Brian Bunting and Sam Kahn.[31] These connections with the – mostly white – socialist circles in Cape Town were later used by the South African regime to claim that the organisation known as the Ovamboland People's Organisation (OPO) was the brainchild of South African communists.

In 1957, the Cape Town-based Namibians formed the Ovamboland People's Congress (OPC). The OPC initiative was largely a political extension of the already existent 'brotherhood' of comprehensive solidarity and mutual support among the group of workers from Owambo. In Cape Town, as in the mines, 'brotherhood' provided the basis for collective responses to employers and administration.[32] The 'brotherhood' of solidarity and cooperation among the group of workers from Owambo found expression in the funds that had been established to support those among the Cape Town-based group who were facing difficulties due to their undocumented status. 'Brotherhood' essentially meant a sense of comprehensive solidarity, unity and mutual support among contract workers in and outside the work situation; in the mines, it provided the basis for collective responses to employers and the administration.[33]

In April 1959, nationalist activity gained a base in Namibia itself with the formation of the Ovamboland People's Organisation in Windhoek, where Sam Nujoma, later President of the South West Africa People's Organisation (SWAPO) and independent Namibia's first president, held regular meetings with contract labourers in the Windhoek workers' compound. OPO's immediate concerns were the labour conditions of the contract workers from Ovamboland. This focus of its early activism was responsible for the broad support OPO quickly gained among the migrant labourers.

While some of the organisation's leadership certainly harboured wider nationalist political interests, the rank and file were primarily concerned with the conditions of workers trapped in the contract labour system. When Nujoma visited Walvis Bay in June 1959, almost all the workers came out to hear him speak. The local OPO chairman, Vinnia Ndadi, who had organised the gatherings, recalled Nujoma's rousing address, which ended with his call out: 'Will you join the struggle to abolish contract labour?' Everyone present shouted, 'Yes! Yes! That's what we want!'[34]

Resistance against the contract labour system fuelled the formation of nationalist organisations in Namibia. However, in the late 1960s, after brutal repression, the flight into exile by many of the founder generation, the 1967–68 Terrorism Trial in Pretoria and the long-term incarceration of leaders such as Ya Toivo on Robben Island, the spirit of resistance seemed broken.

Mobilising against the Contract Labour System

In the early 1970s, however, things changed. Stephen Hayes, a young South African, who worked as a journalist at the *Windhoek Advertiser*, observed a definite change of attitude among the black population in the city and elsewhere in the country. Hayes and Dave de Beer, another young anti-apartheid activist, travelled widely and communicated with workers and residents of black 'reserves'. In 1969, when they had first arrived in Namibia, people had been fearful and reserved in sharing their thoughts, many had been subservient and others were bewildered. By late 1971, however, Hayes recalled that black Namibians were 'becoming conscious of their humanity, and they are walking tall in the streets …, and the word "baas" has disappeared from their vocabulary'.[35]

Two interconnected developments contributed to the enhanced confidence. In June 1971, the International Court of Justice had declared the South African occupation of Namibia illegal. This ruling encouraged a sense of impending change. The leaders of the black Lutheran Churches in Namibia took an unprecedented step and wrote a letter to South Africa's Prime Minister, John Vorster, to protest against the occupation as a violation of human rights. The reorientation of the Churches towards a new theology of liberation signified a tremendous development in intensely Christian Namibia. At the same time, the tightening of the apartheid regime's mobility controls at the end of 1970 diminished the possibility of dodging the racist system even further.[36]

The situation became explosive. A researcher of Namibia's economic and labour history observed that the second half of 1971 was marked by an escalation of anti-colonial political activity.[37] At the heart of this upsurge were demonstrations by high school students in August 1971 in the country's north. In the aftermath of the protests, a number of the student leaders were expelled from schools in Owambo and took up contract labour in the country's southern parts. The expelled students, together with labour and SWAPO activists, immediately set out to mobilise against the contract labour system.

The energetic student activists have been credited for linking the workers' resentment of the contract labour system to demands for liberation.[38] Remarkably, the strike occurred largely spontaneously; mobilising had laid groundwork, but the walk-outs happened without a hierarchical leadership, and workers refused to identify individual leaders. Instead, they expressed their demands collectively in mass meetings. This strategy, which was reported widely in the South African press, also influenced the tactics of the Durban strikes in early 1973, which similarly revolved around collective mass action.[39]

The spark that set the strike off was a remark made by Jannie de Wet, the Commissioner for Ovamboland. In a radio broadcast on 15 November 1971, he claimed that 'contract labour was not a form of slavery because the workers concerned signed their contracts "voluntarily", without anyone forcing them'.[40]

De Wet's statement was in response to growing condemnation of the contract labour system. In early November 1971, Dave de Beer, who was at the time the Anglican Diocesan Secretary in Windhoek, had spoken at a meeting arranged by the NUSAS branch of his alma mater, Wits University in Johannesburg. The young Church worker had drawn on a recent incident at Oamites mine south of Windhoek to make an argument that the contract labour system in Namibia amounted to slavery, where the bosses not only wanted the workers to work for them, but tried to control who they talked to in their spare time, the books they could buy and read, and even their religious belief.[41]

De Beer's statement had been reported widely: *Die Suidwester*, the mouthpiece of the National Party, had splashed it all over its front pages for a whole week, and de Wet had gone on the South West African Broadcasting Corporation's Owambo radio with his speech. Hinananje Nehova, one of the expelled student-turned-worker activists, later recalled that the key slogan and central demand of the workers became, *'Odalate Naiteke'* ('Break the wire' – break the contract system that ties the workers to their bosses like with a wire [*odalate*, oshiWambo, from the Afrikaans *draad*]):

> 'If we break this system with a strike, we could have the freedom to choose our jobs and move freely around the country; to take our families with us and to visit our friends wherever they are.' Everyone supported these ideas.[42]

The strike started in the fish canning factories in Walvis Bay, where 3,200 contract workers were employed. Mass meetings were held, and connections built between different centres of contract labour. The letter written by the workers in Walvis Bay appealed to their comrades in Windhoek: 'Let's take "the boer Jannie de Wet" by his word and do just that, go home.' An ultimatum was set for 12 December. At a Sunday afternoon mass meeting in Windhoek, the workers decided that they would not go to work on the next day. On Monday 13 December 1971, none of the Ovambo workers in Windhoek left the compound. Two days later, the authorities deported the striking workers to Owambo by rail. This was an enforced deportation, yet at the same time it was a tactical return on the part of the workers, a symbolic act of withdrawal, as well as a tactic for extending survival by ensuring a good harvest in the rural north.

By January 1972, 13,000 workers were on strike, and 21 towns and 11 mines were affected. Most of the strikers were Owambo, and at the time the action was often referred to as an 'Ovambo' strike. However, workers of different ethnicities supported the strike.[43]

The far-reaching aims of the strike were the abolition of the contract labour system and an end to influx control. These calls constituted, and were seen thus by the South African regime as, a fundamental challenge to the oppressive state-administered labour regime and apartheid colonialism. The demands were officially adopted at a mass meeting held at Oluno, near the Owambo capital of Ondangwa, which was attended by about 3,500 striking workers who had left their workplaces in southern and central Namibia and returned to Owambo.

The workers demanded an end to the contract labour system, and, practically, freedom of the workers to choose their own workplace. After a decade of enforced acquiescence (at least on the surface), workers and students called again for more than mere improvement; the system had to go altogether. They requested that employment bureaux be established throughout the northern 'homelands' which should advertise vacancies to enable people to find their own jobs.

The workers furthermore demanded the freedom to bring their wives and children along to their places of employment. This request included a call for the abolition of the passbook system and its replacement by identification cards, so it stopped just short of demands for complete abolition of the apartheid influx control system. They also insisted that employees be paid a wage that allowed them to buy their own food (instead of receiving rations, as was the common practice in the compounds) and a cash allowance that recruited workers from the north could use to pay for their own transport to their workplaces in the south.[44]

The South African government responded to the strike with a mixture of partial reform and brutal repression. The hated semi-governmental South West African Native Labour Association was abolished and replaced with tribal 'labour bureaux'; limited freedom to negotiate with employers was now possible. Wages improved, although they remained very low. However, no changes were made to the influx control system, so workers from the north had to leave their families behind.

Limited reforms were juxtaposed with draconian responses to the mobilisation. In January 1972, all public meetings in Ovamboland were banned, and the army was deployed to Owambo. The South African government also announced a blanket news ban, and no-one was allowed to enter the area who was not in possession of a special permit. Finally, on 4 February, the South African government introduced emergency proclamations in Owambo. Proclamation R 17 (1972) prohibited unauthorised meetings of more than five persons; severe restrictions on freedom of political organisation and expression were also imposed. Detention without trial was authorised; informal open-air detention centres known as 'cages' were constructed all across Owambo. By the end of May 1972, 267 Owambo had been detained; 88 were charged with offences, including murder, arson, public violence, incitement, robbery, assault, malicious damage to property and possession of dangerous weapons; 53 people were convicted.[45] Furthermore, a pseudo-traditional form of punishment, public flogging, was instigated by the 'tribal' courts where young activists were subjected to flogging, with up to 30 strikes being administered to the naked buttocks of both men and women.[46] In Windhoek, so-called 'ringleaders' of the strike were hauled before the magistrate's court and charged with 'intimidating' the workers to stay away from work. The state's case collapsed however.

The strike resulted in renewed political mobilisation, and in Owambo, resistance to the contract labour system broadened into a generalised revolt against the South African regime. Vehicles transporting recruits from Angola to replace the striking workers were stoned. Over 100 kilometres of the border fence between Namibia and Angola were cut and flattened by returned workers and other local residents.

Young people rose up in an open revolt, especially after the expelled student activists of the August 1971 school walk-outs, along with some 20,000 striking workers, were deported back to Owambo. This also incited the politicisation of young women in the north. The Namibian historian Martha Akawa argues that:

the presence of about 20,000 politically charged men was one of the most influential factors on women becoming more involved in politics. A woman who became part of the SWAPO Youth League (SYL) in 1972, indicated that, 'when the men got expelled from the South, they held meetings and were talking about politics, how exploitative the contract labour system was and other issues. I got interested and that is how I and other women joined.'[47]

Men, women, and especially young people participated in protests defying the administration. A campaign targeted the government's cattle vaccination points. Many of these were burnt down when people suspected that the vaccinations administered by the colonial apartheid state, rather than protecting from disease, were killing their animals. Akawa concludes that 'the workers made it loud and clear that they were a force to be reckoned with'.[48]

Due to the brutal repression, however, within a few months in 1972 many of the young activists fled into exile and the revolt died down. However, undeniably, the strike of 1971–72 galvanised Namibian liberation politics and brought a new, radical generation to the fore.

Implications of the Namibian Strike for South Africa

Observers have frequently noted that 'the political implications of the strike were also felt in the Republic of South Africa when a series of strikes broke out in Natal'.[49] The Namibian strike was widely reported in the South African press. The news from Namibia was keenly picked up by young leftists in South Africa, who had recently begun to organise in new, radical formations. Omar Badsha recalled that the way the Namibians had conducted the strike had particularly impressed the Durban dockworkers, especially the fact that the workers in Namibia had insisted that everyone was present during negotiations, where the workers shouted their demands collectively. He said that this tactic was then also adopted by the Durban strikes in January 1973.

A FEW CONCLUDING WORDS

The Namibian strike embodied a remarkable resurgence of resistance politics, which received critical attention from the new generation of South African radicals. When radical anti-apartheid 'new left' white students at Wits came up with a campaign for the release of all political prisoners, this self-evidently included the Namibian freedom fighters detained on Robben

Island, and they even invited a recently released former Namibian prisoner, Gerson Veii, to speak on the Johannesburg campus.[50] The all-black South African Students Organisation (SASO), for its part, officially condemned the presence of the apartheid forces in Namibia.[51]

There can be no doubt that the activists of the 'Durban moment' and, overall, the 'new' South African left of the early 1970s were inspired by the events in Namibia. Although factory workers were probably less well informed than leading activists about the developments in the wider southern African region (Omar Badsha interview),[52] the connections between Namibian and South African 'new' anti-apartheid, labour and 'new left' politics in this period were very close.

In Namibia, as in South Africa, the earlier strands of nationalist mobilisation had been brutally crushed with forced removals, police shootings and large trials, which sentenced a generation of liberation fighters to long-term imprisonment on Robben Island. In South Africa, the entrenched structures of the earlier anti-apartheid movement and communist party politics had been struck a decisive blow.

In South Africa and Namibia, young activists drew on new forms of mobilisation. While organisers had laid the groundwork for the Namibian and Durban strikes, the movements were characterised by spontaneity and insistence on tactics of flat leadership. Unsurprisingly, the politics of the early 1970s could not be sustained due to brutal repression through emergency regulations, arrests and public floggings in Namibia; in South Africa, leading activists and activist intellectuals were banned, and thus prevented from speaking out. Those included Rick Turner and Steve Biko, both later murdered by the apartheid state in 1978 and 1977 respectively, and also included their associates in the Black Consciousness movement and the Wages Commission.

What remained was the eruption of new, massive labour and political action in Namibia in 1971, followed by the Durban strikes of early 1973, which put mass resistance back in public view. Movements erupted onto the political scene that were, by necessity and choice, non-sectarian and typically of remarkable openness in their social and political alliances. Their imaginative creativity and reflection on alternatives to apartheid beyond the management of the state remains an inspiration half a century later. This became manifest during the South African student movements of 2015–17, when the young protestors often referred to the writings of the intellectual activists Biko and Turner.

NOTES

1. Peter Cole, *Dockworker Power: Race and Activism in Durban and the San Francisco Bay Area*, Urbana: University of Illinois Press, 2018, xx.

2. Heike Becker, 'Dissent, Disruption, Decolonization: South African Student Protests, 1968 to 2016', *International Socialist Review*, 111, 31–47, at 34–41.

3. Raymond Suttner, *The ANC Underground in South Africa to 1976: A Social and Historical Study*, Johannesburg: Jacana, 2008, 15.

4. Julian Brown, *The Road to Soweto: Resistance and the Uprising of 16 June 1976*, London: James Currey, 2016, 4.

5. Martin Plaut, 'How the 1968 Revolution Reached Cape Town', 1 September 2011, https://martinplaut.wordpress.com/2011/09/01/the-1968-revolution-reaches-cape-town/.

6. Steve Biko, *I Write What I Like: Selected Writings by Steve Biko*, London: Heinemann, 1987, 24.

7. Steve Biko, *I Write What I like. Steve Biko: A Selection of His Writings, 40th Anniversary Edition*, Johannesburg: Picador Africa, 2017, 21.

8. Glenn Moss, *The New Radicals: A Generational Memoir of the 1970s*, Johannesburg: Jacana Media, 2014, 105–120.

9. Ibid., 121–146.

10. William Hemingway Kenniston, *Richard Turner's Contribution to a Socialist Political Culture in South Africa 1968-1978*, MA History thesis, Bellville: University of the Western Cape, 2010, 67–68.

11. Richard Turner, *The Eye of the Needle: Towards Participatory Democracy in South Africa*, London: Seagull Books, 2015 (1972), 100.

12. Ibid., 100.

13. Ibid., 108.

14. Ibid., 10.

15. Ibid., 124.

16. Ibid., 119.

17. Ibid., 122.

18. Kenniston, *Richard Turner's Contribution to a Socialist Political Culture in South Africa 1968–1978*, 85.

19. Ibid., 66.

20. Ibid., 88.

21. Cole, *Dockworker Power*, 118.

22. Moss, *The New Radicals*, 150.

23. Cole, *Dockworker Power*, 127–128.

24. Kenniston, *Richard Turner's Contribution to a Socialist Political Culture in South Africa 1968–1978*, 87.

25. Gillian Cronje and Suzanne Cronje, *The Workers of Namibia*, London: International Defence & Aid Fund, 1979; Robert J. Gordon, *Mines, Masters and Migrants: Life in a Namibian Compound*, Johannesburg: Ravan Press, 1977.

26. Ibid., 79.

27. Zed Ngavirue, *Political Parties and Interest Groups in South West Africa (Namibia): A Study of a Plural Society*, Basle: Schlettwein, 1997, 234.
28. Ibid., 234.
29. 'Owambo' is the spelling more aligned with the local language, and how the people themselves use it. The anglicised spelling 'Ovambo' was generally used by colonial administrators and media before Namibian independence in 1990; the colonial denomination of north-central Namibia was Ovamboland. This spelling was also adopted at the time by the emerging liberation movements, such as the Ovamboland People's Congress and the Ovamboland People's Organisation. I use the colonial spelling where I refer to the institutions, which used it in the 1960s and 1970s. Otherwise, I refer to people and the region as Owambo.
30. Tony Emmett, *Popular Resistance and the Roots of Nationalism in Namibia, 1915–1966*, Basle: Schlettwein, 1999, 274.
31. Ibid., 275.
32. Gordon, *Mines, Masters and Migrants*, 101–142.
33. Ibid.
34. Vinnia Ndadi, *Breaking Contract: The Story of Vinnia Ndadi*, Life Histories from the Revolution, Namibia: SWAPO, Richmond: LSM Information Centre, 1989 (1974), 71.
35. Steven Hayes, *Khanya*, https://khanya.wordpress.com/khanya-blog/.
36. Cronje and Cronje, *The Workers of Namibia*, 80.
37. Richard Moorsom, *Underdevelopment and Labour Migration: The Contract Labour System in Namibia*, Working Paper 10, Bergen: Chr. Michelsen Institute, 1997.
38. Herbert Jauch, *Namibia's Labour Movement: An Overview – History, Challenges and Achievements*, Windhoek: Friedrich-Ebert-Stiftung, 2018, 8.
39. Interview with Omar Badsha, 18 September 2019, Woodstock, Cape Town.
40. Cronje and Cronje, *The Workers of Namibia*, 80–81.
41. Hayes, *Khanya*.
42. Cronje and Cronje, *The Workers of Namibia*, 81.
43. Ibid., 79–80; Kletus Likuwa and Napandulwe Shiweda, 'Okaholo: Contract Labour System and Lessons for Post Colonial Namibia', *Mgbakoigba Journal of African Studies*, 6(2), 2017, 26–47.
44. Cronje and Cronje, *The Workers of Namibia*, 80.
45. André Du Pisani, *SWA/Namibia: The Politics of Continuity and Change*, Johannesburg: Jonathan Ball, 1985, 214–215.
46. Martha Akawa, *The Gender Politics of the Namibian Liberation Struggle*, Basle: Basler Afrika Bibliographien, 2014, 34.
47. Ibid., 33.
48. Ibid.
49. Du Pisani, *SWA/Namibia*, 215.
50. Moss, *The New Radicals*, 121–146.
51. Becker, 'Dissent, Disruption, Decolonization', 40.
52. Interview with Omar Badsha.

15
Dimitri Tsafendas:
An African Revolutionary

Harris Dousemetzis

INTRODUCTION

On 6 September 1966, inside the House of Assembly in Cape Town, Dimitri Tsafendas stabbed to death Hendrik Verwoerd, South Africa's Prime Minister and so-called 'architect of apartheid'. Tsafendas was immediately arrested, and before he had even been questioned by the authorities, they declared him a madman without any political motive for the killing. A communiqué by the South African embassy in Belgium said that the murder had 'manifestly been perpetrated by an unbalanced individual and was therefore devoid of political significance'. The government, it concluded, would carry on the 'peaceful apartheid policy for which Dr. Verwoerd had laid the foundations'.[1]

IN POLICE CUSTODY

Tsafendas was held under the terms of the Criminal Procedure Amendment Act No. 96 of 1965,[2] which meant that the police had the right to detain him without charge or access to a lawyer for up to 180 days.[3] The infamous General Hendrik van den Bergh, head of the Security Police who had received special training in torture techniques from the French in the early 1960s in France and Algeria,[4] was placed in charge of the police investigation into the assassination and personally interrogated Tsafendas the first 48 hours. Van den Bergh claimed that 'no person in South African history has ever been interrogated as much as Demitrios Tsafendas'.[5] When interrogated, Tsafendas said that he had killed Verwoerd because he was 'disgusted' with his 'racial policies', and that he hoped 'a change of policy would take place' after the 'removal of the Prime Minister'.[6] He also told the police that he did not consider Verwoerd to be the 'real representative' of his country and that he wanted to see a government representing 'all the South African people'.[7] His statements to the police were perfectly coherent, and he gave perfectly clear and solid political reasons as to why he had killed Verwoerd. Tsafendas also told the police that he had been a member of the South African Communist Party (SACP) from 1936 to 1942,[8] that he was 'anti-co-lonial, against slavery and in favour of all colonies which were controlled by Belgium, France and Portugal to be afforded self-government', and that while in England, he had participated and had been 'holding the posters up' in 'anti-colonial', 'anti-apartheid' and 'anti-racial' meetings, as well as meetings of 'the Committee of African Organizations'.[9]

Tsafendas also explained perfectly clearly why he had carried out the attack with a knife with no apparent escape plan. He revealed that he had ini-tially planned to shoot Verwoerd on 2 September from some distance inside parliament during a function and then flee to *Eleni*, a Greek tanker docked in Cape Town harbour that was going to sail the following day. However, he was not able to obtain a firearm, and Verwoerd did not attend the event, so he decided to carry out the attack with a knife a few days later; he knew then that there would be no escape, but he also knew that his temporary employ-ment at the parliament was close to finishing and that he would not have another chance again. He told his interrogators: 'I did not care about the consequences for what would happen to me afterwards. I was so disgusted with the racial policy that I went through with my plans to kill the Prime Minister.'[10]

According to the Truth and Reconciliation Commission, 'torture was the dominant form of violation by the apartheid police during the 1960s'; at the time, detainees were routinely tortured for much less serious crimes than that of Tsafendas.[11] Tsafendas was not exempted, and was brutally tortured every day. This was initially done to extract information about his back-ground and any accomplices he might have had, but soon turned into pure revenge. Several times daily, he would be beaten and kicked, and he received daily electric shocks, heightened by water being poured over him while a plastic bag was placed on his head to induce suffocation. His cell had no bed, and he had to lie on the concrete floor, frequently naked and handcuffed. The treatment became harsher and harsher. From the second week onwards, he was subjected to a near-daily ordeal involving a simulated hanging. He would be taken, blindfolded and hands tied, to another room, while the policemen shouted: 'Now, you bastard, now your time has come.' Having been placed on a chair with a rope around his neck, he would be asked for his 'last wish', then the chair would be removed, leaving him dangling from the rope for a few seconds before the gloating policemen allowed him to fall to the ground. Another beating would follow; he would be told that his time had not yet come, but that nevertheless he would never get out alive. Soon he could no longer stand up and had to be carried to his 'hanging'. Sometimes the police would also threaten to throw him out of a window; they would claim, they said, that he had died trying to escape.[12] All these, except possibly for the mock hangings, were standard torture techniques of the South African police at the time. After three weeks of relentless torture, Tsafendas was unable to take any more pain. However, very importantly, the mock hangings had convinced him that one of them would be real, and that the police would then claim that he was a madman who had committed suicide, and that he had killed Verwoerd because of his madness. Tsafendas then decided to change his tune to end the torture and to live as long as possible.

THE POLICE INVESTIGATION

Immediately after the assassination, the South African police embarked on a massive investigation to discover Tsafendas's past; this included questioning over 150 people who had known him, and requesting information about him from the Polícia Internacional e de Defesa do Estado (PIDE, the Portuguese International and State Defence Police), as Tsafendas was born and had lived for almost 20 years in Mozambique, a Portuguese colony at the time. Doubtless to their horror, they confirmed that he was a former member of the SACP,[13] while they also discovered that he had been banned from entering South Africa as he was on the Stop List of the Department of Immigration because of his communist beliefs and activities[14] (this list was also in the possession of PIDE[15]), that the South African authorities had four files on him,[16] that he had been deported and exiled from Mozambique for twelve years due to his communist and anti-colonialist activities there,[17] that he had been arrested several times by the Portuguese police for communist and anti-colonialist activities,[18] that while in South Africa from 1939 to 1942 he had 'engaged actively in Communistic propaganda',[19] that in Mozambique in 1936 he had been dismissed from a job 'owing to his Communist leanings' and that he was suspected of being 'engaged in disseminating Communistic propaganda',[20] that he had fought on the side of the communists during the Greek Civil War,[21] and that while in London he had closely associated with Tennyson Makiwane, the African National Congress (ANC) representative there,[22] as well as with the prominent anti-apartheid activists Canon John Collins, David Gardener and Solly Sachs.[23]

Furthermore, two men had reported Tsafendas to the South African police just over a year before the assassination; Nick Vergos had reported him as a 'dangerous communist'[24] and had characterised him as 'the biggest communist in the Republic of South Africa'[25]; Father Hanno Probst had reported him as a 'Communist and a dangerous person'.[26] In addition, Colonel van Wyk of the South African Police, who was sent to Mozambique and Rhodesia to carry out an investigation into Tsafendas, characterised him in his report as being 'intensely anti-white'.[27] Finally, at least six sailors from the *Eleni* testified to the police that three days before the assassination, Tsafendas had characterised a hypothetical killing of Verwoerd as 'justifiable' because he was 'a dictator and a tyrant who was oppressing his people'.[28] Tsafendas routinely characterised Verwoerd in this fashion.

Several witnesses testified to the police about Tsafendas's deep political convictions and eagerness to fight apartheid and colonialism. For example, Edward Furness, a South African man who had met him in London, testified that Tsafendas wanted 'to create a resistance to the regime of South Africa and mentioned civil disobedience', and had told him that he 'was willing to do anything that would get the South African regime out of power'.[29] Kenneth Ross testified that Tsafendas:

> was very fond of discussing politics and gave me the opinion that he was well versed in politics. Tsafendas objected to the Communists being banished to Robin Island [*sic*] because of their political opinions and actions. In general, Tsafendas was opposed to every decision taken by the South African Government and freely voiced his opinion to me. He was blatantly opposed to the National Party policy, the policy of the present Government, and was definitely pro-Russian.[30]

Robert Smith testified that Tsafendas was a 'Communist' and 'a fanatic on politics and seldom spoke of anything else'.[31] Patrick O'Ryan testified that Tsafendas 'was against the state policy of both South Africa and Portugal' and that he 'labelled the apartheid policies as unfair'.[32] Jacobus Bornman testified that Tsafendas 'stood up a lot for the Coloureds' and 'often criticised the South African government and seemed to have a grudge against Dr. Verwoerd'.[33] Reports in the Mozambican press said that Tsafendas was 'violently anti-Portuguese'.[34] In addition, the Commission of Enquiry appointed to investigate the circumstances of Verwoerd's death discovered that Tsafendas, while in London, had tried to 'recruit people to take part in an uprising in South Africa'. Tsafendas admitted to the commission 'that he did in fact try to recruit people for an uprising', but said 'that his aim was confined to the Territory of Mozambique'.[35]

Immediately after the assassination, General van den Bergh had asked PIDE to provide him with any information it had on Tsafendas. A day after the assassination, the South African embassy in Lisbon sent a top secret telegram to the South African Secretary for Foreign Affairs in Cape Town; this said that according to 'a very reliable local source', Tsafendas 'has a criminal record in Mozambique, where he is said to have been arrested on several occasions after creating public disturbances, including shouting pro-Communist anti-Portuguese slogans'; however, he had 'never been convicted as courts have found him to be of unsound mind'. The telegram concluded with the following sentence: 'If information correct, we suspect Portuguese may play down assassin's previous political activities and we would suggest full details in this connection be sought.'[36] The embassy could not have been more correct in its prediction. The following day, 8 September, the Chief Inspector of PIDE in Lisbon sent a top secret telegram to the Sub-Director of PIDE in Mozambique, instructing him that any 'information indicating Tsafendas as a partisan for the independence of your country should not be transmitted to the South African authorities, despite the relations that exist between your delegation and the South African Police'.[37] Attached to the telegram was a report on Tsafendas that was to be given to the South African authorities. The report lied that PIDE had no file on Tsafendas;[38] in reality, it had had one on him since 1938, which by the time of the assassination consisted of about 130 pages. Tsafendas's PIDE file, No. 10,415, had been opened when Tsafendas was just 20 years old, when he was 'suspected of distributing communist propaganda'.[39] Although PIDE's report concealed important information about Tsafendas's political activities, such as that he had fought in the Greek Civil War, it contained several of his arrests and imprisonments by the Portuguese police and stated that he was 'in favour of the independence of Mocambique'.[40] PIDE could not have concealed these as they were well known to all of his friends and acquaintances, while his arrest and imprisonment in Mozambique in 1964 had been widely reported by the local media.

The information the police had gathered, as well as Tsafendas's statements to them, must have frightened the apartheid authorities, and above all General van den Bergh and his close friend John Vorster (Minister of Police at the time, and the man who succeeded Verwoerd as prime minister), who were both in charge of state security. Thus, Van den Bergh ensured that only a very tiny portion of the information the police had discovered about Tsafendas became publicly known. This was mostly information that had already been published in the press or that was supportive of the image they were trying to project: a schizophrenic man without any political interests who had killed Verwoerd because of his insanity. Tsafendas's statements to the police, as well as his real political views and activism, did not become known at the time, nor during his summary trial and the subsequent Commission of Enquiry. Advocate George Bizos believes that:

> The police at the time would have never allowed it to become known that Tsafendas was a politically minded person who had killed Verwoerd for political reasons; if this had happened, Tsafendas would have instantly become a hero of the anti-apartheid movement. Then, a trial of a politically minded person like Tsafendas would have put apartheid in the dock … it would have also been hugely embarrassing for the police to admit that a dedicated Communist with such a long history of political activism had managed to penetrate what was alleged to be a top security system … Communism was at the time the monster in South Africa, the Number One enemy, and the killing of Verwoerd by a Communist would have been a major blow to the prestige of the regime, but also a big victory for Communism. Verwoerd at the time was adored and accepted by most Whites in this country and the thought that someone had killed him because he disagreed with his policies would have shattered such an image.[41]

SUMMARY TRIAL AND THE COMMISSION OF ENQUIRY

On 25 September, even though Tsafendas had requested George Bizos to be his legal representative, Judge Andries Beyers, the Judge President of the Cape, appointed David Bloomberg, an attorney who supported apartheid, to lead Tsafendas's defence team. The following day, Tsafendas was seen for the first time by his defence team; they quickly concluded that he was mentally unstable, and appointed four psychiatrists and a psychologist to examine him.[42] In the short summary trial that followed, meant to determine whether Tsafendas was fit to stand trial, the defence psychiatrists and psychologist – plus another psychiatrist and another psychologist appointed by the state – testified that they had found him to be a delusional schizophrenic who had believed since he was a little child that a tapeworm lived inside him. They all also found him to be 'unable to function at a reasonable level', 'unable to follow a conversation after fifteen minutes', unable to remember his movements prior to the assassination, unable to give a coherent account of himself, and someone who talked in a disjointed manner and who suffered from thought blocking. Obviously, he was also found to be a completely apolitical madman who had killed Verwoerd because of his madness.[43] However, although the psychiatrists and the psychologists claimed that the tapeworm was dominant in Tsafendas's life and that he was constantly talking about it, none of around 200 witnesses who were questioned by the police and the Commission of Enquiry had ever heard him mentioning it, nor had any of them observed any of the symptoms that were described in court.[44] Furthermore, none of these symptoms had been observed by the ten doctors who examined Tsafendas for his various work and visa applications when he was in South Africa from 1963 onwards. Indeed, all found him perfectly well, both mentally and physically.[45]

The psychiatrists based their diagnosis entirely on what they were told by Tsafendas in three 90-minute sessions, without any third-party information (Tsafendas's medical and criminal records and information from people who knew him). They were not aware that Tsafendas had faked mental illness in the past at least twice in order to escape his predicaments at the time, though the police knew this very well. Dr Harold Cooper, one of the defence's psychiatrists, was discouraged by the police from probing into Tsafendas's past as he was told this was their job. He and the other psychiatrists and psychologists were also told by the police that Tsafendas was a perfectly straightforward case of a schizophrenic. This led Dr Cooper to have serious misgivings about the whole procedure and to wonder if the authorities were perhaps covering up their lax security procedures and pressing for Tsafendas to be declared insane so that they could avoid any responsibility for assassination.[46] Reyner van Zyl, the psychologist who examined Tsafendas on behalf of the defence, told the author about the process of the examination:

We were told, or I was told [by the police] – the group of guys that examined him – that he had been in various mental hospitals all over the world … Yes. Well, you know, we were given this information – that he was a disturbed, schizophrenic man. And that was the background that we had available, and nothing else. The third part [the medical reports] was given to us almost in summary. He has been to this hospital, that hospital, that hospital … I think three or four were mentioned – various hospitals overseas.[47]

Van Zyl also told the author that his diagnosis would have been different if he had seen the statements regarding Tsafendas made by the people who were questioned by the police and all the other evidence gathered during the investigation that contradicted the picture that emerged in the court – for example, that Tsafendas had worked for six months as teacher of English at Limasollu Naci, the most prestigious and famous private college in Turkey at the time. Van Zyl said: 'Yes. Look, obviously that is important information, and information that influences one's findings in the end. There is no doubt about it.'[48]

Judge Beyers found Tsafendas to be unfit to stand trial[49] – a verdict justified on the basis of the evidence presented in court. Subsequently, even though he was declared to be a schizophrenic and in need of treatment, Tsafendas was imprisoned on Robben Island. Although he was not white, he was the only prisoner there ever to be classified as 'white'. A few months later, he was transferred to Pretoria Central Prison.[50] Despite the fact that he was officially found to be mentally unstable and 'unable to function at a reasonable level', Tsafendas's prison service file, A5078, described him as 'a person of Colour, an extremely resourceful and cunning individual who is physically and mentally able to plan and execute escape'.[51] An insight into the government's true beliefs concerning the assassination and Tsafendas emerged on March 1967, about five months after the trial, when Dr J.D. Vorster, the prime minister's brother, speaking to an anti-communist symposium in the USA, said: 'Your President Kennedy and our Dr. Verwoerd were both killed by Communists.'[52] This statement shocked South Africa, which was unaware until then that Tsafendas was a communist, the Johannesburg *Sunday Times*'s front page announcing it with the headline 'Premier's Brother Drops A Bombshell'.[53]

A Commission of Enquiry into the circumstances of Verwoerd's death, headed by Judge Jacques Theodore van Wyk, an enthusiastic supporter of apartheid and one of the most trusted judges of the government, reported its findings in January 1967. Unsurprisingly, it came to the same conclusion as Judge Beyers: that Tsafendas was an apolitical schizophrenic who had killed Verwoerd because of his unstable mind.[54] However, whereas Beyers had based his verdict on the evidence presented to him, Van Wyk concealed and manipulated evidence he had in his possession in order to misportray Tsafendas. To ensure that Tsafendas would not gain public sympathy, Van Wyk concealed his true character – intelligent, generous and politically committed – instead presenting him as a hopeless lunatic, an unsociable, apolitical loser. He also downplayed those aspects of his political activities that were already public knowledge, while largely ignoring the rest.

TSAFENDAS'S LIFE UP TO 1966

Dimitri Tsafendas (born as Dimitrios Tsafantakis)[55] was born in Lourenço Marques (today Maputo) in Mozambique on 14 January 1918 to Michalis Tsafantakis, a white Greek marine engineer, and Amelia Williams, his black Mozambican domestic worker, who belonged to the Shangaan tribe.[56] Tsafendas's family had its origins in Crete, Greece, and had a long history of producing rebels, who in the previous century had fought the Ottoman occupiers there. Michalis named his son Dimitris after his grandfather, Captain Dimitris Tsafantakis, a famed rebel who had fought the Ottomans. Michalis had studied at the University of Padua in Italy; while there, he had become a passionate anarchist and an active member of the anarchist movement.[57] Tsafendas lived with his parents until he was about two. He was then sent by his father to Alexandria, Egypt, to Michalis's mother and sister, until Michalis and his bride-to-be Marika, who was unaware of Dimitri's existence, had their own children. Dimitri spent the next five years in Alexandria under the care of his grandmother and aunt; his favourite thing was listening to their stories about the many family rebels.[58] Young Tsafendas idolised Captain Dimitris and other family rebels, and dreamt of becoming a rebel and a hero like them.[59]

Tsafendas returned to his family in 1925,[60] and the following year he was sent to a boarding school in Middleburg, South Africa.[61] According to psychologist William Mare Volbrecht, a former schoolmate, Tsafendas was 'more advanced than many of his contemporaries and received a good grounding at the school'[62]; 'He was never a loner and mingled freely with us.'[63] Dr Samuel Schmahmann, another classmate, recalled Tsafendas as 'a popular boy who was not the least introverted. I particularly remember him singing a Greek song at a school concert. He was very funny and had us all in stitches.'[64]

Tsafendas grew up in a highly politically conscious environment: his father, still an anarchist and in touch with the anarchist movement in Europe, constantly talked to him about politics and history as he wanted his son to become 'a conscious citizen' and 'a useful member of the society'. When Tsafendas became a teenager, his father gave him political and historical books to read. Michalis even read to him some books that were in Italian by translating them while reading them: one was *Anarchy* by Errico Malatesta, one of Michalis's most admired anarchists. Tsafendas quickly embraced anarchism and the idea of the 'propaganda of the deed', which involved acts of violence, including bombings and assassinations, and especially Luigi Galleani's idea that violence against tyrants and oppressors was justifiable.[65]

Dimitri was very intelligent; psychologists who examined him after the assassination calculated his IQ as 125,[66] placing him in the 'superior' or 'gifted' category, one level above that of average university students and well above the average IQ of 90–110. He loved reading newspapers and literature, and lent books to his friends. The fact that Tsafendas had a wide-ranging collection of books was something witnesses told the South African police after the assassination; for example, Kenneth Ross testified that he was 'aware that Tsafendas possessed a large quantity of literature',[67] while Robert Smith confirmed this.[68] Tsafendas also talked fluently in Afrikaans, Arab, English, German, Greek, Portuguese and Tsonga, had some knowledge of Czech, Italian, French, Russian and Spanish,[69] and spoke Turkish more than adequately.

In 1933, Tsafendas began working for Dimitris Spanos, a dedicated communist, and owner of a newspaper distribution agency and a bookshop in Lourenço Marques. One of Spanos's responsibilities was to distribute the *International* (the newspaper of the International Socialist League) and other communist publications. Tsafendas's talks with Spanos, and his personal experience with poor Mozambicans, gradually moved him closer to communism and further away from anarchism.[70] As Tsafendas grew up, he became eager to participate in a just fight. In the mid-1930s, he was trying to learn how to make bombs when something went wrong and the bomb exploded inside his father's workshop in their house. Miraculously, he escaped with minimal injuries.[71] His step-mother told the South African police after the assassination that the explosion 'nearly blew up our house'.[72] In 1936, Tsafendas got a job at the Chai et Kiosk and turned it into a recruiting post for communism, plying customers with Marxist literature. Eventually, he was dismissed from the job for 'voicing Communist ideas'.[73] The same year, during the Italian invasion of Ethiopia, Tsafendas, along with two friends, committed what he considered to be his first real 'revolutionary' act; they used forks to scratch the paintwork of cars belonging to members of the Italian and German embassies, as well as cars of the local Portuguese administrators.[74]

In 1936, Tsafendas illegally entered South Africa after his official request was turned down,[75] in order to join the SACP.[76] In late 1936 or early 1937, he returned to Mozambique and began working at the Imperial Airways factory.[77] The following year, Mozambique's economy was hit by new government rules for cotton cultivation which boosted the Portuguese textile industry at the expense of the colonies. Tsafendas joined in the widespread opposition to this change. He gave speeches opposing it while giving copies of the *Communist Manifesto* to cotton growers and his fellow factory workers.[78] PIDE heard that Tsafendas was 'spreading Communist propaganda',[79] but the case was 'never proven',[80] as there was 'not sufficient evidence in substantiation of this belief'.[81] The incident had a lasting impact, as it led PIDE to create a file on him: Secret Criminal Record no. 10.415 of Demitrios Tsafantakis.[82] By the late 1930s, Tsafendas's communism and anti-colonialism had become so widely known within the Greek community in Lourenço Marques that he was nicknamed 'The Red'. He often wore a red flower on his lapel, and at times he wrote anti-Portuguese and communist slogans on public walls.[83] In 1939, Tsafendas again illegally entered South Africa, from where his family had moved the year before, after his request for a visa was turned down; the South African Consul-General in Lourenço Marques had informed his country's authorities that Tsafendas was a 'half-caste' with 'Communist leanings', 'suspected of dissemination of Communistic propaganda'.[84] While in South Africa, Tsafendas came to the attention of the police after he had been 'engaged actively in Communistic propaganda'.[85]

In 1942, Tsafendas left South Africa and went on to spend the majority of the Second World War in the USA, serving in liberty ships. In October 1947, Tsafendas arrived in Greece, which at the time was in the middle of a bloody civil war between communists and royalists,[86] and voluntarily joined the Democratic Army, the military wing of the Greek Communist Party.[87] By April 1949, it had become obvious that the communists would lose the war and mass persecutions against them had already begun; Tsafendas decided that it was time to leave Greece.[88]

On 8 November 1949, Tsafendas, carrying a Red Cross passport, was arrested at the Portuguese border post of Barca d'Alva.[89] The police suspected Tsafendas of being a Greek communist militant who had fled after the end of the civil war, as many of his comrades had done. The police in Mozambique informed them that Tsafendas was indeed a communist who had been dismissed from his workplace in Mozambique for 'voicing Communist ideas'.[90] Tsafendas was detained at Barca d'Alva for three months, before being moved for further interrogation to Aljuba Prison in Lisbon,[91] a notorious detention facility for political prisoners, where he was held and interrogated for another six months.[92]

In late 1951, after almost a year of imprisonment in Portugal, Tsafendas travelled to Mozambique, only to learn that he was banned from entering the country due to his being listed as a communist and anti-colonialist because of his activities in the late 1930s.[93] After two weeks in prison in Lourenço Marques, he was deported to Portugal.[94] He arrived in Lisbon on January 1952, only to be re-arrested as the authorities had been informed by the police in Mozambique about his ban, as well as the facts that he was a 'Communist' and was suspected of 'unclear activities' during his time in Mozambique in the 1930s.[95] The police asked him about the 'unclear activities' and if he still believed in communism. It seems that his replies were not satisfactory as he was transferred for more questioning to the Cascais Fort, a notorious detention facility for political prisoners, controlled by PIDE.[96] His interrogation included torture with electric shocks and beatings.[97] At one point, he said, he could not take the pain and so played the madman. The police stopped torturing him;[98] he was then taken to a hospital,[99] and was soon set free.[100]

Remaining in Portugal, PIDE continued watching Tsafendas;[101] his house was searched, and he was frequently subjected to ID checks.[102] Therefore, over the following ten years he twice left the county, seeking a safer environment to live and work. In 1954–55 he lived in Denmark, Sweden and West Germany;[103] in 1958–59 he returned to West Germany, and also went to England.[104] Throughout this period, Tsafendas made numerous applications to be allowed to return to Mozambique or to South Africa, but they were all turned down. His reasons for visiting England included a wish to meet with members of the anti-apartheid movement, which he enthusiastically joined. He frequented the London headquarters of the Anti-Slavery Society, at times giving talks there about the living standards of black South Africans and Mozambicans.[105] He befriended the society's secretary, Commander Thomas Fox-Pitt, a prominent figure in the anti-slavery movement. Fox-Pitt found Tsafendas to be 'very simple-minded and not at all sinister'.[106] He also became a close acquaintance of Tennyson Makiwane, whom he helped by distributing leaflets and putting up posters.[107] In one anti-apartheid demonstration, Tsafendas carried a placard depicting a man in a Ku Klux Klan outfit, labelled 'DR. VERWOERD'. Sometimes, he and other activists battled physically with members of Oswald Mosley's fascist, pro-apartheid Union Movement. In one such fight, Tsafendas was stabbed in the hand; he proudly carried the small scar as a badge of honour.[108] While in London, Tsafendas advocated the use of violence against apartheid and attempted to convince people that an armed uprising in South Africa was necessary to overthrow the apartheid regime; however, he found no sympathy or support for this among other members of the movement, and left London disappointed.[109]

In 1960, in the aftermath of the Sharpeville Massacre, Tsafendas decided that he wanted to 'do something' violent against Verwoerd and apartheid.[110] Since he was banned from entering the country, he decided to get in illegally by travelling via Egypt and Mozambique. However, his plan was foiled when the Portuguese Embassy in Egypt refused to renew his passport. Unable to travel through Africa, he made his way to Turkey via Lebanon.[111] He spent the second half of 1961 in Istanbul, where he worked as an English tutor at Limasollu Naci.[112] From Istanbul, he travelled to Athens, and then in January 1962, to Crete to meet members of his family. Among those he met was Costas Kargakis, who had been a member of the Greek resistance in the Second World War, during which he had taken part in the kidnapping of the Nazi General Heinrich Kreipe. Tsafendas was fascinated by the kidnapping, and got the idea to kidnap Verwoerd and exchange him for political prisoners. In addition, Kargakis, who was an expert bomb-maker, taught Tsafendas how to make bombs with commodities that could be bought in shops.[113] Determined more than ever to return to South Africa and Mozambique to fight apartheid and the Portuguese respectively, Tsafendas returned to Lisbon in February 1962, hoping that he could persuade the authorities to give him amnesty.[114]

Tsafendas's efforts were initially fruitless. However, in late 1963, he was finally given an amnesty by the Portuguese after he convinced them that he was 'a reformed man', no longer a communist or a supporter of the independence of Mozambique. To achieve this, he had stopped associating with leftists and begun publicly denouncing communism and praising the Portuguese dictator Salazar.[115] Thus, in October 1963, he sailed to Mozambique.[116] He had two big suitcases with him; they contained a few clothes, gifts for the family and friends, and anti-apartheid and communist literature. Fearful of searches, Tsafendas had replaced all the book covers with innocent titles.[117]

In Lourenço Marques, Tsafendas was reunited with members of his family. Some of them had come from South Africa to see him as they were aware that he was banned from entering the country, and thus they did not expect him to come there. Tsafendas assured them that he was no longer politically active and asked them for help to enter South Africa so he could visit the grave of his father, who had died about a year ago. His family believed him, and they convinced a South African official in the city's consulate to turn a blind eye to the ban and issue him with a temporary visa for South Africa.[118] Tsafendas entered South Africa on 4 November 1963, and soon obtained a permanent residence permit.[119] Even though he had been aware of what apartheid was and what was happening in the country, he was truly shocked to see its real extent; it made him sad and angry, and even more determined to do something violent against the regime. However, his old comrades shrank from joining any such scheme, while he felt that they did not fully trust him because he had been away from South Africa for so long.[120]

In mid-1964, Tsafendas moved to Beira, Mozambique.[121] Although he wanted to join the recently founded Frente de Libertação Moçambique (FRELIMO, Mozambique Liberation Front) in the struggle for Mozambique's independence, he knew that he would not be able to cope as a guerrilla fighter, being overweight and slow to run and walk.[122] Thus, he decided to contribute to the struggle in a different way. He got a job with the Hume Pipe Company, which laid and operated the pipeline which transported petrol from Beira to Rhodesia,[123] intending to learn all about the company's operations and blow up the pipeline.[124] Furthermore, he began touring the area, preaching communism, while also urging the local people to join FRELIMO and support its struggle. He had with him a suitcase full of communist and anti-colonialist literature, still with different covers.[125]

Tsafendas's activities reached the ears of the Portuguese police. On 16 November 1964, they arrested him in the small town of Maforga while he was urging the people to revolt against the Portuguese and with his suitcase full of 'subversive' literature. He was taken to a police station in Beira and accused of 'making subversive propaganda against the Portuguese government and spreading subversive propaganda among the native masses'.[126] Tsafendas found himself accused of posing as a missionary and of preaching 'under the guise of religion in favour of Mozambique's independence'.[127] Tsafendas denied the charges, but admitted that he supported 'the idea of Mozambique's independence, governed by the natives of that Province, whether they are black or white'.[128] Inspector Horacio Ferreira, the man in charge of the cells at the police station, thought that Tsafendas was 'intensely anti-white' and that he believed 'the Portuguese Government has never done anything for its non-whites'. He also thought he was 'normal' and saw him 'as a very intelligent person'.[129] Due to the severity of the charges against him, Tsafendas was handed to PIDE's Sub-Delegation in Beira.[130] After two months in custody, Tsafendas, since he was accused of pretending to be a missionary, really started pretending to be one; he pretended to be St Peter, Jesus' apostle.[131] He was then transferred to a hospital in Beira.[132] On January 1965, PIDE decided to release him after he convinced them that he was mentally ill.[133] Some weeks afterwards, Tsafendas was arrested again by the Portuguese police as he was reported to have been 'seen in cafes with Coloured political suspects'.[134] Within a few days, he was free again, after convincing the police that he was a harmless madman.[135] Aware that from then on, the police would keep a closer eye on him, he decided to return to South Africa and do something against apartheid. On 5 March 1965, he left Beira by ship for Durban.[136]

While in South Africa, Tsafendas got in touch with anti-apartheid activists, such as Rowley Arenstein.[137] However, none of them was interested in participating in anything violent and helping Tsafendas with his risky plans. Thus, he was forced to abort his plan to kidnap Verwoerd and realised that if he was going to do something violent, he had to do it alone. In July 1966, he started observing the parliament building in Cape Town to explore the possibility of assassinating Verwoerd by shooting at him from afar.[138] Eventually, he managed to get a job inside the parliament as a temporary messenger; this brought him closer to his target.

TSAFENDAS IMPRISONED

Although declared to be a schizophrenic, Tsafendas spent the next 28 years of his life in prison without receiving any medical treatment. Furthermore, he was subjected to the most cruel and inhuman torture, while his cell, which was built specifically for him in Pretoria Central, was right next to the execution chamber, so that he could hear the executions taking place. He believed that he was placed there not only for torture purposes, but also as a warning of what was waiting for him if he ever became 'sane' again.[139] He spent 23 years next to the death chamber, while he was also kept in solitary confinement, sometimes not allowed out of his cell at all; for several years he was not in contact with any fellow prisoner and was not allowed access to newspapers, magazines or books, apart from the Bible.[140] In December 1968, Bernard Mitchell, a former inmate in Pretoria Central, told the British *Observer* about his time in prison and mentioned Tsafendas:

They built a special cell – a flat they called it – for him in the death block in Pretoria Central Prison, where I was at the time ... they put a screen around the landing in front of the cell and 'exercised' Tsafendas there. A screw would stand in each corner and Tsafendas's exercise would consist of dodging their truncheons as they threw him from one side to the other. We used to exercise in the yard below his cell and you could hear him screaming.[141]

In 1971, Professor Barend van Niekerk informed Progressive Party MP Helen Suzman that 'Tsafendas is being subjected to the cruellest possible treatment.'[142] On 1 August 1976, Brian Price, a former prisoner in Pretoria Central, told the *Observer* that Tsafendas 'was treated with gross inhumanity and was a broken man'. He said that the guards urinated in Tsafendas's food before forcing him to eat it, and he was routinely beaten and kicked. 'For the first five years or so, the warders used to lay into Tsafendas. He was a plaything for sadists.'[143] In 1989, the British *Guardian* reported that Tsafendas, 71 years old at the time, was still on Death Row and still being tortured and brutalised.[144]

Tsafendas had no visitors in prison until the late 1970s, when Father Minas Constandinou, a priest assigned by the Greek Orthodox Church in South Africa to be the prison chaplain, began visiting him. Minas had become a very good and trusted friend of Tsafendas in Mozambique in 1963.[145] In 1994, immediately after the collapse of apartheid, efforts were made by Jody Kollapen – then a lawyer who was heading up the Lawyers for Human Rights' Political Prisoner Release Programme, and now a Constitutional Judge – to have Tsafendas released from prison; Tsafendas was at the time South Africa's longest-serving prisoner. Kollapen visited Tsafendas in prison on several occasions, and asked the ANC government to release him. Kollapen wrote to the ANC government in November 1994:

> It remains my belief that Mr. Tsafendas should not die a lonely man in an institution but should spend the last years of his life in the company of people he knows and perhaps trusts … In summation I believe that the man has served his debt to the society (if he owed a debt at all in the first place). His age and disposition certainly do not warrant him being held in an institution and if it was possible to release him either to family or into an old age institution run by the State this might be the best approach to follow at the present time.[146]

The ANC agreed with Kollapen's proposal and asked him to make the necessary arrangements. Kollapen contacted Tsafendas's family and the Greek community in Pretoria so that they could take care of him after his release, as because of his advanced age and failing health, he was not able to look after himself. However, they all refused to care for him.[147] Eventually, because no-one would agree to care for him and because of fears about his life being at risk from white supremacists, the ANC decided in July 1996 to transfer Tsafendas to Sterkfontein, a secure psychiatric hospital.[148] Tsafendas was initially unhappy there, and his health quickly deteriorated. Kollapen remained a visitor, and unsuccessfully attempted to have him released from there also. Tsafendas remained in Sterkfontein until he died on 7 October 1999; he was buried, and still lies, in an unmarked grave,[149] while Verwoerd is still buried in The Heroes' Acre.

TSAFENDAS ON THE KILLING OF VERWOERD

In 1994, Tsafendas was visited by Father Minas; this time he was accompanied by a young priest, Father Ioannis Tsaftaridis. The priests asked him about the killing of Verwoerd. Tsafendas responded that it had been 'an act of profound moral principle', since it was 'morally justifiable' to commit 'tyrannicide'. He cited Frantz Fanon's argument about justifiable violence to back up his argument, quoting extensively from his works and urging the priests to explore them themselves. Since he had had the opportunity to rid the world of a 'monster', he said, it was his 'duty' and 'social responsibility' to act; if he had not done so, he would have been as guilty as Verwoerd, as is the case with anyone who sees a crime he has the power to stop and does not intervene. Minas disagreed, arguing that killing was a mortal sin and could never be acceptable, whatever the dead person might have done. Tsafendas replied:

> Every day, you see a man you know committing a very serious crime for which millions of people suffer. You cannot take him to court or report him to the police, because he is the law in the country. Would you remain silent and let him continue with his crime, or would you do something to stop him? You are guilty not only when you commit a crime, but also when you do nothing to prevent it when you have the chance.[150]

NOTES

1. 'Devoid of Political Meaning', *Rand Daily Mail*, 7 September 1966.
2. '180-Day Prison for Tsafendas?', *The Cape Argus*, 7 September 1966.
3. David Dyzenhaus, *Hard Cases in Wicked Legal Systems: South African Law in the Perspective of Legal Philosophy*, Oxford: Clarendon Press, 1991, 106.
4. Truth and Reconciliation Commission, *Report of the Truth and Reconciliation Commission: Volume Two*, 1998, 195.
5. Gordon Winter, 'Tsafendas Was Ineffective Red – Van den Bergh', *The Citizen*, 26 October 1976.

6. Demetrio Tsafendas, statement to Major Rossouw, 11 September 1966, K150, Report of the Commission of Enquiry into the Circumstances of the Death of the Late Dr. the Honourable Hendrik Frensch Verwoerd (hereafter cited as K150), Vol. 1, File: Verklaring van Demetrio Tsafendas, National Archives of South Africa, Pretoria (hereafter cited as NASA).

7. Tsafendas, statement to Major Rossouw, 11 September 1966.

8. Demetrio Tsafendas, statement to Major Rossouw, 19 September 1966, K150, Vol. 1, File: Verklaring van Demetrio Tsafendas, NASA.

9. Tsafendas, statement to Major Rossouw, 11 September 1966.

10. Ibid.

11. Truth and Reconciliation Commission, *Report of the Truth and Reconciliation Commission: Volume Three*, 1998, 530.

12. Interview with Father Minas Constandinou, 6 February 2013.

13. *Report of the Commission of Enquiry into the Circumstances of the Death of the Late Dr. the Honourable Hendrik Frensch Verwoerd* (hereafter cited as *Report of the COE into Dr. Verwoerd's Death*), December 1966. R.P. 16/1967, Chapter I A, paragraph 23.

14. Ibid., Chapter IV, paragraph 19.

15. General H.J. Den Bergh memorandum to the Commission of Enquiry into Verwoerd's death (hereafter cited as COE), 18 October 1966, K150, Vol. 1, File VDSO 17-64, NASA.

16. *Report of the COE into Dr. Verwoerd's Death*, Chapter XI, paragraphs 4 and 5.

17. Secret telegram from S.A. Embassy, Lisbon, to Secretary of Foreign Affairs, Cape Town, 07 September 1966, K150, Vol. 7, File: 09/04 Suspect Persons Demetrio Tsafendas, NASA; Antony Maw, statement to the police, 7 September 1966, K150, Vol. 4, Sub file: 1/8, NASA; 'Dimitrio a Red, They Alleged', *Pretoria News*, 7 September 1966; 'The Killer: Five Passports and a Record of Subversion', *The Herald* (Melbourne), 8 September 1966; 'Assassin Said to Have Been Deported from P.E.A. for Communist Connections', *Rhodesia Herald*, 8 September 1966.

18. Secret telegram from S.A. Embassy, Lisbon, to Secretary of Foreign Affairs, Cape Town, 07 September 1966. PIDE confidential report regarding Demetrio Tsafendas: no: 2707/64/SR, 25 November 1964, SR, PIDE/DGS, SC, CI (2) 6818, NT 7461, PNA, Arquivo National da Torre do Tombo, Lisbon (hereafter cited as ANTT); Vertaling. Information: Demetrio Tsafendas or Demetrio Tsafandakis, 7 September 1966, K150, Vol. 6, File 3, NASA; PIDE report: Information: Demitrio Tsafendas or Demetrio Tsafandakis, 7 September 1966, PIDE/DGS, SC, CI (2) 6818, NT 7461, PNA, ANTT.

19. *Report of the COE into Dr. Verwoerd's Death*, Chapter II A, paragraph 26.

20. Confidential Report of the Police Body of the Province of Mozambique regarding Demetrio Tsafendas, No: 726/694/PI, 3 May 1955, PIDE/DGS, SC, CI (2) 6818, NT 7461, PNA, ANTT; *Report of the COE into Dr. Verwoerd's Death*, Chapter II A, paragraph 16.

21. *Die Landstem* telegram, n.d. K150, Vol. 5, NASA.

22. Edward Charles Furness, statement to the police, 12 October 1966, K150, Vol. 12, File: Verklarings Demitrio Tsafendas, NASA.

23. Robert Harpur Smith, statement to the police, 7 September 1966, K150, Vol. 12, File: Verklarings Demitrio Tsafendas, NASA.
24. Christoffel Johannes van Vuuren, statement to the police, 14 September 1966, K150, Vol. 12, File: Verklarings Demitrio Tsafendas, NASA.
25. Johannes Jacobus Botha, statement to the police, 15 September 1966, K150, Vol. 12, File: Verklarings Demitrio Tsafendas, NASA.
26. Father Hanno Probst, statement to the COE, 13 October 1966, K150, Vol. 12, File: Verklarings Demitrio Tsafendas, NASA; Christoffel Johannes van Vuuren, statement to the police, 13 September 1966, K150, Vol. 12, File: Verklarings Demitrio Tsafendas, NASA.
27. Col. van Wyk's report regarding the activities of Dimitrio Tsafendas in Mozambique and Rhodesia, 20 September 1966, K150, Vol. 3, Sub file: 1/5, NASA.
28. Interview with Cleanthes Alachiotis, 29 September 2010; interview with Nikolaos Billis, 12 June 2011; interview with Nikolas Kambouris, 17 January 2014; interview with Georgios Kantas, 11 January 2012; interview with Grigoris Pouftis, 28 November 2009; interview with Michalis Vasilakis, 17 March 2016.
29. Edward Furness, statement to the police, 12 October 1966.
30. Kenneth Heugh Ross, statement to the police, 7 September 1966, K150, Vol. 12, File: Verklarings Demitrio Tsafendas, NASA.
31. Robert Harpur Smith, statement to the police, 7 September 1966.
32. Patrick O' Ryan, testimony on Tsafendas's summary trial, 18 October 1966, K150, Vol. 10, File: Trial, NASA.
33. Jacobus Johannes Borman, statement to the police, 3 October 1966, K150, Vol. 12, File: Verklarings Demitrio Tsafendas, NASA.
34. '180-Day Prison for Tsafendas?' *The Cape Argus*, 7 September 1966.
35. *Report of the COE into Dr. Verwoerd's Death*, Chapter II B, paragraph 32.
36. Secret telegram from S.A. Embassy, Lisbon, to Secretary of Foreign Affairs, Cape Town, 07 September 1966.
37. Top secret letter of the Head Inspector of PIDE in Lisbon to the Subdirector of PIDE in Mozambique regarding Demitrio Tsafendas, 8 September 1966, PIDE/DGS, SC, CI (2) 6818, NT 7461, PNA, ANTT.
38. Vertaling, Information: Demitrio Tsafendas or Demetrio Tsafandakis, 7 September 1966; PIDE report: Information: Demitrio Tsafendas or Demetrio Tsafandakis, 7 September 1966.
39. Secret Criminal Record no. 10.415 of Demitrios Tsafantakis, PIDE/DGS, SC, CI (2) 6818, NT 7461, PNA, ANTT.
40. Vertaling, Information: Demitrio Tsafendas or Demetrio Tsafandakis, 7 September 1966; PIDE report: Information: Demitrio Tsafendas or Demetrio Tsafandakis, 7 September 1966.
41. Interview with advocate George Bizos, 18 November 2017.
42. David Bloomberg, *My Times: The Memoirs of David Bloomberg*, Simon's Town: Fernwood Press, 2007, 74–79; Gavin Cooper, *Under Devil's Peak: The Life and Times of Wilfrid Cooper, an Advocate in the Age of Apartheid*, Kenilworth: Burnet Media, 2016, 101–105.
43. Dr. Harold Cooper's testimony on Tsafendas's summary trial, 17 October 1966; Dr. James William MacGregor's testimony on Tsafendas's summary trial, 19

October 1966; Dr. Abraham Aubrey Zabow's testimony on Tsafendas's summary trial, 19 October 1966; all in K150, Vol. 10, File: Trial, NASA.

44. Harris Dousemetzis and Gerry Loughran, *The Man Who Killed Apartheid: The Life of Dimitri Tsafendas*, Johannesburg: Jacana Media, 2018, 240.

45. Dr. G.C. Baker, statement re: Demitrio Tsafendas, G.S.H. 65/014-181, n.d., K150, Vol. 6, File: 4, NASA; Donald Neville Mackay, statement to the COE, 12 October 1966, K150, Vol. 12, File: Verklarings Demitrio Tsafendas, NASA; Memorandum about the application for permanent residence in terms of the Aliens Act from Demetrio Tsafendas, drawn up by the Secretary for Immigration, n.d., K150, Vol. 4, File: 1/7, Departement van immigrasie, NASA; *Report of the COE into Dr. Verwoerd's Death*, Chapter II C, paragraph 64; South African Railways Confidential Medical Examination Certificate of Demitrio Tsafendas, K150, Vol. 7, File: S 83708, Tsafendas: D, NASA; Dr. Leon Solomon's medical report regarding Dimitri Tsafendas, 7 June 1966, K150, Vol. 1, File: 1/1 Departement van Arbeid, NASA; Medical certificate issued by Dr. Solomon for the Employment Insurance Act, 1946, 7 June 1966, K150, Vol. 1, File: 1/1 Departement van Arbeid, NASA; I. Eisenberg statement RE: Demitrio Tsafendas, GS.H. 65/014-181, n.d., K150, Vol. 12, File: Verklarings Demitrio Tsafendas, NASA; Demitrio Tsafendas's Marine Diamond Corporation Application for Employment, 13 January 1966, K150, Vol. 6, File: 3, NASA; Demitrio Tsafendas medical certificate issued by Dr. Been for the Aliens Act, 1937, K150, Vol. 4, File: 1/7, Departement van immigrasie, NASA; Dr. Been statement to the police, 30 September 1966, K150, Vol. 12, File: Verklarings Demitrio Tsafendas, NASA.

46. Peter Lambley, *The Psychology of Apartheid*, Athens, GA: University of Georgia Press, 1980, 239–240, at 273; interview with Reyner van Zyl, 10 April 2016.

47. Ibid.

48. Ibid.

49. Judge Beyers's verdict on Tsafendas's summary trial, 20 October 1966, K150, Vol. 10, File: Trial, NASA.

50. Tsafendas's transfer order from Robben Island to Central Prison, Pretoria, 3 February 1967, Demitrio Tsafendas Mediese Leer A125, NASA.

51. Jaap Marais, *Die Era van Verwoerd*, Pretoria: Aktuele Publikasies, 1992, 208.

52. Brian Bunting, *The Rise of the South African Reich*, London: International and Defence and Aid Fund for South Africa, 1986, 76; 'Premier's Brother Drops a Bombshell', *Sunday Times* (Johannesburg), 19 March 1967.

53. Ibid.

54. *Report of the COE into Dr. Verwoerd's Death*, Chapter III.

55. Tsafantakis was not the real family name. A century earlier, in an attempt to denigrate the troublesome Cretan rebels by portraying them as people of no account, the Ottoman authorities had decreed the adding of the suffix 'akis' – a Greek diminutive used affectionately to refer to a child – to every Cretan surname. Despite Cretan opposition, the change had stuck. Thus Tsafendas had become Tsafantakis. When Dimitri discovered this, he asked his father to restore the true family name, seeing the alterations as humiliating. Michalis understood this, but told him that since the government and all their friends knew the family as Tsafantakis, it would be too difficult to change the name.

However, Dimitri later adopted the name of Tsafendas himself; interview with Katerina Pnefma, 30 March 2015.

56. Demetrio Tsafendas, statement to Major Rossouw, 11 September 1966; Antony Maw statement to the police, 7 September 1966; interview with Katerina Pnefma.
57. Interview with Mary Eintracht, 9 October 2014; interview with Katerina Pnefma; interview with Michael Vlachopoulos, 14 April 2016.
58. Interview with John Michaletos, 16 April 2016.
59. Interview with Mary Eintracht; interview with Antony Michaletos, 2 May 2016; interviews with John Michaletos and Katerina Pnefma.
60. Demetrio Tsafendas, statement to Major Rossouw, 11 September 1966.
61. Marika Tsafantakis, statement to the police, 7 September 1966, K150, Vol. 12, File: Verklarings Demitrio Tsafendas, NASA; Middelburg Primary School report regarding Demitrios Tsafandakis, 17 December 1963, K150, Vol. 4, Sub file: 1/7, Departement van immigrasie, NASA.
62. 'Tsafendas Was of Mixed Origin', Rand Daily Mail, 7 September 1966.
63. William Mare Volbrecht, statement to the police, 3 October 1966, K150, Vol. 3, File: Verklaring deur Majoor Venter, NASA.
64. 'Boyhood Days of Tsafendas', Rand Daily Mail, 8 September 1966.
65. Interview with Minas Constandinou; interview with Nick Papadakis, 30 January 2015; interview with Katerina Pnefma.
66. Reyner van Zyl's testimony on Tsafendas's summary trial, 18 October 1966, K150, Vol. 10, File: Trial, NASA.
67. Kenneth Heugh Ross, statement to the police, 7 September 1966.
68. Robert Harpur Smith, statement to the police, 7 September 1966.
69. Father Hanno Probst, statement to the COE, 13 October 1966.
70. Interview with Andreas Babiolakis, 19 March 2016; interview with Minas Constandinou; interview with Helen Grispos, 22 January 2013; interview with Ira Kyriakakis, 27 March 2015; interview with Katerina Pnefma.
71. Ibid.
72. Marika Tsafantakis, statement to the police, 7 September 1966.
73. PIDE Confidential Report about Demitrio Tsafendas, 7 June 1955, PIDE/DGS, SC, CI (2) 6818, NT 7461, PNA, ANTT.
74. Interview with Helen Grispos.
75. Report of the COE into Dr. Verwoerd's Death, Chapter II A, paragraph 13.
76. Demetrio Tsafendas, statement to Major Rossouw, 11 September 1966.
77. Marika Tsafantakis, statement to the police, 7 September 1966; Secret Criminal Record no. 10.415 of Demitrios Tsafantakis; Confidential Report of the Police Body of the Province of Mozambique regarding Demetrio Tsafendas, No: 726/694/PI, 3 May 1955.
78. Interviews with Andreas Babiolakis, Helen Grispos and Ira Kyriakakis.
79. Secret Criminal Record no. 10.415 of Demitrios Tsafantakis; Confidential Report of the Police Body of the Province of Mozambique regarding Demetrio Tsafendas, No: 726/694/PI, 3 May 1955.
80. Confidential Report of the Police Body of the Province of Mozambique regarding Demetrio Tsafendas, No: 726/694/PI, 3 May 1955.

81. *Report of the COE into Dr. Verwoerd's Death*, Chapter II A, paragraph 16.

82. Secret Criminal Record no. 10.415 of Demitrios Tsafantakis.

83. Interviews with Andreas Babiolakis and Ira Kyriakakis.

84. *Report of the COE into Dr. Verwoerd's Death*, Chapter II A, paragraph 16.

85. Report of the Commissioner for Immigration and Asiatic Affairs regarding Demetrios Tsafandakis, 14 October 1941, K150, Vol. 3, File: W.D. 10/10/4102, Subject: Enquiry regarding Demetrios Tsafandakis, NASA.

86. Demetrio Tsafendas, statement to Major Rossouw. 11 September 1966.

87. *Die Landstem* telegram, n.d.; interview with Father Nikola Banovic, 21 August 2014.

88. Detailed information for a Memorandum regarding Demetrio Tsafendas by Attorney-General W.M. van den Berg, 3 October 1966, K150, Vol. 1, File: VDSO 17/64, Subject: Beweerde Omkopery, NASA; interview with Nikola Banovic.

89. PIDE Confidential Report about Demitrio Tsafendas or Demetrio Tsafantakis, 13 November 1962, PIDE/DGS, SC, CI (2) 6818, NT 7461, PNA, ANTT.

90. PIDE Confidential Report about Demitrio Tsafendas, 7 June 1955.

91. PIDE Confidential Report regarding Demetrio Tsafendas: no: 2707/64/SR, 25 November 1964.

92. 'Brainwashed in Jail Held Man Told *Argus*', *The Cape Argus*, 7 September 1966.

93. Antony Maw, statement to the police, 7 September 1966; PIDE Confidential Report regarding Demetrio Tsafendas: no: 2707/64/SR, 25 November 1964; Portuguese Security Police's report regarding Dimitrio Tsafendas dated 21 February 1962, translated by the South African Department of Defence and sent to the COE on October 12, 1966, K150, Vol. 4, Sub file: 1/6, Department of Defence, NASA.

94. PIDE Record of questions, 25 November 1964, PIDE/DGS, SC, CI (2) 6818, NT 7461, PNA, ANTT; interviews with Antony Michaletos and John Michaletos.

95. 'E Conhesido em Lisboa o Assassino do Dr. Verwoerd', *Diario Popular*, 9 September 1966; PIDE Report regarding Tsafendas, 5 May 1956, PIDE/DGS, SC, CI (2) 6818, NT 7461, PNA, ANTT.

96. Ibid.

97. 'Brainwashed in Jail Held Man Told *Argus*'; interviews with Nikola Banovic and Minas Constandinou; interview with Bishop Ioannis Tsaftaridis, 23 January 2017.

98. Interviews with Nikola Banovic, Minas Constandinou and Ioannis Tsaftaridis.

99. PIDE report: Information: Demitrio Tsafendas or Demetrio Tsafandakis, 12 December 1964; PIDE Report regarding Tsafendas, 5 May 1956.

100. Interviews with Nikola Banovic and Minas Constandinou.

101. Numerous PIDE reports throughout the years regarding Tsafendas's movements and activities, PIDE/DGS, SC, CI (2) 6818, NT 7461, PNA, ANTT.

102. Interview with John Michaletos.

103. *Report of the COE into Dr. Verwoerd's Death*, Chapter II B, paragraph 24.

104. Ibid., paragraph 27.

105. Demetrio Tsafendas, statement to Major Rossouw, 11 September 1966; interview with Father Nikola Banovic, 21 August 2014.

106. 'Winding Back', *The Guardian*, 30 September 1966; interview with Minas Constandinou.
107. Edward Furness, statement to the police, 12 October 1966; interview with Minas Constandinou.
108. Interviews with Antony Michaletos, John Michaletos and Katerina Pnefma.
109. Interviews with Minas Constandinou and Ioannis Tsaftaridis.
110. Interviews with Nikola Banovic and Minas Constandinou.
111. Demetrio Tsafendas, statement to Major Rossouw, 11 September 1966; Confidential Report of the Ministerio Dos Negocios Estrangeiros regarding Dimitri Tsafendas, proc. 518/15/55, Co. 367, 20 October 1961, PIDE/DGS, SC, CI (2) 6818, NT 7461, PNA, ANTT.
112. *Report of the COE into Dr. Verwoerd's Death*, Chapter VI, paragraph 4; Demetrio Tsafendas, statement to Major Rossouw, 11 September 1966; interview with Nikola Banovic.
113. Interview with Minas Constandinou; interview with Alexandros Tsafantakis, 15 February 2016; author interview with Maria and Michalis Tsafantakis, 16 February 2016.
114. Confidential PIDE report regarding Demetrio Tsafendas, No: 3.699-G.U, 13 November 1962, PIDE/DGS, SC, CI (2) 6818, NT 7461, PNA, ANTT; interview with Nikola Banovic.
115. Interviews with Minas Constandinou and Ioannis Tsaftaridis.
116. Demetrio Tsafendas, statement to Major Rossouw, 11 September 1966.
117. Interviews with Antony Michaletos, John Michaletos and Katerina Pnefma.
118. Eleni Vlachopoulos in Manolis Dimelas's documentary film *Live and Let Live*, 2007; interviews with Antony Michaletos, John Michaletos and Katerina Pnefma.
119. *Report of the COE into Dr. Verwoerd's Death*, Chapter II C, paragraph 1.
120. Interview with Fotini Gavasiadis, 6 May 2015.
121. Confidential Security Report of the Special Branch of the British South African Police in Umtali, Subject: Assassination of Dr. Verwoerd, 10 September 1966, K150, Vol. 3, Sub file: 1/5, NASA; South African Police report regarding the activities of Dimitrio Tsafendas in Mozambique and Rhodesia, 20 September 1966, K150, Vol. 3, File: 1/5, FILE Suid Afrikaanse Polisie, NASA.
122. Interview with Nick Papadakis; interview with Costas Poriazis, 5 April 2016.
123. Demetrio Tsafendas, statement to Major Rossouw, 11 September 1966; South African Police report regarding the activities of Dimitrio Tsafendas in Mozambique and Rhodesia, 20 September 1966; interview with Nick Papadakis.
124. Interviews with Minas Constandinou and Ioannis Tsaftaridis.
125. Interviews with Andreas Babiolakis, Minas Constandinou and Nick Papadakis.
126. PIDE Confidential Report regarding Demetrio Tsafendas: no: 2707/64/SR, 25 November 1964; Vertaling. Information: Demitrio Tsafendas or Demetrio Tsafandakis, 7 September 1966; PIDE report: Information: Demitrio Tsafendas or Demetrio Tsafandakis, 7 September 1966.
127. PIDE Confidential Report regarding Demetrio Tsafendas: no: 2707/64/SR, 25 November 1964.
128. Ibid.

129. South African Police report regarding the activities of Dimitrio Tsafendas in Mozambique and Rhodesia, 20 September 1966.

130. PIDE report about the Defendant: Demitrio Tsafendas or Dimitrius Tsafendakis, 19 January 1965, SR, PIDE/DGS, SC, CI (2) 6818, NT 7461, PNA, ANTT.

131. Interviews with Andreas Babiolakis, Minas Constandinou and Nick Papadakis.

132. Demetrio Tsafendas, statement to Major Rossouw, 11 September 1966.

133. Alberto Henriques de Matos Rodrigues conclusion to the Subdirector, 23 January 1965, PIDE/DGS, SC, CI (2) 6818, NT 7461, PNA, ANTT.

134. 'The Clouded Past of an Assassin', *Daily Mirror*, 9 September 1966.

135. Interviews with Andreas Babiolakis, Nick Papadakis and Costas Poriazis.

136. Demetrio Tsafendas, statement to Major Rossouw, 11 September 1966; South African Police report regarding the activities of Dimitrio Tsafendas in Mozambique and Rhodesia, 20 September 1966.

137. *Report of the COE into Dr. Verwoerd's Death*, Chapter II C, paragraph 33; Eperanza Theron, statement to the police, 24 September 1966, K150, Vol. 12, File: Verklarings Demitrio Tsafendas, NASA.

138. Interview with Minas Constandinou.

139. Interviews with Minas Constandinou and Ioannis Tsaftaridis.

140. Interview with Alexander Moumbaris, 13 December 2015.

141. John de St Jorre, 'I Was Glad That Cancer Got Me Out of Vorster's Jail', *The Observer*, 1 December 1968.

142. Letter to Helen Suzman from Professor Barend D. van Niekerk of Wits, 9 April 1971, Helen Suzman Papers 1944–2009, Mb2.10.1.5, University of the Witwatersrand.

143. Ian Mather, 'Horror in Black and White', *The Observer*, 1 August 1976.

144. David Beresford, 'Dr. Verwoerd's Insane Killer Being Brutalised on SA Death Row: Cell Next to Gallows for 71-Year Old Prisoner', *The Guardian*, 9 June 1989.

145. Interview with Minas Constandinou.

146. Memorandum of Jody Kollapen of Lawyers for Human Rights, 24 November 1994, Tsafendas's file in the Lawyers for Human Rights collection (AL3183), SAHA.

147. Memorandum of Jody Kollapen of Lawyers for Human Rights, 24 November 1994.

148. Tsafendas's order for removal, 5 July 1994, Demitrio Tsafendas Mediese Leer A125, NASA; interview with George Bizos.

149. Henk van Woerden, *A Mouthful of Glass*, London: Granta Books, 2000, 152–156.

150. Interviews with Minas Constandinou and Ioannis Tsaftaridis.

Conclusion: A Tribute to Two 'Great Witnesses' Invited to the Dakar Conference in 2019, Moctar Fofana Niang and Eugénie Rokhaya Aw

Pascal Bianchini, Ndongo Samba Sylla and Leo Zeilig

Two great personalities of the Senegalese left whom we invited to give their accounts on the first day of the Dakar Conference in 2019 have passed away, Moctar Fofana Niang on 20 March 2021 and Eugénie Rokhaya Aw on 3 July 2022. We could not publish this book without paying tribute to their memories, so it is dedicated to their memories and activism.

MOCTAR FOFANA NIANG

Born in 1939 in Koulikoro, Mali, Moctar Fofana Niang moved to Senegal during his childhood. Although he was not one of the first 23 signatories of the Parti africain de l'indépendance (PAI, African Independence Party) manifesto on 15 September 1957, he was one of the first to disseminate this founding document. While he was a student at Delafosse Technical High School in Dakar, he was one of the leaders of the strike at this school, which was the first of its kind to have a national impact and reach. When he entered working life, he was employed in the field of agricultural cooperatives in eastern Senegal, where he opposed the dominant Parti socialiste du Sénégal (Socialist Party of Senegal) led by Léopold Senghor, which used to appoint leaders in its pay instead of those elected by the peasants themselves.

At the same time, Niang helped to develop the PAI underground. He was one of the party activists sent to the USSR for higher studies. On his return, in 1965, he was arrested by the police on the Bamako–Dakar express train and taken to Dakar, where he was tortured like other PAI militants suspected of attempting to establish a maquis in the Casamance or in eastern Senegal, in the south of the country.

Later, having resumed his professional activity, Niang was still active with the PAI in the underground, and later in the legal framework with the Parti de l'indépendance et du travail (PIT, Party of Independence and Labour), one of the formations that emerged out of the PAI. During these years, he was also a leading trade union activist in the Union of Commerce Workers, where he held the post of deputy general secretary for several years.

At the end of his life, having left the PIT, he joined Yonnu Askan Wi, a formation bringing together different currents of the Marxist left that remained in opposition to the regimes of Abdoulaye Wade and then Macky Sall. He was also president of the National Preparatory Committee for the commemoration of the 50th anniversary of the PAI manifesto. After a colloquium in 2008, this committee continued to organise meetings in the following years to make the younger generations aware of the struggles led by PAI militants.

For those who knew him, Moctar was a man of remarkable kindness and modesty, even though he had been a leading militant and was one of the most knowledgeable persons about the history of the PAI and the revolutionary left in Senegal. He leaves us two remarkable volumes in which he combines the use of internal party documents and his own personal memories in his account.[1]

EUGÉNIE ROKHAYA AW

Eugénie Rokhaya Aw was born in Paris in 1952, from the marriage between her Senegalese father and her mother, originally from Martinique. She spent part of her childhood in Niger, where her father moved for work. As an activist in France within the Fédération des étudiants d'Afrique noire en France (Black African Students Federation in France), she continued her commitment to the anti-colonial Sawaba. Sensitised to the colonial question from an early age, when she arrived at the University of Dakar in the early 1970s to study philosophy, she took part in the Maoist movement within the clandestine organisation Réénu Réew (The Roots of the Country), which later gave rise to one of the major formations of the Marxist left in Senegal: And-Jëf (Unite to Act). In this context, she developed contacts with women workers in the fishing industry through literacy programmes.

At the same time, during her student years, Aw began working as a journalist, specialising mainly in arts columns. She worked for the newspaper *Dakar-matin*, which later became *Le Soleil*, the only authorised daily and unofficial newspaper of the regime. At the same time, the clandestine printing press of the newspaper *Xare Bi* was set up at her home. When a large number of activists from the organisation that published this newspaper were arrested in 1975, Aw and her companion at the time were also apprehended and sentenced to prison.

After being released, Aw continued to work as a journalist. After completing her higher education in Canada, she became an academic, and in 2005 was the first woman to be appointed as head of the well-known journalism school the Centre d'études des sciences et techniques de l'information (Centre for Science and Technology Studies) in Dakar. At the same time, she was involved in feminist struggles, notably by leading women's organisations such as the Association of African Women Communication Professionals.

Despite the acclaim she acquired over the decades in the media and in international institutions, Aw never turned her back on her youthful commitments, as shown by the striking testimony she gave in 2019 to Yannek Simalla on the torture and imprisonment of political prisoners under the Senghor regime.[2]

We dedicate this volume to these two great fighters and revolutionaries.

NOTES

1. Moctar Fofana Niang, *Trajectoires et documents du Parti africain de l'indépendance (P.A.I.) au Sénégal*, Dakar: Editions de la Brousse, 2014; Moctar Fofana Niang, *Parti africain de l'indépendance (P.A.I.): evénements et acteurs sur la route de la décolonisation*, Dakar: Nielbeen, 2020.
2. See Yannek Simalla, 'Trois femmes prisonnières politiques au temps de Léopold Sédar Senghor: Eugénie Aw', https://www.youtube.com/watch?v=SUv9c1rL3Kc. https://roape.net/2023/09/12/underground-politics-in-senegal-a-posthumous-interview-with-eugenie-rokhaya-aw/

Notes on Contributors

Moussa Bicharra Ahmed defended his thesis in history on the Chad–Libya conflict at the University of Kiev, Ukraine in 1992. He works at the University of N'Djamena, Chad. From 1979 to 1984, he held several positions in the National Liberation Front of Chad, such as Secretary to the Revolutionary Council.

Baba Aye is a trade unionist, eco-socialist and poet. He is currently the health and social sector policy officer of a global union federation, and co-president of the Geneva Global Health Hub. He was spokesperson of the National Association of Nigerian Students and a member of the leadership of Campaign for Democracy (the first united front body of the left) during the 'June 12 Struggle' in Nigeria. After the reinstatement of civil rule, he served at different times as Deputy National Secretary of the Labour Party of Nigeria and National Convener of United Action for Democracy. Over the years, he has edited several left-wing periodicals in Nigeria, including *Cuba Si* (organ of the Nigeria-Cuba Friendship and Cultural Association), *Working People's Vanguard* (organ of the All-Nigeria Socialist Alliance), and he currently edits the *Socialist Worker* (Nigeria). He is a contributing editor of the *Review of African Political Economy* and the author of *Era of Crises and Revolts: Perspectives for Workers and Youths* (2012) and *Drafts of Becoming* (a collection of poems, 2021).

Heike Becker is a writer and scholar based at the University of the Western Cape, Cape Town, South Africa, where she teaches Social and Cultural Anthropology. Her work explores themes at the interface between culture and politics. She focuses on the politics of memory, decolonisation and social movements of resistance in southern Africa (South Africa and Namibia). She has also conducted research on decolonising the public space in Germany and the UK. Over the past few years, she has been involved in many decolonial and antiracist protests in Berlin. Otherwise, her militant commitment is evident in blog articles she writes for the *Review of African Political Economy* and the Rosa-Luxemburg-Foundation.

Adrian J. Browne is an archives sector worker and a member of the Public and Commercial Services Union. He completed his PhD in 2020 at the Department of History, Durham University, UK. An Economic and Social Research Council Post-Doctoral Fellowship followed in 2021–22. He has published articles in *History in Africa* and, with co-authors, the *Journal of Eastern African Studies* and *Journal of Critical African Studies*. He lives in south London.

Moussa Diallo, born in 1977 in Zouma, Burkina Faso, is a teacher-researcher at the University Center of Manga, Burkina Faso. He teaches the History of Modern and Contemporary Philosophy, and Moral and Political Philosophy. His research interests include the history of philosophy, moral and political philosophy, and the problems of collective action in Burkina Faso. He is also a trade unionist in Burkina Faso, and was the General Delegate of the National Association of Burkinabe Students from 2001 to 2004, Deputy Confederal Secretary in charge of social issues from 2006 to 2013, Confederal Secretary in charge of monitoring labour legislation and social standards from 2013 to 2021, and since 27 November 2021 he has served as the Confederal Secretary General of the General Confederation of Labour of Burkina.

Harris Dousemetzis is a tutor at the School of Government and International Affairs at Durham University, UK, and holds a PhD in politics from the same university. He spent nearly ten years researching Dimitri Tsafendas and Verwoerd's assassination. He is also the author of *The Man who Killed Apartheid: The Life of Dimitri Tsafendas* (2018), the *Report to the Minister of Justice in the Matter of Dr. Verwoerd's Assassination* (2018) and *Gay Rights under Jimmy Carter: The Revolution That Dared Not Speak Its Name* (2023).

George Klay Kieh, Jr is Dean of the Barbara Jordan Mickey Leland School of Public Affairs and Professor of Political Science at Texas Southern University, Houston, Texas, USA. His revolutionary activities included membership in the Movement for Justice in Africa – Liberia and serving as President of the University of Liberia Student Union. Because of his revolutionary activities, he was a political prisoner in Liberia in 1979 and 1984.

Nicki Kindersley is a Lecturer in African History at Cardiff University, UK, working on histories of labour, migration and political thought, focused on South Sudan and its borderlands. Her research projects are all collaborations with the Rift Valley Institute, Nairobi, Kenya and the University of Juba, South Sudan. She is currently secretary of the Direct Action Community Union ACORN Cardiff, and an University and College Union member.

Héloïse Kiriakou is a secondary school teacher and researcher associated with the Institut des mondes africains at the University of Paris 1-Sorbonne, France. Her PhD dissertation (2019) focused on the history of Brazzaville, the laboratory of the Congolese revolution, between 1963 and 1977.

Djiddi Allahi Mahamat was a member of the National Liberation Front of Chad in opposition to the regime of Hissène Habré. In 1984, he went to the Soviet Union to study political economy in Minsk until 1990. He was Member of Parliament for the Tibesti West constituency in Chad until 2021.

Adam Mayer works as Assistant Professor of International Studies at the American University of Iraq – Baghdad, and as a researcher at Szechenyi Istvan University, Győr, Hungary. He also supervises PhDs at both Óbuda University, Budapest, Hungary and at the Universidad Nacional de Educación a Distancia, Madrid, Spain. He focuses on radical intellectual history of African Marxist thought. His book *Naija Marxisms: Revolutionary Thought in Nigeria* was published by Pluto Press in 2016. Since then, his articles on radical and socialist African political economy, feminism, activism and protest have appeared in the *Review of African Political Economy*, *Canadian Journal of African Studies*, Journal of *the African Literature Association*, International Journal of Arts and Humanities Studies, *African Identities*, as well as the *Review of African Political Economy*, *Jacobin*, *Tablet* and other academic and popular media. He is working on a history of Anglophone West African Marxisms and their cross-regional entanglements on the continent as well as the diaspora, with a special interest in Africa's own agency and contribution to global Marxist theory from the 1940s to today. He also co-edits the *Journal of Central and Eastern European African Studies*, Hungary's only English-language academic journal on the subject, where he campaigns for radical re-humanisation for Afro-Europeans in an illiberal context.

Tilman Musch works, among other topics, on human–environment relationships in the Central Sahara and on customary law in the Tibesti, Chad. After a thesis on Buryat-Siberian nomadism (Paris, 2007), he specialised in nomadic and Saharan civilisations.

Zeyad el Nabolsy is a PhD candidate in Africana Studies at Cornell University, Ithaca, New York State, USA. He has an MA in philosophy and a BEng. in Chemical Engineering from McMaster University, Hamilton, Ontario, Canada. He specialises in modern African intellectual history and philosophy. He has published on the intellectual history of Afro-Asian solidarity, philosophy of culture, scientific dependency, debates about the theory of imperialism, Amílcar Cabral, and the history of African studies in Egypt, among other topics. He is actively involved in public education efforts aimed at recognising the epistemic damage colonialism has inflicted on the African continent.

Issa N'Diaye is Professor of Philosophy at the University of Bamako, Mali. He was a member of the underground Malian Workers Party, a student leader and later leader of the higher education union under the dictatorship, Minister of National Education during the 1991–92 transition, and Minister of Culture and Scientific Research in the first post-dictatorship government. He was a political prisoner several times under the military dictatorship of Moussa Traoré, subject to frequent arbitrary transfers and finally expulsion from the civil service. He played an active part in the fall of the dictatorship and the advent of multi-party democracy in Mali. He is the author of numerous publications, including *Démocratie et fractures sociales au Mali, tome 1: Silence, on démocratise!* (2018) and *Démocratie et fractures sociales au Mali, tome 2: Le festival des brigands* (2018), which bear witness to more than 50 years of social and political struggles and reflection as a leader, trade unionist, journalist, political training leader, community activist, etc.

Patrick Norberg is a doctoral researcher in the Department of International Development, Kings College London, where he is researching Marxist theories of working-class formation. He is active in left-wing causes in east London.

Irène Rabenoro is Professor of Sociolinguistics at the Department of Anglophone Studies, University of Antananarivo, Madagascar. In her youth, she took part in the May 1972 peaceful students' movement which eventually overthrew the president of the First Republic of Madagascar. As an activist for the Mpitolona ho an'ny Fanjakan'ny Madinika (Party for the Power of the Proletariat), she was arrested seven times within five months. She was the Ambassador of Madagascar to the United Nations Educational, Scientific and Cultural Organization (UNESCO) and Representative of the

President of Madagascar to Francophony (2007–10). As President of the Group of 77 and China at UNESCO (2008), she was viewed as *the* spokesperson of the developing world, especially in the field of education and science. Her research works include Malagasy political discourse analyses of the revolutionary events of May 1972. In 2022, as President of the Organising Committee at the University of Antananarivo, Madagascar of the 50th anniversary celebration of 13 May 1972, she gathered the main actors of May 1972 and had them deliver testimonials, thus raising a debate on the outcome of the movement.

Tatiana Smirnova is a postdoctoral researcher at Center FrancoPaix, Université de Québec à Montréal, Canada and a research associate at the Sahel Research Group, University of Florida, Gainesville, Florida, USA. For her PhD thesis at the Ecole des hautes études en sciences sociales, Paris, France she studied the history of the student movement in Niger and its role in politics from 1960 to 2010. Currently, she is continuing her research at the Sahel Research Group on different forms of violence as well as Russia–Africa relations. She is the author of many publications in peer-reviewed journals and reports. She has also worked as a consultant for various international non-governmental organisations.

Matt Swagler is a socialist activist in New York City, USA and an Assistant Professor at Connecticut College, New London, Connecticut, USA, where he teaches courses on African and Global History. He is currently preparing a book on radical youth and student movements in postcolonial Congo-Brazzaville and Senegal.

Ibrahima Wane holds doctorates in Modern Literature and Oral Literature. He is Professor of African Literature and Civilisations at Cheikh Anta Diop University in Dakar, Senegal, where he is in charge of the master's degree programme in African Literature at the Department of Modern Literature. He also heads the African and Francophone Studies programme of the Doctoral School of Arts, Cultures and Civilisations. His research interests include popular poetry and music in West Africa, literature written in African languages, urban cultures and the political imagination. His recent publications include *Le 1er Festival mondial des arts nègres: mémoire et actualité*, co-edited with Saliou Mbaye (2020).

Index

The Pluto Press Newsletter

Hello friend of Pluto!

Want to stay on top of the best radical books
we publish?

Then sign up to be the first to hear about our
new books, as well as special events,
podcasts and videos.

You'll also get 50% off your first order with us
when you sign up.

Come and join us!

Go to bit.ly/PlutoNewsletter

Thanks to our Patreon subscriber:

Ciaran Kane

Who has shown generosity and
comradeship in support of our publishing.

Check out the other perks you get by subscribing
to our Patreon – visit patreon.com/plutopress.

Subscriptions start from £3 a month.